Mobile Urbanity

Integration and Conflict Studies
Published in association with the Max Planck Institute for Social Anthropology, Halle/Saale

Series Editor: Günther Schlee, Director at the Max Planck Institute for Social Anthropology

Editorial Board: Brian Donahoe (Max Planck Institute for Social Anthropology), John Eidson (Max Planck Institute for Social Anthropology), Peter Finke (University of Zurich), Joachim Görlich (Max Planck Institute for Social Anthropology), Jacqueline Knörr (Max Planck Institute for Social Anthropology), Bettina Mann (Max Planck Institute for Social Anthropology), Stephen Reyna (Max Planck Institute for Social Anthropology)

Assisted by: Cornelia Schnepel and Viktoria Zeng (Max Planck Institute for Social Anthropology)

The objective of the Max Planck Institute for Social Anthropology is to advance anthropological fieldwork and enhance theory building. 'Integration' and 'conflict', the central themes of this series, are major concerns of the contemporary social sciences and of significant interest to the general public. They have also been among the main research areas of the institute since its foundation. Bringing together international experts, *Integration and Conflict Studies* includes both monographs and edited volumes, and offers a forum for studies that contribute to a better understanding of processes of identification and inter-group relations.

Recent volumes:

Volume 20
Mobile Urbanity: Somali Presence in Urban East Africa
  Edited by Neil Carrier and Tabea Scharrer

Volume 19
Playing the Marginality Game: Identity Politics in West Africa
  Anita Schroven

Volume 18
The Wheel of Autonomy: Rhetoric and Ethnicity in the Omo Valley
  Felix Girke

Volume 17
Bishkek Boys: Neighbourhood Youth and Urban Change in Kyrgyzstan's Capital
  Philipp Schröder

Volume 16
Difference and Sameness as Modes of Integration: Anthropological Perspectives on Ethnicity and Religion
  Edited by Günther Schlee and Alexander Horstmann

Volume 15
On Retaliation: Towards an Interdisciplinary Understanding of a Basic Human Condition
  Edited by Bertram Turner and Günther Schlee

Volume 14
'City of the Future': Built Space, Modernity and Urban Change in Astana
  Mateusz Laszczkowski

Volume 13
Staying at Home: Identities, Memories and Social Networks of Kazakhstani Germans
  Rita Sanders

Volume 12
The Upper Guinea Coast in Global Perspective
  Edited by Jacqueline Knörr and Christoph Kohl

Volume 11
Masks and Staffs: Identity Politics in the Cameroon Grassfields
  Michaela Pelican

For a full volume listing, please see the series page on our website: http://www.berghahnbooks.com/series/integration-and-conflict-studies

Mobile Urbanity
Somali Presence in Urban East Africa

Edited by Neil Carrier and Tabea Scharrer

berghahn
NEW YORK • OXFORD
www.berghahnbooks.com

First published in 2019 by
Berghahn Books
www.berghahnbooks.com

© 2019, 2022 Neil Carrier and Tabea Scharrer
First paperback edition published in 2022

All rights reserved. Except for the quotation of short passages
for the purposes of criticism and review, no part of this book
may be reproduced in any form or by any means, electronic or
mechanical, including photocopying, recording, or any information
storage and retrieval system now known or to be invented,
without written permission of the publisher.

Library of Congress Cataloging-in-Publication Data
Names: Carrier, Neil C. M., editor, author. | Scharrer, Tabea, editor, author.
Title: Mobile urbanity : Somali presence in urban East Africa / edited by
  Neil Carrier and Tabea Scharrer.
Description: New York : Berghahn Books, 2019. | Series: Integration and
  conflict studies ; v. 20 | Includes bibliographical references and index.
Identifiers: LCCN 2019009573 (print) | LCCN 2019011827 (ebook) | ISBN
  9781789202977 (ebook) | ISBN 9781789202960 (hardback : alk. paper)
Subjects: LCSH: Labor mobility--Africa, East. | Somalis--Africa, East. |
  Immigrants--Africa, East. | Somalis--Migrations. | City and town
  life--Africa, East. | Africa, East--Emigration and immigration--Economic
  aspects.
Classification: LCC JV8998.7 (ebook) | LCC JV8998.7 .M63 2019 (print) | DDC
  305.89354067--dc23
LC record available at https://lccn.loc.gov/2019009573

British Library Cataloguing in Publication Data
A catalogue record for this book is available from the British Library

ISBN 978-1-78920-296-0 hardback
ISBN 978-1-80073-443-2 paperback
ISBN 978-1-78920-297-7 ebook

https://doi.org/10.3167/9781789202960

Contents

List of Illustrations   vii

Acknowledgements   viii

List of Abbreviations   x

Part I. Introductions

Introduction. Mobile Urbanity: Somali Presence in Urban East Africa   3
   Tabea Scharrer and Neil Carrier

Interlude. Being and Becoming Mobile   26
   Yusuf Hassan

Part II. Urbanity

Chapter 1. The Somali Factor in Urban Kenya: A History   41
   Hannah Whittaker

Chapter 2. The Port and the Island: Cosmopolitan and Vernacular Identity Constructions among Somali Women in Nairobi and Johannesburg   58
   Nereida Ripero-Muñiz

Chapter 3. Being Oromo in Nairobi's 'Little Mogadishu': Superdiversity, Moral Community and the Open Economy   76
Neil Carrier and Hassan H. Kochore

Part III. Economic Networks

Chapter 4. Demanding and Commanding Goods: The Eastleigh Transformation Told through the 'Lives' of Its Commodities   97
Neil Carrier and Hannah Elliott

Chapter 5. Capital Mobilization among the Somali Refugee Business Community in Eastleigh, Nairobi   118
John Mwangi Githigaro and Kenneth Omeje

Chapter 6. Challenging the Status Quo from the Bottom Up? Gender and Enterprise in Somali Migrant Communities in Nairobi, Kenya   135
Holly A. Ritchie

Chapter 7. Reinventing Retail: 'Somali' Shopping Centres in Kenya   157
Tabea Scharrer

Part IV. The Politics of Somali Mobility

Chapter 8. Perpetually in Transit: Somalian Refugees in a Context of Increasing Hostility   181
Lucy Lowe and Mark Yarnell

Chapter 9. Framing the Swoop: A Comparative Analysis of Operation Usalama Watch in Muslim and Secular Print Media in Kenya   200
Joseph Wandera and Halkano Abdi Wario

Chapter 10. Beyond Eastleigh: A New Little Mogadishu in Uganda?   219
Gianluca Iazzolino

Afterword   238
Günther Schlee

Glossary   244
Index   247

Illustrations

Maps
0.1 Map of Kenya. 5
0.2 Map of Nairobi. 13
1.1 Somali villages in colonial Nairobi. 46

Figures
0.1 Eastleigh viewed from the Grand Royal Hotel, 2011. 16
6.1 Three Somali refugee women taking part in an NGO training course on business development skills (BDS) in Eastleigh, January 2014. 138
7.1 Construction work does not prevent trade (Eastleigh, Second Avenue). 160
7.2 Upper floor in Al-Mujtahid Shopping Centre, Nakuru. 163
7.3 The Dubai Shopping Centre in Nakuru. 165

Acknowledgements

The editors owe many people a debt of gratitude for helping to produce this volume. This book would not exist without the assistance of the many people in East (and South) Africa who shared their time and opinion with us for the various empirical investigations which form the basis of this volume. Furthermore, we gratefully acknowledge the work of all the people involved in producing this edited collection. These are of course first and foremost the contributors of the various chapters, with whom it was a pleasure to work. Some of them had already presented early versions of their chapters at a forum on Somalis in Urban East Africa held at the British Institute in Eastern Africa (BIEA) in Nairobi in September 2014, which was kindly sponsored by the Max Planck Institute for Social Anthropology, the Rift Valley Institute, the BIEA and the Oxford Diasporas Programme funded by the Leverhulme Trust. This meeting brought together researchers, practitioners of international and nongovernmental organizations and Eastleigh stalwarts such as Yusuf Hassan, Lul Issack, Ahmed Mohamed, Burhan Iman, Mohamed Ali, Elias Issack and others. Many thanks also to the staff at the BIEA and RVI for their organizational expertise. At the Max Planck Institute for Social Anthropology we thank Prof. Günther Schlee in particular for helping us publish this volume in the department's series 'Integration and Conflict Studies' at Berghahn Books. Cornelia Schnepel, Jutta Turner and Franziska Sandkühler assisted ably in the editing process of this book, and we are very grateful for their assistance in the project. Finally, thanks to the many reviewers of the book manuscript, those reviewing the book internally at the Max Planck Institute for Social Anthropology as well as Anna Lindley and the second external reviewer of Berghahn, for their very helpful and constructive comments.

Abbreviations

AMISOM	African Union Mission to Somalia
ATPU	Anti-Terrorism Police Unit
CARA	Control of Alien Refugees Act
CBD	Central Business District
DRA	Kenyan Department of Refugee Affairs
EBDA	Eastleigh Business District Association
EPRDF	Ethiopian People's Revolutionary Democratic Front
FGM	Female Genital Mutilation
GoK	Government of Kenya
HRW	Human Rights Watch
IGAD	Intergovernmental Authority on Development
IPOA	Kenya's Independent Policing Authority
IRC	International Rescue Committee
KANU	Kenya African National Union
KAR	King's African Rifles
KAU	Kenya African Union
KICC	Kenyatta International Conference Centre
KMYA	Kenya Muslim Youth Alliance
KNBS	Kenya National Bureau of Statistics
KNCHR	Kenya National Commission on Human Rights
KRA	Kenya Revenue Authority
LEGCO	Kenya Legislative Assembly
MRC	Mandate Refugee Certificate

MSE	Micro and Small Enterprises
MUHURI	Muslim Human Rights
NEP	North Eastern Province of Kenya
NFD	Northern Frontier District
NPPPP	Northern Province Peoples Progressive Party
OLF	Oromo Liberation Front
RAS	Kenya's Refugee Affairs Secretariat
ROSCAs	Rotating Savings and Credit Associations
SUPKEM	Supreme Council of Kenya Muslims
TPLF	Tigray People's Liberation Front
UNGU	United Nations Guard Unit
UNHCR	UN High Commissioner for Refugees
UPU	Universal Postal Union
USA	United Somali Association

Part I
Introductions

Introduction

Mobile Urbanity

Somali Presence in Urban East Africa

Tabea Scharrer and Neil Carrier

This is a book about how complex patterns of mobility shape and reshape urban landscapes and the lives of those who live within them, and how urban landscapes in turn shape and reshape patterns of mobility. Migrants, mobile goods, capital and ideas constantly reach, pass through or sojourn in urban spaces, while also connecting cities with other places through their movement. From New York to Guangzhou, cities bear the marks of all this movement, and attract further movement in turn.[1] In some ways urbanity itself is mobile – inhabitants of urban areas not only take with them an urban lifestyle and habitus when they move elsewhere, they often rebuild familiar urban features wherever they settle.[2] This connection of mobility and urban transformation is ever more obvious in cities and towns throughout the contemporary world, although archaeological and historical evidence shows that the two have always been linked.[3] In addition, cities are increasingly the focus of migration policy debates, as demonstrated by a recent International Organisation of Migration (IOM) conference and report on the topic focussing on cities and 'managing mobility' (IOM 2015). Likewise, the city now looms large in migration scholarship, not just as a backdrop for migrants and mobility, but also as a key agent constituted by, and generating new forms of movement (Glick Schiller and Çağlar 2010). In this book we focus on these themes through a case-study of the impact people more commonly associated with mobility rather than urbanity have had on towns and cities in East Africa: Somalis.

Somalis are perceived as people on the move. This is not just due to the romantic image of them as nomadic pastoralists. They have long since left the

Horn of Africa in search of various types of opportunities. As Muslims, many have made pilgrimage to the Arabian Peninsula over the years – shared religion has encouraged patterns of mobility of people, beliefs and practices. As seafarers, others reached distant shores from India to Wales (see for instance Lodhi 1992 or Turton 1974). The proximity of Somali territories to the Gulf, has led to much work and trade migration over the years to that region, especially in the boom oil years (Abdi 2015). Others went to study in the USSR when the government of Siad Barre had close ties to the Eastern Bloc during the Cold War. With the outbreak of civil war in Somalia in the late 1980s, Somalis spread further still, mainly as refugees, forming in the process a vast diaspora with communities in towns and cities from Australia to North America. So-called 'Little Mogadishus' have sprouted in the process in places such as Minneapolis and Toronto where these communities are especially dense. Somalis have thus changed the fabric of much urban life in such places, bringing Somali identity, language, food and business to all corners of the globe.

Perhaps the greatest impact of Somalis beyond their home regions in the Horn has been on the neighbouring countries of East Africa, including Ethiopia, Uganda and Tanzania, but most especially, Kenya. Somalis have lived in the areas belonging to what is now Ethiopia and Kenya since pre-colonial times, and spread to Uganda and Tanzania during British colonialism in these two countries. In recent times Somalis have been a major focus of the politics of this region as continuing conflict – and the occasional drought – in Somalia has maintained a near diaspora of refugees. While in the early 1990s about 300,000 Somalians[4] were officially registered as refugees in Kenya, this number decreased to about 200,000 people in the mid-1990s. Their numbers rose again from 2007–08 onwards and peaked in 2011 (a time of severe drought) at about 500,000. In February 2019 there were still about 260,000 refugees from Somalia registered in Kenya. In addition, there are an unknown number of unregistered forced migrants living in Kenya.[5] Since 2006 (Ethiopia) and 2007 (AMISOM) respectively, troops from various East African countries have operated inside Somalia attempting to defeat the Islamist group Al-Shabaab within an African Union mission. Al-Shabaab has reacted to this military intervention with its own operation within these countries. This is true for Uganda, but especially for Kenya where there have been a number of attacks perpetrated by the group (including those on the Westgate Shopping Mall in Nairobi in 2013, the Garissa University College in 2015 and the 14 Riverside complex in Nairobi in 2019).

The presence of Somalian refugees in Kenya is most conspicuous in the refugee camps of Dadaab and Kakuma, located in remote parts of the country and home to hundreds of thousands of refugees for almost thirty years (Horst 2006, Rawlence 2016). These camps have long been threatened with closure by the Kenyan government who depict them as breeding grounds of insecurity. The

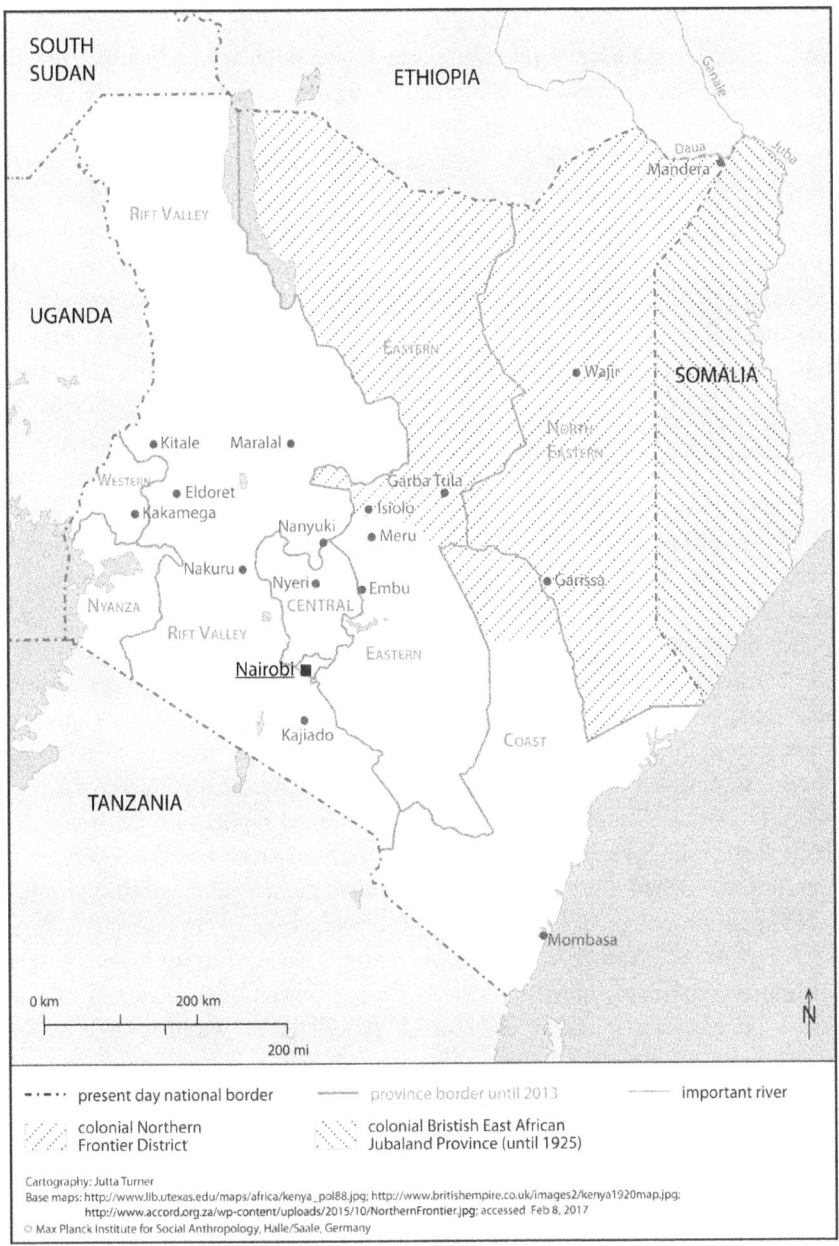

Map 0.1 Map of Kenya.

vast logistical effort required to manage these camps, combined with the national and international politics surrounding them and the humanitarian needs of people trying to survive in them, means they have come to dominate much recent telling of the story of Somalis in Kenya.

However, Somali migrants have also had an enormous impact on the towns and cities of East Africa. While Kenya has a large population of ethnic Somalis indigenous to its northeastern region and its towns such as Garissa and Mandera, Somali presence is more and more conspicuous in urban areas within the rest of the country and beyond into Uganda and Tanzania. Chief among these urban areas is the now famous district of Nairobi known as Eastleigh. This quarter has become a major commercial zone for East Africa through Somali trade. It is now populated with Somali-owned and run shopping centres and thousands of East Africans come to shop there daily. Eastleigh is not the only urban area, which has changed due to Somali migration. Similar processes of urban transformation have occurred in other areas of Nairobi, in cities such as Nakuru and Mombasa with significant Somali populations, and even in parts of Kampala and Dar es Salaam. Somali mobility has led them into many East African urban areas, bringing transformation in their wake. Such transformation has been controversial and contested, especially that of Eastleigh, which is often portrayed within Kenya as a place of foreigners, a part of the Somali Republic somehow dropped into Nairobi. Concern about Al-Shabaab also means its economic transformation is seen through a highly securitized prism, both within Kenya, and by international policy makers and media.

Somali presence in Kenya has long been viewed with concern by the authorities from colonial times onwards (Scharrer 2018). In the postcolonial period, their place within the Kenyan nation was seen as precarious in the years following the secessionist war of the 1960s, where many in the northeastern parts of Kenya wished to secede. The legacy of this war and its brutal suppression has been long lasting, and even Somalis born and bred within Kenya have had their citizenship questioned. Lochery (2012) has vividly described the screening operations of the 1980s that made many Kenyan Somalis feel second-class or 'ambiguous' citizens (Scharrer 2018). More recently fears of terrorism have led to further screenings of Somalis in Kenya, most notoriously during Operation Usalama Watch in 2014 (see chapters by Lowe and Yarnell as well as by Wandera and Wario, this volume). While raids on Eastleigh and elsewhere appear to come in waves, harassment of urban Somalis by police and other state security forces has been the norm. Somalian refugees in particular are targeted as they are seen as both wealthy yet vulnerable. The link of Somalians with Indian Ocean piracy has also affected how they are seen in Kenya and beyond, and there are suspicions that piracy and other forms of criminality underlie their apparent wealth. This image gives less visibility to the majority of Somalis in urban Kenya who live under conditions of poverty or lower middle-class livelihoods.

It is in this context that our volume emerges, a volume that intends to demystify Somali presence in urban East Africa, showing its historical depth and the deeper underpinnings of the urban transformations it has wrought. While Somali-led urban transformation has not always been a positive story, it is a far more complicated one than is often portrayed. When we started to work on this edited volume, with the aim of bringing together as many of the researchers working on issues of Somali urbanity in East Africa as possible, tensions were extremely high in the aftermath of Operation Usalama Watch, and so a number of papers study this political context in detail. Others are more focused on the historical and socio-economic aspects of Somali urban presence in East Africa. This combination allows for a rounded look at how towns and cities have shaped Somali life and society in East Africa, but also how their presence has in turn shaped these same towns and cities and broader urban practices. However, the volume has much wider implications beyond the particular case-study of Somalis in urban East Africa.

These wider implications are summed up in our concept of *mobile urbanity*. Through this concept and its application to the case of Somalis and East African urban transformation, we hope to contribute to growing debates on the interface between migration and urbanization, both being seen as critical social processes in our contemporary world. The already mentioned report of the International Organisation of Migration (IOM) focussing on cities and 'managing mobility' implies a need to tighten control of this movement despite acknowledgement in the same document of the benefits migrants often bring to cities and their economies (IOM 2015). In the African context too, there have been calls for a deeper exploration of the links between mobility and the city (Bakewell and Jonsson 2011). Furthermore, as we shall elaborate below, recent scholarship suggests that there is a need to move beyond seeing the city as simply a backdrop for migrants and migration, but to study them as mutually constituted (Glick Schiller and Çağlar 2016).

Migration has always been a constitutive part of urbanization processes. This entanglement has also long been a focus of academic research, as the vast literature on rural–urban migration and ethnic enclaves – the 'Chinatowns' and 'Little Italys' of the world – suggests. Now it is getting more attention than ever. However, this new attention is very much 'transnational', exploring not just how migrants integrate into a particular urban context – as the literature on ethnic enclaves tended to do – but also on how social and economic ties maintained to other urban sites across the world affect all the places linked to migration. We argue that the Somali case in East Africa is highly resonant with these wider debates on migration and the city, showing how socially, historically and politically complex such a relationship is. Indeed, the case offers a lens to think through the challenges and opportunities urban migrants both face and bring through their mobility.

Mobility

Mobility is a complicated and multifaceted phenomenon in our contemporary world. The Syrian and Rohingya refugee crises have brought *forced migration* into focus, while anti-migrant sentiment in developed and developing countries alike echoes in the rhetoric of populist politicians, and in the xenophobia and increasing recourse to discourses of autochthony in Africa, Europe and elsewhere (Crush and Ramachandran 2010; Geschiere 2009). However, the term *mobility* covers a far wider range of forms of movement, and not just those of people (Urry 2000). Mobility conveys a degree of agency, suggesting the ability to move, and so brings to mind those with at least some social and economic capital. As a term its open-endedness is useful, conveying not just migration to settled lives in other places, but also the intricate patterns of movement that constitute many contemporary lives – and have constituted many lives in the past too, despite the framing of our age as the 'age of migration' in the words of Castles, de Haas and Miller (2017 [1993]). Work on transnationalism and diaspora by authors including Glick Schiller, Basch and Szanton (1992), Levitt (2001) and Cohen (2008) has for two decades highlighted how many people live transnationally, for example working in one country but remaining tied through family and other forms of belonging to places of origin or to other countries. This engagement is even being praised as a means of development, harnessing the flows of remittances constantly moving back to the regions of origin. Others leave the diaspora and move 'home' to start businesses or NGOs, or enter politics, sometimes with an explicit developmental aim: such 'return migrants' are seen by some as the 'new developers' (for a nuanced analysis of this in regards to Africa, see Akesson and Baaz 2015).

The emphasis on remittances as a stream of potential developmental capital shows how one form of mobility can generate another – in this case that of money as well as people. Likewise, spatial mobility can lead to social mobility. Human mobility also increases the mobility of trade goods. Unlike people, goods and capital seem to flow relatively unimpeded. Trade deals at national and super-national levels attempt to facilitate this movement, while clearly there is concern that this mobility has its shady side. Indeed, the flow of arms, drugs and 'conflict goods' (such as 'blood diamonds', coltan and the like [Cooper 2001]) – the 'dark side of globalization' in the words of van Schendel and Abraham (2005) – is aided greatly by the sheer volume of global trade and the corruptibility of the global trade system. Contraband crosses borders, while tax and duties are often easily evaded, and borders become resources for those who can control these flows. Money criss-crosses the world with ease, both in hard cash and electronically. The Panama Papers released in 2016 highlighted only too strongly how the capital of the world's elite is remarkably mobile, being transferred from jurisdiction to jurisdiction in attempts to evade tax.

As Ferguson argues (2006), the supposed intensification of globalization excludes many from its key benefits, while exposing the less fortunate to its risks; it is a phenomenon that leaps and hops, rather than a seamless integration of our planet and its people. Meanwhile, as Nyamnjoh argues in regards to the African context, some people are represented and imagined as only passively mobile:

'nothing African moves unless provoked by forces beyond their control' (2013: 659). Yet migration and the flow of goods and capital have certainly not just been the preserve of the rich, although the poor face far more barriers to their own movement and trade, especially in an era where such movement is increasingly securitized (Kibreab 2014) and demonised, not just in North America and Europe, but within Africa too. While the type of globalization of multinational corporations and those transferring money from one tax haven to another has come to dominate how the phenomenon is imagined, for many globalization is experienced in different ways, often through what has been termed by Portes, Mathews and others as 'low-end globalization' or 'globalization from below' (Portes 1997; Schlee 2001; Mathews 2011; Mathews, Ribeiro and Vega 2012). Mathews' focus is on small-scale (and some large-scale too) traders who crisscross borders – usually to the manufacturing and trade hubs of Asia – in search of cheap consumer goods popular not just in India and Africa, but in western countries as well. Such goods, as Mathews argues, allow access to the products of globalization by the world's poor. But there is also much mobility beyond such trade, with people travelling too for work and business opportunities, or to provide care for family members.

The case of Somalis highlights all these mobile complexities. The collapse of the Somali state in the late 1980s and ensuing conflict and other crises (including drought) have meant that many Somalians have become refugees, and the hundreds of thousands of residents in Dadaab and Kakuma refugee camps in northern Kenya have become symbolic of the Somali experience of the last two decades (Horst 2006). While protracted displacement in such camps has been the experience of migration for far too many, Somali mobility is much more multifaceted than this might suggest. Of course, as people associated with pastoralist livelihoods and nomadic patterns of life, movement has been a feature of life for many Somalis, as evoked by the classic ethnographies of I.M. Lewis (e.g. Lewis 1961). The romantic vision of Somalis as a nomadic people, however, is somewhat misleading.[6] This is not only true for the many generations that led more sedentary lives (including the 'Somali Bantu' whose livelihood was principally agricultural, and town dwellers such as the inhabitants of Mogadishu and other urban areas in precolonial Somalia), but also for those having become more sedentarized during the late colonial period and after independence (Hogg 1986; Besteman 1998). However, the nomadic imaginary still remains a key aspect of identification for many, also for those now living very different lives in towns and cities. An urban life, however, does not preclude mobility – there is a rather high mobility within Somali families, mainly for care-giving reasons, and people might move from one urban area to the next for education or economic reasons (for example see Hassan, this volume).

Displacement following civil war in Somalia itself has led to the creation of a vast Somali diaspora, which has settled in many countries around the world from the USA to Australia, as well as in other parts of Africa, including a significant population in South Africa (Steinberg 2015; Abdi 2015; see also the chapter by Ripero-Muñiz in this volume). Currently, more than 10 per cent of the Somalian population lives outside the country. Transnational ties are woven throughout this diaspora, and remittances sent in support of family members or for investment flow through the networks of which it is made (Lindley 2010). Such remittances and other forms of investment by those who have become wealthy in the diaspora have provided much support for development initiatives inside Somalia and in Somali regions elsewhere, including northeastern Kenya, as well as the refugee camps and the cities of Kenya and Ethiopia. In the process, links to the 'low-end global' manufacturing powerhouses of the East have also grown as Somali mobility encompasses China and Thailand, as well as the trans-shipment hub of Dubai. Thus, out of displacement have sprung many opportunities for economic growth that Somali businesspeople have exploited skilfully, an example of what Hammar (2014) terms 'displacement economy'.

All these varied forms of Somali mobility come strongly into focus in Kenya. As its territory contains land criss-crossed for many decades by Somali pastoralists, it is home to traditional patterns of Somali mobility and nomadism. It has also long been a destination and centre for Somali migration within East Africa and the continent more broadly, a temporal dimension we aim to tackle by showing the historical depth of this migration. The marginalization of its indigenous Somali population (Lochery 2012; Scharrer 2018), and the fraying tolerance shown towards Somalian refugees by the Kenyan state (see Lowe and Yarnell, this volume), are highly suggestive of the contemporary politics of migration, especially in the securitization of these politics in the wake of attacks by Somali militant groups. The economic implications of Somali displacement are also evident in Kenya, including the refugee camps of Dadaab, themselves the hub of trade (Pérouse de Montclos and Kagwanja 2000).

But it is the effects of all this migration upon urban Kenya that most interests us in this volume. From the early settlement of Somalis in Nairobi and the politics of where they should live (Whittaker, this volume), to the urban impact of new forms of trade goods (Carrier and Elliott, this volume) and ways of doing trade (Scharrer, this volume), as well as remittances and other forms of support from the recently formed diaspora (Mwangi, this volume), Somalis and their mobility have played a huge role in forming and transforming urban Kenya. Indeed, they constitute a major case-study of the conjuncture of mobility and the urban and all the dynamics therein.

Urbanity

The urban itself is constituted by mobility. When people started to settle, new nodes of connection emerged, linking people from different origins, and urban areas of 'relatively large, dense, and permanent settlement[s] of socially heterogeneous individuals' (Wirth 1938: 8) developed. Such urban areas are generally characterized not just by a high population size and density, but also by a greater specialization of economic structures and occupations beyond agriculture (including animal-husbandry, see Potts 2017), and by a change in social relations and lifestyle. Knowing all other town dwellers is impossible in these bigger settlements, making voluntary associations more important and reducing the dependency upon particular persons often associated with kinship ties (see Wirth 1938: 12; for an example from Zambian colonial cities see Gluckman 2009 [1961]). Heterogeneity in urban areas mainly results from immigration, but is also due to spatial and social differentiation and mobility in the urban areas (Wirth 1938: 16). It is, however, not only people who shape urban structures and city life, but their lives are equally influenced by city structures, old and new, and the logics of city life taking place in these structures. Indeed, urban life impacts on the way people move: the 'city acts as a forge for migratory behaviour' (Bakewell and Jonsson 2011: 13).

For a long time, African cities were, with some notable exception, either not the focus of research or were treated as a deviation from the norm, as different from what cities ought to be. Mbembe and Nuttall (2004: 353) criticize the (academic) discourse about contemporary African cities, arguing that it is still overshadowed by the 'metanarrative of urbanization, modernization, and crisis'. Likewise, they bemoan that Africans have for a long time been depicted in anthropological and historical writings as 'essentially rural creatures'. This is especially true for pastoral people, as Whittaker shows in this volume. Mbembe and Nuttall (2004) therefore call for a deprovincializing of the scholarship on Africa, meaning less focus on the originality and difference of African cities, and more on the fundamental connections to other regional and global places, that is to say, on the 'worldliness' of African life.

Nonetheless, even authors who aim at challenging this notion of African cities as deviating from an abstract (euro-centric) norm, end up depicting sub-Saharan Africa cities as different from those in other parts of the world. Danny Hoffman (2007), for instance, uses his research area, the war-torn cities of Freetown (Sierra Leone) and Monrovia (Liberia), to generalize about the future of the postcolonial (African) city itself. He argues that armed conflicts do not lead to a 'temporary suspension of the "normal" functioning of the city', but that they create one possible 'manifestation of the way economies and governmentalities are organized in the contemporary period' (Hoffman 2007: 404). Within the city he describes zones of legal exception with which the state had reached an ambiguous, and ambivalent, accommodation. These zones, which are 'beyond the reach of the law' protect those living inside from the reach of the state, but appear threatening and lawless from the outside (ibid.: 414). Meanwhile, Abdumaliq Simone (2006: 358) speaks of a 'generalised practice of piracy' in everyday African urban life.

While urban physical and social infrastructures are underfunded, in some cases purposefully, urban populations not only experience uncertainty, but also make use of the very unpredictability and the unregulated practices as resources. Piracy, as an 'act of taking things out of their normal ... frameworks of circulation and use' (ibid.: 357), whether through using the pavement as a market (in the case of informal traders) or by appropriating cinemas as churches, thus becomes part of normal everyday life.

So, do African cities work differently from those elsewhere? A way to bring these two different notions, of African specificity and of African worldliness, together is the idea that all cities, no matter where they are situated, follow their own specific intrinsic logic (*Eigenlogik der Städte*, Löw 2012), allowing one to see the heterogeneous experiences within African cities. Löw argues that in every city a distinct constellation of knowledge and forms of expressions develop. These emerging contexts of meanings influence the practices of people as well as their 'identity, emotions, attitudes, and thinking' (Löw 2012: 310). These practices in turn 'reproduce a logic specific to the given city' (ibid.). When thinking with the idea of an 'intrinsic logic' of cities one has to make sure, however, not to overlook other aspects of city life, such as the internal heterogeneity of urban areas, the changes taking place in them or their involvement in global processes.

Is there an intrinsic logic to Nairobi, the major focus of this current volume? First of all, as a city founded during the colonial era, Nairobi is still very much shaped by a colonial partitioning, sub-dividing the city into different racially and ethnically segregated neighbourhoods. In addition, there was a sharp contrast between functional and residential zones. After independence this sectioning remained, the post-'apartheid' grid building the base for the growing city and further fragmentation now more along the lines of class. Similar urban histories and structures can be traced in Nakuru (Kenya), Kampala (Uganda) and Johannesburg (South Africa), that feature in the chapters by Tabea Scharrer, Gianluca Iazzolino and Nereida Muñiz-Ripero, respectively.

Nairobi itself is important for the study of various types of urban development. These include such famous 'slums' as Kibera and Mathare, such informal settlements having long been studied, among others by Andrew Hake (1977). He described Nairobi as a 'self-help city', referring to the informal settlements that emerged around Nairobi over the twentieth century and their relationship with the more formal city. By contrast, since the 1990s, Nairobi has also become a regional hub for international organizations and multinational companies, serving as their headquarters for East Africa, and in some cases for the whole sub-Saharan African region or even globally. Many of these international organizations work in the humanitarian sector, especially in the field of refugee protection. In this way too, Nairobi became part of a 'displacement economy' (Hammar 2014) – not only as an area of refuge and settlement for forced

Introduction 13

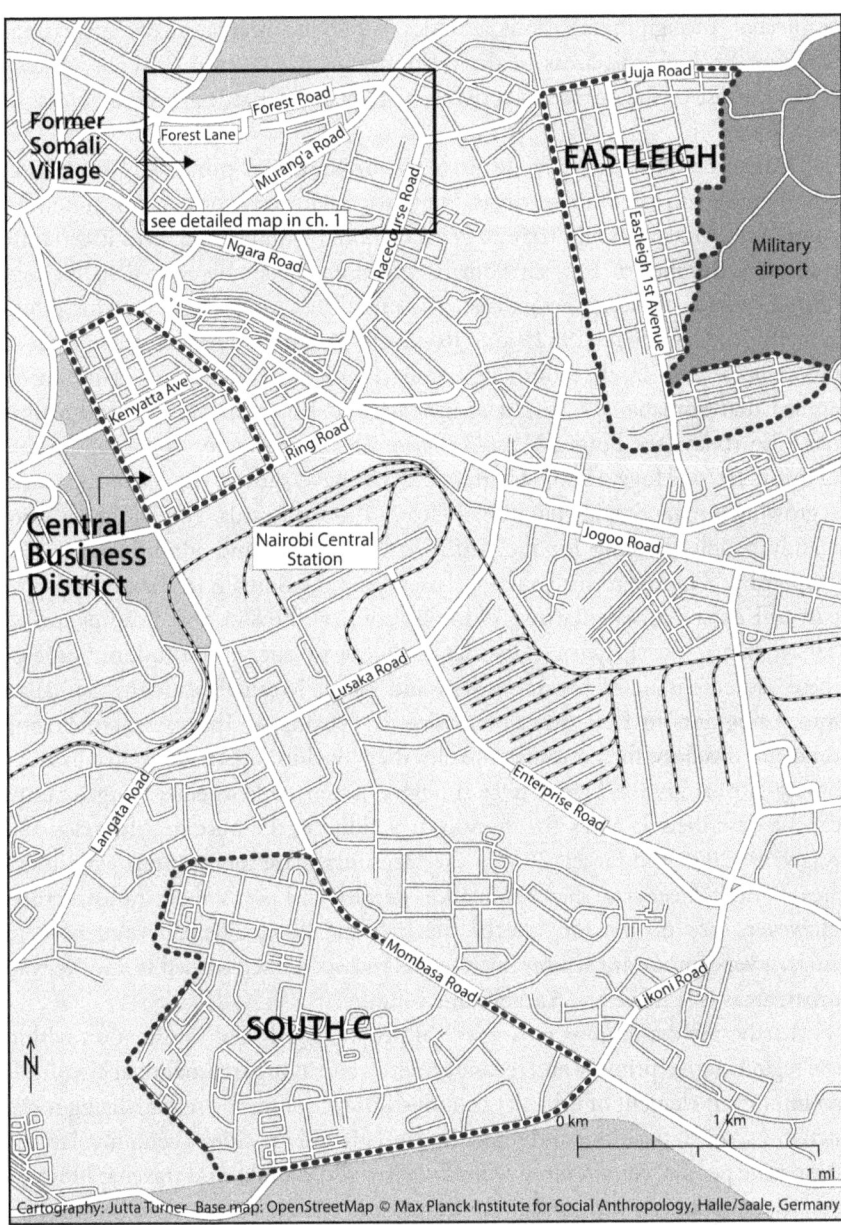

Map 0.2 Map of Nairobi.

migrants, but also as a place of transit for much international humanitarian aid, a place where political deals between warring parties were brokered and a place where money coming from the war-torn regions could be secured and reused for commercial deals. Many of these activities took place in different parts of the city, whose inhabitants normally live rather segregated lives, yet became connected through these various activities. While the international organizations work in the high-end areas in the northwest of the Central Business District (CBD), most of the Somalian activities take place in Eastleigh, situated east of the CBD.

Migration into the cities leads to an urbanization process. Urbanization describes the growth of urban areas, but is also a subjective process for those who come from rural areas and have to get acquainted with city life. This is certainly true for a number of Kenyan Somalis and Somalians who moved to Nairobi having previously been pastoralists. It is not clear though, how big this group actually is. Cassanelli (1982) and Reese (1996) have shown the importance of urban centres in the South of Somlia in precolonial times and it can be argued that Somalia was at least as urbanized as Kenya in the 1950s (which is true also today, see Potts 2017: 73, figure 2). Furthermore, as several authors (Turton 1974; Hogg 1986; Whittaker 2012) have shown, in Kenya there was a growing urban Somali population from 1900 onwards. At first these were mainly people working for the British colonial army and administration (see chapter by Whittaker, this volume). Later on many Somalis in the northeastern part of Kenya also sedentarized, either by political force in closed camps (called 'villages'), to participate in the wider economy or out of destitution. Some of these settlements later became towns and cities. Meanwhile, many Somalian forced migrants in East Africa were already urbanized. They were either long time city dwellers, forced to flee the city they lived in, or started to live in cities or city-like camps as refugees. Even though it is debatable whether refugee camps can be described as cities (in the way it is done by Pérouse de Montclos and Kagwanja 2000 and Jansen 2016),[7] they certainly share some aspects with urban areas – their sheer size, their population density and partly their infrastructure. However, they do not provide the freedom and independence experienced in cities, a very important reason for refugees to become self-settled in the Kenyan urban areas (see Lowe and Yarnell, this volume).

Lastly, the continuous movement of people, goods and information within the region, across primary and secondary cities and along transnational circuits, is an important element of urbanity (Simone 2011), constantly respatializing social networks, social positions and resources, and gives these cities a certain volatility. Alongside people, certain *forms of urbanity* are also mobile, and travel as lifestyles and spatial practices with those who move from one area to another. In this way, once rural practices become urbanized, Ethiopian restaurants become meeting points for people from different regions from the Horn of Africa, and Somali shopping centres are being built not only in East Africa (see the chapters by Scharrer and Iazzolino, this volume), but also in South Africa, Arab countries or in the USA.

Eastleigh

While our book has a wide focus on Somali urbanity in Kenya and Africa more broadly (as well as their links to urban sites shaped by Somali migration throughout the world), several of the chapters focus on one place in particular: Eastleigh (often written as Islii in Somali spelling). This has become the archetypal Somali urban space beyond Somalia (for a book-length historical ethnography of the estate, see Carrier 2017) and one symbol of the urban transformation that migration can bring. Eastleigh has long been one of the urban places of 'uncertain trajectories … simultaneously demonstrating marked development and decline' (Simone 2011: 380). It began when land speculators bought up the land in the early twentieth century, intending it to become a European populated township. However, few Europeans ever settled there, and instead much of it was bought up by Asian investors in the late 1910s and settled by their countrymen. Soon people of Asian origin dominated the estate. Maps from the colonial period show how Indianized the estate was at that time, many street names reflecting links to the Indian subcontinent (Carrier 2017). Importantly, alongside this Indian population was a smaller contingent of Somalis who had settled there as early as anyone else (ibid; Whittaker, this volume). This population would form a magnet for later Somali influxes.

In the late colonial and early period after independence, Swahili and other urbanized East Africans moved into the area, while better off Asians relocated to other quarters in Nairobi.[8] In the Kenyatta era, Kikuyus would come into the estate in large numbers, and still to this day they own much property in the estate. Thus, from the beginning onwards Eastleigh has been a multicultural and cosmopolitan estate. Like other parts of Nairobi too, Eastleigh suffered from infrastructural deterioration during the 1980s, which led again to demographic change, as the more affluent moved to more salubrious areas of the city. Soon the estate's demographics would shift yet again through migration.

On the one hand, military conflicts in the Horn of Africa led to an increased influx of refugees to Kenya (Ethiopian and Somalian), a great number of whom passed through or settled in Eastleigh. On the other hand, the economic system in northern Kenya changed as well due to these conflicts (and drought), increasing internal migration to the bigger towns. The pre-existing Somali population of Eastleigh would act as a draw for Somalian refugees and Somali internal migrants from northeastern Kenya.[9] It was in this age that Somali identity and dominance of the estate grew, leading some to dub it 'Mogadishu Ndogo' or 'Little Mogadishu', a nickname perceived with ambivalence by many in the estate (Carrier 2017), and one that hides other populations resident there, including a large population of Ethiopian Oromo (Carrier and Kochore, this volume). It was also at this time that the estate transformed into a commercial hub, as its shopping centres began to sprout (see the chapters by Hassan and by

16 *Tabea Scharrer and Neil Carrier*

Figure 0.1 Eastleigh viewed from the Grand Royal Hotel, 2011 (by now the road has been repaired) (photo: T. Scharrer).

Scharrer, this volume; Carrier and Lochery 2013), built upon remittances from the West (Mwangi, this volume) and cheaply manufactured goods of the East (Carrier and Elliott, this volume), processes that we describe in the chapters that follow.

Chapter Overview

Following the introduction, Yusuf Hassan, the Member of Parliament of Kamukunji Constituency in Nairobi (within which Eastleigh is located), gives a personal perspective on the history of Somalis in urban Kenya and their growing contribution to Kenya's politics and economy, a contribution symbolized by the transformation of Eastleigh. In doing so he combines his own personal history with that of the broader Somali community in Kenya, showing also the connection between mobility and urbanity.

The second part of the book focuses on the theme of urbanity and its role for Somali mobility, and also places the spatial epicentre of this book, Eastleigh, into a wider context. Hannah Whittaker (*The Somali Factor in Urban Kenya: A History*) provides an overview of early Somali migration into Nairobi and other urban areas of Kenya. It deals with migration to these towns, settlement patterns within them, the political mobilizations around resettlement programs by the colonial authorities, the position of Somalis in Kenyan society and economic struggles (especially regarding grazing rights). This historical contextualization of Somali mobile urbanity focuses on two aspects of early Somali urban settlement: the precarity of their legal status and the agency of Somali townspeople. It shows that the colonial discourses about Somali urbanity resemble to some extent contemporary discussions.

Next, Nereida Ripero-Muñiz (*The Port and the Island: Cosmopolitan and Vernacular Identity Constructions among Somali Women in Nairobi and Johannesburg*) places Eastleigh into a wider African landscape by shedding light on the similarities and differences between Nairobi and Johannesburg and the life of migrants within them. Both cities share certain characteristics for Somalis: they have become transitional places, as Somalis journey through or temporally inhabit these two cities on their way to somewhere else. They also find hostility in both cities from members of the local population and governmental organizations: their mobile urbanity is resisted. However, Nairobi and Johannesburg also offer cosmopolitan contexts for Somalis to interact, adding cosmopolitan practices to their vernacular ones. Nairobi has become a port of Somalia, an entry and exit point into and out of the country, not only for people but also for goods, money, ideas and practices. The Somali community here is bigger and more established than the one in Johannesburg, offering a larger network of economic and emotional support. Meanwhile in Johannesburg, a much smaller Somali community is found and isolation seems to be the main collective feeling. The city and its surroundings are perceived as a land of opportunities; its thriving economy, quite unique in the African context, makes it a 'treasure island' for many African migrants. This is also the case for Somalis, who endure a tough journey through the African continent full of great expectations that often melt away upon arrival (see also Cawo Abdi's 2015 book *Elusive Jannah* on the mixed fortunes that can await migrants upon reaching such destinations).

The third chapter by Neil Carrier and Hassan H. Kochore (*Being Oromo in Nairobi's 'Little Mogadishu': Superdiversity, Moral Community and the Open Economy*) situates Eastleigh in the wider ethnic landscape of Kenya by describing life in Eastleigh for a non-Somali population. Eastleigh is a much more heterogeneous and cosmopolitan place than is often realized, and many non-Somalis live and work in the estate, including a substantial population of Oromo refugees from Ethiopia. They have transformed parts of the estate into a 'Little Ethiopia' and make a substantial contribution to the Eastleigh economy. This chapter considers the journeys the Oromo make to Eastleigh as well as the religious and social factors that enable them to integrate within the Somali-dominated economy. It will also show how patterns of urban life in Eastleigh are replicated in other parts of the Oromo world, as elements of the estate's economy have been transplanted to Johannesburg in an important demonstration of mobile urbanity. Furthermore, interactions with Somalis continue as the two groups find their lives interwoven in other parts of the world including the UK and USA where many have been resettled.

The third part of the book turns towards the economic networks built up and used by the Somali community in the urban areas and through their mobility. Neil Carrier and Hannah Elliott (*Demanding and Commanding Goods: The Eastleigh Transformation Told through the 'Lives' of Its Commodities*) focus on the goods that Somali businesspeople import and export through their, often transnational, networks. Situating their chapter within the anthropological literature on commodities – including Appadurai's famous volume *The Social Life of Things* (1986) – they show how understanding the 'social life' of the items that criss-cross Eastleigh reveals the importance of growing production of cheap clothes and electronics in Asia, and the increasing demand for these products in East Africa. Access to both the supply and demand side of these products has been leveraged by Somalis into the kinds of urban transformation we see in Eastleigh. Thus, a key focus of the chapter is on these products, situated in what Gordon Mathews terms 'low-end globalization'. The chapter looks also at other goods whose flow impacts the estate, from *miraa* (the stimulant more widely known as khat) to gold, a holder of much economic and cultural value for Somali women.

The chapter by John Mwangi Githigaro and Kenneth Omeje (*Capital Mobilization among the Somali Refugee Business Community in Eastleigh, Nairobi*) looks in depth at how Somalis in Eastleigh have raised the capital that has created such a booming economy in this former residential area of Nairobi. Mwangi punctures the rumours as to the source of the money behind this transformation by showing how the Eastleigh economy represents a convergence of local and international capital of various forms – financial and social. The chapter describes how this capital is mobilized through clan and kinship networks (that often stretch around the globe), through rotating credit associations (known as *ayuuto* in Somali), community contingency funds known as *qaran* among Somalis, business partnerships (often again linked to clan and kinship), personal savings, capital from other business ventures, and even, on rarer occasions, through bank loans. Mwangi also argues that rather than being a drain on Kenyan society, Somali mobile capital has made much positive contribution to the Kenyan economy.

Holly A. Ritchie focuses in her chapter (*Challenging the Status Quo from the Bottom Up? Gender and Enterprise in Somali Migrant Communities in Nairobi, Kenya*) on the situation of refugee women. She looks at how they try to survive through entrepreneurship despite their insecure legal status and the many challenges they face, including violence and other forms of abuse. Ritchie's focus is on the petty refugee traders, who actually form a great proportion of those operating in the Eastleigh economy. She highlights how their businesses operate, many combining different sorts of occupations. Most of her interviewees were focused more on survival rather than business growth. Such humble enterprises are beset with challenges, from raids by the City Council (checking for valid business permits), gang violence and harassment, but most especially navigating the changing religious norms within a society where Salafist teachings have much influence on how women conduct their business and lives in general. Ritchie thus shows how Eastleigh remains a challenging urban environment for its refugee residents, despite the evident wealth.

The last chapter of this section, by Tabea Scharrer (*Reinventing Retail: 'Somali' Shopping Centres in Kenya*), explores how changes in the Eastleigh business sector, which rely very much on a transformation of the notion and usage of space, became a model for Kenya in general and the whole East African region. Using the example of Nakuru, it is shown that these Somali shopping centres follow a different spatial logic than the markets and shops that used to dominate Kenya's retail sector. Coming mainly from Mogadishu with hardly more than their knowledge on how to do business, Somalian refugees transformed hotel rooms in Eastleigh to shops during daytime, bigger shops were subdivided into smaller stalls and later on shopping complexes were built, where every inch is made use of. These shopping centres combine elements of open-air markets and Western style shopping malls. Lacking the glamour of the latter, 'Somali' shopping centres have one or more floors with traders either renting a shop, a table, or a place outside a shop. While open-air markets are open, public places, shopping centres are privately owned and driven, often with a rather long chain of brokers, owners, leasers and subleasers. Contrary to Western style malls, there are often no places for recreation or public meetings, the pragmatism of trade reigns supreme. These transformations were taken up as a model quickly spreading throughout Kenya and beyond: such urban transformations are themselves mobile.

In the fourth and last section of the book, different aspects of the politics of Somali mobility are examined. All three chapters in this section are heavily influenced by the period in which they were written. Following spates of terror-related violence since 2011, including the Westgate Mall attack of 2013 and intermittent attacks in Nairobi, Mombasa and in parts of northeastern Kenya, the security forces of the Kenyan Government embarked on a large-scale crackdown on Eastleigh and other urban areas in 2014. In an operation called Usalama ('Peace') Watch, Kenya's security forces raided houses and caused shops to be closed. Hundreds of residents were incarcerated at the Safaricom Kasarani Stadium, from where they were sent to the refugee camps or were deported to Somalia. Lucy Lowe and Mark Yarnell (*Perpetually in Transit: Somalian Refugees in a Context of Increasing Hostility*) focus on the life of urban Somalians in Eastleigh. On the one hand, they focus on a time of heightened political tension with many assaults by the police. On the other, they provide an answer to why people opt to live in cities in contrast to life in refugee camps, even though they cannot profit from humanitarian aid provided in camps, and suffer from a challenging security situation. Living in the city, and specifically within a predominantly Somali neighbourhood, allowed Somalian forced migrants to gain an existence as non-refugees. There, through private businesses and corruption, they are able to purchase goods, health care, education and even a particular sense of freedom. The perception by Kenyans and non-Kenyans that Eastleigh was ethnically Somali, established an environment in which people could be Somalis, rather than refugees. The temporality of this space, which could be understood as rented rather than owned, the ambiguous legality of residency and the ubiquitous insecurity meant that the boundaries and definitions of who was, or was not, Somali had to be continually reinforced.

Joseph Wandera and Halkano Abdi Wario (*Framing the Swoop: A Comparative Analysis of Operation Usalama Watch in Muslim and Secular Print Media in Kenya*) focus on the public discussion of the security operation Usalama Watch. There was unprecedented media coverage of the operation, with secular and faith-based media channels covering the government's action in diverging ways. This chapter analyses the framing of the swoop in Eastleigh and other urban areas inhabited by Somalis by the *Daily Nation*, a leading secular newspaper, and by the *Friday Bulletin*, a journal published by the Jamia Mosque in Nairobi. Embedding the chapter in the theoretical framework of 'securitization', the authors ask how far the particular publishers are willing to buy in and to support the state's effort to frame the security situation in Kenya in a way that allows for extraordinary security measures.

The tenth and last chapter in this volume, by Gianluca Iazzolino (*Beyond Eastleigh: A New Little Mogadishu in Uganda?*), focuses on recent changes in Somali migration flows to Uganda. It examines the Somali routes to Kampala, which provide an interesting case-study to reflect on: the complex interweaving of factors shaping migration/mobility patterns; the often not so clear-cut separation between forced and voluntary migration categories; and the influence of low-end globalization (Mathews, Ribeiro and Vega 2012), referring to transnational networks based on low-capital and informal business. The chapter retraces the historical origins of the Somali presence in Uganda and the development of a new 'Little Mogadishu' in Kampala's Kisenyi district. The recent influx to Uganda was driven by several factors at a regional level: the growing pressure on Somalian refugees in Kenya, as well as the ease of access from Uganda to neighbouring areas, particularly the Democratic Republic of Congo, Rwanda and, until recent upheavals, South Sudan – but also to Somalia, thanks to a visa policy which allows Somali passport-holders to re-enter Uganda. The immigration of Somalians to Uganda is also facilitated by the legal framework of the latter, especially the implementation of Uganda's 2006 refugee law. Therefore, the case of the Somali diaspora in Uganda offers insights into the relation between the state security apparatus and refugee populations and offers a counterpoint to the manner in which Kenya has attempted to deal with its Somali population and their mobile urbanity.

In an *Afterword* Günther Schlee provides some concluding remarks to the collection of papers in this volume. He focuses his discussion on two main issues: the question of how far the people presented in this volume can be discussed as part of a 'global Somali community' (therefore widening the scope of this volume to a global one), and the importance of urban life for the Somali diaspora. He argues that the heterogeneous background of Somalis, spatially and historically, makes it difficult to talk about one community. Furthermore, patrilineal links and clanship are still highly important features, dividing Somalis into several segments. This division is somewhat dissolved in the urban settings of East Africa, as the relative peace there seems to favour inter-clan cooperation. In addition, Schlee contends that urbanity has become a global lifestyle of Somalis, who often choose well-connected cities as a place for settling down, cities that facilitate their mobile urbanity.

Neil Carrier is Lecturer in Social Anthropology at the University of Bristol (UK). After finishing his PhD in Social Anthropology at the University of St Andrews, he moved to the African Studies Centre at the University of Oxford. He has published two monographs, on Khat (*Kenyan Khat: The Social Life of a Stimulant*, Brill, 2007) and on Eastleigh (*Little Mogadishu: Eastleigh, Nairobi's Global Somali Hub*, Oxford University Press, 2017).

Tabea Scharrer is a postdoctoral researcher at the Max Planck Institute for Social Anthropology, Halle (Germany). She has conducted research in Tanzania and Kenya on Islamic missionary movements as well as on migration-related issues in refugee camps as well as in urban areas. Her publications include the monograph *Narrative islamischer Konversion: Biographische Erzählungen konvertierter Muslime in Ostafrika* (transcript, 2013) and a co-edited volume on *Middle Classes in Africa* (Palgrave, 2018).

Notes

1. On Guangzhou and how its rapid growth links to the mobility of people and goods, see Mathews, Dan Lin and Yang (2017).
2. This also means that our concept of 'mobile urbanity' is quite different from that of Piscitelli, for whom, following De Certeau, it is a 'heuristic tool to read the city through the everyday life experiences of mobile subjects' (2018: 34).
3. For the southern African examples of Mapungubwe and Great Zimbabwe, see Pikirayi (2017).
4. The term 'Somali' designates an ambiguous category that straddles ethnic and national levels. In Kenya there are many who are ethnic Somalis but Kenyan by nationality –

Somalis now form the sixth-biggest ethnic group in Kenya according to the (contested) census conducted in 2009. Yet the term Somali can also refer to someone from the Republic of Somalia. Many refugees in Kenya are Somali by ethnicity and nationality (though some of these refugees were born in Kenya). To complicate matters further, some come from other Somali parts of the Horn of Africa, including the Ogaden in Ethiopia, the Republic of Somaliland and Djibouti. Thus, in this book we use Somali to refer to a broader category that encompasses Somali speakers or people from Somali families whether from Somalia, Somaliland, Kenya or from the Somali diaspora abroad. When referring specifically to Somalis of Kenyan origin, we use the term 'Kenyan Somali', and when referring to Somalis from the Republic of Somalia in particular, we use the term Somalian. Even these labels cannot avoid some ambiguity, as so many people and their families have long straddled identities as Kenyan and Somalian purely by dint of the arbitrary colonial placement of the border between the two countries.

5. For a comprehensive summary of the presence of Somalian refugees in Kenya and the changing Kenyan refugee policy see Scharrer (forthcoming).
6. See Schlee (2001: 23) who argues that it is often difficult to distinguish 'migrant knowledge', deriving from the adaptation to often precarious situations in the course of migration, from effects of socialization (be it in the region where people grew up or where they settled later in their lives).
7. See also the blog entry by Jeff Crisp who argues against the idea that refugee camps can be considered as cities (http://www.refugeesinternational.org/blog/zaatari-camp-and-not-city; retrieved 16 September 2016).
8. Carrier (2017: Chapter 1), P. Goldsmith (2008), 'Kenya: Eastleigh Goes Global', *The East African*, 17 August. http://allafrica.com/stories/printable/200808190301.html, retrieved 26 January 2010.
9. According to a Somali politician (interviewed in September 2014), there were about 200,000 Somalis living in Eastleigh, half of whom were Somalian refugees. Many of them were either registered in the refugee camps, but living in Eastleigh, or they were not registered at all (see also Scharrer 2018).

References

Abdi, C.M. 2015. *Elusive Jannah: The Somali Diaspora and a Borderless Muslim Identity.* Minneapolis: Minnesota University Press.
Akesson, L., and M.E. Baaz. 2015. *Africa's Return Migrants: The New Developers?* London: Zed Books.
Appadurai, A. (ed.). 1986. *The Social Life of Things: Commodities in Cultural Perspective.* Cambridge: Cambridge University Press.
Bakewell, O., and G. Jonsson. 2011. *Migration, Mobility and the African City.* Oxford: International Migration Institute.
Besteman, C. 1998. 'Primordialist Blinders: A Reply to IM Lewis', *Cultural Anthropology* 13(1): 109–20.
Carrier, N. 2017. *Little Mogadishu: Eastleigh, Nairobi's Global Somali Hub.* New York: Oxford University Press.
Carrier, N., and E. Lochery. 2013. 'Missing States? Somali Trade Networks and the Eastleigh Transformation', *Journal of Eastern African Studies* 7(2): 334–52.
Cassanelli, L. 1982. *The Shaping of Somali Society. Reconstructing the History of a Pastoral People, 1600 to 1900.* Philadelphia: University of Pennsylvania Press.

Castles, S., H. de Haas and M.J. Miller. 2017. *The Age of Migration: International Population Movements in the Modern World*. London: Palgrave Macmillan.
Cohen, R. 2008. *Global Diasporas: An Introduction*. London: Routledge.
Cooper, N. 2001. 'Conflict Goods: The Challenges for Peacekeeping and Conflict Prevention', *International Peacekeeping* 8(3): 21–38.
Crush, J., and S. Ramachandran. 2010. 'Xenophobia, International Migration and Development', *Journal of Human Development and Capabilities* 11(2): 209–28.
Ferguson, J. 2006. *Global Shadows: Africa in the Neoliberal World Order*. Durham, NC: Duke University Press.
Geschiere, P. 2009. *The Perils of Belonging: Autochthony, Citizenship and Exclusion in Africa and Europe*. Chicago: Chicago University Press.
Glick Schiller, N., L. Basch and C. Blanc-Szanton. 1992. 'Transnationalism: A New Analytic Framework for Understanding Migration', *Annals of the New York Academy of Sciences* 645: 1–24.
Glick Schiller, N., and A. Çağlar. 2010. *Locating Migration: Rescaling Cities and Migrants*. Ithaca, NY: Cornell University Press.
———. 2016. 'Displacement, Emplacement and Migrant Newcomers: Rethinking Urban Sociabilities within Multiscalar Power', *Identities* 23(1): 17–34.
Gluckman, M. 2009. 'Anthropological Problems Arising from the African Industrial Revolution', in M. Mollona, G.D. Neve and J. Parry (eds), *Industrial Work and Life: An Anthropological Reader*. Oxford, New York: Berg, pp. 299–309.
Hake, A. 1977. *African Metropolis: Nairobi's Self-Help City*. London: Palgrave Macmillan.
Hammar, A. 2014. 'Introduction', in A. Hammar (ed.), *Displacement Economies: Paradoxes of Crisis and Creativity in Africa*. London, New York: Zed Books, pp. 3–32.
Hogg, R. 1986. 'The New Pastoralism: Poverty and Dependency in Northern Kenya', *Africa* 56(3): 319–33.
Hoffman, D. 2007. 'The City as Barracks: Freetown, Monrovia, and the Organization of Violence in Postcolonial African Cities', *Cultural Anthropology* 22(3): 400–28.
Horst, C. 2006. *Transnational Nomads: How Somalis Cope with Refugee Life in the Dadaab Camps of Kenya*. Oxford, New York: Berghahn.
IOM. 2015. *World Migration Report 2015*. Geneva: IOM Publications. Retrieved 23 September 2018 from http://www.iom.int/world-migration-report-2015.
Jansen, B.J. 2016. '"Digging Aid": The Camp as an Option in East and the Horn of Africa', *Journal of Refugee Studies* 29(2): 149–65.
Kibreab, G. 2014. 'Forced Migration in the Great Lakes and Horn of Africa', in E. Fiddian-Qasimeyeh, et al. (eds), *The Oxford Handbook of Refugee and Forced Migration Studies*. Oxford: Oxford University Press.
Levitt, P. 2001. *The Transnational Villagers*. Berkeley: University of California Press.
Lewis, I.M. 1961. *A Pastoral Democracy: A Study of Pastoralism and Politics among the Northern Somali of the Horn of Africa*. London: Oxford University Press.
Lindley, A. 2010. *The Early Morning Phone Call: Somali Refugees' Remittances*. Oxford, New York: Berghahn.
Lochery, E. 2012. 'Rendering Difference Visible: The Kenyan State and its Somali Citizens', *African Affairs* 111(445): 615–39.
Lodhi, A.Y. 1992. 'African Settlements in India', *Nordic Journal of African Studies* 1(1): 83–86.
Löw, M. 2012. 'The Intrinsic Logic of Cities: Towards a New Theory on Urbanism', *Urban Research & Practice* 5(3): 303–15.

Mathews, G. 2011. *Ghetto at the Centre of the World: Chungking Mansions, Hong Kong*. Chicago: University of Chicago Press.

Mathews, G., G.L. Ribeiro and C.A. Vega. 2012. *Globalization from Below: The World's Other Economy*. London: Routledge.

Mathews, G., Dan Lin, L. and Yang Yang. 2017. *The World in Guangzhou: Africans and other Foreigners in South China's Global Marketplace*. Chicago: University of Chicago Press.

Mbembe, A., and S. Nuttall. 2004. 'Writing the World from an African Metropolis', *Public Culture* 16(3): 347–72.

Nyamnjoh, F.B. 2013. 'Fiction and Reality of Mobility in Africa', *Citizenship Studies* 17(6–7): 653–80, doi:10.1080/13621025.2013.834121.

Pérouse de Montclos, M.-A., and P.M. Kagwanja. 2000. 'Refugee Camps or Cities? The Socio-Economic Dynamics of the Dadaab and Kakuma Camps in Northern Kenya', *Journal of Refugee Studies* 13(2): 205–22.

Pikirayi, I. 2017. 'Trade, Globalisation and the Archaic State in Southern Africa', *Journal of Southern African Studies* 43(5): 879–93.

Piscitelli, P. 2018. 'Mobile Urbanity in Southern Africa. The Socio-Spatial Practices of Informal Cross-Border Traders Between Johannesburg and Maputo', in A. Petrillo and P. Bellaviti (eds), *Sustainable Urban Development and Globalization*. Cham: Springer, pp. 33–47.

Portes, A. 1997. 'Globalization from Below: The Rise of Transnational Communities', *Working Paper*. Retrieved 14 October 2016 from http://www.transcomm.ox.ac.uk/working%20papers/portes.pdf.

Potts, D. 2017. 'Conflict and Collisions in Sub-Saharan African Urban Definitions: Interpreting Recent Urbanization Data From Kenya', *World Development* 97: 67–78, doi:10.1016/j.worlddev.2017.03.036.

Rawlence, B. 2016. *City of Thorns. Nine Lives in the World's Largest Refugee Camp*. London: Picador.

Reese, S.S. 1996. *Patricians of the Benaadir: Islamic Learning, Commerce and Somali Urban Identity in the Nineteenth Century*. Philadelphia: University of Pennsylvania Press.

Scharrer, T. forthcoming. 'Leaving the Camp Behind? The Case of Somalian Refugees in Kenya', *European Union Trust Fund for Africa, Research and Evidence Facility Working Paper No. 3*. London and Nairobi: EUTF Research and Evidence Facility.

Scharrer, T. 2018. '"Ambiguous Citizens": Kenyan Somalis and the Question of Belonging', *Journal of Eastern African Studies* 12(3): 494–513, doi:10.1080/17531055.2018.14838 64.

van Schendel, W., and I. Abraham. 2005. *Illicit Flows and Criminal Things: States, Borders and the Other Side of Globalization*. Bloomington: Indiana University Press.

Schlee, G. 2001. '"Globalisierung von unten": Strategien und mentale Landkarten von afrikanischen Migranten in Europa'. Retrieved 3 July 2017 from https://www.eth.mpg.de/3660038/project01.pdf.

Simone, A. 2006. 'Pirate Towns: Reworking Social and Symbolic Infrastructures in Johannesburg and Douala', *Urban Studies* 43(2): 357–70.

———. 2011. 'The Urbanity of Movement: Dynamic Frontiers in Contemporary Africa', *Journal of Planning Education and Research* 31(4): 379–91.

Steinberg, J. 2015. *A Man of Good Hope*. Johannesburg: Jonathan Ball.

Turton, E.R. 1974. 'The Isaq Somali Diaspora and Poll-Tax Agitation in Kenya, 1936–41', *African Affairs* 73(292): 325–46.

Urry, J. 2000. *Sociology Beyond Societies: Mobilities for the Twenty-First Century*. London: Routledge.
Whittaker, H. 2012. 'Forced Villagization during the Shifta Conflict in Kenya, ca. 1963–1968', *The International Journal of African Historical Studies* 45(3): 343–64.
Wirth, L. 1938. 'Urbanism as a Way of Life', *American Journal of Sociology* 44(1): 1–24.

Interlude
Being and Becoming Mobile

Yusuf Hassan

This volume is about how mobility and urbanity come together in the lives of Somalis living in Kenya, Uganda and elsewhere in East Africa, and looks at how Somalis have been highly influential townspeople in the region. In this interlude I offer my own take on this *mobile urbanity*, detailing how Somalis have built up such a key presence in East African towns and cities, and accounting for the recent rise in Somali economic and political power that such important urban sites as Eastleigh symbolize. In what follows, I draw not only on my recent experiences as Member of Parliament for Kamukunji (the constituency within which Eastleigh is situated), but also my own life story as a Somali growing up as part of a highly mobile family in various settlements within Kenya and beyond.

My earliest recollection is leaving Nairobi on the back of a lorry heading to Garissa with my mother, for what must have been an early version of *dhaqan celin* (a form of cultural education involving a return to Somali homeland regions, popular now with Somalis in the global diaspora) to learn the Quran and the Somali language in a *dugsi* (a school with an emphasis on Islamic teaching). Shortly after, we had to flee the escalating conflict in northern Kenya. The Kenyan state was at war against its Somali citizens to quell an armed revolt in the region. This was during what became officially known as the 'Shifta war' (see below) and Kenya was increasingly a hostile place for all Somalis regardless of which side of the conflict they were on.

My family fled to Tanzania and settled in Tarime, which is just on the other side of the Kenyan border. At the end of the war, we returned to Kenya and moved to Nyamtiro, a village in Kuria on the Kenyan–Tanzanian border. We were so close to the border that the back of our house touched the beam separating the two countries.

Disgruntled by Kenya's role in the collapse of the East African Community, President Julius Nyerere permanently shut Tanzania's border with Kenya. With that the cross-border trade dried up. We had to move again, this time to Busia on the Kenya–Uganda border. In Busia, the border was marked by a small dirt road. When one of the Somali shops in Uganda ran out of an item, they could literally shout out to the Somali shop on the Kenyan side and the item would be promptly delivered across. Often the shops were owned by Somalis of the same family. I was saved from these periodic relocations and enjoyed some stability after I was sent to a boarding school.

Eventually, my family moved to Namanga on the Kenyan–Tanzanian border. I recall my elder brother Abdikadir leaving home to work for an uncle in Tororo, Uganda, another frontier town. After raising sufficient money to set-up his own business, he outdid our parents and emigrated to Congo and set up shop in the border town of Bunia.

My mother was herself a mobile trader of some sort, a long-distance hawker. She regularly travelled to Mombasa and Nairobi to buy clothes and shoes for women. She would sell the stuff to customers living along the route. At times, she would run out of merchandise and return to Mombasa while being only half way through her journey.

This story was typical of the lives of many Somalis who in their search for new opportunities and as a result of political pressures found it difficult to establish roots and a sense of locality, belonging and continuity. This, of course, links to the wider context of the tense relationship between the Kenyan state and its Somali population.

Kenyan Somalis: Strangers in Their Own Country

Somalis have lived in Kenya long before its creation as a country. In the census of 2009 they numbered almost two and a half million,[1] and they occupy about 40 per cent of Kenyan territory. Yet they remain on the margins of the society.

Both the British colonial regime and the post-colonial state employed a raft of repressive policies and measures to deter, prevent and deny Somalis from becoming part of the Kenyan story. Somalis have had a precarious existence as 'ambiguous citizens' (Scharrer 2018) and 'strangers' in their own country. For years, they have been engaged in a protracted struggle for space, recognition and belonging in Kenya.

The exclusion and othering of Somalis is a complicated, historical and deeply structural problem (see also Weitzberg 2017). It is rooted in Kenya's past when the colonial regime categorized Somalis as 'aliens' and 'undesirables' and quarantined them to the area known as the Northern Frontier District (NFD). As a consequence, the area was neglected and marginalized. The fiercely independent Somalis did not fit into the colonial project and the British imposed repressive and exclusionist practices to keep them at bay. These practices continue to inform and shape Kenya's approach to its Somali citizens.

At the end of colonial rule, Somalis felt no emotional attachment to or affection for Kenya, and in 1962, when Kenyan Somalis got the chance to freely express their views on their future in a referendum, they overwhelmingly voiced their wish to secede to Somalia.[2]

The British rejected their demand and the NFD remained part of Kenya, the Somali-majority Garissa, Wajir and Mandera districts becoming the North Eastern Province (NEP). This decision sparked an armed revolt for Somali self-determination in what in Kenya became known as the 'Shifta war' (1963–1968). This war caused the deaths of thousands of Somalis, massive displacement and economic destruction and further complicated the case of Somalis in Kenya. They were now viewed as a 'fifth column' and the 'enemy within', as an existential threat to the new Kenya. They not only suffered crippling inequality and marginality but also unspeakable brutality at the hands of the security forces and local administration. Having boycotted the 1963 Kenya elections, they were also unrepresented in the political system. In any case, with a state of emergency declared, a string of punitive laws hastily passed by the new Kenya parliament ensured that they enjoyed no rights whatsoever. The NEP was governed like an occupied territory and its population treated not as citizens but rather as subjects. The state was determined to crush the rebellion by any means necessary, and was relentless in its scorched earth campaign (see Whittaker 2014). This triggered a humanitarian crisis of huge proportions. Thousands fled to Somalia and Ethiopia, while the rest were rounded up and forcibly settled in what the government described as 'protected villages' similar to the detention camps established by the British during the Mau Mau uprising. The triple scourge of war, drought and diseases took its toll on the population and decimated their livestock, so breaking their economic lifeline. This led to increased pauperization and forced them to seek employment opportunities in Nairobi, Mombasa, Nakuru and beyond. Indeed, Somali settlement and urbanization in Kenya has owed much to such harsh policies meted out by the state.

The cruel and degrading actions of the government continued long after the end of the war. In the 1980s, during Moi's regime, the state carried out the worst atrocities in the history of independent Kenya. In what were acts of collective punishment, security forces killed thousands of civilians and burnt homesteads in the Bulla Karatasi massacre in Garissa of November 1980, the Malka Mari massacres in Mandera of 1981/2 and the Wagalla massacre in Wajir of February 1984 (see TJRC Report 2013: 101–44).[3] The Moi regime also conducted a major screening exercise in 1989 which forced Somalis to carry a separate pink coloured identification card and created 'hierarchies of citizenry' (Lochery 2012; Lind, Mutahi and Oosterom 2017).

In the 1990s and 2000s, Somalis made incremental social and political gains, raising hope that they were at last coming out of the cold. They increasingly became visible in the business sector and started to assert their democratic rights. However, the rise of Somalis was viewed with suspicion and seen as a threat, fuelling growing xenophobia, amplified by the narrative that their success was driven by illicit trade and piracy money.

The emergence of Al-Shabaab, the Somalia-based militant group, and Kenya's military invasion of Somalia once again put them under a negative spotlight. Somalis had come full circle and just like in the 1960s and 1970s were being accused of disloyalty. In the eyes of the state they were now all 'Al-Shabaab sympathizers' and 'terrorists', who posed a threat to the peace and security of Kenya.

The worst experience was in April 2014 when the state launched the widespread security crackdown codenamed Usalama Watch targeting the Somali community (see chapters by Lowe and Yarnell, and by Wario and Wandera in this volume). This ill-advised and counter-productive campaign sparked outrage and deepened the mistrust and tension between Somalis and the state.

The state has since reintroduced stringent screening procedures to sift the 'indigenous' Somali from the 'alien' Somali and prevent 'outsiders' from acquiring Kenyan identity papers and passports. Many young Somalis who are unable to acquire identity documents have been thrown into a legal black hole and remain in a state of limbo.

Urban Somali Pioneers

This Kenyan-Somali history – so fraught with adversity – has rarely been portrayed as an urban one, as Somalis are viewed mainly as pastoralist nomads of the north. Indeed, the marginalization of Somalis from the history of Kenya has also marginalized the story of their contribution to the country's towns and cities. Yet they have long been important townspeople. One movement that has left an indelible mark on urban Kenya is that of Somalis who came from Somaliland with the British in 1890s and early 1900s. They were part and parcel of the colonial project and played an active role in the making of the new Kenya and its small and large urban settlements. They settled along the new Kenya–Uganda Railway from Nairobi, Naivasha, Nakuru, Kisumu, Kakamega, Eldoret, Nyeri, Nanyuki and Rumuruti among other places, creating urban residential enclaves known as Kambi ya Somali. They were few in numbers but were quickly able to extend their reach to many parts of Kenya.

Despite their growing affluence, influence and urbanity, they remained mobile and were often in motion in quest for new opportunities. They had left their pastoral life behind but somehow found it impossible to establish a locality of belonging. Many of them had little sense of attachment or permanence in the places they settled in. Paradoxically, the more urbanized they became, the more mobile they were. They seamlessly adopted their mobile nomadic background to their new urbanity. The title of this volume – mobile urbanity – rings true in many respects.

Many of these Somalis settled in dangerous and remote frontier outposts, which provided opportunities for informal trading: buying cheap contraband goods from one country to the next, using unofficial crossings and unregulated routes. Being an oral society there was no paperwork or records, they flourished mostly in informality. Much of the Somali trading was therefore outside state control.

Long before the rise of Eastleigh as a major Somali business hub, Somalis had established economic networks linking with Somalia, the Somali region of Ethiopia, the NFD and extending further into Tanzania and Uganda. Somalis' first foray into business in the new colony was to trade in cattle, goats, sheep and horses to meet the demand created by the new settlers in the white highlands of Kenya. Later, when the British colonial authorities banned the movement of livestock, Somalis were quick to find new trading routes and markets, first between the Gikuyus and Maasais in the reserves, whose stocks were decimated by droughts and outbreaks of diseases, and later among the increasingly urbanized Africans (Kitching 1980: 212-33). A Somali merchant established the first known butchery in Dagoretti, a part of Nairobi. Later Somalis opened butcheries and groceries in other new commercial centres[4] and were instrumental in popularizing the widespread culture of *nyama choma* (roast meat) in Kenya. Somalis later made headway into other businesses and accumulated enough capital to acquire land in new urban centres such as Nairobi (Ngong, Mbagathi, Kileleshwa, Ngara and later Eastleigh), Nakuru, Naivasha and established a new urban settlement in Isiolo.

These Somalis not only challenged the colonial authority and fought to advance their rights but also supported Kenya's liberation. Several of them were actively engaged in Kenya's nationalist politics. They provided financial and material support to the Kenya African Union (KAU, later Kenya African National Union, KANU) and the Mau Mau movement. In the 1940s, Mohamed Hassan (who was the first Somali to study at the elite Alliance High School) was a senior member of KAU and the Mau Mau movement. He was detained and dispossessed of his business and property by the British colonial authorities.[5] Ali Aden Lord, the first Somali to be elected from northern Kenya to the Kenya Legislative Assembly (LEGCO) in 1960, was another well-known supporter of the Mau Mau.

A century later, Somalis have once again led the way in revolutionizing consumer habits in Kenya and beyond by introducing a new shopping experience exemplified by the Garissa Lodge business model in Eastleigh that sparked the commercial growth of this Nairobi district, symbolic of the rising economic and political power of Somalis in Kenya.

Eastleigh Metamorphosis

The Eastleigh that I knew in the 1970 and1980s was a very different place to the one I returned back to after two decades of living in exile. Eastleigh was then a sleepy residential neighbourhood dominated by South Asians – Goans, Sikhs, Hindus and Muslims. The Goans lived in Eastleigh Section I and had their social and cultural base around the imposing St Teresa Catholic Church on the corner of First Avenue and Juja Road; the Sunni Muslims were next door on Second Avenue around the 3rd and 8th Street Mosques; and the Ismailis were centred around the Khoja Mosque on 4th Street. The Sikhs lived mostly in Section I and parts of neighbouring Pangani, while the Hindus lived in the heart of the neighbourhood in Section II. A mixed group of South Asians spread into Section III. A significant number of Yemeni and Seychellois immigrants also lived there. Although Somalis were among the first occupants of Eastleigh, until then they were a minority.

Upon my return in 2006, I was astounded by how much the neighbourhood had changed. The most visible shift was the demography. Gone were almost all the South Asians and with them all their cultural manifestations including the large weekend family picnics in Eastleigh and Pangani playgrounds, women in saris, children playing cricket and the *paan*, samosa and *bajia* vendors. Instead of Gujarati, Urdu, Hindi and Punjabi, the languages in the air now were Somali and Oromo. The neighbourhood had undergone a metamorphosis.

Eastleigh was now a crowded, chaotic and noisy commercial place, the old single-storey Indian family houses had been torn down and replaced by high-rise multi-storey buildings. The iconic Kenya Bus terminal was gone, in its place now stood the glassy blue Eastleigh Mall, one of the many that dominate the neighbourhood.

The driving forces behind this remarkable transformation were Somali immigrants. The first wave of these migrants came to Kenya after the 1969 military coup in Somalia and the overthrow of the Ethiopian Emperor Haile Selassie in 1974. But the largest influx of refugees into Kenya from both Somalia and Ethiopia happened after the collapse of the Somali state and the demise of the military regime in Ethiopia in the early 1990s.

The new immigrants were attracted to Eastleigh because it was already home to a large Somali population, which gave them a sense of comfort and belonging. They were quick to seize on the business opportunities it offered and injected new life into the neighbourhood. Although there are highly successful entrepreneurs who have forged business partnerships with outsiders (across ethnic lines), most businesses in Eastleigh are based on family and kinship, clanship and ethnic ties. Out of these have emerged a new class of merchants with global links.

With the flow of capital, goods, people, information and ideas, and trading networks straddling several continents, Eastleigh had changed into a dynamic global economic hub (Carrier 2017). It was now a super-diverse and culturally vibrant place that rivalled the Nairobi Central Business District and Westlands. Taking advantage of globalization and regionalization, Somalis have developed complex transnational and transregional networks linking East Africa with nodes in Asia, Middle East, Europe and North America. They import from Dubai, China, Turkey, Egypt, India, Brazil, Thailand and Pakistan. And they have export markets in Saudi Arabia, UAE and Qatar, as well as to Somalia. They have overcome multiple barriers in Kenya and in the foreign markets where they buy their supplies. They have forged business alliances with local partners. To stay competitive, they constantly scan for cheaper products and new markets. To promote and advance their business interests, they also formed the Eastleigh Business District Association.

Since 2012, Eastleigh has undergone yet another remarkable urban renewal. All around, there are visible signs of improvement in its infrastructure. The completion of First Avenue and General Waruingi's dual-carriage roads and the reconstruction of Second Avenue and Muratina Roads has spurred the economic growth of the neighbourhood. This is reflected in ongoing construction projects and the many businesses that open in the neighbourhood every month. Eastleigh's growth and economic robustness is a big attraction to investors especially those in the Somali diaspora.

Eastleigh now has over 55 shopping malls, many of which have opened in the last five years. Amal Plaza is the biggest with more than 600 retail outlets.[6] Altogether Eastleigh has more than 15,000 shops, 3,000 food stores, 90 hotels, lodges and restaurants, including some upmarket facilities popular with the middle-class diaspora and non-Somali tourists, such as the Grand Royal Hotel (which is shown on the front cover of this book), the Nomad Palace Hotel and the Diamond Palace Hotel.[7] Twenty-five banks (including all the major banks in Kenya, such as KCB, Equity, Barclays, Stanbic, or Family Bank) and *hawalas* (Money Transfer agencies; among them Dahabshiil, Kaah, Amal, Amana, Tawakal, Continental and Iftin) have branches in the business hub.

It is also a growing medical hub attracting clients from all over Kenya and neighbouring countries. It boasts of some of the best doctors, as well as well-equipped and affordable medical facilities in Kenya. Some 30 hospitals, health centres, clinics and pharmacies are located in Eastleigh.[8]

Furthermore, Eastleigh has more than 40 educational and cultural centres. Some of these are religious-based but integrated schools (that means that they also teach the Kenyan curriculum), which have produced some of the top KCPE and KSCE (primary and secondary school certificate) results in the country.[9]

Increasing Economic and Political Influence in Kenya

This Eastleigh transformation is also symbolic of wider inroads Somalis have made into Kenyan economic and political life, inroads that might have seemed impossible only a few decades earlier. Somalis have witnessed an incredible turn around in their social, economic and political fortunes and have experienced a dramatic transformation in their lives.

Somalis have over the years founded many important and well-known businesses in Kenya, such as Hass Petroleum (1997), Bluebird Aviation (1997) or Interpel Investments (2001), and some are among the wealthiest tycoons in Kenya.[10] They have also made inroads into the banking sector. In 2007, one of the leading Somali bankers, Nathif Jama Adam, founded the First Community Bank (FCB), the first Shariah complaint institution in Kenya. And in 2011, Hassan Bashir launched the first Islamic insurance company in East Africa, Takaful, which has since become one of the leading insurance companies in the region.

Somalis own about 50 per cent of the fleets in the Kenyan aviation industry,[11] and now dominate the cargo business.[12] Somalis also run some of the biggest transport and energy companies in Kenya and the East African region.[13] Furthermore, they have ventured into the telecommunications and media business. More than 50 per cent of all the Safaricom and Airtel dealerships in Kenya are Somali-owned. They also hold some of the largest fibre optic companies in East Africa.[14] In the construction industry and real estate, Somalis own companies undertaking some of the biggest infrastructure projects in the country.[15] Somali-run companies have built new estates in Nairobi South C, South B, Kilimani, Hurlingham, Kileleshwa and Parklands.

Somalis are increasingly moving into the manufacturing sector, producing pharmaceuticals, paint, pasta, toilet papers, edible oil, flour and owning juice processing plants, plastic and gas cylinder factories and milk processing plants.[16]

Another very visible sign of Somali presence in Nairobi is the restaurant business. Many of the latest restaurants in the CBD and Upper Hill are Somali-owned, including chains like Kilimanjaro, Pronto, City Gava and Savannah, Al-Yusra, Grand Cafe and the upper-market CJs Cafe. Some of these eateries have introduced Somali cuisines including camel meat and milk to wider Kenyan society.

Last but not least, Somalis are also very present in the public sphere. There are several Somali-owned radio and TV stations operating in Kenya.[17] And there are more than 100 Somali lawyers practicing in Kenya today, some owning leading Kenyan legal firms.[18]

Another area where Somalis have made some considerable progress is in politics. Even though Somalis boycotted the first elections and therefore had no political representation in parliament, in 1964 the government nominated several

Somali MPs to parliament. The 2017 general elections, in contrast, returned one of the biggest representations of Somalis to the Kenyan parliament. Some 34 Somali MPs and Senators were elected or nominated for office (among 415 MPs and Senators in total), making them one of the largest political blocks in parliament. They include three Somalis elected from predominately non-Somali areas outside of northern Kenya – Yusuf Hassan, the MP for Kamukunji in Nairobi, Junet Mohamed from Suna East in Migori and Amin Mohamed from Nanyuki in Laikipia.

There is no longer a state position that is out of reach for Somalis. Since 1983, when the first ever Somali was appointed to the Cabinet, Somalis have occupied some of the most sensitive state and political posts in the country, such as the Ministry for Defence or the directorship of the National Intelligence Service.[19]

Somalis also occupy high-ranking positions in international organizations and companies. The Secretary General of the Kenya Red Cross is Abbas Gullet, who is accredited with turning around the fortunes of the ailing organization and developing its capacity and resources to handle multiple humanitarian crises. Other Somalis who hold international and regional jobs are the Director-General of the Universal Postal Union (UPU), Bishar Abdirahman Hussein, and the Executive Secretary of the Intergovernmental Authority on Development (IGAD), Mahboub Mohamed.

The devolved system of governance, which was introduced in 2013, is likely to greatly benefit Somalis. Out of the 47 counties in Kenya, Somalis are a majority in three counties: Garissa, Wajir and Mandera. Each county is led by a directly elected Governor and a local assembly. In the 2017 elections, Ali Roba was re-elected as Governor of Mandera, Mohamed Abdi was elected in Wajir and Ali Korane in Garissa. The three counties have received some 115 billion shillings from the national budget since 2013. Devolution has expanded political spaces and is already positively impacting on the rural economies of marginalized communities including Somalis.

In 1963 when Kenya attained its independence, northern Kenya did not have a single secondary school. Today there are many secondary schools and colleges in Garissa, Wajir and Mandera. There are also several higher education institutes in the region, such as the Northern Technical Training College and the Garissa University, the first public university. There are also two Somali-run universities, the Umma University with campuses in Kajiado and Thika under the leadership of Chancellor Abbas Gullet and Vice-Chancellor Professor Idle Omar Farah and the RAF International University (financed by a Qatari organization) in Kajiado under Chancellor Sheikh Mohamed Osman. Somali academics and scholars teach at public universities such as Nairobi University, Kenyatta University and Moi University, and at private ones such as United States International University and Mount Kenya University. There are more than 33,000 Somali students at universities and colleges in Kenya today.[20]

Conclusion

Somalis have survived many upheavals and are remarkably resilient. Through their grit, guile and entrepreneurial acumen they have overcome monumental challenges. They have put behind them the painful past and the terrible memories of the 'Shifta war' and the horrible atrocities inflicted upon them by successive Kenyan regimes, and are rapidly moving upwards in every sector of Kenyan life. There is no area closed to Somalis in Kenya today and individual Somalis have reached the top in business, politics, academia, the media and law. Increasingly, they are politically active and assertive in defence of their fundamental rights. Over the years they have fought and rolled back some of the worst policies and practices that have denied them equality and inclusion in Kenya. And yet they are still not well-integrated and remain outsiders and strangers in their own country.

Despite the ups and downs, many Somalis have high expectations of the 2010 Kenyan Constitution, especially the bill of rights and the expanding democratic space in the country, and hope that with time they will come to enjoy full citizen rights and become an integral part of the Kenyan story.

Yusuf Hassan is a Kenyan politician, diplomat and journalist. In 2011 he was elected Member of Parliament for Kamukunji in Nairobi and is serving his third term. He has worked for the United Nations (UNHCR, OCHA and IRIN) and as a journalist with the BBC, Africa Events, Namibian National Radio and TV and the Voice of America. He was one of founders of the Committee for the Release of Political Prisoners in Kenya and the first Chairperson of UKENYA/UMOJA opposition group.

Notes

1. The large growth in the Somali population suggested by the 2009 census was seen as controversial and disputed by some (Scharrer 2018: 499).
2. The results of this referendum were published in the following: *The Report of the NFD Commission*, Her Majesty's government, London 1962.
3. On these massacres, see: Damian Clarke and Mohammed Adow, *Not Yet Kenyan*, Al-Jazeera. 14 September 2013, available at: https://www.aljazeera.com/programmes/aljazeeracorrespondent/2013/10/not-yet-kenyan-2013102885818441218.html (accessed 28 February 2019); Mohammed Adow, *Revisiting Kenya's Forgotten Progroms*, Al-Jazeera, 15 Dec 2013, available at: https://www.aljazeera.com/programmes/aljazeeracorrespondent/2013/11/revisiting-kenya-forgotten-pogroms-20131111101457765 43.html (accessed 28 February 2019); Iqra Salah, *Bulla Karatasi: The Forgotten Massacre*, Africa Uncensored, 4 December 2018, available at: http://africauncensored.net/bulla-karatasi/ (accessed 28 February 2019); Judy Kibinge, *SCARRED: The Anatomy of a Massacre*, a documentary film the trailer for which can be seen here: https://hangout.co.ke/film-screening-scarred-the-anatomy-of-a-massacre-by-judy-kibinge/ (accessed 28 February 2019). For a book-length treatment of the Wagalla Massacre, see Sheik (2007).

4. The Hashi family and Mohamed Haji Adan 'Dansee' family, for instance, opened a grocery and butchery in Karen. They were the first Somalis permitted to operate a business in a Whites-only neighbourhood.
5. 'Hassan, the Mysterious Somali Trader Who Funded Mau Mau Fighters' by J. Kamau (*Daily Nation*, 9 April 2017), https://www.nation.co.ke/news/Hassan-mysterious-Somali-trader-who-funded-Mau-Mau-fighters/1056-3882956-ev05ha/index.html, retrieved 16 November 2018.
6. Currently these are the major shopping centres: Amal plaza (Jama Orshe), Bangkok and Hong Kong (Yusuf Abdi Adan), AMCO (Abdullahi Mohamed Dahir), Yare Business Park (Ahmed Abdullahi Yare), Olympic (Hussein Bood), King's (Abdi Muhumad Jelle), Tokyo (Aden Adow), Tasneem & Iftin (Abdullahi Jama and Haji Ali Noor Gab), Mega & Sunrise (Abdi Mohamed Isburash), Prime (Haji Ismail Hassan), Day-to-Day (Abdirizak Idle), Moyale (Duran Hassan Madobe and Hassan Ige Musa), Eastleigh Mall (Sheikh Mahamud Shibli) and Madina Mall (Sheikh Mohamed Ibrahim Shakul).
7. Personal Communication: Omar Bangkok of Eastleigh Business District Association, Nairobi, 28 October 2018. The major hotels are the following: Grand Royal Hotel (Samow Edin Osman), Nomad Palace Hotel (Nur Bare Duale, the brother of Adan Bare Duale), Gulf Palace Hotel (Sharif Mohamed), Dubai Hotel (Yusuf Abdi Adan) and Diamond Palace Hotel (Dahir Ahmed Hussein).
8. 'Eastleigh is Shaping up as New Medical Hub for the Capital' by E. Omete (*Business Daily*, 7 March 2018), https://www.businessdailyafrica.com/lifestyle/fitness/Eastleigh-is-shaping-up-as-new-medical-hub/4258372-4331750-format-xhtml-wqy8nmz/index.html; retrieved 16 November 2018. Among these medical facilities are the Alliance Medical Centre in Madina Mall (CEO Dr Liiban Ahmed), Ladnan Hospital (co-founded by Dr Abdi Mohamed, who is also the Chairman of the Kenya Association of Private Hospitals), Nairobi East Hospital (Salat Garad Mohamed) and Al-Amin Hospital.
9. Among the most prominent schools and cultural centres are: Atlas College (Abdikadir Mohamud Ibrahim), Moya Institute of Technology (Mohamed Adam Abdi), Aw Jama Omar Cultural and Research Centre (Fardosa Aw Jama). Some of the major integrated schools are: Ansaru Sunnah Group of Schools (established by Sheikh Abdirizak Jir), Rabbani Schools (Sheikh Abdirahman Adani and Maalim Maulid Ahmed), and California Academy (Sheikh Mahamud Shibli).
10. Abdinasir Ali Hassan, the founder and CEO of Hass Petroleum, is closely connected to the business group White Lotus; both companies are currently developing the landmark Pinnacle Tower in Nairobi Upper Hill. Yusuf Abdi Adan, Hussein Unshur Mohamed, Hussein Ahmed Farah and Mohamed Abdikadir Aden are co-owners of Bluebird Aviation Services, Abdirahman Haji Abass has founded Interpel Investments and many other businesses. Other high-ranking businesspeople are Ahmed Rashid Jibril, chairman and co-founder of 748 Air Services, Amina Hersi Moghe, an industrialist and entrepreneur with extensive commercial interests in Kenya and Uganda, Musa Hassan Bulhan, owner of African Express Airways, Ahmed Abdullahi Dakawi, owner of the largest LPG Transport Company in Kenya and Premier Hospital in Mombasa, as well as Mahat Kuno Roble, Abbas Sheikh Mohamed Ali and Khalif Buko.
11. Companies in the aviation industry include Bluebird Aviation, 748 Air Services, African Express Airways, Silverstone Air Services (Managing Director Mohamed Somow), Skywards Express (Chairman Mohammed Abdi and Managing Director Isaack Somow), Freedom Airlines (General Manager Iman Shallow Abukar) and Ocean Airlines (Managing Director Mohamed Burale).

12. Among the prominent cargo companies are: Focus/Interpel Investments (Faisal Abass, Managing Director), Salihiya Cargo and Shipping Line Agency (Ibrahim Abdullahi), Golden Gate (Mohamed Bule), Salama Cargo (Omar Hussein), African Salihiya Cargo and Clearing (Mohamed-Dahir Sheikh Abdirahman, Managing Director), Nurex Cargo (Nuh Abdille) and GN Cargo (Guled Aden).
13. These include Hass Petroleum, Tecaflex, Tosha, Raegonal, Texas, Trojan International and Hashi in the energy sector, and Awale Transport (Awale Jimale), Tanad (Musa Said Hassan), Aina Shamis and Rhino Transport (Abdirahman Sheikh and Yusuf Sheikh).
14. Such as Soliton Telmec (Abdirahman Omar Sheikh, managing director) or Frontier Optical Network (Jama Mohamed, managing director).
15. For example, the Lafey and Diamond Construction (owned by Mohamed Kulmiye and Mohamed Khalif), Concordia Building and Civil Engineering Co. (owned by the Bare Duale family) and Tosha Holdings (Abdisirad Khalif Ali). Some of the new multi-storey office blocks owned by Somalis in the CBD and Kilimani in Nairobi include Lenana Towers and Yalaha Towers (Yusuf Abdi Adan) and Bihi Towers (Sheikh Ahmed Nur Bihi).
16. Among these are Skylight Chemicals (founded by Abdulwahab Ahmed Nur), Gas Cylinders (Ali Noor Gab), Tamu Fruit & Juice Processing, Nuug Camel Milk (Bashir Warsame), White Gold Camel Milk (Jama Warsame) and Edible Oil Processing (Billow Kerrow).
17. Such as Star FM and STN TV (founded by Mohamed Osman), Ebru TV (founded by a Turkish businessman and later bought by Ali Jamah), Nairobi Law Monthly and Nairobi Business Monthly (published by Ahmednasir Abdullahi, who also founded RTN TV).
18. These include Ahmednasir Abdullahi (Ahmednasir-Abdikadir & Co Associates), Abdullahi Garane and Mahat Somane (Garane & Somane), Ahmed Adan (Wetangula, Adan, Makokha & Co Advocates), Aden Daud (Michael, Daud & Associates), Abdikadir Hussein Mohamed (Abdikadir Associates), Abdiwahid Biriq (Sagana, Biriq & Co) as well as Mohamed Ibrahim and Ahmed Issack Hassan (Ibrahim, Issack & Co).
19. These positions include Defence Minister (Yusuf Haji 2008–2013), Foreign Affairs Minister (Amina Mohamed 2013-2017); Trade, Investment and Industrialisation Minister (Adan Mohamed 2013–2018); Commander of the Kenya Defence Forces (General Mohamud Mohamed 1986–1996); National Police Commissioner (General Mohamed Hussein Ali 2004–2009), Chair of the Independent Electoral and Boundaries Commission (Ahmed Issack Hassan 2011–2016); Senior Advisor to the President (Abdikadir Hussein Mohamed 2013–2017); and a Director in the National Intelligence Service (Noordin Yusuf Haji 2013–2018). Some of the key positions occupied by Somalis in Uhuru Kenyatta's administration (since 2017) include the Education Minister (Amina Mohamed), Cabinet Secretary for East Africa Community and Northern Corridor Development Minister (Adan Mohamed), Leader of Majority in the National Assembly (Aden Bare Duale), Chief Administrative Secretaries (equivalent to Deputy Minister position, Mohamed Elmi, Dr Rashid Aman and Hassan Noor), Director of Public Prosecutions (Noordin Yusuf Haji), Deputy Inspector General Administration Police Service (Noor Gabow), Supreme Court Judge (Mohamed Ibrahim), High Court Judge (Mohamed Warsame), Principal Secretaries Labour and Social Protection (Dr Ibrahim Mohamed), Broadcasting and Telecommunication (Fatuma Hirsi) and Environment (Ali Noor Ismail), three Ambassadors and three representatives in the East African parliament known as EALA.

20. Personal communication, Farah Maalim, former Deputy Speaker of Kenya National Assembly, 28 November 2018.

References

Carrier, N. 2016. *Little Mogadishu: Eastleigh, Nairobi's Global Somali Hub*. London: Hurst.
Kitching, G. 1980. *Class and Economic Change in Kenya*. London: Yale University Press.
Lind, J., P. Mutahi, Patr and M. Oosterom. 2017. '"Killing a Mosquito with a Hammer": Al-Shabaab Violence and State Security Responses in Kenya', *Peacebuilding* 5(2): 1–18.
Lochery, E. 2012. 'Rendering Difference Visible: The Kenyan State and its Somali Citizens', *African Affairs* 111(445): 615–39.
Report of the Truth, Justice and Reconciliation Commission (TJRC). 2013.Volume IIA. Nairobi, pp. 101–44.
Scharrer, T. 2018. '"Ambiguous Citizens": Kenyan Somalis and the Question of Belonging', *Journal of Eastern African Studies* 12(3): 494–513.
Sheik, S.A. 2007. *Blood on the Runway: The Wagalla Masscare of 1984*. Nairobi: Northern Publishing House.
Weitzberg, K. 2017. *We Do Not Have Borders: Greater Somalia and the Predicaments of Belonging in Kenya*. Athens, OH: Ohio University Press.
Whittaker, H. 2014. *Insurgency and Counterinsurgency in Kenya: A Social History of the Shifta Conflict, C. 1963–1968*. Leiden: Brill.

Part II
Urbanity

Chapter 1

The Somali Factor in Urban Kenya
A History

Hannah Whittaker

Introduction

Nairobi is home to one of the largest Somali communities outside of Somalia. This community combines Kenyan Somalis, Somali refugees from Ethiopia and Somali nationals, many of whom went there following the collapse of the Somali state in 1991. Recent waves of Somali migration to Nairobi have transformed suburbs like Eastleigh. What was primarily a residential area is now a regional hub for trade networks that operate across East Africa and into Asia and the Middle East that have contributed significantly to the growth of the Kenyan economy (Carrier and Lochery 2013: 346).[1]

The Somali presence in Nairobi is nonetheless controversial. Eastleigh's transformation since Somalia's state collapse has earned the estate the nickname 'Little Mogadishu' (ibid.: 334). This is a problematic label. It suggests that the estate is more a part of the neighbouring state of Somalia, and by extension has come to be regarded as a place of refugees, 'illegal' immigrants and insecurity. The label 'Little Mogadishu' also belies the cosmopolitanism of Eastleigh, which is home to many non-Somalis (see Carrier and Kochore, this volume), and it obscures the fact that many of the Somalis that do live there are Kenyan by birth and descent (Carrier 2015). This has compounded historical patterns of othering and discrimination against Kenyan Somalis. By virtue of their shared ethnicity with people arriving from Somalia over the past couple of decades, Kenyan Somalis are now often stereotyped as interlopers, and since the rise of Al-Shabaab, conduits for terrorism.

This chapter takes the questions that are currently being asked of the right of Somali people to live and work in Nairobi, as an opportunity to re-focus attention on the longer history of Somali urban migration and settlement in Kenya (see also Whittaker 2015). While at first view, the 'mobile urbanity' of Somalis (see Carrier and Scharrer, this volume) may appear to be relatively recent, gaining prominence through current debates about migration and urban transformation, this chapter makes clear that many of the contemporary aspects of Somali 'mobile urbanity' (including notions of 'ambiguous' citizenship, (il) legality, resilience and insecurity) have long historical roots. In doing so, the chapter establishes three fundamental points. First, ethnic Somalis have always formed part of Kenya's indigenous population. Second, urban Somalis have lived in Nairobi since the very first establishment of the British East Africa Protectorate (EAP) in 1895, and third, Somali people have lived and worked in the Eastleigh estate since its inception in 1921. What is more, Somali networks of trade and kinship connected these urban Somalis to kinsmen living in the north of the country, many of whom also came to settle in Nairobi in the decades before and after Kenyan independence.

This chapter is framed around two themes that characterize the history of Somali urban settlement in Kenya, as well as the concept of 'mobile urbanity' more broadly. The first is precarity. The notion of precarity has increased in prominence in recent years (Paret and Gleeson 2016: 278). In its most prevalent usage the focus is on employment and the labour market, and the linking of precarity to economic insecurity (insecure jobs, low wages and few benefits). In this chapter precarity is understood to be more synonymous with uncertainty and unpredictability, as well as with human vulnerability (ibid.: 280). For example, the fact that many of the Somalis that currently live and work in Nairobi have Kenyan nationality but are obscured from discussions about the Somali presence in Kenya reflects the current precarity of their citizenship. However, as this chapter shows, the tenuous nature of Somali belonging in Kenya is nothing new. Although the Nairobi Somalis were given permission to live within the city in the early years of the British protectorate, their presence was constantly under review, and required repeated renegotiation. As with other mobile populations, urban Somalis in Kenya were therefore vulnerable to state policies of exclusion, especially as colonial officials regarded them as essentially 'rural creatures'.

Despite official attempts to exclude them, Somali people living in Nairobi have nonetheless repeatedly asserted their right to live and work in the city. The second theme of the chapter is therefore Somali agency, though it is important to note that this term is not meant in an idyllic or romanticized way. Current scholarship is mixed about the possibilities for resistance to conditions of precarity (Standing 2014; Waite 2009). In particular, migrants or mobile populations are believed to prefer a life 'under the radar', rather than push for social change. By contrast, the evidence presented in this chapter reinforces an idea that precarity can become a reference point for collective action that drives social change (Paret and Gleeson 2016: 282). In the African context, a number of scholars have already extolled the virtues of self-help and entrepreneurship among African urban dwellers, especially those living in informal estates or slums (Cooper 1983: 8). Andrew Hake (1977: 35) famously described Nairobi as a 'self-help city'. He argued that to provide for their social needs, the people of Nairobi 'showed great resilience in evolving responses in the face of enormous difficulties and frustrations'. Likewise, given the prime causes of Somali displacement (war, famine and humanitarian crises) there is also much emphasis on self-help and entrepreneurship within Somali studies. Carrier (2017) shows how these ideas and concepts are just as important to how Somalis see themselves, as to how others perceive them. The recent growth of Somali business and entrepreneurship in Nairobi (much of which is built on networks of trust, 'goodwill' and 'informal' mechanism of raising capital (see Crisis Group Report 2015: 4)), is emblematic of this. Similar strategies of self-help and entrepreneurship were also used by the Nairobi Somalis to manage the uncertainty and precarity of their legal status and were characteristic of the way in which the urban Somalis dealt with colonial resettlement programmes, and attempts to limit their claims to a place in the city.

This chapter is based on research conducted since 2008, into the colonial and postcolonial relationship between Kenyan Somalis and the state. The main part of the data was collected from archives in London and Nairobi during 2013 and 2014. The chapter begins by outlining the history and settlement of Somali people in Kenya. It then moves to consider some of the contested aspects of the history of the urban Somalis in Kenya. In particular it highlights the connections between the precariousness of Somali citizenship (which may have sometimes given urban Somalis the ability to access increased privileges, but has also meant that their position in the colony was insecure), and Somali agency; the ways in which Somali people have historically made demands on the state, as well as asserted their rights to recognition as Kenyan citizens.

The History and Settlement of Kenyan Somalis

The majority of Kenyan Somalis are pastoralists living in the northeastern part of Kenya, the area which formed the North Eastern Province of Kenya (NEP) until 2013 (see map in the introduction). This is the eastern half of what was known during the colonial period as the Northern Frontier District (NFD). Somali groups began arriving in what became the NFD in the years after 1860, when they crossed over the River Daua following a long migration southwards and westwards from the Gulf of Aden (Lewis 1960: 213). Most of these Somalis were members of Hawiye and Darood lineages.

As was common across the continent, the imperial partition in eastern Africa resulted in some of the most 'bizarre territorial entities in modern global history'

(Reid 2009: 145). The British sphere of influence in eastern Africa was formalized by the Anglo–Italian agreements of 1891 and 1894. These agreements defined the northern limit of the British EAP as the River Daua, and the eastern limit as the River Juba. When Jubaland province was ceded to the Italians in 1925, the international frontier between Kenya and Italian Somaliland shifted westwards and became the eastern boundary of the NFD. However, economically speaking the NFD, Jubaland and adjacent areas of Ethiopia and Italian Somaliland formed a single region (Schlee with Shongolo 2014: 1; Thompson 2015: 20). For centuries before the imperial partition, this region was characterized by shifting populations relating to the requirements of pastoral mobility. Many people therefore failed to comply with the new imperial frontiers and continued to move in and out of the British sphere of influence (see Schlee 1989). For example, in 1909, a large number of Somalis crossed into the NFD with their livestock as a consequence of drought further east, and then moved back again after the rains (Moyse-Bartlett 1956: 212). Rather than invest the necessary resources to attempt to effectively limit these cross-border movements, or integrate the region with the rest of Kenya, the British preferred to govern it as a 'closed district'. This was an area without serious economic potential, and had been incorporated into the EAP as a buffer against the rival expansionist imperial powers of Ethiopia and Italy to the north and east (Schlee with Shongolo 2014: 2). Non-resident travel to and from the NFD was prohibited, except with the permission of the provincial commissioner. This policy can help to explain the ambivalence of the pastoral Somalis towards the colonial state, as well as their involvement in pan-Somali irredentism when Kenya gained independence in 1963 (see Mburu 2005; Whittaker 2014; Thompson 2015).

At around the same time as the Darood and Hawiye Somalis moved south of the River Daua, groups of Isaaq and Herti Somalis from the northern coast of the Somali peninsular and southern Arabia, also gradually migrated southwards down the coast from Aden to Kismayu, Mombasa and Zanzibar (Turton 1974a: 326). British administrative officials believed that one of the reasons for this southwards population movement was the gradual deterioration of pasture in areas further north.[2] Many Isaaq Somalis also travelled as hired *askaris* (soldiers) or gun-bearers with European explorers (Turton 1972: 120). Henry Morton Stanley first recruited Isaaq Somalis in 1874, when he stopped at Aden before his Congo expedition, and Richard Burton, Frederick Lugard, and J. W. Gregory also employed them (Turton 1974a: 326). The first Isaaq Somalis to arrive in Kenya are thought to have accompanied Lord Delamare on his expedition into the Rift Valley in 1897 (Weitzberg 2013: 183).[3] A number later entered government service as clerks and interpreters, or were recruited as soldiers in the Kings African Rifles (KAR) (ibid.). After their service in the KAR, many of these Isaaq and Herti Somalis settled as stock traders in townships and trading centres. The first settlements were at Nairobi, Dagoretti, Laikipia, Rumuruti, Isiolo,

Wajir and Garba Tulla.⁴ Subsequent waves of Isaaq and Herti Somalis also came to Kenya from British Somaliland after service in the KAR during World War I and World War II. By the 1920s, there were Isaaq and Herti communities living in Nanyuki, Nyeri, Kakamega, Kajiado, Maralal, Nakuru, Embu, Kitale and Eldoret (Turton 1974a: 326).

Outside of Nairobi, the largest urban Somali settlement was at Isiolo Town. Isiolo was initially developed as a strategic base for the KAR, and in 1929 it became the regional headquarters for the NFD. The British also wanted to develop Isiolo as a central settlement for Isaaq and Herti Somalis living in other urban areas, where it was believed that their accumulation of livestock had damaged local grazing. Isaaq and Herti Somali living in Rumuruti were moved to Isiolo in 1924, followed by those residing in Wajir in 1925, and Garba Tulla in 1931.⁵ However, the resettlement scheme was abandoned in the early 1930s. In part this was the consequence of the fact that administrative officials erroneously located Isiolo Town in the NFD, when it was actually part of Meru district (Hjort 1979; Boye and Kaarhus 2011: 111). The scheme was also abandoned because of concerns about 'overcrowding'.⁶ The porosity of the border between Kenya and Somalia, as well as between Kenya and Ethiopia meant that it was relatively easy for Isaaq and Herti Somalis to move across imperial frontiers, and in 1929, the district commissioner of Isiolo warned that one of the possible consequences of formally gazetting a Somali Reserve at Isiolo would be an 'infiltration from northern Somaliland'.⁷ Despite efforts to control mobility, Somali migration to Isiolo nonetheless continued, though the actual size of the Somali population at Isiolo, or in the Kenya colony more broadly, was never known with any certainty (see Weitzberg 2015). In 1937 it was estimated that in total (men, women, and children) there were 532 Isaaq and 253 Herti residing at Isiolo.⁸ In 1952, a similar estimate of 800 Isaaq and Herti was made, though officials acknowledged that the figure was likely to be much higher in reality.⁹ The uncertainty that surrounded colonial attempts to enumerate the Somali population in Kenya has certainly fed into state anxieties.¹⁰

As the colonial capital, Nairobi became home to the largest population of urban Somalis. When a census of the urban Somali population living in areas outside of the NFD was conducted in 1956, it was estimated that 28 per cent (1,532) lived in Nairobi.¹¹ Like other early colonial towns in Kenya, the initial growth of Nairobi was linked to the construction of the Mombasa–Kisumu railway. The first permanent buildings were erected in 1896, and Nairobi developed into an important administrative centre (Obudho 1997: 8; Furedi 1973: 276). The building of the railway, and the development of Nairobi also provided opportunities for employment and trade for the indigenous population. In 1898, groups like the Isaaq and Herti Somalis that had already played important roles as clerks, interpreters and soldiers, were given permission to construct a number of buildings in the town, and by 1899 records show that 'a number' of Somalis

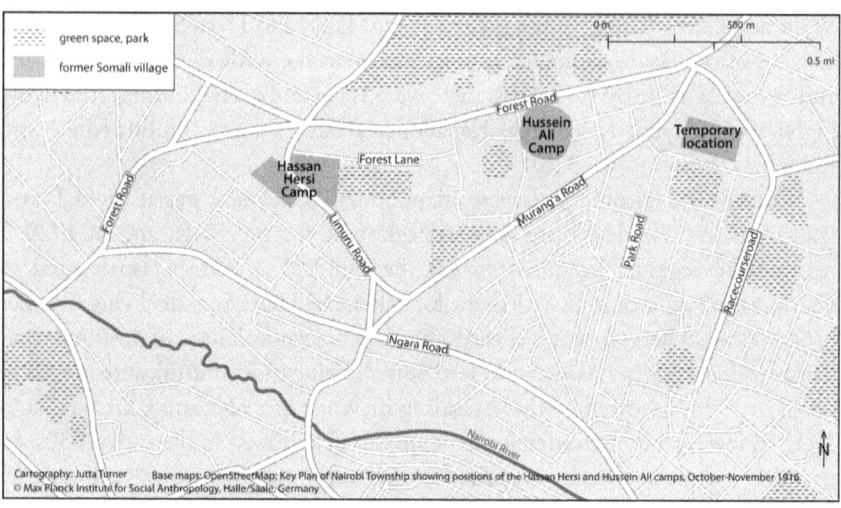

Map 1.1 Somali villages in colonial Nairobi.

were living there.¹² In 1902 they began paying rent to the Land Office, before becoming liable for the hut and poll tax in 1907.¹³ By the outbreak of World War I, the number of Somalis living in Nairobi had grown to around 400 (of a total estimated population of 16,107).¹⁴

Like many other colonial cities, Nairobi was racially segregated, and Asians, Europeans and Africans lived in distinct residential areas (Furedi 1973: 276). Most of the non-European population lived either in the Indian Bazaar, or in one of a number of African 'villages'. These included the informal African estates of Kileleshwa, Mji wa Mombasa, Masikini and Pangani, as well as four Somali villages, which were located in the area that is now framed by Murang'a road to the north and Ngara road to the west (Hake 1977: 35).¹⁵ British administrative reports describe the two larger Somali villages by the names of their headmen, Hussein Ali and Hassan Hersi, both of whom were regarded as being 'sound and reliable men'.¹⁶

By 1916, these villages were made up of 64 houses and 44 houses respectively.¹⁷ Most of the buildings were constructed of corrugated iron supported by timber, and had ceilings and floors made of matchboarding. There were also four stone houses, and a number of buildings had electricity. According to Henry Belfield, the protectorate commissioner, the furniture, clothes and general standard of buildings within the Somali villages suggested great prosperity.¹⁸ It is certainly the case that most of the Somalis residing in Nairobi were successfully involved in the livestock trade, for which they benefitted from kinship connections to pastoral areas further north in the colony.¹⁹

Despite being regarded as a relatively prosperous community, the position of the Somalis (as well as of other non-European groups) within Nairobi was nonetheless threatened by broader imperial urban policies in Africa that aimed to restrict as much as possible permanent African residence (Murunga 2005: 102). In the case of Nairobi, European speculators had acquired plots in the early years of the settlement of the city and they did not want to see their investments compromised by letting Africans build houses (Anderson 2002: 140). At the same time, colonial efforts to improve sanitation in the city drew on racial stereotypes that cast Africans and Indians as 'inherently unhygienic' (Murunga 2005: 98, 100). The combination of economic policy and sanitary 'science' was used as a motivation and justification to expel Africans from 'European' towns, and for the development of segregationist policies (Curtin 1985; Swanson 1977; Ngalamulume 2004).

Nonetheless, protectorate and colonial officials had to balance the desire to restrict African housing with the need to maintain labour supply (Anderson 2002). In the years before and after World War I, numerous attempts were made to replace the informal African estates that had grown up in Nairobi with a publically funded housing project. Financial constraints initially prevented any scheme from progressing, but by the second decade of the twentieth century, the relative scarcity of African housing was thought to be adversely affecting the labour supply to Nairobi (ibid.). As such, in 1921, a new African Location was established at Pumwani, and the four Somali villages were demolished and many of the latter's former residents were relocated there, along with the residents of Mombasa and Masikini (Achola 2002: 123; Murunga 2009: 213; Hake 1977: 136). A continued lack of housing, combined with rural–urban migration soon led to overcrowding in Pumwani, which spread out into River Road and Canal Road (Furedi 1973: 276). By 1939, Nairobi's population had swollen to an estimated 65,500 people, and officials calculated that there were well over 8,000 people residing in Pumwani. This was more than double the number originally intended (Hake 1977: 50; Anderson 2002: 144).

After 1921, Eastleigh estate also developed as an important Somali residential area. Eastleigh was originally established in 1921 as a place where Indians could settle when the Indian Bazaar was closed (Hake 1977: 101). However, according to Godwin Murunga, other groups ended up living there (Murunga 2009: 213). Many of the wealthier Indians eschewed Eastleigh for Parklands, and a number of Isaaq Somalis were among those that bought a share of over 3,000 plots (Carrier and Lochery 2013: 336). Isaaq connections to kinsmen in other urban centres as well as to other Somalis and Muslim pastoralists living in the north of the country meant that many other Somalis also visited and settled (ibid.). By the 1940s and 1950s, Eastleigh, and in particular Eastleigh Section III, was the largest settlement of Somalis in Nairobi (Murunga 2009: 214). In 1971, it was estimated that Eastleigh Section III was home to 10,965 people, with another 12,280 people living in other parts of the estate (Hake 1977: 102–103).

Contested Histories of Kenya's Urban Somalis

Modern urban Kenya has therefore always had an indigenous Somali population. However, the Somali presence in Kenya, especially in urban centres outside of the NFD, has also always been contested. On the one hand, Isaaq and Herti Somalis had a history of imperial service, and many Europeans held them in high regard (Turton 1974a: 326). The Commissioner of the East Africa Protectorate, Charles Eliot, reflected in 1905 that 'there can be no doubt that they are the most intelligent race in the protectorate' (Eliot 1905: 188). Yet at the same time, because Isaaq and Herti Somalis belonged to lineages that originated from areas outside of the protectorate, they were referred to as the 'Alien' Somalis, and were regarded as migrants. The ambivalent attitude of the protectorate authorities towards the Somalis was also bound up with a broader administrative concern over 'detribalized' Africans. Groups like the Nairobi Somalis were not subject to the jurisdiction of 'native tribunals' and there were fears that they would become too numerous for the British to effectively govern (Parsons 1997: 90). In 1916, one former sub-commissioner commented that detribalized *askaris* (soldiers) would degenerate into a class of 'professional beggars and hangers on' (ibid.).

Somalis living in Kenya therefore not only faced urban exclusion as a consequence of colonial racial policies, but also because of the precarious legal status they acquired under British rule, which created additional insecurities. The categorization of Isaaq and Herti Somalis as 'aliens', 'migrants', and 'detribalized' Africans, conceptually limited their claims to 'belong', and meant that it was easy for officials to call their presence in Kenya into question. In 1944, for instance, one official argued that although the government had an obligation to old government servants, the younger generation of Somalis should be encouraged to return to Somaliland.[20] In 1945, there was discussion about the possibility of repatriating 'all Alien Somalis to their territory of origin'.[21]

As with today, the precarity of the Somali urban presence in Nairobi was a consequence of their vulnerability to the power of the state to detain or remove those that are regarded as migrants. For instance, the language that was used in colonial debates about the Isaaq and Herti resembles current rhetoric about Somalis living in Kenya (as the following chapters of this volume attest). Officials stationed in the north of the colony made reference to their fears of 'illegal' Somali migration to Kenya, which was facilitated by the size of the NFD, and the fact that many Isaaq and Herti Somalis living in Kenya maintained strong links with kinsmen living elsewhere in the Horn of Africa and beyond. Fears about 'illegal' Somali migration to Kenya appeared to be confirmed during an attempted census in 1938 and 1940. Administrative officials reported that less than half of the Somalis counted in Isiolo were born in Kenya, or were legally entitled to be there. The other half was believed to have 'infiltrated' from British or Italian Somaliland.²² Officials reported similar 'problems' elsewhere in Kenya, and in Nairobi the problem was thought to be 'acute'.²³

It is however important to note the context within which these debates were taking place. While current concerns over the Somali presence in Nairobi focus on regional insecurity and Al-Shabaab related terrorist activity (see Lowe and Yarnell in this volume), much of the British paranoia over 'illegal' Somali migration into the colony during the inter-war years reflected the growing influence of developmental discourse on colonial policy. After 1930, African societies became the objects of state intervention and 'expert' knowledge, which shaped the implementation of development schemes that were meant to transform African societies, making them more compliant and more productive (Bonneuil 2000: 260–69). In British East Africa, there was a particular concern with a perceived threat to the productive capacity of African land by overcrowding and soil erosion, which legitimized attempts to reorganize and standardize land use systems, including limiting stocks and grazing rights (ibid.: 265, 269; Anderson 1984: 322). One of the reasons why the Somali presence in Isiolo and Nairobi was considered so contentious was the supposed impact of unregulated Somali mobility on the rangelands.²⁴

Despite the precariousness of the presence of Isaaq and Herti Somalis in Kenya, it is also the case that Isaaq and Herti Somalis developed strategies to manage the risk and uncertainty of their legal position, in particular by collectively mobilizing and petitioning for greater inclusion. The position of Isaaq and Herti Somalis as 'legal' migrants, together with the fact that many had played important roles as intermediaries in the early stages of British imperial expansion, meant that at various times they were able to negotiate greater rights and privileges in the context of a colonial struggle to define an evolving racial hierarchy (Weitzberg 2013: 184). Somalis were exempt from the 1915 Native Registration Ordinance, after the Isaaq and Herti leaders expressed grievances at having to carry a *kipande* (an identity card that restricted African mobility). In 1919, the Isaaq and Herti Somalis also successfully lobbied protectorate authorities for 'non-native' status, and the Somali Exemption Ordinance was passed. This gave the Somalis similar rights to Arabs and Indians living in the protectorate, such as access to special hospital wards, greater mobility, and the right to legal and permanent settlement in towns and cities (ibid., 184–6).

The relatively privileged position of the Isaaq and Herti Somalis within the colony, which was based primarily on their history of imperial service, was nonetheless fragile. It remained constantly under review, and required repeated renegotiation. In this way, the precariousness of the Somali urban presence became a reference point for mobilization, exemplifying the way that the Nairobi Somalis have been able to express agency. In particular, the need for the repeated renegotiation of their presence in the city shows how they have developed strategies to navigate structures of state power. The precedent was set as early as 1916, when protectorate officials attempted to have the Nairobi Somalis removed from the city centre to a 'nomadic camp' at M'bagathi. The pretext for the eviction was concern over public health, following the discovery of smallpox in Hassan Hersi's village in January 1915.[25] This came just a year after Professor J. Simpson published his report on the sanitary conditions of Nairobi. The conclusions were damning. Nairobi was 'one of the most insanitary [towns] I have ever seen' (Simpson 1914). Nonetheless, protectorate officials also pointed to the ambiguous status of Isaaq and Herti Somalis as de facto 'non-natives' to justify the eviction. Henry Belfield made clear in his correspondence with the colonial office, that the Somali presence in Nairobi Township was looked upon as subject to the will of the administration, and that they had no claim of any description to the land that they occupied.[26]

Although the Nairobi Somalis were unable to challenge the legality of the eviction, they did seek legal representation from the solicitors Shapely and Schwartz to contest the proposed relocation to what was described as a 'nomadic camp'. This terminology reflects the way that colonial officials depicted Africans as essentially 'rural' people. This was especially the case for those populations like the Somalis that were associated with pastoralism. However, as a number of scholars have already shown, urbanity and processes of sedentarization are also fundamental to Somali society and history (Cassanelli 1982; Reese 1996; Whittaker 2012). Many Nairobi Somalis were engaged in the livestock trade, and maintained strong connections to rural kinsmen, but they nonetheless saw themselves as part of the city. Instead of the nomadic camp, the Nairobi Somalis demanded relocation to an area closer to the city centre; they demanded permanent houses made of stone or cement, with 99-year leases for the owners.[27] This was an unequivocal demand for security of tenure within the city, as well as a rejection of the government's use of a one-dimensional image of the Somalis as pastoralists and nomads, and therefore not 'natural' urban dwellers, in order to have them removed. The architects Tate, Smith and Henderson were also employed to construct plans for an alternative 'model village' located on the Nairobi River.[28]

By contesting the terms of the eviction, if not the eviction itself, the Nairobi Somalis succeeded in securing redress (in the form of compensation), and they caused enough of a delay in the process that the plans eventually fell into abeyance. Nonetheless, housing remained a key site of contestation between the urban Somalis and colonial authorities, and the Nairobi Somalis continued to use this to their advantage. When demolition orders were served on 22 Somali houses that were judged to be a public health 'problem' in Eastleigh during the 1950s, the United Somali Association (USA), a Nairobi based political association, negotiated a more favourable solution. Rather than let the houses be demolished and condemned, the USA lobbied Nairobi city council for financial assistance to rebuild them.[29] The Association justified the demand for assistance by arguing that the poor state of Somali housing at Eastleigh was a consequence of government policy, particularly restrictions on Somali participation in the livestock trade after 1945. The USA succeeded in securing an offer for loans of up to £1,200 per house to cover the costs of redevelopment.[30]

Urban Somalis living in Kenya also periodically mobilized to extract various other benefits and entitlements from the state. The Nairobi Somalis made the earliest demands for the establishment of Somali schools in Kenya. A school was embedded within the architectural plans for a model Somali village in 1916,[31] but Somalis living in the NFD, as well as those living in Nairobi were without a primary or secondary school until after the World War II (Turton 1974b: 347). Again, one of the factors working against the establishment of a school for the Somalis was their 'non-native' status, which the colonial office used as an excuse to not invest in Somali education in Kenya (ibid.: 349). However, when an Indian school was opened in 1930 (Indians in Kenya also had 'non-native' status), Isaaq and Herti groups petitioned the British King, George V about the lack of a Somali school (ibid.). They repeated their request to the colonial government in 1934, and in 1938 drew upon their own plans for a school at Nakuru (ibid.). A school specifically designed for the Somalis was eventually opened at Isiolo in 1946 (ibid.: 350).

According to E.R. Turton (ibid.: 349), Isaaq agitation over the lack of Somali schools in Kenya was part of a 'wearying flow of memoranda, memorials and petitions to all sections of the administration' during the 1930s, which also included a campaign for 'Asiatic' status. Keren Weitzberg (2013) has dealt in detail with the Isaaq campaign for 'Asiatic' status. Weitzberg (ibid.: 188) argues that British attempts to shore up the imperial racial order in the inter-war years proved problematic for Isaaq and Herti Somalis. In 1937, a new Non-Native Poll Tax was introduced, which established a sliding scale of tax obligations for Europeans, Asians and 'other' non-natives (Arabs, Swahilis and Somalis). This reduced Somali tax from thirty to twenty shillings. Fearing that paying the reduced amount of tax would lead to a loss of privileges, the Isaaq began a campaign to pay the higher tax rate of thirty shillings. As part of the campaign, Isaaq leaders claimed 'Asiatic' origin. They also adopted the name Isahaakia, and rallied around the Isahaakia Association. As Weitzberg (ibid.) has argued, the label 'Asiatic' was a conflation between territorial, racial and legal categories and was designed to underscore Isaaq connections to Aden, where British colonial subjects were legally considered Asian.

The participation of the Isaaq Somalis in the poll-tax campaign and their repeated demand to be considered 'Asiatic', and therefore not African, nor even Somali, does complicate the history and memory of Somali urban belonging in Kenya. However, as Weitzberg (ibid.: 190) also argues, use of the term was an appropriation of colonial vocabularies, and it is very difficult to know if the term Asiatic was widely used by the Nairobi Somalis, beyond its use by Somali leaders to make claims on the state, in light of their already precarious status. It is the case that in the context of current xenophobia, members of the Isaaq community have suppressed public memories of participation in the poll tax campaign in order to situate themselves within the Kenyan nationalist narrative (Weitzberg 2013).

The British never resolved the legal status of Isaaq and Herti Somalis in Kenya, nor were they ever able to control the movement and settlement of Somalis in urban areas (Weitzberg 2015). It was not until the late 1950s that the authorities registered Somali people living in areas of Kenya that were outside of the NFD, or issue them with identity cards (ibid.: 425). By this time, the repatriation of Isaaq and Herti Somalis to Somaliland was no longer being considered. Officials acknowledged the fact that a large number of those living in Kenya could claim to be domiciled there, and that concerns about overstocking would not be solved by repatriation, since a large number of people would simply leave their stock with kinsmen in Kenya, if they were forced to return to Somaliland.[32] However, these concessions came during the final years of British rule in Kenya, and were not enough to secure urban Somalis living in Nairobi recognition as full Kenyan citizens in the emerging postcolonial order. Instead, through networks of trade and kinship that linked urban Somalis in Kenya to those living in the NFD and the recently independent Republic of Somalia, many became associated with pan-Somali nationalism and the campaign for the creation of a 'Greater Somali' state. This is not to suggest that support for pan-Somali irredentism amongst urban Somalis in Kenya (as well as Kenyan Somalis more broadly) was unanimous. During the 1960s, Somali people living in Kenya found themselves caught between two competing nationalist visions of the future (see Whittaker 2014). However, the emergence of a pan-Somali movement and the separatist insurgency that developed within the NFD after Kenyan independence in 1963 increased the vulnerability of all Somali people in Kenya by giving rise to a persisting idea that they have dubious loyalty to the Kenyan state.

Conclusion

In the years since Kenyan independence, the ambiguous legal status of urban Somalis that was established but never resolved by the colonial authorities has taken on renewed significance. Volatility and periodic conflict in the neighbouring states of Ethiopia and Somalia has increased Somali migration to Kenya, and destabilized areas along the border. At the same time, state capacity to distinguish between those Somalis that are citizens and those that are not has not strengthened; neither have mechanisms for controlling migration. The increased presence and influence of Somali refugees in places like Nairobi, has also given rise to an idea that they are temporarily encamped there. These developments, coupled with the growing economic power of Somalis in Kenya, as well as the rise of Al-Shabaab, have had particularly negative implications for Kenyan Somalis, whose citizenship was already questioned following the campaign for NFD secession. Somalis living in Kenya have to go through additional vetting in order to gain a national identity card, which simply serves to make the access of Kenyan Somalis to the rights and protections of citizenship more precarious, especially those for whose lineage is not indigenous to Kenya (Lochery 2012). It is perhaps ironic that over the same period, and as a consequence of some of the same dynamics that have fuelled state anxieties about Somali people in Kenya, Somalis themselves have sought closer identification as Kenyans. One indication of this is the tendency for Kenyan Somalis to express regret or downplay the historical significance of Somali separatism (Whittaker 2014). Recent narratives of the secessionist conflict have focused instead on the history and memory of government harassment during counterinsurgency operations, which positions Somalis as a victimized Kenyan minority (ibid.). The point is not made to suggest that these memories of the secessionist conflict are simply revised versions of the past to suit present needs. The war that was fought between 1963 and 1968 has tended to reduce Somali participation in the politics of independence in Kenya to the campaign for NFD secession. Yet many Somalis did also campaign to remain within Kenya under some sort of federal arrangement, while others simply used the opportunities and uncertainties that the independence negotiations provided to make additional claims on the state (ibid.). This was particularly the case in Nairobi, where the USA and the Somali National Association worked to secure bureaucratic recognition and political representation for Somali people living there. Both campaigned about municipal housing, the need for Somali schools, and the desire for more Somali representatives on the legislative council.[33] Even the Northern Province Peoples Progressive Party (NPPPP), the largest pro-secession party to emerge in the NFD, used the campaign for secession as leverage for securing greater economic and political rights as Kenyans. Between 1961 and 1963, the NPPPP campaigned for the development of NFD areas, more schools, hospitals, employment opportunities, and the end to the government monopoly of the livestock economy.[34] The positioning of the NPPPP as belonging both within and outside of the Kenyan state reflects both the transnational associations of Somali people, and the uncertainties that surrounded the independence process in Kenya. It is also symptomatic of Somali 'mobile urbanity' and the way that Kenyan Somalis have evolved creative responses to the precariousness of their citizenship.

Hannah Whittaker works as a senior lecturer in History at Brunel University, London (UK). She holds a PhD in African studies from SOAS, for research on the so-called Shifta war. This was published as a monograph in 2014 (*Insurgency and Counterinsurgency in Kenya: A Social History of the Shifta Conflict, c. 1963–1968*,

Brill). Her current research on the history of northern Kenya is focused on the relationship between development and security.

Notes

1. According to Carrier and Lochery, Eastleigh brings in the second highest revenue for the Kenya Revenue Agency behind the Central Business District.
2. Kenya National Archive (KNA), DC/WAJ 2/9/1, Officer in Charge NFD to Chief Secretary Nairobi, 29 July 1944.
3. See also KNA, DC/MBT 7/1/2, H.B. Sharpe, 'Further Notes on Marsabit District', March 1928.
4. KNA, PC/EST/2/11/16, The Secretariat, 'The Position of Alien Somalis in Kenya Colony', 25 April 1945.
5. KNA, PC/EST/2/11/16, 'The Position of Alien Somalis'.
6. Ibid.
7. Ibid.
8. KNA, DC/ISO 2/3/7, District Commissioner Isiolo to Office in Charge of NFD, 26 May 1938.
9. This was of an estimated total population of 14,785 (Somalis, Boran, Sakuye, Arabs, Asians and Europeans). KNA, PC/GRSSA 2/1/17, Provincial Commissioner Northern Province to Divisional Engineer, Public Works Department, 16 January 1952.
10. The recent decision to nullify the results of the 2009 Kenya census in districts with large Somali populations is a continued reflection of this anxiety.
11. Of this figure 782 were listed as Isaaq, 422 as Herti, 215 as Hawiye and 53 others. The second largest provincial concentration of Somalis was given as Rift Valley, where there were thought to be 1,473 in residence. In Coast Province 828 were counted, 664 in Central Province, 480 in Nyanza Province and 451 in Southern Province. KNA, PC/NFD 4/2/9/7, Report on the census of the Somali population of Kenya Colony (excluding the Northern Province), 1956.
12. British National Archive (BNA), FO 533/171, unsigned letter to district commissioner Nairobi, 2 October 1916.
13. BNA, FO 533/170, Governor of Kenya to Secretary of State for the Colonies, 13 October 1916.
14. The Somali population was given as 303 males, 48 females, and 50 children. KNA, DC/NBI 1/1/1, Nairobi Political Record Book, 1912.
15. Also see BNA, MPGG 1/65, Keyplan of Nairobi Township.
16. The smaller villages were simply referred to as 'other'. KNA, DC/NBI 1/1/1, Nairobi Political Record Book, 1912.
17. BNA, FO 533/170, Governor of Kenya to Secretary of State for the Colonies, 13 October 1916.
18. Ibid.
19. In the early years of the protectorate Somali livestock traders were known to buy camels, mules, sheep and goats also from the Boran in northern Kenya and Ethiopia. KNA, DC/NBI 1/1/1, Nairobi Political Record Book, 1912.
20. KNA, PC/EST/2/11/16, 'The Position of the Alien Somali'.
21. Ibid.
22. Ibid.
23. Ibid.

24. KNA, PC/EST/2/11/16, 'The Position of the Alien Somali'.
25. BNA, CO 533/170, Governor to Secretary of State for the Colonies, 30 September 1916.
26. BNA, CO 533/171, Governor to Secretary of State for the Colonies, 16 October 1916.
27. BNA, CO 533/171, 'Somali Villages in Nairobi, British East Africa', report prepared by Shapely and Schwartz, 10 October 1916.
28. BNA, CO 533/171, 'Somali Villages in Nairobi, British East Africa', report prepared by Shapely and Schwartz, 10 October 1916; BNA, MPGG 1/65, proposed model village for the Somali near Nairobi.
29. KNA, NHC/1/93, City Treasurer to Secretary of the Central Housing Board, 23 October 1959; KNA, NHC/1/93, City Treasurer to Secretary of the Central Housing Board, 10 November 1959.
30. KNA, NHC/1/93, Notes of a meeting between the Minister for Housing and the United Somali Association, 13 December 1958; KNA, NHC/1/93, City Treasurer to Secretary of the Central Housing Board, 23 October 1959.
31. BNA, MPGG 1/65, proposed model village for the Somali near Nairobi.
32. Another factor working against repatriation was the need to compensate those willing to leave. KNA, PC/EST/2/11/16, 'The Position of the Alien Somali'.
33. KNA, CS/8/22/1, Associations and Public Bodies, United Somali Association; KNA, CS/8/22/2, Somali National Association to Chief Secretary, 24 February 1959.
34. For example see KNA, BB/1/98, Abdi Rashid Khalif to PC Northern Province, 10 March 1961; BNA, FCO 141/6657, NPPPP Petition to Secretary of State for the Colonies, 1961; BNA, FCO 141/6840, NPPPP to Chief Commissioner, 4 October 1961. KNA, PC/GRSSA/3/1/69, NPPPP Chairman to PC Northern Province, 2 August 1963. BNA, FCO141/7120, Nairobi to Secretary of State for the Colonies, 26 March 1963.

References

Achola, M.A. 2002. 'Colonial Policy and Urban Health: The Case of Colonial Nairobi', in A. Burton (ed.), *The Urban Experience in Eastern Africa, c. 1750–2000*. Nairobi: The British Institute in Eastern Africa, pp. 119–37.

Anderson, D. 1984. 'Depression, Dust Bowl, Demography and Drought: The Colonial State and Soil Conservation in East Africa during the 1930s', *African Affairs* 83(332): 321–43.

———. 2002. 'Corruption at City Hall: African Housing and Urban Development in Colonial Nairobi', in A. Burton (ed.), *The Urban Experience in Eastern Africa, c. 1750–2000*. Nairobi: The British Institute in Eastern Africa, pp. 138–54.

Bonneuil, C. 2000. 'Development as Experiment: Science and State-Building in Late Colonial and Postcolonial Africa, 1930–1979', *Osiris* 15: 258–81.

Boye, S.R., and R. Kaarhus. 2011. 'Competing Claims and Contested Boundaries: Legitimating Land Rights in Isiolo District, Northern Kenya', *Africa Spectrum* 46(2): 99–124.

Carrier, N. 2015. 'Citizenship, Place and Identity in Nairobi's "Little Mogadishu"', *Conference on Urban Property, Governance and Citizenship in the Global South*. Copenhagen: Copenhagen University.

———. 2017. *Little Mogadishu: Eastleigh, Nairobi's Global Somali Hub*. New York: Oxford University Press.

Carrier, N., and E. Lochery. 2013. 'Missing States? Somali Trade Networks and the Eastleigh Transformation', *Journal of Eastern African Studies* 7(2): 334–52.

Cassanelli, L. 1982. *The Shaping of Somali Society. Reconstructing the History of a Pastoral People, 1600 to 1900*. Philadelphia: University of Pennsylvania Press.

Cooper, F. 1983. 'Urban Space, Industrial Time and Wage Labour in Africa', in F. Cooper (ed.), *Struggle for the City: Migrant Labour, Capital and the State in Urban Africa*. London: Sage Publications, pp. 7–50.

Crisis Group Report. 2015. *Kenya's Somali North East: Devolution and Security*. Nairobi, Brussels: International Crisis Group.

Curtin, P. 1985. 'Medical Knowledge and Urban Planning in Tropical Africa', *American Historical Review* 90(3): 594–613.

Eliot, C. 1905. *The East Africa Protectorate*. London: E. Arnold.

Furedi, F. 1973. 'The African Crowd in Nairobi: Popular Movements and Elite Politics', *Journal of African History* 14(2): 275–90.

Hake, A. 1977. *African Metropolis: Nairobi's Self-Help City*. New York: St Martin's Press.

Hjort, A. 1979. *Savanna Town: Rural Ties and Urban Opportunities in Northern Kenya*. Stockholm: University of Stockholm.

Lewis, I.M. 1960. 'The Somali Conquest of the Horn of Africa', *Journal of African History* 1(2): 213–29.

Lochery, E. 2012. 'Rendering Difference Visible: The Kenyan State and Its Somali Citizens', *African Affairs* 111(445): 615–39.

Mburu, N. 2005. *Bandits on the Border: The Last Frontier in the Search for Somali Unity*. New Jersey: Red Sea Press.

Moyse-Bartlett, H. 1956. *King's African Rifles: A Study in the Military History of East and Central Africa, 1890–1945*. Aldershot: Gale and Polden.

Murunga, G. 2005. '"Inherently Unhygienic Races": Plague and the Origins of Settler Dominance in Nairobi, 1899–1907', in S. Salm and T. Falola (eds), *African Urban Spaces in Historical Perspective*. Suffolk: University of Rochester Press, pp. 98–130.

Murunga, G. 2009. 'Refugees at Home? Coping with Somalia Conflict in Nairobi, Kenya', in M. Ben Arrous and L. Ki-Zerbo (eds), *African Studies in Geography from Below*. Dakar: Codesria, pp. 198–232.

Ngalamulume, K. 2004. 'Keeping the City Totally Clean: Yellow Fever and the Politics of Prevention in Colonial Saint-Louis-de-Senegal, 1850–1914', *Journal of African History* 45: 183–202.

Obudho, R.A. 1997. *Urbanization and Management of Kenya's Urban Centres in the 21st Century*. Nairobi: Centre for Urban Research.

Paret, M., and S. Gleeson. 2016. 'Precarity and Agency Through a Migration Lens', *Citizenship Studies* 20(3-4): 277–94.

Parsons, T. 1997. '"Kibera Is Our Blood": The Sudanese Military Legacy in Nairobi's Kibera Location, 1902–1968', *The International Journal of African Historical Studies* 30(1): 87–122.

Reese, S. 1996. *Patricians of the Benaadir. Islamic Learning, Commerce and Somali Urban Identity in the Nineteenth Century*. Philadelphia: University of Pennsylvania Press.

Reid, R. 2009. *A History of Modern Africa, 1800-Present*. Oxford: Wiley-Blackwell.

Schlee, G. 1989. *Identities on the Move: Clanship and Pastoralism in Northern Kenya*. Manchester: Manchester University Press.

Schlee, G. with A. Shongolo. 2014. *Islam and Ethnicity in Northern Kenya and Southern Ethiopia*. Oxford: James Currey.

Simpson, W.J. 1914. *Report on Sanitary Matters in the East Africa Protectorate, Uganda and Zanzibar*. London: Colonial Office.

Standing, G. 2014. *A Precariat Charter: From Denizens to Citizens*. London: Bloomsbury Academic.

Swanson, M. 1977. 'The Sanitation Syndrome: Bubonic Plague and Urban Native Policy in Cape Colony, 1900–1909', *Journal of African History* 18: 387–410.

Thompson, V. 2015. *Conflict in the Horn of Africa: The Kenya-Somalia Border Problem, 1941–2015*. New York: University Press of America.

Turton, E.R. 1972. 'Somali Resistance to Colonial Rule and the Development of Somali Political Activity in Kenya, 1893–1960', *Journal of African History* 13(1): 119–43.

———. 1974a. 'The Isaaq Somali Diaspora and Poll-Tax Agitation in Kenya, 1936–41', *African Affairs* 73(292): 325–46.

———. 1974b. 'The Introduction and Development of Educational Facilities for the Somali in Kenya', *History of Education Quarterly* 14(3): 347–65.

Waite, L. 2009. 'A Place and Space for a Critical Geography of Precarity?', *Geography Compass* 3(1): 412–433.

Weitzberg, K. 2013. 'Producing History from Elisions, Fragments and Silences: Public Testimony, the Asiatic Poll-Tax Campaign, and the Isaaq Somali Population of Kenya', *Northeast African Studies* 13(2): 177–206.

———. 2015. 'The Unaccountable Census: Colonial Enumeration and Its Implications for the Somali People of Kenya', *Journal of African History* 56(3): 409–28.

Whittaker, H. 2012. 'Forced Villagization during the *Shifta* Conflict in Kenya, c. 1963–1968', *International Journal of African Historical Studies* 45(3): 343–64.

———. 2014. *Insurgency and Counterinsurgency in Kenya: A Social History of the Shifta Conflict, 1963–68*. Leiden: Brill.

———. 2015. 'A New Model Village? Nairobi Development and the Somali Question in Kenya, c. 1915–17', *Northeast African Studies* 15(2): 117–40.

Chapter 2

The Port and the Island

Cosmopolitan and Vernacular Identity Constructions among Somali Women in Nairobi and Johannesburg

Nereida Ripero-Muñiz

Introduction

I met Hibo in Tawakal clinic in Eastleigh. She is a twenty-two year old Kenyan Somali student of Islamic Studies at UMMA University in Thika, and on weekends she runs the women's meetings taking place at the clinic. I had attended one of the meetings and was talking to her afterwards. Our conversation took place in January 2014, when the Kenyan police were starting to raid Eastleigh looking for undocumented migrants and Al-Shabaab members. Hibo was outraged by those raids, which were a repressive response of the Kenyan government to the terrorist attack perpetrated by Al-Shabaab at the Westgate mall.

She angrily referred to the stereotypical image many people have of Somalis as ignorant refugees and Muslims with terrorist affiliations. 'People think we are stupid, that we don't even know who Rihanna is!', she exclaimed loudly, taking out her arms from below the jilbab covering her head and half of her body as she shook violently the smartphone held in her hands.

Hibo's words showcase the great dichotomy that exists between the public image about Somalis the media has helped to create and the way Somalis see themselves. In the global imagination, Somalis tend to be seen as helpless refugees from a war-torn country, Indian Ocean pirates, radical Muslims or Al-Shabaab terrorists. However, Somalis see themselves as proud people of nomadic origin with transnational families, great business entrepreneurs and as committed Muslims.

Hibo's complaint about the stereotyping of Somalis is shared by many young Somali women residing in Nairobi and Johannesburg. This is not just a result of transnationalism or globalization, but can also be ascribed to the cosmopolitan experiences of a part of the Somali diaspora.

For Somalis, the two cities of Nairobi and Johannesburg are interconnected at different transnational levels: through the commercial routes of goods that leave the Kenyan capital in the direction of South Africa – such as textiles, clothes, non-perishable food and even khat (see Carrier and Elliott, this volume) and most importantly through the migration routes of Somalis. Many of those living in Johannesburg have journeyed through or resided previously in Nairobi, which gave rise to strong social networks linking these two cities. Both cities have also become transitional places for Somalis as many use them as platforms to get to Western countries or the Middle East. Last but not least, in both cities Somalis have transformed neighbourhoods (Eastleigh in Nairobi, Mayfair in Johannesburg) into two 'Little Mogadishus', translocally connected to the rest of the world where Somalis can be found. This showcases the urbanity of the Somali diaspora and how different urban centres are connected through everyday practices performed by Somali migrants around the world.

This chapter examines how Somaliness is constructed, experienced and expressed in the two urban African contexts of Nairobi and Johannesburg. It explores how the cosmopolitan conditions offered in these two African cities affect urban refugees' sense of identity. I firstly review some literature on cosmopolitanism and explore how this concept can be used to approach refugee identities; I then present a brief overview of the situation of Somalis in Kenya and South Africa, and more specifically in Eastleigh, Nairobi, and Mayfair, Johannesburg, to finally focus on how Somaliness is expressed and constructed in these two African urban contexts in relation to the cosmopolitan aspirations of Somali migrant women.

The findings presented here build on my PhD research exploring the dynamics of identity construction in diasporic spaces. They are based on ethnographic data and 40 life-stories and in-depth interviews with adult Somali women in Mayfair, Johannesburg and Eastleigh, Nairobi conducted between 2012 and 2015. All original names have been changed to protect confidentiality. The body of narrative data was approached using a thematic analysis. I grouped the narratives collected in Nairobi and Johannesburg and compared what was said in the two contexts in order to find similarities and differences between the two interlinked cities. Most of the narratives produced by the women in both cities show a complex scenario of identifications in which hyphenated identities, feelings of belonging and non-belonging and reproduction of vernacular and cosmopolitan practices play a key role in the construction of Somaliness.

The Cosmopolitan Refugee

The theme of cosmopolitanism had a revival in the social sciences some years ago (Appadurai 2013; Appiah 1997 and 2006; Beck 2006; Beck and Sznaider

2006; Darieva, Glick Schiller and Gruner-Domic 2012; Furia 2005; Gilroy 2005; Pollock 2000; Pollock et al. 2000; Waldron 2000; Werbner 2008), and the vast use of the concept 'cosmopolitanism' has made its meanings multiply. As Vertovec and Cohen summarize, cosmopolitanism can be understood as 'a socio-cultural condition, a philosophy, a political project, an attitude or a practice' (2002). Moreover, as Skrbis, Kendall and Woodward (2004) note: 'cosmopolitanism is not only embodied, but also felt, imagined, consumed and fantasized' (p. 121).

Cosmopolitanism has generally tended to be associated with the cultivated elite from western countries (Appadurai 2013; Skrbis and Woodward 2007; Waldron 2000; Hannerz 1996). This is an elite embodied in the traveller or the expatriate. This conception of cosmopolitanism is too narrow and incomplete as it leaves out of the picture other forms of cosmopolitanism that should be taken into account in the interconnected world in which we now live. Some authors have challenged the Eurocentric connotations of the term: for example, Gilroy proposes South Africa, and specially Johannesburg, as the cradle for 'a new cosmopolitanism centred in the global South' (2005: 289), an idea that is developed further by Achille Mbembe through his concept of 'afropolitanism' (2007; see also Nuttall and Mbembe 2008). This is a cosmopolitanism born and practiced in Africa in which Johannesburg is presented as the main cosmopolitan hub of the continent.

Authors such as Malkki (1995), Werbner (1999), Kothari (2008) and Landau and Freemantle (2010) have applied the concept of cosmopolitanism to migrants or refugees in Africa. While Landau and Freemantle argue that cosmopolitanism is often a mere 'tactical cosmopolitanism' adopted by many migrants in South Africa as a strategy 'to negotiate partial inclusion in South Africa's transforming society without becoming bounded by it' (2010: 4), others propose that the experience of migration actually influences how people perceive the world and act in it. Kothari (2008) noted that this kind of migrant cosmopolitanism can be observed among peddlers from South Asia and West Africa living in Barcelona, and Liisa Malkki, in her 1995 book *Purity and Exile*, explored the cosmopolitan constructions of identity that Hutu refugees experienced in Kigoma, observing that, 'in the process of managing these "rootless" identities in a township life, they were creating not a heroized national identity but a lively cosmopolitanism' (1995: 36).

Something similar could be said about many of the Somali women I talked to in Nairobi and Johannesburg, where I observed that cosmopolitanism was not only a strategy, but also the result of a transnational experience in which women reinvent themselves in the diaspora.

There is one more important aspect that should be taken into account to understand the dynamics of identity formation among the Somali diaspora: the role hope plays in this process. Appadurai describes cosmopolitanism from below as a cosmopolitanism that 'builds on the practices of the local ... but is imbued with a politics of hope ... it builds towards global affinities' (2013: 198). This is a grounded cosmopolitanism in which the vernacular and the local interweave with the 'politics of hope', a desire for membership in the 'new world order' (Ferguson 2006) in which people can work, study and move freely around the world. Imagination plays an important role in this process. Somalis keep contact with relatives residing in the West and are aware of the rights and entitlements that citizenship in a western country can give them, which itself became a powerful engine for migration (Abdi 2015).

This cosmopolitanism is not incompatible with a strong sense of Somaliness. As Anthony Appiah (1997) points out, the cosmopolitan ideal implies taking one's roots to wherever one goes. Therefore the two apparently contradictory conditions of patriotism and cosmopolitanism can actually cohabit in the mind of the same person. Embracing cosmopolitanism does not make Somalis leave their national and vernacular identifications behind. Rihanna may be one of Hibo's favourite singers, but for her that is perfectly compatible with wearing the jilbab, having henna applied for a special occasion and studying the Qur'an.

Between Hostility and Cosmopolitanism: The Situation of Somalis in Kenya and South Africa

Kenya and South Africa are just two of the countries in Africa that host Somali migrants. Kenya has a longer history as a nation hosting Somalian refugees, due to its geographical proximity to Somalia, its historical ties and its own large indigenous Somali population (see also Lowe and Yarnell, this volume). While in the case of Kenya there are official numbers concerning the Somalian refugee population (see introduction to this volume), there are only estimates as to the numbers of Somalis in South Africa. In January 2015 the UNHCR calculated that there are about 24,000 living as refugees in South Africa (UNHCR 2015). Somalis started arriving in South Africa after the beginning of the civil war in Somalia and the droughts that devastated the country during the early nineties. Jinnah (2010) identifies and describes three other waves of Somali migration to South Africa: in the mid-1990s; in 2000, when Ethiopia invaded Somalia; and the last wave of arrivals in 2010–2011 as a result of droughts and famines.

Even if South Africa and Kenya represent very different destinations for Somalis, both countries also share certain characteristics for them. To start with, the geographical position of Kenya and South Africa in relation to Somalia and the permeable African borders make them more accessible to reach from Somalia than Western countries. And in many cases both countries become an initial base to relocate later to the US, Canada, Europe or the Middle East.

In both countries, Somalis encounter hostility from members of the local population and governmental organizations (Abdi 2015; Jinnah 2010; Sadouni

2009; Murunga 2009), as the recurrent xenophobic attacks on Somali shopkeepers in South African townships and the massive arrests by the Kenyan police taking place from time to time (see chapters by Lowe and Yarnell and by Wandera and Wario, this volume) show. However, the reasons behind these hostilities are different in the two contexts. In the case of Kenya, hostility against ethnic Somalis, either Somalian refugees or Kenyan Somalis, is not a new phenomenon, as they have been stigmatized both by the government and police for long.

South Africa does not share Kenya's conflict-ridden history with Somalia. Nevertheless, as Jinnah notes, the hostility Somalis encounter in South Africa comes not only from 'ordinary citizens', but also from 'government officials, public servants, hospitals and government departments' (2010: 93). South Africa, being the most prosperous country in sub-Saharan Africa, attracts a great number of migrants from the rest of the continent. But it is also a country of great social and economic inequalities. As happens in many other places, the immigrant population is willing to undertake low-paid jobs or to start businesses where they offer products at low prices, as is the case with Somalis. Due to the aforementioned inequalities, this is not well received by some of the local population, and hostility against migrants has tragically materialized in recurrent xenophobic attacks (Landau 2012). Probably the most significant attacks took place in May 2008, leaving 64 dead and thousands displaced (Hassim, Kupe and Worby 2008) and more recently in January 2015.

The wave of attacks in 2015 happened during the time I was undertaking fieldwork in South Africa. They were instigated by King Goodwill Zwelithini, a Zulu traditional leader who declared in vernacular language that all foreigners must pack and leave the country.[1] Following this declaration, migrants from different nationalities were attacked in the whole country over several weeks and many of them, such as Zimbabweans or Malawians, went back to their countries of origin. Somalis around the country were also attacked with most of them seeking refuge in Mayfair after fleeing the rural areas and townships where they run successful *spaza* shops.[2] After the wave of attacks passed, some Somalis returned to their businesses in the townships. Many others decided to leave the country in search of a better and less threatened life somewhere else.

However, despite this hostility, xenophobia and marginalization, Somalis in Kenya and South Africa find Nairobi and Johannesburg two cosmopolitan cities where an African modernity flourishes. At the same time, in these places their Somaliness is negotiated, contested and transformed, while the urban areas of Eastleigh and Mayfair become ever more translocally connected.

Where Is Mogadishu?

Nairobi and Johannesburg are deeply connected by the migration routes of Somalis, as many of those living in Johannesburg have journeyed through or resided previously in Nairobi. This route is sometimes also taken the other way round, as happened during the wave of xenophobic attacks in South Africa at the beginning of 2015, when many Somalis staying in South Africa went back to Nairobi after temporarily transiting through Mayfair.

There is also a significant population of Somalis living in or transiting through both cities.[3] In Nairobi, even if ethnic Somalis can be found in different areas of the city – such as South C, Kilimani or Komorock – a vast majority are concentrated in Eastleigh or 'Isili', as it is popularly known (for more information about the Somali population in Nairobi and the history of Eastleigh see the Introduction and the chapter by Whittaker in this volume).

In the case of Johannesburg, Somalis chose Mayfair for settling down in the city. This is, like Eastleigh, a formerly Indian neighbourhood. In contrast to Nairobi the Indian population was the very reason why Somalis opted to stay in this area, as they found religious links with the Muslim Indian population who inhabited this area (Abdi 2015; Jinnah 2010; Sadouni 2009). Even if some Indian families still live there, nowadays the population of Mayfair is mostly made up of Somalis and Ethiopian Muslims.

In both cities, Somalis inhabiting these spaces have transformed the neighbourhoods, creating what are commonly known as 'Little Mogadishus'. The businesses, objects of consumption and recreational places (such as restaurants or tea houses) rebuild at a small scale the social, economic and cultural everyday life of a peaceful Mogadishu that no longer exists. Moreover, these symbolic recreations of the lost city, spaces in which everyday practices take place, also maintain some of the commercial and cosmopolitan spirit that the Somali capital once had as one of the main hubs in the Indian Ocean. Eastleigh and Mayfair have likewise become commercial and economic global hubs for the Somali diaspora. These city quarters can be considered as material reproductions at a small scale of Mogadishu's lifestyle and street life created by the combination of strong cultural, national and religious identifications with ideas about a lost homeland among Somalis living in Nairobi and Johannesburg. Here Somaliness becomes a materialization of a way of being that transforms spaces into very distinctive places (see chapter by Scharrer). At the same time, the two neighbourhoods are interconnected through migration routes and flows of goods, but they are also linked to Mogadishu and other major cities in Somalia in the collective imagination of Somalis residing in both neighbourhoods.

Both cities have also become transitional places for Somalis as many of them journey through or temporarily inhabit these two cities on their way to somewhere else. From this perspective Nairobi has become one of the most important ports of Somalia. Its geographical position together with the historical, cultural and social links between the city and Somalia have made it an entry and exit point into and out of the country, not only for people but also for goods, money, ideas and practices. The Somali community there, formed by Somalian refugees,

Kenyan Somalis and Somali diaspora returnees, is bigger and more established than the one in Johannesburg, and offers a larger network of economic and emotional support for Somalis transiting through or living in the city.

Somalian refugees have made of Eastleigh a transitional place par excellence: some Somalians are happy to stay there, but most arrive in Nairobi with a desire to go somewhere else, a period of transit that can last from just a couple of weeks to several years. Newcomers to Eastleigh normally rely on the help of their relatives. This help can take many forms, from offering a space to sleep in Eastleigh during the time of transit, to sending remittances so the person can live. If the family is wealthy some distant uncle or cousin living abroad can decide to invest in a business in Eastleigh for his relative to run. Relatives and clansmen often (but not always) decide which will be the next destination of the person in transit and sponsor their journey. Sometimes this decision can take long or things can go wrong, for instance a relative that was supposed to sponsor someone is no longer able to do so, thereby prolonging the period of transit.

This was the case for Samira, who left Bossaso in Puntland, following in the footsteps of her sisters, one of whom lives in Johannesburg, the other in Addis Ababa. A distant cousin offered to sponsor her to go to London, but after she arrived in Eastleigh her cousin changed his mind. According to the stories related by other informants and supported by my Somali research assistant, this is a situation that happens often. Samira then stayed in a room she shared with other women from the same clan, receiving some 'little' money from her sisters when they could spare some. After the London plan did not work out, Samira thought of going to Libya via Sudan so she could reach Europe from there. Her sisters persuaded her not to, as this route is very dangerous and she could be robbed, raped, kidnapped for ransom or killed at sea. Therefore she kept staying in Eastleigh suffering from *buufis*.[4]

Nairobi (and especially Eastleigh) functions as a central port for the Somali diaspora who use its proximity to Somalia either to leave the country, as refugees do, or to get into it, as diaspora returnees are increasingly doing. It also functions as a cargo port, a major node of commerce for the Somali diaspora, providing goods not only for Kenya but also for East and Southern Africa, and even to other places around the globe where Somalis can be found, such as Minneapolis or Helsinki (see Carrier and Elliot, this volume).

Meanwhile in Johannesburg, a much smaller Somali community can be found, and isolation seems to be the main general feeling among Somalis living in Mayfair. South Africa is perceived as a land of opportunities; and Johannesburg's thriving economy makes it a 'treasure island' for many African migrants. This is also the case for Somalis, who endure a tough journey through the African continent full of great expectations that can dissolve as soon as they reach the city.

For Somalis, the journey to Johannesburg, as to many other places, begins in Nairobi. Somalians come to Eastleigh from different regions of East Africa.

Some cross the permeable border between Somalia and Kenya, others pass by Ethiopia first – depending on the region of Somalia they are leaving, or where their family is living. From there they continue to Nairobi, although some may stay in the Kenyan refugee camps for a while (see chapter by Lowe and Yarnell). Once in Nairobi the journey to South Africa is organized through *mukhalasiin* or smugglers, who charge a considerable amount of money to smuggle people through the different borders they have to cross before reaching South Africa. The journey can be organized in two ways. Some migrants pay the full amount to a *mukhalas* at the beginning of the journey, normally in Nairobi. This full amount includes transport, accommodation along the journey, bribes to pay border officials plus the *mukhalas'* commission. Others pay instead bit by bit as they reach the different countries that the journey entails. In 2014 the price from Nairobi to Johannesburg was around USD 800.

There are three possible main routes to South Africa. Most commonly Somalis undertake this journey by road. After passing from Kenya to Tanzania, there are two possible ways: either crossing directly to northern Mozambique and from there going to Maputo where the last steps of the journey are organized; or from Tanzania they detour to Zambia, Malawi and finally Zimbabwe. However, a small minority is also able to fly from Nairobi or Addis Ababa to Maputo and from there cross the border to South Africa by road. In some other cases, people arrive by boat from Somalia or Kenya to northern Mozambique.

The journey can take from a couple of weeks to years, depending on whether migrants have the money to pay for the full journey upfront or if they stop at different places along the way. Small Somali enclaves are found along the route, such as in Dar es Salaam or Nampula. People who have paid just for parts of the journey may need to stay in these enclaves, relying on other Somalis' help and hospitality until they raise the necessary funds to continue the journey. During this time they might work for somebody or wait for the sponsorship of some relative that sends money through *hawala*, or the common money transfer facilities of MoneyGram or Western Union.

This is a journey full of perils. Migrants, normally travelling individually, join together in small groups of ten or fifteen people. The border authorities or the police are some of the main concerns along the journey, but actually the *mukhalasiin* can become a problem as well. Even if they are normally reliable, in the sense that they deliver the service they have been paid for, there is no guarantee this will actually happen. Many of them are described as criminals that might drop undocumented migrants in the middle of nowhere.

Once Somalis arrive in Johannesburg, normally at Park Station, a family member picks them up or they call one of the Somali taxi drivers operating in Mayfair, whose number they were giving during the journey. A driver will come and pick them up, and on the way to Mayfair they will figure out what clan and sub-clan the person belongs to, and drop them at a house of someone related to them. In case no kinsmen are found in the city, they attempt to find possible friends or acquaintances. In Johannesburg, Somalis also get their asylum seeker permit or refugee permit and either continue to somewhere else in the country, like Port Elisabeth, Cape Town, or a township where they can start a business, or they settle in Mayfair.

Johannesburg, a city normally portrayed as the most modern, multicultural and cosmopolitan hub south of the Sahara (Nuttall and Mbembe 2008), even considered the cradle of 'afropolitanism', is actually a city that constantly excludes. Johannesburg evolved as a city demarcating strong ethnic enclaves, making very clear who belonged where. Even if the spatial boundaries according to race imposed by the apartheid regime no longer exist, its consequences are still much felt in the life of the city. These boundaries continue to exist in the collective imagination of the city, fed by narratives of fear, that become as difficult to surpass as the multiple electric fences anchored to its grounds, and it is still very clear who belongs where. This exclusion becomes even more apparent for migrants, as Grant and Thompson note: 'Paradoxically, Johannesburg is a quintessentially migrant city and also ranks among the least immigrant-friendly cities in the world' (2015: 181).

Mayfair, which is situated close to the city centre, has transformed very quickly during the last couple of years. When I started doing research in the area in January 2012 only a couple of lodges, cybercafés and restaurants could be found around Amal, the Somali shopping centre at the heart of the neighbourhood. These businesses, run by Somalis or Oromo, have doubled in numbers in the last years, especially along 8th Avenue.

Even if Mayfair has transformed into another 'Little Mogadishu', the hostile and xenophobic situation Somalis face in South Africa, the spatial boundaries that still exist in the post-apartheid city together with the lack of direct family support all create a strong feeling of insecurity, alienation and isolation among the Somali community living there. This generates a strong collective feeling of *buufis*.

In this sense, Mayfair becomes a small island from which it is difficult to leave. Most Somalis residing in the neighbourhood, especially women, rarely leave the area – unless they work in the central business district (CBD). As Grant and Thompson (2015) remark, Somalis will be eager to give you directions to get to any township in the country, but will not know how to get further than Fordsburg or the CBD in the inner city of Johannesburg. This sense of Mayfair as an island is reinforced by the fact that the area is rarely visited by any South African, except for the few Indians still residing in the area – contrary to Eastleigh where many Kenyans choose to shop due to the cheap prices found nowhere else in the city. In this sense, Somalis living in Mayfair feel quite isolated, with few links, if any, to the rest of the city. This isolation contrasts enormously with the different commercial and social connections they keep with other Somalis spread across South Africa and with the tight transnational social networks maintained with Somalia and other Somali diasporic spaces in the continent and around the world. As Grant and Thompson also corroborate: '[Mayfair] appears as an enclave less connected to an urban or national grid, but operates more widely in transnational networks that link dispersed spaces to immigrant enclaves, creating specific local milieus' (Grant and Thompson 2015: 197).

Nevertheless, the isolation Somalis feel and create in Mayfair with respect to the rest of the city also offers a kind of protection. Some Somali businessmen in Mayfair are aware that they could be making much more money opening shops in townships but they choose to stay in the quarter as they feel more secure inside this island. Moreover, during the xenophobic attacks of 2008 and 2015 shopkeepers from the townships came to the area in big numbers looking for protection. In January 2015 the numbers of Somalis in the area multiplied, with lodges full to their capacity, hosting people for free, who even had to sleep in the corridors.

But islands also have ports, and weeks later Mayfair became empty again, with many Somalis leaving South Africa, either back to Somalia or to Kenya or to Brazil – in order to reach the US, a new extended migration route among Somalis. So in this sense Mayfair also works as a transitional place in order to get somewhere else. In a period of a few months, the island became first a protective nest, and soon after a temporary port, a busy transitional place from which to leave South Africa, demonstrating the ephemeral nature of this place, open to constant transformation depending on the always changing circumstances of the people inhabiting its streets.

Constructing Somaliness Outside Somalia: Vernacular and Cosmopolitan Identities

> If I don't have tradition, technically I am a lost person. I need to have tradition. If not, I can follow anybody from another culture. I can follow any culture. I'm lost … It's like identity. I am called Zahara Somebody Somebody so if I come here and say 'I will change my identity', I'll become like a Shona and all those people. … As a Somalian, we don't leave our culture behind. Anywhere you go, you know this person is a Somalian. The way we dress and everything … I'm still a Somalian and I will always be Somalian.
>
> —Interview with Zahara, Johannesburg

Zahara, a twenty-eight year-old born in Mogadishu, got separated from her family at an early age. When the war broke out in the capital city, a bomb hit her house and in the chaos that came immediately after, she thought that she had lost all the members of her family. She was then 'adopted' by a family of distant relatives who used her as a house help and mistreated her. When she was old enough she got into a boat in Kismayo and after a journey full of perils by sea and land that took several years, she reached Johannesburg four years ago. After her arrival in the country she found out through distant relatives that her mother was still alive and living in Ethiopia, and that some of her brothers lived in Norway. Once she sorted her 'travelling documents' she took the journey back by road from Johannesburg to Ethiopia to meet with her mother. On her return to South Africa she opened a small convenience shop in Mayfair as she waited to be resettled in the US by the UNHCR.

Even if she had crossed parts of the African continent a couple of times, had family in different parts of the world and was expecting to go to the US, for the moment she was a refugee in a hostile and xenophobic country, her everyday life was full of uncertainties and her Somali origin 'and way of being' was one of the few things she was fully certain about, thus her 'Somali identity' became a secure reference point in a very uncertain world.

Zahara's vision of her Somali identity, as an immoveable characteristic inherited from her parents and passed from generation to generation, is not unique among Somalis living in Johannesburg. Lula, a young mother from Puntland who came to South Africa for an arranged marriage, explained her Somaliness in the following way:

> You are born into it. Like this child, she was born here but you cannot call her South African because her mother was born there in Somalia. Our origin is Somali, and our culture is different. Something you cannot change. Even if you have an American passport you are still Somali. (Interview with Lula, Johannesburg)

Being Somali was portrayed by both women as a fixed characteristic, 'something that you are born into' and which you will stay from the cradle to the grave, regardless of where you go and where you live. These narratives present 'national culture' as a pillar from which their identity unfolds and in which 'tradition' passing from generation to generation constitutes the base of Somaliness. 'Tradition' is seen as a kind of unchangeable set of practices chained and repeated over generations, reinforcing a strong sense of collective identity.

In the extremely xenophobic and hostile context of Johannesburg, where the Somali population is much smaller than in Nairobi and consists mostly of Somalian refugees and asylum seekers, collective identity becomes an anchor connecting Somalis to a lost homeland, to the diasporic community living all around the world, and to other Somalis living in South Africa. That is why it becomes so important to strengthen certain characteristics of Somaliness, to ensure oneself a certain place among a collectivity. As Stuart Hall declares, these kinds of narratives 'construct identities which are ambiguously placed between past and future' (Hall, Held and McGrew 1992: 295). Sentences like 'I was born Somali and I always will be a Somali' reinforce a sense of continuity in an always changing and uncertain world. These narratives emanate from a strong nationalist identification, in which the nation has become 'a system of cultural representation ... a discourse, a way of constructing meanings' (Hall, Held and McGrew 1992: 292).

In Nairobi, where the population of ethnic Somalis is much bigger, including Somalian refugees but also Kenyan Somalis and Somali diaspora returnees, the sense of identity becomes more fluid and performative. I next present, to illustrate this point further, the cases of Amal, transiting through Eastleigh on her way to the UK, and Samia, a diaspora returnee from Canada.

I met Amal after one of the meetings at Tawakal clinic in Eastleigh. She came from Mogadishu to Nairobi a couple of years ago, where she now lives with her sister and her family. She was also learning English and I walked with her to Dallas International College of Modern Teaching, in the heart of Eastleigh, to collect her degree. 'Your way to success' reads the motto of the school. She was leaving soon to Addis Ababa. There she was supposed to meet and marry her future husband, a distant cousin staying in the UK. After the wedding in Addis she wanted to relocate with him to the UK. She told me how Eastleigh felt so much like home, 'it's almost the same', and how eager she was to go overseas to have 'a better life', even if that implied getting married with a man she did not know yet and who had been chosen for her. My Kenyan Somali research assistant was quick to clarify that this practice of arranged marriage was decreasing among Somali women in Nairobi as 'they are more exposed to cosmopolitanism'. Many of them now decide to elope with a man of their choice, causing great grievance to the family. This was not the case for Amal – for her the marriage was to fulfil the cosmopolitan aspirations she was looking for.

Even if Nairobi is the exit port of many Somalis wishing to relocate to a Western county, the Middle East or to South Africa, it is also an entry port back into Somalia, especially for diaspora returnees who also bring with them different sets of practices and believes.

Samia is a forty years old diaspora returnee who went to Canada to study when the conflict in Somalia escalated in the 1990s. She spent almost fifteen years abroad. After completing her PhD she decided to go back to East Africa, where she now lives between Nairobi and Mogadishu, running an NGO which seeks to empower Somali women. When asked about her Somali identity she declared:

> I am a woman with two identities, actually multiple identities: I am an African. I am a Muslim. I am from East Africa, from the Horn of Africa. I am a Somali. I am a Canadian. I am a feminist. I am an environmentalist. I am a social activist. You Know? (Interview with Samia, Nairobi)

Samia presents a very different way of being Somali than Zahara or Lula. Zahara associated her identity with the culture and nation she was born into, something static that cannot be changed, otherwise the self would get lost: her Somali identity became an anchor in a world full of changes and she stuck to it in order to make some sense of it. However, for Samia, her life experiences, class and education made her recognize the multiplicity of identifications forming her own self.

To talk about Somaliness nowadays we have to take into account these two different approaches to identity that Somali women take – one, which rests on an idea of a fixed tradition coexisting alongside another, which rests on a more postmodern approach. Samia described herself as a woman of multiple identities; actually she defined herself as 'hyphenated'. She considered herself both as an outsider as an insider. As she explained:

> You become stateless. Somali passport is not valid. You cannot travel with it. You don't have the state protection or access to opportunities. But I was lucky. I worked hard, I ended up going to Canada … to start a whole new life … The sky is the limit … it's up to you to build your life … And of course you struggle. I wasn't a white woman. … You are always an outsider, you are always the other, you are always asked the question, 'where are you from?', for the way I dress and the colour of my skin. … After 20 years of exile I came back to Somalia and I see myself both as an outsider and as insider … Because I changed, I am wearing different glasses. Sometimes when I am in Somalia I feel I don't belong there. Also the conflict changes people. And the same thing when I am in Canada, I am an insider and an outsider and I think is good. It gives me advantage, room to manoeuvre. (Interview with Samia, Nairobi)

For Samia, her diasporic experience in the West and the fact that she returned to East Africa have made her an outsider as well as an insider at the same time both in Canada and in Somalia. Even if she feels she doesn't belong fully to any of the countries, she portrayed this distance as benefitting her as she is able to successfully navigate two very different worlds. The fact that she is always 'the other', both in Canada and in Somalia, doesn't make her question her 'roots' or where she belongs. She admitted openly that she belongs to both worlds and that this is actually something that works in her favour. As Stuart Hall pointed out, diasporic people are:

> People from different cultural backgrounds, who have been obliged to live somewhere else but who remain in some deep ways also connected to their homes, cultures and places of origin, and consequently develop

what I would call a diasporic form of consciousness and way of life …
what DuBois called 'double consciousness'. (Hall 2006: 347)

This 'double consciousness' is sometimes not well received by other Somalis defending a 'pure sense' of Somaliness, and women like Samia are accused of being westernized. She is an example of someone with a diasporic identity that incorporates different sets of vernacular, religious and cosmopolitan identifications to create a new 'hybrid' self – sometimes made of contradictory practices and ways of being. Samia sees an advantage in this duality. As Avtar Brah points out: 'diasporic identities are at once local and global. They are networks of transnational identification encompassing "imagined" and "encountered" communities' (Brah 1996: 196). The relationship between the local and the global expressed by Somali women when talking about their different identifications varies, depending on their particular life stories and the intersections surrounding their lives such as class or the level of education.

Places also become an intersection to be taken into account. Nairobi, seen here as a port, where Somalis with very different backgrounds live together, allows these kinds of fluid and multiple identifications to emerge. Meanwhile the sense of an island that Mayfair represents for Somalis in Johannesburg reinforces a strong sense of collective identity based on common traditions and national identity.

However, what both Samia and Zahara share, regardless of their visions of identity, is a strong sense of belonging to an 'imagined community' (Anderson 1983), that of 'Somalis', the group of people they belong to no matter where they are in the world. Here the vision of the nation as a discourse or 'system of cultural representation' (Hall, Held and McGrew 1992) explains well how 'Somali' national identity flourishes all around the world, constructed around narratives and practices, in spite of the collapse of the nation-state.

Conclusion

This chapter has briefly presented the situation of Somalis in Kenya and South Africa, explored the existing connections and mobile urbanity between Eastleigh in Nairobi and Mayfair in Johannesburg, and discussed some of the processes of identity-formation Somalis undergo in the contexts of two cities that offer a cosmopolitan but at the same time hostile environment for Somalis.

In both cities Somalis have transformed the urban landscapes, creating what are popularly known as 'Little Mogadishus' in Eastleigh and Mayfair. These two neighbourhoods are not just themselves deeply connected, but are also connected to the rest of the world in which Somalis can be found, showcasing the tight relationships among distant urban centres created by the transitional experience of Somali migration in African cities. Moreover, the findings in both cities show collective identification processes that transcend physical boundaries.

Based on the meaning these two cities have for Somalis, I have proposed the metaphors of Nairobi as a port and Mayfair as an island to describe the different dynamics Somalis experience in each place, which has some implications for collective identity formation processes.

Due to the large Somali population living in Eastleigh, Somalis, even if they are in transit, often develop greater feelings of belonging and the city quarter has become an, at least temporary, home away from home for many. At the same time, the fluidity of Eastleigh, in which ethnic Somalis from different backgrounds live together with non-Somali Kenyans and non-Kenyans, makes it a cosmopolitan hub for the Somali diaspora. Furthermore the transit of people, goods and money on the streets of Nairobi, arriving to and leaving the city for many other places around the world, makes Nairobi, and especially Eastleigh, one or the busiest ports of the Horn of Africa.

In Johannesburg, Somalis do not develop similar feelings of belonging compared to Nairobi. Mayfair only becomes a shelter and therefore something akin to a home away from home in difficult times, when Somalis staying in other parts of the country come to Mayfair to look for protection among their compatriots. Mayfair operates much like a small island, where Somalis feel some sense of safety but still none of belonging. Johannesburg, the city considered the afropolitan city par excellence, is actually a conglomerate of islands, a heritage of the spatial distributions imposed during apartheid. The xenophobic situation Somalis face in South Africa together with these spatial boundaries of the post-apartheid city reinforces the sense of Mayfair as an island.

All this has implications for collective identification processes. In Mayfair Somaliness tends to be expressed and experienced as a primordial tradition, which becomes a unifying factor and a way of resilience in a hostile environment. The fact that the Somali community here is smaller than in Nairobi and formed mostly by refugees and asylum seekers makes them perceive 'tradition' as a fixed characteristic they use to reinforce their sense of identity in a xenophobic context. At the same time they reinforce their membership in the Somali community of Mayfair, to stay connected to a collectivity that will be the only structure on which they can rely in case of trouble.

Meanwhile in Nairobi, where the Somali population consists of Somalian refugees, Kenyan Somalis and diaspora returnees coming from different backgrounds of class, status, nationality and migration experience, the sense of identity is more fluid and performative. Here the 'hybrid identity of Somaliness' becomes more noticeable; with individuals negotiating between different sets of identities, as a result of a transnational life where the global and the local maintain a different, more open and fluid dialogue than in Johannesburg. This is also due to the nature of Nairobi as a 'port', more open to cosmopolitan ways of being and where different expressions of being Somali coexist in a city in which they also interact more freely than in Johannesburg.

In the case of the Somali diaspora in both cities, cosmopolitanism operates in a double way: on the one hand it depends on the personal experience of the migrant, either as directly lived or as they are exposed to it by relatives living all around the world, whilst on the other hand it is influenced by the cosmopolitan nature of these two African metropolises. However, even if Johannesburg is generally considered the most cosmopolitan city south of the Sahara, in the case of Somalis Nairobi appears as a more cosmopolitan context than Johannesburg.

Nevertheless, in both cities Somalis expressed a strong sense of belonging to an 'imagined community' (Anderson 1983) sustained by narratives of national and cultural identification with a lost homeland and implemented in everyday practices. The Somali diaspora shares a strong sense of being transnationally connected all around the world where Somaliness seems to flourish without being contained by the territorial boundaries of the nation-state. Whatever the urban setting, 'Somaliness' appears strong among Somalis in exile, and a constant in their mobile lives.

Nereida Ripero-Muñiz is a lecturer and researcher based at the School of Literature, Language and Media at the University of the Witwatersrand (South Africa). She was awarded a PhD degree by the same university in 2016; her dissertation explored identity construction among Somali women living in Nairobi and Johannesburg and will be published as a monograph by Berghahn Books. Her current research focuses on the transnational links of the global Somali diaspora and how it affects placemaking, cultural production and collective identities across borders.

Notes

1. *Times Live*. 2015. 'Listen to Exactly What King Goodwill Zwelithini Said about Foreigners'. Retrieved 16 April 2015 from http://www.timeslive.co.za/local/2015/04/16/listen-to-exactly-what-king-goodwill-zwelithini-said-about-foreigners.
2. Spaza shops are small convenience stores in townships and informal settlements often run by Somalian or Ethiopian nationals. These are very successful businesses, constituting the most important aspect of the Somali economy in South Africa. The recurrent hostility that from time to time materializes in fatal xenophobic attacks, makes them a dangerous destination and only men tend to go to work there, while women stay in the safer urban areas. See Abdi (2015) and Steinberg (2014) for a more detailed description of Somalis living and working in spaza shops in South African townships.
3. There is no reliable data of how many Somalis live in each city.
4. *Buufis* is a Somali word meaning the unfulfilled desire of migration and the anxiety generated by the impossibility to move that sometimes can even result in a strong depression. Cindy Horst (2006) argues that *buufis* can result from the strong transnational connections of the Somali diaspora. Those staying in Somalia or refugee camps get regular reports about

better living standards from relatives residing in Western countries, creating a constant desire for improvement by migrating.

References

Abdi, C.M. 2015. *Elusive Jannah: The Somali Diaspora and a Borderless Muslim Identity*. Minneapolis: University of Minnesota Press.
Anderson, B.R. 1983. *Imagined Communities: Reflections on the Origin and Spread of Nationalism*, rev. ed. London, New York: Verso.
Appadurai, A. 2013. *The Future as Cultural Fact: Essays on the Global Condition*. London, New York: Verso Books.
Appiah, K.A. 1997 'Cosmopolitan Patriots', *Critical Inquiry* 23(3): 617–39.
———. 2006. *Cosmopolitanism: Ethics in a World of Strangers*. New York: W.W. Norton & Co.
Beck, U. 2006. *Cosmopolitan Vision*. Cambridge: Polity.
Beck, U., and N. Sznaider. 2006. 'Unpacking Cosmopolitanism for the Social Sciences: A Research Agenda', *The British Journal of Sociology* 57(1): 1–23.
Brah, A. 1996. *Cartographies of Diaspora: Contesting Identities*. London, New York: Routledge.
Darieva, T., N.G. Schiller and S. Gruner-Domic. 2012. *Cosmopolitan Sociability: Locating Transnational Religious and Diasporic Networks*. London, New York: Routledge.
Ferguson, J. 2006. *Global Shadows: Africa in the Neoliberal World Order*. Durham, NC and London: Duke University Press.
Furia, P.A. 2005. 'Global Citizenship, Anyone? Cosmopolitanism, Privilege and Public Opinion', *Global Society* 19(4): 331–59.
Gilroy, P. 2005. 'A New Cosmopolitanism', *Interventions* 7(3): 287–92.
Grant R., and D. Thompson. 2015. 'City on Edge: Immigrant Businesses and the Right to Urban Space in Inner-City Johannesburg', *Urban Geography* 36(2): 181–200.
Hall, S., D. Held and T. McGrew. 1992. *Modernity and Its Futures: Understanding Modern Societies, Book IV*. Cambridge: Polity.
Hall, S. 2006. 'Cosmopolitanism Globalization and Diaspora. Stuart Hall in Conversation with Pnina Werbner, March 2006,' in P. Werbner (ed), *Anthropology and the New Cosmopolitanism. Rooted, Feminist and Vernacular Perspectives*. Oxford and New York: Berg, pp. 260–345.
Hannerz, U. 1996. *Transnational Connections: Culture, People, Places*. London and New York: Routledge.
Hassim, S., T. Kupe and E. Worby. 2008. *Go Home or Die Here: Violence, Xenophobia and the Reinvention of Difference in South Africa*. Johannesburg: Wits University Press.
Horst, C. 2006. '*Buufis* amongst Somalis in Dadaab: The Transnational and Historical Logics behind Resettlement Dreams', *Journal of Refugee Studies* 19(2): 143–57.
Jinnah, Z. 2010. 'Making Home in a Hostile Land: Understanding Somali Identity, Integration, Livelihood and Risks in Johannesburg', *Journal of Sociology and Anthropology* 1(1): 91–99.
Kothari, U. 2008. 'Global Peddlers and Local Networks: Migrant Cosmopolitanisms', *Environment and Planning D: Society and Space* 26(3): 500–516.
Landau, L.B. 2012. *Exorcising the Demons Within: Xenophobia, Violence and Statecraft in Contemporary South Africa*. Tokyo, New York and Paris: United Nations University Press.

Landau, L.B., and I. Freemantle. 2010. 'Tactical Cosmopolitanism and Idioms of Belonging: Insertion and Self-Exclusion in Johannesburg', *Journal of Ethnic and Migration Studies* 36(3): 375–90.
Malkki, L.H. 1995. *Purity and Exile: Violence, Memory, and National Cosmology among Hutu Refugees in Tanzania*. Chicago: University of Chicago Press.
Murunga, G.R. 2009. 'Refugees at Home? Coping with Somalia Conflict in Nairobi, Kenya', in M. Ben Arrous and L. Ki-Zerbo (eds), *African Studies in Geography from Below*. Dakar, Sénégal: CODESRIA, pp. 198–232.
Mbembe, A. 2007. 'Afropolitanism', in N. Simon and L. Durán, *Africa Remix: Contemporary Art of a Continent*. Johannesburg: Jacana Media, pp. 26–30.
Nuttall, S., and A. Mbembe. 2008. *Johannesburg: The Elusive Metropolis*. Durham, NC: Duke University Press.
Pollock, S. 2000. 'Cosmopolitan and Vernacular in History', *Public Culture* 12(3): 591–625.
Pollock, S., H.K. Bhabha, C.A. Breckenridge and D. Chakrabarty. 2000. 'Cosmopolitanisms', *Public Culture* 12(3): 577–89.
Sadouni, S. 2009. '"God Is Not Unemployed": Journeys of Somali Refugees in Johannesburg', *African Studies* 68(2): 235–49.
Skrbis, Z., G. Kendall and I. Woodward. 2004. 'Locating Cosmopolitanism Between Humanist Ideal and Grounded Social Category', *Theory, Culture & Society* 21(6): 115–36.
Skrbis, Z., and I. Woodward. 2007. 'The Ambivalence of Ordinary Cosmopolitanism: Investigating the Limits of Cosmopolitan Openness', *The Sociological Review* 55(4): 730–47.
Steinberg, J. 2014. *A Man of Good Hope*. Johannesburg and Cape Town: Jonathan Ball Publishers.
UNHCR. 2015. *Country Operations Profile – South Africa*. Retrieved 30 October 2015 from http://www.unhcr.org/5461e604b.pdf.
Vertovec, S., and R. Cohen. 2002. *Conceiving Cosmopolitanism: Theory, Context and Practice*. Oxford: Oxford University Press.
Waldron, J. 2000. 'What Is Cosmopolitan?', *Journal of Political Philosophy* 8(2): 227–43.
Werbner, P. 1999. 'Global Pathways. Working Class Cosmopolitans and the Creation of Transnational Ethnic Worlds', *Social Anthropology* 7(1): 17–35.
———. 2008. *Anthropology and the New Cosmopolitanism: Rooted, Feminist and Vernacular Perspectives*. London: Bloomsbury Academic.

Chapter 3

Being Oromo in Nairobi's 'Little Mogadishu'

Superdiversity, Moral Community and the Open Economy

Neil Carrier and Hassan H. Kochore

Somali presence in urban Kenya has brought great demographic, political and economic change over recent decades. Kenyan Somalis, Somalian refugees and the wider Somali diaspora have formed networks that bring investment, business acumen and imported goods to places like Eastleigh, transforming the urban landscape in the process. This pattern of recent change certainly has a Somali blueprint which is visible in Eastleigh, a place soaked with Somaliness: Somali language is spoken on every corner, shopping malls and hotels are named after key places in the Somali global geography, while other elements of Somali identity – religion, dress and food – are also highly conspicuous. It is this dominant identity that led some to refer to Eastleigh as 'Little Mogadishu' from the mid-1990s onwards. This equation of Eastleigh with Somaliness can, however, obscure crucial aspects of identification in the estate.

Indeed, while a superficial visit might lead to an impression of Eastleigh as a mono-ethnic Somali enclave, more time spent there opens up a much wider 'ethnoscape'.[1] It is a place of what Vertovec has dubbed 'superdiversity' (Vertovec 2007), a term that highlights the increasing complexity of places of migration in the West where intersectional identities appear to have multiplied. An emphasis on this superdiversity is important as it demonstrates how Somali mobile urbanity is intertwined with that of others. Eastleigh has provided opportunities for many, and in fact relies greatly on the comings and goings of many non-Somalis. Viewing Eastleigh as a mono-ethnic place only linked to the story of one particular people does a disservice to understanding the complexities of urban life in contemporary Africa, and the different migrations and mobilities that underpin African urbanity.

This chapter explores this ethnic complexity through the story of Eastleigh's Oromo and their migrations into and out of the estate. It shows how life in exile in Eastleigh generates bonds and a 'moral community' (Durkheim 1915) within which there are strong pressures to help fellow Oromo. However, bonds of trust are also forged between them and Eastleigh's Somali population. Eastleigh's economic growth and the wider expansion of Somali business interests in East Africa depends on such interchange and on opening its economy beyond the confines of one ethnicity. We argue that the Oromo are representative both of the cosmopolitan complexion of the estate and of the openness of the Eastleigh economy, even if there are limits – as we show – to this openness. Indeed, their example suggests a more legitimate comparison of Eastleigh to Mogadishu: not the Mogadishu that has suffered so much in recent decades, but the pre-war Mogadishu, for centuries a cosmopolitan hub of trade that Nuruddin Farah nostalgically remembers in his essay 'Of Tamarind and Cosmopolitanism' (Farah 2002). Eastleigh's economy relies and thrives on its multi-ethnic make-up and its openness, just as the Somali economy within Kenya relies on opening up to others. A closed mono-ethnic economy – one that did not offer opportunities to members of minority communities such as the Oromo and other non-Somalis – could scarcely have thrived in the way it has done. The chapter begins with a wider look at the ways in which this famous Somali urban space is far more cosmopolitan than the name 'Little Mogadishu' might suggest.

More than Little Mogadishu

To begin with, while 'Little Mogadishu' might suggest a place of people and culture uprooted from the Somali Republic, it is important to point out that even the Somalian population of the estate is obviously more varied than this term suggests. There certainly are many Somalians in Eastleigh. Even though there were only 20,171 Somalian refugees officially registered in Nairobi in 2018,[2] tens of thousands of refugees registered in the Dadaab and Kakuma camps unofficially also live in the urban areas or between there and the camps. Many of these Somalians do originate in Mogadishu, but others come from a variety of places in Somalia: Kismayo, Afmadow and other cities and towns, and even villages inside Somalia. Furthermore, much of its Somali population is Kenyan by birth and nationality. The very name of the original Eastleigh shopping centre – 'Garissa Lodge' (after the northeastern Kenyan town of Garissa) – shows how connected the place is to a very 'Kenyan' Somali geography. Yet its superdiversity goes beyond Somali diversity, and within Eastleigh there are many older residents of other Kenyan ethnicities who have remained there throughout all the commercial and demographic transformation. For example, Kikuyu have long had stakes in the estate to the degree that a Kenyan Somali businessman suggested during a discussion about the estate that instead of 'Little Mogadishu' Eastleigh could just as easily be known as 'Little Kiambu'. Eastleigh also continues to attract migrants from many other parts of the country, and in sections of the estate – especially south of the airbase – there are many Kamba, Luo and others. One significant population in the estate – and one highly integrated into its economy – are Meru from the khat-growing region of Kenya who have come over many decades in large numbers to sell a commodity ubiquitous and popular in the estate (Carrier 2017: Chapter 3).

The diversity is also reflected among Eastleigh's refugee population, not all of whom are from Somalia. While there are some Congolese, Rwandese and Sudanese refugees in Eastleigh, its most significant non-Somali refugee population consists of Ethiopians. Amhara and Tigray have long come to the estate (at least since the 1970s), some becoming influential in Nairobi's *matatu* (public service vehicle) industry (Kagwanja 1998). But it is Eastleigh's large population of Oromo refugees, many of whom might be mistaken for being Somali by outsiders, on which we focus our chapter. These Oromo have integrated into the Somali-dominated economy of the estate, and even carry aspects of its urban form with them during onward migrations.

In what follows, we explore the Ethiopian side of 'Little Mogadishu', highlighting the reasons for Oromo in-migration to Eastleigh and the arduous journeys they take to get there. This chapter builds on both ethnographic and survey work in the estate from 2011 onwards.[3] We conducted interviews with around twenty Oromo – men and women – living in the estate, and commissioned a local Oromo to conduct a survey of sixty Eastleigh Oromo that focused on their journeys into the estate, their experience of life there and forms of support.[4] This work was challenging, as Oromo in Eastleigh are fearful of both Kenyan and Ethiopian authorities. However, through contacts in local organizations working with refugees we were able to build trusting relations with a network of research participants, though many of these were keen to ensure anonymity given their fears.[5] Such participants helped us understand how a 'moral community' of being Oromo binds this refugee population together, and how they integrate into the Eastleigh economy through relations of trust often supported by Islam and knowledge of the Somali language. Oromo even recreate something of a home in this new place, albeit a precarious one: fear for their safety and suspicions of both the Kenyan state and a shadowy network of the Ethiopian security forces lurk in the background. For this and other reasons, Oromo have strong ambitions and desires to leave Eastleigh. We therefore also attempt to trace some of the routes out of the estate, arguing that unlike those Somalis who root themselves in Eastleigh and establish more permanent businesses and livelihoods, the Oromo have little desire to linger there. Many attempt to reach southern Africa, where in a part of Johannesburg's Central Business District they have recreated something of the Eastleigh economy.[6]

The Oromo: The People and Their Journeys

Oromo are the largest ethnic group in Ethiopia, albeit one constituted by several smaller groups, including the 'Raya, Wollo, Karaiyu, Kotu, Leka, Mecha, Tulama, Guji, Arssi and Boran' (Baxter 1978: 284). There is much variety among them in terms of livelihoods (some are pastoralists, others agriculturalists), and in terms of religion (some Muslim, some Christian and others practising 'traditional religion'). They are spread throughout much of Ethiopia (some – like the Boran – spreading over into Kenya too). Their territory in Ethiopia is now known as Oromia, which forms one of the nine regional states of Ethiopia, and the biggest in terms of population and area.

Despite their size, the Oromo have found themselves marginalized from power under successive regimes,[7] most recently by the Ethiopian People's Revolutionary Democratic Front (EPRDF), which came to power following the 1991 revolution which brought down the authoritarian Derg regime of Mengistu. While EPRDF presents itself as an all-inclusive national coalition of parties, the Tigray People's Liberation Front (TPLF) have been dominant (Jones et al. 2012; International Crisis Group 2009). There has been much political and economic oppression in Oromia following the withdrawal of the Oromo Liberation Front (OLF) from the Transitional Government of Ethiopia in 1992, and their subsequent labelling as a terrorist organization. This oppression has forced unknown numbers to leave the country, meaning that many Oromo now live abroad, some as far afield as USA and Australia following refugee resettlement there (Elliott 2012). For many, heading south to Kenya is an important first step on their migratory journey.

There have been peaks and troughs to this movement from Ethiopia to and through Kenya. Indeed, Oromo have come to Kenya in waves over the years: some came in the 1980s during the time of the Derg; many arrived in Kenya in the early 1990s, while another wave came in the run-up to the 2005 elections. But the push and pull factors influencing the decisions to leave seem to remain constant, and Oromo migration to Kenya continues. The Kenyan media consistently carry reports of 'Ethiopians'[8] or 'aliens'[9] arrested at various points en route to Nairobi, mainly along the Nairobi–Moyale route. There are only estimates as to how many Oromo now live in Nairobi. For example out of the 56,000 registered refugees in Nairobi in 2013, 10,568 were Ethiopian.[10] A large proportion of these would be Oromo, and a great proportion again would live in Eastleigh. In the next section we explore some of the reasons why Oromo leave Ethiopia, and how they reach Eastleigh.

Running to Kenya: The Fear of Detention and Persecution

Eastleigh Oromo interviewed in 2012 gave vivid accounts of detention and worse in Ethiopia that precipitated their flight to Kenya. As one of our informants put it, remaining in Ethiopia meant *dhuumaf id'amum* – death and detention. Several described being imprisoned following accusations of association with the OLF. One reported that he used to work for a disabled people's charity in Ethiopia that distributed wheelchairs. They did not discriminate as to whom they gave the wheelchairs, and some might have been handed to injured OLF veterans – on suspicion of this he was detained for two years. Women too faced detention; one now living in Eastleigh reported being detained in the town of Nango for two months. In fact, in mapping out other places that connect to Eastleigh, Ethiopian detention centres loom large in importance, especially notorious ones like the Federal Prison of Mekalawi. Oromo also complain of the lack of educational opportunities for them in Ethiopia, which they argue is an attempt by the authorities to keep them marginalized and submissive. The below story of a man called Gennemmi is emblematic:

> He was detained in Dire Dawa in the late 1990s after leading a student protest against conscription for military service in the Ethiopian–Eritrean war. As a member of the student council, he called a meeting to object to the conscription of students as it would interrupt their education. The meeting was disrupted by the military and many students ran away. He was accused of sending them off to fight for the OLF, and was abducted during a night raid before being detained and tortured in a military camp for 18 months. After failing to get evidence against him, they released him, but with strict conditions restricting his movements. He was told to return to his education, where he was expected to inform on Oromo teachers. Upon gaining sufficient qualifications for entering university, he was refused permission to leave Dire Dawa to attend, and he was subsequently arrested and detained once more after protesting. Released soon after – again with the precondition not to leave Dire Dawa – Gennemmi defied these restrictions, and registered at a university near Harar. He was subsequently tracked by the authorities, and it was then that he decided to leave for Kenya, helped by his aunt who gave him money for the journey.

Another Oromo called Duba – from a family who owned a successful shop in the Bale region of Oromia – related this account of his detention and flight to Nairobi:

> Duba's father was assassinated in 1999 on account of accusations of a link to the OLF, and two years later – when he was twenty years old – the same people came for him and detained him in a place called Malka Waqana for over two months. He was eventually released, following which he continued to work for the family business, visiting Addis to

buy stock. However, his life would change in 2005, the time of the elections. Duba used to sell sacks of maize, and was accused by the authorities of hiding guns in the sacks for the militia. Around this time his stepbrother, his cousin and another man were killed. He had to bury these three men, and was warned by his mother that he would be next as he was seen as a threat by the authorities. He fled.

All Oromo interviewed described similar factors behind their decisions to leave. These factors are emphasized strongly too in wider discussions of the contemporary experience of Oromo within Ethiopia, and activists like the British chair of the Oromia Support Group give these accounts a platform in the wider world.[11]

Most of the Oromo interviewed gave very similar accounts of their journeys to Kenya and Eastleigh. Indeed, so common is the journey made by these migrants that an industry has developed in Moyale, the town that straddles the Ethiopia–Kenya border, for facilitating onward travel to Nairobi and beyond. Brokers there charge between 400–2000 Birr (USD 20–100) to help people cross the border and continue south. One man we interviewed paid a broker 2000 Birr for the journey to Nairobi on a cattle truck. He was able to afford this as he had 5000 Birr (USD 250) with him for the journey. Some manage to secure a free passage to Nairobi by travelling on trucks carrying livestock and tending to any animals that fall over on the journey. An Eastleigh Oromo described how he barely slept for three days on the journey from Moyale to Nairobi while tending goats transported on a truck. Meanwhile, Duba travelled to Moyale via Shashamane, and Yabelo. There he saw porters carrying things over the border, and pretended to be one and crossed.

Not all Oromo reach Eastleigh through Moyale, however: others take much more tortuous routes. One man we interviewed had fled to Somaliland from his home region of Ethiopia,[12] but faced continuing difficulties there. He narrated how Ethiopian security services operate freely in Somaliland, as the current political arrangement between the two countries allows. Facing the threat of repatriation to Ethiopia, he set out on the long and treacherous journey to Kenya through Somaliland and Somalia, finally reaching the Kenya–Somali border at Mandera, and finding onward transportation to Nairobi.

Moyale Airport and the Moral Community

Few Oromo said that they had heard of Eastleigh while in Ethiopia, and most simply head south to cross into Kenya and onwards to Nairobi, albeit with three crucial pieces of advice for coping with Nairobi: make sure to take warm clothes to cope with the cold; be careful travelling on the notorious *matatu* public transport vehicles; and watch out for the Kenyan police. However, of those who flee to Kenya, most arrive and seek to survive in Eastleigh. This is because, while they come from many different parts of Ethiopia (though a majority of our respondents came from Harar and Dire Dawa), most of their journeys south funnel them through Moyale, and most trucks and buses that connect Moyale to Nairobi end their journeys in the heart of Eastleigh. Specifically, they arrive on Tenth Street, nicknamed 'Moyale Airport' for its role as a transport hub to the north.

Tenth Street is the heart of Ethiopian (and Eritrean) Eastleigh. Along this street are Eritrean and Ethiopian-owned restaurants that do a brisk trade in the classic Ethiopian dish of *injera* and spicy stew, sold at rates far lower than in city centre Ethiopian restaurants. Smaller shacks run mainly by Oromo sell Ethiopian commodities like *teff flour*, *shiro* and *berbery* spices, while also serving small glasses of coffee, whereas Oromo and Somali women sell bundles of khat from tables outside. The Ethiopian feel of this area is augmented further by the profusion of Amharic and Oromo names painted on several businesses, often in Amharic script. The area is suffused too with distinctly Oromo sounds emitted from speakers placed outside the 'studios' selling music, as well as the majority of voices there speaking the Oromo language. Given all the sights, sounds, smells and tastes in this part of Eastleigh, some might be tempted to dub it 'Little Addis'.

With this Ethiopian vibe, Moyale Airport provides a soft landing for Oromo, who can stop at any of these shops or coffee kiosks to find people who can help them get their bearings. It does not have to be someone they knew back at home in Ethiopia – though sometimes they have a contact – but anybody from their home district or even the Oromia region in general. Almost always they are able to find people from their home area who can accommodate them and teach them the geography of Nairobi (especially guiding them to the UNHCR offices). Often they are taken to stay in another section of Eastleigh (to the north of the estate, known as Section I) where many reside around an Oromo mosque. Christian Oromo, on the other hand, usually find their way to another part of Nairobi where there is a Coptic Church.

While regional and other differences in identity among Oromo might be salient in Ethiopia, in Eastleigh there seems to be a palpable sense of a moral community amongst them. 'Moral community' was a term Durkheim used to refer to the solidarity created by religion (Durkheim 1915: 62) through shared practices and beliefs, but it also well conveys the sense of community and mutual obligation that can be generated by other social processes, including shared experiences of exile. In the case of Eastleigh Oromo, moral community reflects the shared notion that fellow Oromo should be supported, partly created by narratives created in exile, similar to those described by Lisa Malkki for Burundian refugees in Tanzania (Malkki 1995). A moral community was reflected in the most common response to our survey question asking if the respondent had relatives in Eastleigh when they arrived: 'Oromo are my family' was a popular response. As with Somalis, in the face of a potentially hostile environment in Eastleigh, solidarity is a much-needed resource, and one bolstered in the case of Oromo by a strong political consciousness. Most in Eastleigh are deeply aware of the wider context and discourse of Oromo persecution, and of the global dimensions of the Oromo cause. They deeply engage with, and reproduce, this discourse in their own accounts, and, as Haneke (2002: 136) notes, this acts as a unifying factor. For example, almost all of our respondents knew of Trevor Truman, the British campaigner for Oromo rights, and there is much communication through Facebook between Oromo around the world.

Although they maintain connections to Oromo in the wider diaspora, the Eastleigh Oromo we interviewed stated that they did not maintain communication with family in Ethiopia. This was explained as a necessity, as there is a fear that by getting in touch they might be putting families at risk should the authorities find that they have been communicating with an exiled 'subversive'. This contrasts markedly with life for Somalians in Eastleigh who generally maintain strong connections to home regions. There is much fear too in Eastleigh that Ethiopian and Kenyan authorities work together to repatriate Oromo: talk of Ethiopian 'agents' is common, and there are numerous cases of abductions and disappearances (Horne 2017), including of an Oromo scholar and leader who had been living in Kenya for many years, Dabasa Guyo (Oromo Relief Association 2011).

In relation to the 'omnipresent' nature of the Ethiopian spies in Eastleigh, one informant stated that, 'this country has started to smell like Ethiopia'. On further enquiry about what he meant, he explained that he referred to the general climate of fear and suspicion of being watched by Ethiopian government agents. At the time of the research, Oromo were disadvantaged compared to Somalian refugees in that they did not get 'prima facie' refugee status in Kenya. Instead they had to be processed to get their Mandate Refugee Certificate (MRC) issued by UNHCR. Since 2016 procedures have changed and Kenya's Refugee Affairs Secretariat (RAS) has taken the lead in registering refugees in Nairobi.[13] Now and before the refugee status determination process could take months or even years. The MRC was a document that gave some – albeit often flimsy – legal protections as refugees recognized by the UNHCR and some rights (including education, but not the right to work – for which a separate work permit is required). Many refugees lived in Eastleigh without MRCs, having been declined by UNHCR, and, in a climate where an encampment policy for refugees is pursued, the risk of being sent to the remote refugee camps is a real threat. Another real fear is general insecurity, and a number of interviewees reported being attacked by thieves in Eastleigh and on nearby Juja Road.

Thus solidarity is a necessity for what one of our informants aptly summarized as *jirachuf barbathis* (survival and searching for a livelihood), and such solidarity is certainly much in evidence. Those who arrive alone at Tenth Street can expect to be taken in by other Oromo, the latter perhaps reciprocating for good deeds done to them. Sometimes Oromo newcomers find not just fictive kin within a wider 'Oromo family', but also actual kin. One young man who came as a refugee unexpectedly found his father who had lived in Eastleigh for well over a decade having fled following detention in Mekalawi. He had been told to forget about his father as he was 'probably dead' having had no contact since 1993 when he was detained. Eventually, however, he himself became the target of the authorities and decided to flee to Kenya where they were reunited. This story recounted to us by father and son separated for more than a decade in Ethiopia and reunited in the Eastleigh context was illustrative of the total 'uprooting' some Oromo refugees undergo as it becomes risky to stay in touch with relatives in Ethiopia monitored by a strong, authoritarian state, again contrasting markedly with Somalis and their continued links to family in home regions.

Economic Integration

One key attraction of Eastleigh for Oromo is the ability to integrate into its economy. While there is an Oromo diaspora in western countries that provides some Eastleigh Oromo with remittances, most have to earn a living. Oromo form a significant proportion of the Eastleigh workforce, often working in Somali or Ethiopian restaurants (in particular there are many young Oromo men working as waiters in mostly Somali-owned restaurants), being salespersons or shop attendants in the shopping centres, or hawking khat or coffee (our fieldwork in one shopping centre in particular was rendered much more pleasant by the coffee provided by an Oromo woman who hawked coffee there at the equivalent of just 5¢ a cup). Barbershops (which are now proliferating in Eastleigh in general and Tenth Street in particular) attract some Oromo youth. A number also work as taxi drivers, although this is felt to be a risky livelihood, as many Oromo fear leaving Eastleigh, being so distrustful of the rest of Nairobi (this somewhat resembles the situation of Somalis in Johannesburg, for whom Mayfair is an island of protection, see chapter by Ripero-Muñiz in this volume). Aside from trips to the UNHCR offices in the Westlands part of the city (situated northwest of the CBD, the Central Business District) – another key part of the refugee geography in Nairobi – many Oromo limit themselves to the confines of Eastleigh. Here we see what might be termed 'immobile urbanity', as Oromo limit themselves to the relatively safe urban enclave of Eastleigh: after the mobility of their migration journeys, migrants often find themselves relatively constrained in receiving countries. Oromo taxi drivers are also cautious as to whom they transport: one told us how he only accepted other Oromo or Somalis having been carjacked when transporting 'Kenyans'.

There are some, however, who manage to join the Eastleigh economy at a higher level, some integrating into the estate's petty bourgeoisie of shopkeepers

(Carrier 2017: chapter 5). This is difficult, as some have no experience in business at home, and obtaining the resources for business permits and start-up capital is also not easy. Whatever type of employment they secure, established Oromo networks can help, as can the wider Somali networks that dominate the estate, especially for those who know some Somali language.

Indeed, in an area where Somalis are economically and socially powerful, knowing the Somali language can be an invaluable resource in gaining employment in the Somali shopping centres: speaking Somali can bring you closer to the Somalis and therefore winning their *aman* – trust. 'Trust' is a major part of all successful informal economies, and also many formal economies too, and there is a common emphasis on the need for trust among Somalis and others in Eastleigh. While many argue that the Eastleigh economy has been successful precisely because there is much trust among Somalis, it is clear that this talk of trust is idealized, and as much normative as descriptive, as accounts of deceit and mistrust among Somalis are also common (Carrier and Lochery 2013; Carrier 2017, chapter 5; Carrier and Elliott 2018). Some Oromo from regions with a substantial Somali population can have an advantage in gaining the *aman* of Somalis, for example those from the city of Harar. In that cosmopolitan Ethiopian city, in the words of Christine Gibb, 'centuries of common residence and religious worship have … served to minimize differences, or, more accurately, contributed to aspects of common culture shared between residents in Harar [be they Somali, Oromo, Harari or Arabs]' (Gibb 1999: 89–90).

From the interviews in our study, the story of how Oromo from Harar integrate into Eastleigh stood out as their narratives suggest they gained entry relatively easily because of what one might call the 'Harariness of Eastleigh' – they were used to an urbanity very similar to that of Eastleigh. Just like Harar, Eastleigh is a major commercial centre connected to much of the Horn of Africa and the outside world. The interaction between Eastleigh inhabitants has created an intricate web of trading and consumer communities through the different commodities they deal with. Oromo we met claimed Oromo and Somali have no problems interacting, and very occasionally even intermarry, although they also said there was generally little affection between them: one summarized the relationship as neutral saying *jibansi injíru, jalali injíru* (Oromo: 'there is no love, there is no hate').

There are particularly close working relations between the Harar Oromo and the Somali. These Oromo have connected into the mainstream Eastleigh economy of small retail shops in the shopping centres and the wider estate, allowing access to other Oromo. Indeed, some of the shopping centres have a large proportion of Oromo shopkeepers, many working especially as tailors and even employing local Kenyans in their businesses. For example, Ibsa, a young Harari man, first worked as a shop assistant at a Somali-owned shop in one of the shopping centres. His familiarity with the basics of the Somali language was useful as he could both ask for work from the Somalis and interact with Somali customers. Working in the shop enabled him to perfect his Somali language, and after saving for some time, he earned enough capital to buy a small kiosk from another Oromo who had been resettled.

Even without Somali language skills, some Oromo can communicate with Somalis through shared knowledge of Arabic, even if this knowledge is often rudimentary. An Oromo who now runs a shop in one of the bigger shopping centres reported that he first entered the Eastleigh economy working for a Somali clothes shop as a tailor, securing this employment through communicating with the owner in Arabic. From this he could save sufficient money and gain enough knowledge of how the economy works to start his own business.

Other Oromo take advantage of their linguistic closeness to a group of Somali, called the Garre, who are powerful in Eastleigh. Their origins lie in the border region between Ethiopia, Kenya and Somalia, and some of them are more comfortable speaking Oromo than standard Somali. Others speak varieties of southern Somali (Schlee 2010: 100–101). While there are some debates as to their ethnic classification (whether Somali, Oromo, or a separate group), Garre in Nairobi strongly emphasize their Somaliness (Carrier 2017: chapter 3). However, with a shared language, Oromo sometimes find work alongside Garre – an Oromo friend of ours, for instance, obtained work in a Garre hotel.

Islam is a key factor underpinning Oromo integration into the Eastleigh economy. Muslim Oromo have integrated into the estate through the religion they share with Somalis and with each other. This shared Islam is referred to in Oromo as *islantiti*. A number of Oromo have exploited this shared religious practice with Somalis to aid survival. In one case a Harari woman related how, after being dropped in Eastleigh by the truck from Isiolo, she just turned up at a Somali family's doorstep. She said she identified herself as a refugee seeking help. She reckoned that because she was dressed in a *buibui* (a robe-like black dress), they automatically assumed she was a Muslim and therefore helped her out of *islantiti*. She helped them with house chores until she found out about the 'Oromo mosque' on Second Street where she found fellow Oromo who helped her get work in a restaurant on Fourth Street.

Oromo can make headway in the Eastleigh economy even without strong pre-existing connections to Somalis, some relating rags to (relative) riches accounts of their business history. One case study is of Hassan, an Oromo who was running a shop within one of the Eastleigh shopping centres:

> Hassan came as a refugee to Eastleigh in 2005, arriving alone with few belongings. His first employment was at a Somali restaurant where he worked as a cleaner. He was paid poorly, but was given a place to stay and food. Next he moved to an Ethiopian restaurant where he felt more at home as he could understand the language. He earned 3000

Kenyan Shillings (about USD 45) per month as a cook and was given accommodation. He worked at this restaurant for just over a year, before getting a job in a Somali shop in Garissa Lodge shopping centre. By then he understood Somali and Kiswahili fairly well, at least knowing the words for clothes, and secured work through an Oromo contact. Having worked there for a year and a half and saved much of his salary, his next enterprise was to make juice. He bought a blender and sold juice to shoppers and traders at a large shopping centre. This enterprise became profitable, eventually allowing him to secure a shop in that shopping centre where he sold men's clothes with an Oromo partner. They took over the shop from another Oromo who was moving to the USA. Hassan and his partner had USD 1000 capital between them, but only needed a fraction of this for the rent and deposit. They had to buy outright their initial stock, but soon built up a name for themselves among wholesalers allowing them to obtain credit.

Thus, despite usually lacking direct kin in the estate, Oromo can integrate into Eastleigh through a shared moral community as Oromo and as Muslims, and through other connections to Somalis. An enterprising spirit such as Hassan's can also help with integrating into the Eastleigh economy. However, despite these possibilities of integration into Eastleigh in terms of livelihoods, and despite the apparent moral community among them there, no Oromo we met expressed any desire to integrate permanently into Eastleigh or wider Kenyan society.

Transience and Liminality

In the survey we conducted, few respondents of the sixty had been in the estate for more than a few years. The high proportion of relative newcomers amongst those surveyed fits the impression that most do not stay for long in Eastleigh before moving on, whether through the legal channel of refugee resettlement to a third country, or through illegal channels to places like South Africa. Resettlement is a complicated process (Elliott 2012), involving a maze of different bureaucracies and decision-makers, and subject to the policy whims of receiving countries, but it is often the goal of Eastleigh Oromo. Like Somalis and their feelings of *buufis* – a desire to move to 'greener pastures' like Europe and America which can lead to mental instability if unfulfilled (Horst 2006) – Oromo in Eastleigh are highly focused on reaching places seen as offering more opportunity. For those lucky enough to get resettlement in the West, they often find themselves again alongside Somalis: for example, Bolton in the UK has recently seen an influx of Oromo and Somali refugees, a number of whom, from both communities, have spent time in Eastleigh. For those following an illicit onward path, the dangers are great – tragically illustrated by the deaths of 43 Ethiopians and Somalis in a container in Tanzania in 2012 – and financial costs high. Many take the plunge, however. An estimated 17,000–20,000 people from East Africa and the Horn are smuggled to southern Africa each year (Long and Crisp 2011: 6).

Certainly, most Eastleigh Oromo perceive the estate as a waystation on journeys elsewhere. Even those with shops apparently feel little attachment to the estate, sometimes simply leaving businesses to others once the opportunity to move comes along. In the words of one of our interviewees, compared with the opportunity to move abroad, a shop in Eastleigh is a small thing indeed. Desperation can ensue if stays are protracted, which is often the case as resettlement can be denied, especially for those with political pasts. For example, the increased securitization since the Patriot Act of the Bush administration (in 2001) means that anyone associated with groups like the OLF (classified by the US as a terrorist organization) will not be granted resettlement in the USA, a key sponsor of resettlement (Elliott 2012: 16–17), or at least it was before the Trump administration capped numbers drastically.[14]

The story of Aseffa, an Oromo in his 50s, illustrates the psychological damage that such unwanted permanency in Eastleigh can do.

> Aseffa spent his days at an Ethiopian restaurant in Eastleigh watching the world go by, making a sparse living from advising others informally on how to navigate the resettlement process. A member of a Muslim organization banned in the country, he fled Ethiopia and arrived in Eastleigh in 1993. Initially optimistic that he would be resettled, constant setbacks began to sap his confidence. In the late 1990s, he attributed the reluctance of the UNHCR to process his resettlement claim to the immense corruption of the era, but later also thought that he had been labelled a terrorist, and this had held back his claim. Disappointment at his plight had descended into paranoia. An eloquent man with good English, he talked of helicopters searching for him in Eastleigh, and how a range of people from UNHCR to evangelical Christians were intent on sabotaging his life.

While Aseffa constitutes an extreme example, narratives of victimhood and conspiracy are common among Oromo in Eastleigh, and further reinforce the sense of Oromo moral community that helps them survive in an estate to which they have only tenuous feelings of attachment.

Indeed, this tenuous attachment to the place is evident in how returning to Eastleigh after reaching dreamed of destinations abroad is unthinkable for Oromo, in contrast to the nostalgia some diaspora Somalis can have for the estate. Cawo Abdi recounts how many Somalis migrate in search of what she calls an 'elusive Jannah' (paradise), placing great hope in the USA as somewhere they can find security and a life worth living (Abdi 2015). Disappointment in such places – where many face social and economic marginalization within a non-Muslim land – can lead to nostalgia for either home, or else for places like Eastleigh that are close to home. As research among Oromo in the USA suggests, they are far less ambivalent about staying in that country given their history of marginalization and harassment within Ethiopia itself (Halcon et al. 2004: 22).

Somali attachment to the estate – albeit also soaked with ambivalence – is much stronger: many Somalis are also focused on leaving Eastleigh and making it to the West (see chapter by Lowe and Yarnell in this volume), but many can make a home and a decent living – though precariously – in 'Little Mogadishu'. Also, a number of Somalis who gain secure citizenship in the West return to Eastleigh and start businesses such as hotels and restaurants. Many are drawn there both for financial reasons – much more can be done with their money in East Africa than in the West – and because even the real dangers of police harassment are somewhat easier to negotiate given the greater financial power of 'returnee' Somalis compared with Oromo. Interest in the estate among the Somali diaspora also generates one of the key investment strands in the estate's economy.

Neither of these pull factors exist for Oromo who have transited through the estate. It is simply a place of refuge for them, albeit a precarious one where they feel unsafe and threatened both by the Kenyan state security services, crime, and the ever-present fear of shadowy Ethiopian agents. On top of this, Oromo are not integrated into the elite of the Eastleigh economy, a stratum dominated by the Somali owners of the shopping centres and other businesses. For Oromo, its economy mostly offers opportunities for survival rather than wealth, and there are few obvious avenues for diaspora Oromo to invest, and hence little financial pull for those who manage to save money in wealthier parts of the world. Thus, while Eastleigh is an open economy in some ways for Oromo, especially at the level of the Eastleigh proletariat, and for a luckier few, as members of the Eastleigh petty bourgeoisie, there are only limited opportunities to penetrate into the class of mall owners and real estate developers.

However, in some ways Oromo take Eastleigh with them on their journeys, not just in memories and links to family and friends still there, but also in the blueprint of its economy which has itself proved mobile. In Johannesburg Oromo refugees have created a mini Eastleigh in the centre of the city.[15] There, many Oromo have transformed a number of buildings into shopping centres selling 'low-end' goods (see chapters by Carrier and Elliott as well as by Scharrer, this volume) with business practices very similar to those of Eastleigh. While the economy in Johannesburg is not simply a copy of that in Eastleigh, it would not be surprising if aspects of its blueprint had been transplanted there, given that so many Oromo travel through Eastleigh and gain experience in its economy. Oromo have no intention of returning to Eastleigh once they have left, but they take various aspects of this urban economy along with them.

Conclusion

While interesting in its own right as an example of refugee livelihoods, the Oromo presence and movement through Eastleigh clearly shows how it is not a monolithic Somali place or economy, despite the tag of 'Little Mogadishu' that has been attached to it. In fact, it could not possibly have become so successful were it so monolithic: such an economy requires a degree of openness to others, and it does indeed welcome shoppers, traders and investors of all ethnicities. Somalis might dominate in the retail and wholesale outlets of the estate, but Somali to non-Somali business relations are also extremely common as wholesalers and mall owners are dependent on these for the continual expansion of their businesses.

The case of the Oromo is a good example of how a non-Somali group can integrate within this economy. Of course, as demonstrated through the example of Harari Oromo in particular, many share much in common with Somalis in the estate. Some speak a little of the Somali language, others communicate across ethnic lines through Arabic; some rely on shared Islam to integrate themselves in the economy, allowing them to generate the trust needed to get goods on credit or be entrusted with running a shop. They also share the experience of many Somalians in urban Kenya of being refugees trying to survive in exile.

This is not to say that integrating into the estate and its economy is easy. The Oromo again illustrate this need for caution well: their lives are difficult in the estate, caught as they are between state harassment (or the fear of it), and the crime that is common in the area. Eastleigh is certainly no heaven for them, even if it is a haven (compare with chapter by Ripero-Muñiz in this volume, who calls Eastleigh a port). Eastleigh's dusty streets offer only a tenuous security. Much work for Eastleigh Oromo is of a very menial type within its informal economy as waiters, coffee-sellers and so forth. Although a lucky few fulfil the 'Eastleigh dream' (Carrier 2017, chapter 5) and become rich indeed, and some few Oromo make it into the shop-keeping class, for most it is a place to survive while hoping that further migration will bring social mobility in the future. The openness of its economy that we describe here has obvious limits.

Neil Carrier is Lecturer in Social Anthropology at the University of Bristol (UK). After finishing his PhD in Social Anthropology at the University of St Andrews, he moved to the African Studies Centre at the University of Oxford. He has published two monographs, on Khat (*Kenyan Khat: The Social Life of a Stimulant*, Brill, 2007) and on Eastleigh (*Little Mogadishu: Eastleigh, Nairobi's Global Somali Hub*, Oxford University Press, 2017).

Hassan H. Kochore is a PhD candidate at the Max Planck Institute for Social Anthropology. He holds a Bachelor's Degree in Anthropology from the University of Nairobi and an MSc in African Studies from Oxford University. His research experience includes conducting ethnographic fieldwork, archival, literature and media-based research. He has (co-)authored several peer-reviewed journal articles and book chapters regarding the anthropology, history and politics of northern Kenya.

Notes

1. 'Ethnoscape' being Appadurai's term (1996) for the shifting ethnic composition of many places in our contemporary world (though it is also a term apt for many of the cosmopolitan places of the past too).
2. See UNHCR statistical summary of 'Refugees and Asylum Seekers in Kenya' for 2018. Available online (retrieved 4 August 2018): http://www.unhcr.org/ke/wp-content/uploads/sites/2/2018/03/KENYA-Statistics-Package-February-2018-1.pdf.
3. It is important to note that the political situation in Ethiopia has changed significantly since the submission of this chapter. Abiy Ahmed, an Oromo, took the reins as Prime Minister on 2 April 2018. However, there has been a new wave of violence and displacement of populations in places like Kamashiand Assosa (Benishangul Gumuz) and East and West Wollega (Oromia). Furthermore, Ethiopian migrants (Oromo amongst them) continue to be intercepted in the country *en route* to Nairobi or destined for other places outside of Kenya.
4. This research was part of the Leverhulme-funded project 'Diaspora, Trade and Trust: Eastleigh, Nairobi's "Little Mogadishu"' within the Oxford Diasporas Programme. We are very grateful to the Leverhulme, the wider Oxford Diasporas Project, and of course the many Oromo who took time to talk with us or completed the survey. We are especially grateful to Kemal for his work conducting the survey. All names below are anonymized, reflecting the fear many Oromo feel living in Eastleigh.
5. That Kochore is an Oromo-speaker (being Borana, an Oromo-speaking people of southern Ethiopia and northern Kenya) significantly aided our acceptance by Eastleigh Oromo.
6. This is the area between Jeppe and Bree Street (Le Roux 2009; see also the chapter by Scharrer in this volume).
7. For an in-depth history of the *longue durée* of being Oromo in Ethiopia, see Hassen (1990, 2015). Also see the edited collection *Being and Becoming Oromo* by Baxter, Hultin and Triulzi (1996).
8. Ngetich, D. 2015. '40 Ethiopian Aliens Arrested in Meru', *citizentv.co.ke*, 27 August 2015. Retrieved 8 June 2017 from https://citizentv.co.ke/news/40-ethiopian-aliens-arrested-in-meru-99148/.
9. 'Police Arrest 15 Aliens in Samburu', *Daily Nation*, 20 October 2015. Retrieved 8 June 2017 from http://www.nation.co.ke/news/Police-arrest-15-aliens-in-Samburu/-/1056/2923370/-/137v6wt/-/index.html.
10. UNHCR data retrieved 8 June 2017 from http://www.unhcr.org/510275a09.html.
11. For example, see the following online article: 'Persecuted in Ethopia: No refuge in Africa'. *Amnesty.org.uk*, 13 September 2013. Retrieved 9 December 2015 from http://www.amnesty.org.uk/groups/lytham-st-annes-and-blackpool/persecuted-ethiopia-no-refuge-africa-0.
12. On Oromo in Somaliland, see Lindley (2010).
13. In addition the Kenyan government stopped giving 'prima facie' refugee status to Somalians in the same year.

14. On the Trump administration's cuts to refugee resettlement numbers, see article 'Trump's Refugee Fiasco' by Malley and Pomper in *Politico Magazine*, 18 September 2018, available online: https://www.politico.com/magazine/story/2018/09/18/trumps-refugees-announcement-220063 (accessed 10 October 2018).
15. See the photo essay by Tanya Zack on the Oxford Diasporas Programme website: http://www.migration.ox.ac.uk/odp/johannesburgs-ethiopian-district-photo-essay.shtml#&panel1-1 (accessed 5 December 2015).

References

Abdi, C. 2015. *Elusive Jannah: The Somali Diaspora and a Borderless Muslim Identity*. Minneapolis: University of Minnesota Press.
Appadurai, A. 1996. *Modernity at Large: Cultural Dimensions of Globalization*. Minneapolis: Minnesota University Press.
Baxter, P.T.W. 1978. 'Ethiopia's Unacknowledged Problem: The Oromo', *African Affairs* 77(308): 283–96.
Baxter, P.T.W., J. Hultin and A. Triulzi. 1996. *Being and Becoming Oromo: Historical and Anthropological Enquiries*. Lawrenceville, NJ: Red Sea Press.
Carrier, N.C.M. 2017. *Little Mogadishu: Eastleigh, Nairobi's Global Somali Hub*. London, New York: Hurst, Oxford University Press.
Carrier, N.C.M., and E. Lochery. 2013. 'Missing States? Somali Trade Networks and the Eastleigh Transformation', *Journal of Eastern African Studies* 7(2): 334–52.
Carrier, N.C.M. and H. Elliott. 2018. 'Entrust we Must: The Role of "Trust" in Somali Economic Life', *Working paper* 2018: 2, *Dansk Institut for Internationale Studier*. Retrieved 10 August 2018 from https://www.diis.dk/publikationer/in-business-we-trust
Durkheim, E. 1915. *The Elementary Forms of the Religious Life*. London: George Allen & Unwin.
Elliott, H.R. 2012. 'Refugee Resettlement: The View from Kenya. Findings from Field Research in Nairobi and Kakuma Refugee Camp', *Research Report* for KNOW RESET. Retrieved 10 April 2016 from http://www.know-reset.eu/files/texts/00695_20130530121940_carim-knowresetrr-2012-01.pdf.
Farah, N. 2002. 'Of Tamarind and Cosmopolitanism!', in H. Engdahl (ed.), *Witness Literature: Proceedings of the Nobel Centennial Symposium*. London: World Scientific, pp. 69–76.
Gibb, C. 1999. 'Baraka without Borders: Integrating Communities in the City of Saints', *Journal of Religion in Africa* 29(1): 88–108.
Halcon, L.L., et al. 2004. 'Trauma and Coping in Somali and Oromo Refugee Youth', *Journal of Adolescent Health* 35(1): 17–25.
Haneke, G. 2002. 'The Multidimensionality of Oromo Identity', in G. Schlee (ed.), *Imagined Differences: Hatred and the Construction of Identity*. Hamburg: Lit, pp. 133–53.
Hassen, M. 1990. *The Oromo of Ethiopia: A History, 1570–1860*. Cambridge: Cambridge University Press.
———. 2015. *The Oromo and the Christian Kingdom of Ethiopia 1300–1700*. Woodbridge: James Currey.
Horne, F. 2017. 'The Long Arm of Ethiopia Reaches for Those Who Fled', *Report for Human Rights Watch*, 20 September 2017. Retrieved 10 August 2018 from https://www.hrw.org/news/2017/09/20/long-arm-ethiopia-reaches-those-who-fled.
Horst, C. 2006. '*Buufis* amongst Somalis in Dadaab: The Transnational and Historical Logics behind Resettlement Dreams', *Journal of Refugee Studies* 19(2): 143–57.

International Crisis Group. 2009. 'Ethiopia: Ethnic Federalism and its Discontents', *Africa Report No. 153*. Nairobi and Brussels: International Crisis Group.

Jones, W., R. Soares de Oliveira and H. Verhoeven. 2012. 'Africa's Illiberal State-Builders', *Refugee Studies Centre Working Paper Series*. Oxford: Oxford University. Retrieved 5 June 2016 from https://www.rsc.ox.ac.uk/files/publications/working-paper-series/wp89-africas-illiberal-state-builders-2013.pdf.

Kagwanja, P.M. 1998. 'Investing in Asylum: Ethiopian Forced Migrants and the *Matatu* Industry in Nairobi', *Les Cahiers d'Afrique de l'Est* 10: 51–69.

Le Roux, H. 2009. 'Coffeemanifesto: Sampling Instant and Slow Spaces in the African City', *African Perspectives 2009, The African Inner City: [Re]sourced, International Conference, Pretoria 25–28 September 2009*. University of Pretoria. Retrieved 4 October 2018 from https://repository.up.ac.za/handle/2263/59966.

Lindley, A. 2010. 'Seeking Refuge in an Unrecognized State: Oromos in Somaliland', *Refuge: Canada's Periodical on Refugees* 26(1): 187–89.

Long, K., and J. Crisp. 2011. 'In Harm's Way: The Irregular Movement of Migrants to Southern Africa from the Horn and Great Lakes Regions', *UNHCR Research Paper*. Retrieved 10 April 2016 from http://www.unhcr.org/4d395af89.html.

Malkki, L.H. 1995. *Purity and Exile: Violence, Memory, and National Cosmology among Hutu Refugees in Tanzania*. Chicago: University of Chicago Press.

Oromo Relief Association. 2011. *Ethiopia Exports More Than Coffee: Oromo Refugees, Fear and Destitution in Kenya*. Report available online. Retrieved 4 October 2018 from https://de.scribd.com/document/223306867/Ethiopia-Exports-More-Than-Coffee.

Schlee, G. 2010. *How Enemies are Made: Towards a Theory of Ethnic and Religious Conflicts*. Oxford, New York: Berghahn.

Vertovec, S. 2007. 'Super-Diversity and Its Implications', *Ethnic and Racial Studies* 30(6): 1024–54.

Part III
Economic Networks

Chapter 4

Demanding and Commanding Goods

The Eastleigh Transformation Told through the 'Lives' of Its Commodities

Neil Carrier and Hannah Elliott

> Garissa Lodge ... the place in Africa where you can buy everything from Sony TVs to AK-47s to nuclear secrets thanks to Somalis.
> —Contributor to the Somali.net online forum, 2010

Commerce has long been at the heart of Somali urbanity in Kenya. Somali trade networks now link Kenya to Dubai, Bangkok, Istanbul, Guangzhou and many other global trade hubs, importing a wide range of goods through Mombasa port, Eldoret airport and over the Somali–Kenya border from Kismayu and Mogadishu.[1] Global Somali trade infrastructure – including freight and clearing companies, and *hawala* money transfer agencies such as Dahabshiil – ensures a smooth flow of goods and capital across oceans and national borders. Such goods and capital are a crucial element in the transformation of Somali urban space in East Africa, with Eastleigh being a prime example. It is the main Nairobi hub for these goods; linking in turn many other places within Kenya (including the shopping centres of Nakuru, see Scharrer, this volume) and East and Central Africa, and containers brimming with clothes, electronics and other consumer goods are delivered daily to the estate.

With all these goods entering the estate, Eastleigh has become famous as somewhere Somalis sell just about anything, as the above tongue-in-cheek epigraph referencing Eastleigh's archetypal mall, Garissa Lodge, attests. While the availability of weapons is often associated with Eastleigh[2] and serves to reinforce its image as a wild and lawless place, these are assuredly not an integral part of its economy. Nevertheless, the claim that anything can be bought in Eastleigh speaks to the dynamic marketization taking place there and the creativity of its predominantly Somali population in identifying lucrative market niches. Indeed, this is an estate where even interviews with fake pirates can be bought and sold,[3] as can identity itself in the form of fake passports and other identity documents as well as resettlement abroad (see Carrier 2017; Rasmussen and Wafer forthcoming).

As this chapter will show, however, it is rather more mundane commodities that have built the estate historically and transformed it into what it is today. Indeed, Eastleigh is most visited for the affordable consumer goods it offers, in particular clothes and textiles, which attract customers from across the region. These are usually cheaply manufactured examples of 'low-end globalization' – a phenomenon described by Mathews (2011a) as crucial in giving access to global consumer goods to those who can least afford them. Indeed, such globally mobile goods are crucial for the transformation of not just Eastleigh, but similar urban environments around the world.

This chapter takes a 'commodity-eye' view of Eastleigh, looking at the making of the estate from the perspective of the commodities that pass through it. It is based on several spells of ethnographic fieldwork conducted in Eastleigh between 2010 to 2014, both as part of Elliott's 2011 MA dissertation project on camel milk, and the project *Diaspora, Trade and Trust: Eastleigh, Nairobi's Little Mogadishu* which Carrier led at the University of Oxford. By looking at Eastleigh through the lens of some of the mobile commodities, which form the estate's lifeblood, we elucidate and demystify the processes of its formation, growth and transformation. This commodity focus shows how this economic hub is simultaneously made up of highly localized relations and networks as well as transnational ones, which have developed at different historical moments. This complicates the notion that Eastleigh is a product of Somalia's collapse into civil war in 1991, and the related 'Little Mogadishu' label by which the estate has become famously known (Carrier 2017). The properties of the goods themselves are crucial in driving the nature of these flows: their temporalities and the relations underpinning them. Moreover, their 'perspectives' reveal the broader shifting social, political and economic conditions which have determined and continue to determine which goods reach Eastleigh and how. In this sense, while we argue that the goods that reach Eastleigh have agency in that they demand and command particular trading styles, relations and dynamics, our commodity-eye view by no means tells a story of a market rationale or logic driven only by the goods themselves.

In this chapter, we first situate our 'commodity-eye view' in a broader theoretical literature on the 'social life of things' (Appadurai 1986). We then go on to examine the particular lives of different key commodities in the estate. Here we trace the trajectories and relations through which the commodities reach their destination. These trajectories and relations and their varying geographical scope speak of the global reach of Somali networks in the twenty-first century, and the role of these commodities in the story of their mobile urbanity.

Situating a 'Commodity-Eye View' Approach to Eastleigh

The theoretical and methodological approach of 'following the thing' has largely been inspired by Appadurai's (1986) volume *The Social Life of Things*, which introduced new ways of making sense of commodities and commodity economies. It challenged the classic anthropological gift/commodity dichotomy by arguing that 'things' should be examined in terms of their full 'life histories' or biographies (Kopytoff 1986) from production to consumption, and not only at the moment of their commodification. Tracing commodities' trajectories outside of the marketplace enabled scholars to elucidate the social relations and the political and economic conditions underpinning their commodification. Consequently, commodities are revealed as far more socially complex than simply things with monetary value that are bought and sold.

Appadurai's approach also challenged Marxist-inspired debates around commodity economies and commodification. Appadurai's commodity-centred approach took seriously the thing itself – its very materiality – arguing that things had a spirit or life of sorts. This differed from Marxist notions of commodity fetishism; while here commodities could become animated, this was as a consequence of the capitalist mode of production and labourers' alienation from the goods they produced (e.g. Taussig 2010). Things for Marx could thus come to life, but this was a life projected onto them by humans rather than one inherent to the characteristics or properties of the things themselves. As Gregory (2014) notes, Appadurai's 'social life of things' marked a post-humanist turn in anthropology and the discussions and debates over the extent to which we can think of things as having agency.

The post-humanist debate has introduced new theoretical approaches, which challenge the very notion of humans being primary agents in the world and towards seeing agency as emanating from human and non-human 'networks'. We are influenced by Appadurai's and post-humanists' approach of taking 'things' seriously, looking at the way the material properties of commodities determine the nature of their flows and the relations surrounding them. At the same time, these flows are also determined by political, social and economic conditions to which Somalis and others connected to Eastleigh's economy have creatively adapted and manoeuvred in responding to and carving out market niches. Although our 'commodity-eye view' thus shifts our perspective of Eastleigh to the 'things' themselves, it does not seek to tell a story that is primarily about the properties and agency of things. Rather it takes these things as an entry point into looking at the bigger picture of Eastleigh's formation and transformation – especially its relation to regional and global trade networks of varied scales forged through Somali mobility.

While Appadurai's approach called for scholars to trace the full trajectories that things follow (1986: 17) to better understand their (multifaceted) meanings and value, our approach is a little different. Rather than taking a multisited approach (Marcus 1995) to the study of a single commodity (e.g. Mintz 1986), we focus on several key commodities and what they can tell us about Eastleigh, our approach therefore being more emplaced. Far from viewing this 'field' as a single, bounded space, however, we seek to elucidate how Eastleigh is a manifestation of flows, networks and relations (Candea 2007).

The academic debate around flow versus fixity when thinking about place seems fitting in relation to the Eastleigh context, not only due to the mobile nature of many of those who make up its population but also to the estate's historical relationship with nomadic pastoralist economies in northern Kenya and elsewhere in the Horn. The British assumed that Nairobi's early Somali population was better placed outside of the city due to their categorization as livestock people, and this was opposed by Nairobi-based Somalis who, while certainly tied into a pastoral economy through the livestock trade also considered themselves distinctly urban (Whittaker 2015, and this volume). It is to this livestock economy that we first turn.

Livestock

Livestock are rarely present in Eastleigh itself, but the livestock economy was instrumental in the estate's early formation. Given Eastleigh's close links to pastoralist peoples, the products of livestock feature prominently in the diet of the estate, and meat and milk are consumed and sold in its many restaurants and outlets. They have a symbolic presence too. The romance of pastoralism endures for many Somalis, evident, for example, in the naming of 'Nomad Palace', one of the estate's high-end hotels. For many Somali groups, camels have long been a highly culturally symbolic and valued exchange item, vital in the inter-family and clan negotiations around brideprice; in the settlement of *diya* payments (blood money as compensation in case of a death); and regarding health, as we will see below when we explore Eastleigh's camel milk economy.

Most livestock arriving from northern Kenya and Somalia arrives in Kariobangi, a kilometre or two from Eastleigh, rather than in Eastleigh itself. Livestock trade has had a strong impact on Eastleigh's transformed landscape, however: capital raised from the sale of cattle, camels, sheep and goats circulates through the estate, while livestock remains – together with buildings – are an attractive investment for the estate's businesspeople. Historically livestock have been important for the estate's economy too; livestock wealth was used to fund the purchase of early plots and buildings. Somalis in early colonial Kenya had grown relatively wealthy thanks to the livestock trade, and supplied much meat to Nairobi's early population. For example, the Nairobi District Annual Report of 1912–13 noted how active Somalis were in this trade, reporting that '[o]ne caravan has just arrived with 3,000 sheep from Samburu, this party is said to have another 3,000 sheep in Kenya ready to come here, and 4,000 in Samburu to go to Jubaland. They have also 800 cattle in Samburu to exchange for more sheep'. This mobile wealth allowed them to buy up plots in Nairobi East Township when they came on the market (Carrier 2017). In earlier times, too, livestock roamed Eastleigh: the land that is now the airbase was a place of pasture for Somali livestock.

However, as with all aspects of the estate's economy, the collapse of the Somali state boosted the importance of livestock for Eastleigh, and for a town to which it is intimately connected: Garissa. Peter Little emphasizes how the livestock trade – like that of other commerce – has boomed in Somalia's stateless years, forming a key commodity in the country's 'economy without state'. As Somalia collapsed, Kenya's livestock industry was liberalized, opening up a large market for Somali-bred cattle, mainly routed through Garissa (Little 2003: 170). Indeed, ever-growing demand for meat in Nairobi and other Kenyan towns has long spurred the cross-border livestock trade with Somalia (Cassanelli 2010: 143), no doubt generating and cementing social networks used in the transport of other goods too. Such trade was a major factor in a population surge in Garissa over the same period (alongside a rise in the number of refugees living in the town), and a major source of funding for Eastleigh developments. While many could earn enough from the sale of livestock to provide start-up capital for small shops – helping to construct malls in the process through goodwill payments (see Carrier 2017; Carrier and Lochery 2013) – enough money could be raised for large-scale traders to invest in larger ventures including hotels. Little (2003: 172) provides some examples:

> Abdinoor, the owner of one of the largest hotels in Garissa, used profits from livestock trade to finance the establishment's construction. Despite his hotel and other investments, including in the Eastleigh neighbourhood of Nairobi, he remained active in livestock trade during the 2000s … Abdullah, another prominent businessman and hotel owner in Garissa town, also amassed his initial capital through livestock trade and transport, and he also has investments and businesses in Eastleigh.

The linkages between trade in Somali livestock and Eastleigh businesses are common, and operating a business in Eastleigh and trading livestock are not mutually exclusive. Campbell relates how a Garissa cattle trader operates a shop in Eastleigh selling women's clothes (which he also sells in Garissa) in the dry season when cattle are more sedentary (2006: 24–25). Little comments on this intriguing case: 'Such is the perplexing world of Somali businesses in Eastleigh, where a male Muslim trader imports and sells women's fashionable clothes, but also operates a cattle business with ties deep inside Somalia's rangelands' (2003: 128). Many traders in Eastleigh have diversified portfolios of business interests, but owning livestock – still so culturally valued a commodity among Somalis – is one to which many in Eastleigh still turn.

Khat

While the livestock trade has played a crucial yet inconspicuous role in the development of the estate, another significant trade item is seen on almost every street corner: *khat*, more usually known as *miraa* in Kenya. This is the ever more controversial stimulant substance that consists of the stems and leaves of the tree *Catha edulis*. It is hugely popular throughout Somalia and Kenya, both as a stimulant used by nightwatchmen and lorrydrivers in their work, and as a sociable substance whose effects – known as *handas* in Kenya, and as *mirqaan* by Somalis – can ease conversation in recreational contexts. It is also a demanding commodity, whose active compounds and palatability degrades rapidly after harvesting, necessitating swift transport and sale (Carrier 2005). Khat is viewed with great ambivalence wherever it is found (principally in the Horn of Africa, Yemen, East Africa and Madagascar), reflecting the ambiguities of its potential for harm. While moderate consumption is fairly innocuous, there are medical[4] and social harms associated with excessive use; socially it can act to bring people together, it can also prove divisive; economically it earns much for producers and traders, yet can be a burden on household finances as some chew beyond their own and their family's means.

Meru are the principal growers and traders in Kenya, especially the Tigania and Igembe subgroups of the Nyambene Hills region to the northeast of Mount Kenya (Carrier 2014). The twentieth century was a period of rapid growth for khat from this region, spreading throughout Kenya, East Africa and the Horn as the road network expanded. Archival records show how Eastleigh was very much a centre of the trade by the early 1940s: Meru traders brought the substance there for Somalis and others. By the late 1940s, an Eastleigh-based Somali named Mohamed Hassan was one of the few licensed to trade the substance, and for a while he appears to have had a monopoly on its distribution in Nairobi.[5] There were many Isaaq Somali who traded legally in the substance at this time, who, being based in towns throughout East Africa, had a decisive advantage in facilitating its trade.

As an item of consumption, the substance was not just popular among Somalis in the estate, but also among its Muslim Asian population. However, Somali consumption was such as to limit supplies to others: an Arab trader in Pumwani complained that his customers could not get supplies in 1947 as the supply that reached the city mainly went to Somalis.[6] But khat has long had its detractors in Eastleigh too, and growing consumption in Nairobi in the 1950s prompted some Somalis there to campaign against it and call for a total ban.[7] Consumption remained popular despite this opposition to the extent that hundreds of Meru traders have started businesses in the estate over the years selling the commodity supplied from their home district, many more moving there since the arrival of so many more Somalis in the 1990s.

Today khat chewing forms one of the main Eastleigh pastimes, albeit one that many regard as hardly 'respectable'. Much consumption occurs in the evening as activity switches from the shopping epicentre of First Avenue to Second Avenue, a street filled more with khat kiosks and restaurants than malls. Khat kiosks stock up with fresh supplies from Meru in the early evening, advertising the fact with a banana leaf hanging from the door that, earlier in the day, served as wrapping for the commodity in transit. Many Eastleigh residents buy khat from these traders, adjourning to either private rooms and cars, or, in the case of men, often to such public areas as *shaah macaan*. This translates as 'sweet tea' from Somali, and is a small area located on Thirteenth Street, near such Eastleigh landmarks as the ten-storey Grand Royal Hotel. One can indeed buy sweet tea at *shaah macaan*, as well as indulge in shisha, khat and, most importantly, chat.

Some who frequent such spots as *shaah macaan* are diaspora Somalis (mainly Somalian, but some Kenyan Somali in origin) visiting the estate on holiday and for whom chewing khat is a rare treat when they often live in Western countries where khat consumption is illegal and consequently expensive and risky. This now includes those from the UK, where it was only recently banned. Many others are Kenyan Somalis and Somalians resident in the estate, some sealing business deals over a chew, discussing politics, or relaxing after a day's business. Such khat consumption continues apace despite its dubious reputation among certain segments of Eastleigh society.

Such consumption within the estate has provided business opportunities for many Somali, Meru and for Oromo (see Carrier and Kochore, this volume). However, it is the international trade in the commodity that has played a key role in the Eastleigh transformation itself. The international trade was spurred by the spread of the Somali diaspora to Europe and North America in the 1990s and 2000s, creating markets for Kenyan khat in these regions. The institution of the *mafrish* – khat-chewing venues – in the diaspora became key sites of sociality for some, despite the condemnation of khat consumption by others. The scale of demand was so great that by the end of the 2000s, Kenya was supplying around 7,000 boxes weekly to the UK alone, all of which would have been processed in Eastleigh or nearby Pumwani (Anderson and Carrier 2011).

Some of the earliest malls are said to have been capitalized by this trade, in particular that to Somalia and to Europe and beyond. Indeed, as well as forming a key market for the commodity through its large khat-chewing population,

Eastleigh has for over two decades formed the main hub for this international trade, just as it was a hub for the growing national and regional trade in colonial times. A fleet of Toyota Hilux vehicles bring large supplies of the commodity daily from Meru, in particular the town of Maua, itself transformed into something of a Somali-enclave since the collapse of the Somali state (Carrier 2007). For the now illegal UK and Netherlands markets, some of this was then processed at a number of establishments in the estate, being standardized into small bundles and boxed up ready for delivery to the airport. This reprocessing was another source of income for those trying to survive in the estate: before the European bans they were paid piecemeal rates working for around forty export companies. This Somali-led expansion (which, like Eastleigh business more broadly, combined Somalian and Kenyan Somali interests) created tension with Meru in the late 1990s, as some of the latter resented the Somali monopoly of the international export, shutting down the trade at various points in protest (Carrier 2007).

A few became rich from the trade (and from the older trade to Somalia itself, routing khat through Nairobi's Wilson Airport), especially those exporting large numbers of boxes, and some invested profits in malls and other businesses. It is reckoned that Garissa Lodge, Hong Kong and Bangkok malls owe their current form at least partially to the khat trade. However, money made from khat is often considered tainted; the substance has long been subject to debate as to whether it is 'haram' or 'halal', with more rigid Islamic scholars arguing for the former. To give another example, one khat exporter was said to have been preparing for Hajj, only to be told that he must only finance the trip with money not derived from khat, while also being told by a prominent sheikh that to purify the money he should give half away to the poor. For Eastleigh businesspeople, khat can be something to move away from once established in business.

The future of khat is far from certain, especially given the recent prohibitions in the UK and Netherlands. The loss of the legal UK market will potentially have a dramatic effect on Eastleigh's khat economy; indeed, reports already suggest that some of this khat is now flooding the national market, reducing prices in Nairobi and elsewhere, while much is redirected to Mogadishu. Also, khat has been illegal in most other European and North American countries for some time, but still finds its way there (Anderson and Carrier 2011): such prohibitions have not stopped Eastleigh-based traders supplying the continuing demand, and consignments destined to be smuggled are also processed in the estate. Smuggled khat attracts the highest prices, and it is likely that some will try their hand at smuggling it into the UK where demand remains. Furthermore, khat consumption in the estate itself is hardly likely to diminish anytime soon, even if it is increasingly seen as a vice. Khat will remain a part of life for many there, whether through refugees chewing time away while hoping for resettlement, or businesspeople sealing deals over a bundle or two.

Eating and Drinking Culture

While not seen as an archetypal Eastleigh commodity, food is very much an important and valued aspect of the estate's social and economic life. As Caplan suggests, 'food is never "just food" and its significance can never be purely nutritional' (1997: 3). Eastleigh residents and visitors ascribe much value to certain cultural foodstuffs. More mundanely, Eastleigh's inhabitants need feeding, and selling food in the estate can be profitable. Furthermore, much Eastleigh food is sold in bulk as commodities destined for consumption elsewhere. Indeed, Eastleigh contains many small shops selling foodstuffs – especially cooking oil, rice, pasta, sugar and spices – as well as street stalls selling fruit and dates, and larger supermarkets selling a wider range of goods. Such supermarkets are mainly Somali run, and include the Amana chain run by a Somali family with a history of business in China. However, Eastleigh links into the wider Kenyan economy too as far as food shopping goes, as it also has a branch of Tuskys at Madina Mall, a major Kenyan supermarket chain.

Many foodstuffs sold in the estate are Kenyan in origin, including tea, fruit and vegetables, bread and so forth. However, there are many imported foodstuffs sold too, some of which are linked to the contraband economy. For example, it is well known that much sugar circulating in Kenya is smuggled over the Somali border having travelled the world from Brazil, through Dubai and Kismayu before entering Kenya (see Rasmussen 2017). Eastleigh is not a major hub for this smuggled sugar – much of which is taken directly from Mandera to other towns in northern Kenya, as well as the Dadaab camps – but no doubt it is sold and consumed in the estate, while some residents have been involved in this lucrative business. Pakistani rice is also smuggled cross-border, and can be found in food shops and supermarkets in Eastleigh. Sugar and rice are particularly troublesome for Kenya as the country is itself a major producer of these commodities; such cheap imported varieties can undermine local industry, especially in northern towns where Kenyan equivalents are more expensive.[8] Kenya has also been concerned about the role of the sugar trade in supporting Al-Shabaab.

Much Eastleigh food has strong links to 'homes' elsewhere, as seems fitting in an estate with such a large refugee and diaspora population: tastes are also mobile. For those visiting from the West, supermarkets sell many familiar products, such as Maryland Cookies, while numerous restaurants cater for diaspora tastes by serving burgers and pizza, albeit with some Somali twists such as camel meat pizza topping, or a milkshake made with camel milk. For Ethiopian refugees, many small shops stock popular foods from north of the border, for example the barley grain snack known as *kolo*, while Ethiopian-style coffee is sold throughout the estate, including by refugees hawking it in flasks. Such niche foods not only provide a welcoming taste of home: they also offer yet more opportunities for survival.

Of course, Somali food is available in profusion in the estate, especially meat and rice (*bariis*) or pasta dishes available in all scales of establishment. Camel meat is especially popular for the wealthier. However, perhaps the most interesting foodstuff – certainly in terms of its commodification – is camel milk, or *caano geel* as it is known in Somali. Elliott's (2014) study of the 'social life' of camel milk revealed how its commodification has been crucial to camel herders' ability to remain livestock keepers in the face of numerous threats to pastoralist ways of life, and how it has also been incorporated into the survival strategies of women in Eastleigh (see Anderson et al 2012). Camel milk also often features in narratives of a wider Somali identity; the good has become strongly resonant of the *badia* (rural areas) often romanticized by urbanized and diaspora Somalis, and is a substance consequently imbued with a sense of 'authentic Somaliness'.[9]

Camel milk is deemed medicinal amongst Somalis – linked, they claim, to the trees and plants camels consume. In Eastleigh its popularity is evident everywhere, from the many restaurants in which it is sold, to the women selling it in yellow jerry cans around Seventh Street and Thirteenth Street. There is also a milk bar on Seventh Street selling glasses of camel milk to mainly male clientele. Camel milk tea is more popular than cow's milk tea among Somalis, and by early evening restaurants have often sold out (Elliott 2014). Camel milk adds a creamy richness to tea, as well as a smokiness derived from the gourds used to collect it when milking which are smoked to keep sterile.

Traditionally camel milk was something that should not be commodified but was restricted to family consumption. Resorting to selling milk was seen as a form of desperation. However, the collapse of the Somali state spurred the creation of a vibrant camel milk market in Somalia and in centres like Eastleigh (Anderson et al. 2012; Elliott 2014). Elliott (ibid.: 135ff) documents how Kenyan Somali women from Isiolo and Garissa became involved in the trade, spotting its market potential in Nairobi as some milk was brought to the estate for those with families in the north who owned camels. As more and more Somalis came to Eastleigh – from northern Kenya, Somalia and later from the wider diaspora – commodified camel milk became a trade item offering livelihood opportunities, both for those needing an income in Eastleigh and for women able to leverage connections between suppliers in the north and these sellers in the city. Some of these intermediaries organized themselves into a cooperative to facilitate its supply on the buses that run between the estate and the north. Garre women have been especially involved in the trade, as they are able to speak both Boran and Somali, and so communicate with camel herders from a number of different ethnicities (Somali, Boran, Sakuye and Gabra). As it was regarded as a petty trade, and milk was further traditionally considered the domain of women, men generally left these women to it. There has however been an increasing formalization of the trade, pioneered by one company which marketed processed camel milk derived from herds in ranches around Nanyuki (Anderson et al. 2012). One could now buy homogenized camel milk in Nairobi city centre supermarkets.

Thus, like khat, the popularity of camel milk in Eastleigh has created an informal trade that many can enter given that it requires little start-up capital. The trade nevertheless remains reliant on personalized networks. As Elliott (2014) found, many of the women operating the trade were Kenyan Somalis, although refugee women had also entered the trade. Camel milk links many disparate groups together, from suppliers and middlewomen elsewhere in the country, to women from different backgrounds in Eastleigh itself, and despite its commodification, it remains an item of consumption full of cultural and social as well as economic value for many. Like khat, it is also a perishable substance that must be traded and entrusted swiftly before spoiling, its material qualities once more generating momentum. It resembles khat in another way too in being another part of the Eastleigh economy embedded within very Kenyan networks. In this case, it is a key commodity linking the estate to the pastoral economy of northern Kenya. Camel milk's transformation into a lucrative commodity has, more recently, attracted men to the trade, and Elliott found that there was a growing trend towards camel herds owned by businesspeople directly supplying restaurants in Eastleigh and elsewhere in the city, bypassing the 'middlewomen' petty traders upon whom the trade initially depended. Camels are said to increasingly be 'livestock of business'. Diversification between city-based enterprises and keeping camels for milk trade appears to echo or mirror an earlier splitting of business interests between a (changing) pastoral economy and Eastleigh as we described in the section on livestock. What differentiates the camel milk and livestock economies is that the trade in camel milk developed in the wake of the Somali civil war and the surge in demand that was created by the growth of Eastleigh's population and is thus particularly emblematic of this 'displacement economy' (Elliott 2014; Hammar 2014).

Gold

The next commodity we consider is one that comes to Eastleigh after travelling much longer distances, and one valued for its longevity: gold, or *dhahabu* as it is known in Kiswahili. Gold is one of the first goods sold in the estate at the beginning of its transformation, and it is of great social significance within Somali society. It has also become ever more significant to the Eastleigh economy in the form of jewellery sourced from the Middle East, mostly from Dubai although more recently sourced from Bahrain, Jeddah and Singapore. While jewellery is bought in these places, it is hard to know where the source material originates: possibly some of the gold itself originates in Africa. The quality of gold sold in Eastleigh varies greatly, though traders thought that most customers were only interested in 22 or 21 carat items: 18 carat items are sometimes bought by traders to return to Dubai where it can be mixed with other gold to make it 21 carat. Of course, many items sold are much cheaper gold-plated products. Retailers reported that they test the purity of items bought from wholesalers using chemicals, although they said that their customers usually trust retailers and do not demand to see the gold tested.

Wholesaling and retailing gold jewellery in Eastleigh is mainly the preserve of Somali women, though there are men who sell gold from bigger shops and some Somali retailers also buy from Asian and Swahili wholesalers. Women sellers can be seen at a number of malls, usually retailing from small makeshift stalls, often in the same space where informal currency exchange takes place, a trade operated almost entirely by young men. This is much needed in an estate where money itself is a crucial commodity, with so many different currencies circulating through its transnational networks. The gendered division between gold sellers and currency exchangers is striking, especially in a building known as Al Kowther near Garissa Lodge.

For Somali women, gold jewellery has long been a key item received from a husband as *mehar*, the essential payment from a man or his kin to the bride herself (an Islamic practice known as *mahr* as transliterated from Arabic). It is seen as a form of insurance in case of divorce or difficult times, providing an independent resource that can be tapped when needed. As something that can hold economic value in the long term, gold is especially well suited in this regard, unlike money that can fluctuate so much in value over the years. Potential wives' demand for gold jewellery can be experienced by men as a burden, especially in the context of a transnational space such as Eastleigh where they are in competition with diaspora men who can often pay more than most locals, and also offer the chance of resettlement abroad through family reunification. However, the importance of gold economically in Eastleigh continues to derive from its cultural importance: as a key item of exchange between men and women, there will always be demand for it from the estate's Somali residents who, in everyday market life, appear to be its key consumers.

Of course, it is not just Somalis for whom gold sourced in the Middle East has this significance: the use of gold jewellery in Indian and Pakistani dowries also has a long history, and demand in these countries boosted the gold trade in Dubai from the 1940s, already making it an important market for the commodity. Also, towns along the Swahili coast – including ports such as Brava – have long been hubs for gold jewellery, itself an important source of financial power for women in pre-colonial times (Hecht 1987: 6). The importance of jewellery as a store of value, and not just as something of beauty, certainly rings true with gold retailers Elliott met in Eastleigh. One, for example, had come recently from Toronto after living there since 1992. The retailer was divorced, and came alone with her four children with the intention of doing some business and giving her children what she deemed was a better education than they would receive in Canada. Needing to establish herself in business, she sold half her collection of 400 grams of gold jewellery, earning USD 8,000 that she used for the start-up costs. She kept the other half of her collection in reserve in case she needed more money in the future.

Gold sellers act as informal bankers within this gendered economy, and women's social networks are strengthened through various sorts of exchanges. For example, those with personal relationships with gold sellers in Eastleigh can sometimes use them informally to get cash advances by leaving sets of jewellery with sellers on the proviso that they will not be sold until after a certain timeframe, rather like a pawnbroker system, but without interest payments. One woman Elliott met in 2012 – Asli – had a large hospital bill to pay and no cash with which to do so. She had a large piece of jewellery bought for a wedding and took it to a friend of hers who sells gold. This friend gave her 100,000 Kenyan shillings (around USD 1,200) for the piece – actually rather more than it was worth – and Asli bought it back for the same price before the two-month period they had agreed upon elapsed. As they were friends, and Asli a regular customer, there was no payment for this service, though some sellers might charge a fee of 1,000 shillings. In purchasing desired items of jewellery, women sometimes also make use of personal relations with traders. Asli had a relationship with another trader whereby she could give her money in increments whenever she had some to spare, and these payments acted as a deposit for a certain piece or set of jewellery which the trader agreed not to sell until Asli had paid in full. In this way, Asli would not divert money she saved to other purposes.

Like other Eastleigh commodities and Eastleigh trade in general, there is concern over how to ensure the trade in gold is Islamically correct. Unlike khat, gold is a very respectable commodity, but one that must be traded according to certain rules derived from the sayings of the Prophet. A particular verse is referenced in the *Sahih Muslim* that stipulates that no usury can be applied to gold for gold transactions (and transactions of other monetary instruments), and that transactions must be 'hand to hand'. There is debate as to exactly how to interpret this, but the stipulation 'hand to hand' is generally taken to mean the transaction must be completed in person at one time. This interpretation is known among Somali gold traders and their customers, and as a consequence the common form of trade relations based on trust and credit in Eastleigh is, it would seem, precluded. In theory retailers must buy their stock outright before they trade it, and so often buy from whoever is wholesaling gold at a decent price, rather than necessarily building long term trusting business relations. In practice, those with pre-existing relations of trust might bend the rules a little, perhaps giving a retailer gold in advance of payment the following day. Apparently, gold sells so fast in Eastleigh that such short-term credit arrangements are easy to manage.

Thus, gold is another commodity bursting with meaning for Somalis themselves, and forming a crucial store of value among women's economic networks. It demonstrates strongly the interpenetration of the social, cultural and religious in Eastleigh's economy. While gold, camel milk and khat are commodities brought to the estate chiefly for Somali consumption, we now turn to commodities chiefly imported to attract non-Somali customers: clothes and textiles, the archetypal Eastleigh goods.

Clothing East Africa

Imported clothing is the most commonly sold item both in the earliest incarnation of Eastleigh's original mall, Garissa Lodge, and in the shopping malls of today. Nowadays numerous Somali-owned shipping and freight companies bring in large numbers of containers from Dubai, Hong Kong and elsewhere, many filled with the clothing sold in the many malls and thousands of small shops. A proportion of the clothes sold – and designed and embroidered by its many (typically non-Somali) tailors – are Muslim-style dress, and these are mainly bought by Somalis and other Muslims in the estate, as well as feeding networks leading to other Somali trade hubs, including Eldoret, Kisumu and Kampala. International Islamic fashion is everywhere in Eastleigh, as huge demand exists for such items as *abaya* and *hijab* for women, and *galabbiya* and *kufi* (skull cap) for men. This demand seems to be increasing as the influence of stricter forms of Islam grows.[10] These items clearly have much symbolic value, linking Somalis to the broader Islamic world, and have strong political significance, reflecting the increasing strength of Islam politically for Somalis since the 1970s. Indeed, items now common amongst Somalis – such as the *jilbab* (a long, loose-fitting coat or over-dress) for women and *macawis* (a form of sarong) for men – became widespread under the influence of other Islamic societies in the last four decades rather than reflecting pre-existing Somali styles of clothing (Akou 2011: 75–76). Other items specifically appealing to Somalis are also common, including football shirts designed with the Somali or Somaliland national colours.

However, it is non-Islamic clothing that has been the major catalyst for the estate's transformation. This clothing appeals not just to Eastleigh residents, but also to a wider population in East Africa, and includes jeans, t-shirts, football shirts, smart shirts, shoes of all types, dresses (often tailor-made from fabric sold in the estate), underwear and suits. Almost all of these products sold in the estate are exemplars of the goods sold through 'low-end globalization', to use Mathews' (2011a) term. Other goods sold also form part of this phenomenon of goods manufactured cheaply in factories in China, Thailand, India and elsewhere that are often traded in South–South networks – especially electronics, perfumes and cosmetics – but it is clothing and textiles for which the estate is most famous.[11]

These commodities form the key connection between manufacturers and agents in Dubai, Hong Kong and, most recently, Turkey; wholesalers and retailers in Eastleigh; and the East African customers keen to buy them. Clothes are perhaps the most socially significant and symbolic of all these commodities. As Hansen describes in relation to the second-hand clothes trade in Zambia, clothing is especially powerful 'in mediating notions of self and society, which make this commodity different from any other in terms of indexing welfare and development'. In effect, Hansen argues, people in Zambia want 'well-dressed bodies' (2000: 90–91). The same is true of Kenyans, and Somalis in Eastleigh have provided an accessible route to the well-dressed body, one reliant on new rather than second-hand clothes.

Eastleigh's imported clothes cater for both men and women. Indeed, most shops in the malls specialize in either menswear or womenswear, aside from bigger shops that have separate sections for each. For men, suits in particular are a prime reason to visit Eastleigh, and it is known for their trade throughout East Africa. Womenswear in the estate is very varied, from ready-made dresses, skirts and jeans, to underwear, shoes and accessories such as handbags.

These typical Eastleigh clothes are worn by Somalis themselves: women sometimes wear non-Islamic clothes under their *abaya* or at home, while Somali men in the estate are often sharply dressed in suits. Diaspora Somalis also shop in Eastleigh to buy clothes to take back to the West. However, most Eastleigh stock is worn all over Nairobi, Kenya and the wider region, being bought in the estate directly by customers, or sourced there wholesale to be sold elsewhere. Indeed, many items of clothing sold in shops in central Nairobi, as well as towns in northern Kenya, the Dadaab and Kakuma refugee camps, Kampala and elsewhere, are sourced in Eastleigh.

This centrality of Eastleigh to clothing Kenya and East Africa arose because the estate provided new clothes at such cheap prices. Indeed, price is key, and Eastleigh traders have long sought out ways to reduce costs. Earlier networks that were built on labour migration links between Somalia and the Gulf through which smuggled imported clothes and other consumables entered Kenya were recentred on the estate with the revolution in shopping malls pioneered by Garissa Lodge in the early 1990s (Carrier 2017; Carrier and Lochery 2013), providing intense competition to the more expensive Indian shops in town. Smuggling was a source of comparative advantage early on but, as Somali networks solidified, it was their ability to source in bulk and ship cheaply from hubs such as Dubai that became a major reason why these clothes were sold so cheaply. Of course, there are other factors behind the cheap prices, including lower business overheads and, crucially, the fact that much of the clothing consists of cheaply manufactured items. These goods could be imported in larger quantities thanks to the trade liberalization and lower import tariffs of the early 1990s (Carrier and Lochery 2013).

Indeed, the very affordable nature of the clothes that Somali networks began to bring in at the time of liberalization has been crucial to Eastleigh's success, paralleling that of another post-liberalization clothing boom in East Africa: '*mitumba*', the Kiswahili term for second-hand clothes. As trade tariffs designed to protect Kenya's own manufacturing industries were dropped, imports of both *mitumba* and new, cheap clothes increased dramatically. While new clothes transformed the landscape of Eastleigh, *mitumba* led to the expansion of the Gikomba market, now a major centre for the trade, located only a couple of kilometres away from Eastleigh.[12] While blamed by some for the decline of the Kenyan textile industry, *mitumba* – like the clothes of Eastleigh – has generated much business and informal employment throughout the country, from wealthy importers to more lowly street hawkers. The sudden availability of such cheap goods at Eastleigh and Gikomba allowed a flourishing of Kenyan consumerism, affordable goods allowing not just the rich to indulge in the purchase of great quantities of clothing and to follow fashions. Eastleigh and Gikomba goods provide affordable ways towards the 'well-dressed body' (Hansen 2000: 91).

One might assume that the clothes and shoes sold in Eastleigh would be more desired than *mitumba*, being new items. However, many Kenyans – even those of means – reckon Gikomba clothes the more desirable. This links to the often-perceived inferior quality of Eastleigh goods – many thought to be poor copies of fashionable brands – and to the desired brands that find their way into *mitumba* markets. Most new clothes in Eastleigh come directly from Asian factories, often through Dubai, Hong Kong and other such hubs.[13] Most customers are aware of this origin and can be quite sceptical about their quality. Although so many high-end goods are now manufactured in China – including fashionable electronic brands such as Apple – there is a widespread notion in Kenya as elsewhere that 'made in China' equals low-quality goods. It is hard to generalize too much about the quality of Eastleigh goods, as there are many different gradations of quality sold: not all could be dubbed low-end global products. For example, tailor shops stock a wide range of fabrics, from high-end material to use for wealthy weddings, to cheap synthetics used to make dresses for the lower-end of the market. While people may be more concerned about buying cheap electronics or phones, which may prove unreliable, even the cheapest Eastleigh clothes will have their uses, especially where a functional look and feel are more important than designer-fashioned elegance. Nevertheless, many customers do want clothing resembling the high-end fashions seen in the media and especially in music videos.

As well as offering obscurely branded goods, Eastleigh offers many brand names that satisfy customers' desires to be part of wider global fashions: labels like Lacoste, Polo and Gucci are seen on much Eastleigh clothing, as well as on bags and shoes. While some of these goods might be genuine, many of them – of course – are copies, part of the counterfeiting industry that has thrived in recent years, especially in China where such goods are known as *shanzai*. The scale of this counterfeit trade (including electronics and medicines as well as clothes) is enormous, reckoned by some to be worth around USD 600 billion in annual sales (Lin 2011: 7). Some brands seek to use international property rights legislation to fight back against copies, while some see copies as adding value to the genuine brands by raising awareness of their labels (Lin 2011).

Labels are certainly sought-after in Eastleigh, even where there is awareness that a product is not a genuine Polo or Lacoste. Suits sold as Dunhill and Marks and Spencer are very popular with men: so much so that if one has a suit with such a label, one often leaves it on the sleeve tag.[14] As with the many watches and electronic items also sold in the estate[15] – some of which rather than being Citizen or Panasonic are Citizien or Panasoanic – there are many more obvious 'knock-offs', the term used by Mathews for goods sold under slightly altered names (2011a: 114). Eastleigh suits display a good range of such brand names, such as Markspencer blazers, as well as trousers and suits labelled Prada Milano that gave their fakeness away by describing themselves as 'Made in Lialy'.

It is easy to dismiss the value of these clothes, given their often low quality, comical misspellings and dubious relationship with 'genuine' articles of the global fashion trade. Some Kenyans would rather seek out the 'authentic' in the *mitumba* stalls, rather than wear the 'fake' of Eastleigh. Across Kenya, labelling things, and even actions, attitudes and sentiments of dubious quality as 'fake' has become part of an everyday language, and there is much expression of nostalgia for goods of the past remembered as being of better quality. But for the vast majority of Eastleigh shoppers, and those who buy the same items further along its distribution networks, these goods offer an affordable way of participating in a global community around which these brand names, whether 'fake' or 'original', circulate. As Mathews puts it, the market in cheap goods offers a means through which people can taste 'the fruits of globalization at prices they can afford' (2011b: 165).

Conclusion

Eastleigh has faced much difficulty in the face of state suspicion and crackdowns attempting to 'clean up' the estate.[16] Despite this it demonstrates remarkable resilience. Even following the April 2014 period of police surveillance and violence in the area that was officially named 'Operation Usalama Watch' (see chapters by Lowe and Yarnell and by Wandera and Wario in this volume), the estate was soon buzzing again with customers and in many ways appeared more vibrant than ever. This is in part a testimony to the demand for the goods that it supplies, which have rendered it an indispensable hub to the region. These highly-mobile goods have themselves been potent actors in the Somali-led transformation of Eastleigh and other urban areas of East Africa. Such goods may in general be cheap, but when sold in great quantities as a result of their great demand, money can be made and shopping malls built. In this way, the demand for such global goods is a crucial part of the Eastleigh equation that gets ignored in analyses of its transformation: Kenyan and East African shoppers – especially those of lesser means – are in many ways the key drivers of its success. While other Kenyans also travel to China and elsewhere to bring such goods, Somalis have proven dynamic intermediaries between the Asian manufacturing revolution and the East African demand for such fruits of 'low-end globalization'.

As we noted earlier, the story of Eastleigh told from the perspective of its commodities is not intended to tell a story of the agency of the goods themselves, or of the robustness of 'the market'. It rather tells of the agency and resilience of Somalis themselves, their adaptability and their creativity in having rendered their businesses so crucial to East Africa's economy. Furthermore, the story highlights a history of Somali ties and trading networks linking the Horn to other economic nodes across the globe, long preceding the collapse of the Somali state. These networks were built upon and strengthened as Somalis were dispersed during Somalia's crisis. It is through these networks that the 'fruits of globalization' have become so readily available to eastern Africans. At the same time, trade in commodities which meet more specifically Somali demands attest to the fact that the estate to many offers a taste of 'home' away from home, and opportunities to 'be Somali' in a cultural sense. The different trajectories of the goods reaching and passing through Eastleigh reveal that places are always translocal (Candea 2007) and made up of linkages to a plethora of 'elsewheres', some nearby, others a world away.

Neil Carrier is Lecturer in Social Anthropology at the University of Bristol (UK). After finishing his PhD in Social Anthropology at the University of St Andrews, he moved to the African Studies Centre at the University of Oxford. He has published two monographs, on Khat (*Kenyan Khat: The Social Life of a Stimulant*, Brill, 2007) and on Eastleigh (*Little Mogadishu: Eastleigh, Nairobi's Global Somali Hub*, Oxford University Press, 2017).

Hannah Elliott is Postdoctoral Research Fellow at the Copenhagen Business School, where she is researching tea and notions of sustainability in Kenya. She holds a PhD from the University of Copenhagen, where she wrote her thesis on anticipation in Isiolo, the gateway to Kenya's 'new frontier'. Before embarking on her PhD she conducted ethnographic research in Eastleigh, focusing in particular on the estate's camel milk market ('Somali Displacements and Shifting Markets: Camel Milk in Nairobi's Eastleigh Estate', in A. Hammar (ed.), *Displacement Economies*, 2014, Zed Books).

Notes

1. See Carrier and Lochery (2013) and Little (2014: chapter 7) on the expansion of Somali trade networks. Initially many of the goods imported by Somalis into Kenya and Eastleigh came through Mogadishu and Kismayu, though with increasing formalization of this import since the late 1990s, Somalis started importing more goods directly through Kenyan (air)ports such as Mombasa and Eldoret.
2. See, for example, Jones, T. (2011), 'Little Mogadishu', *AfricanLens*, 17 June 2011. Retrieved 8 August 2016 from http://www.africanlens.com/stories/photo_story/little_mogadishu.
3. Osman, J. 2013. 'The 'Somali Pirates' who are not what they seem', *channel4.com*, 2 April 2013. Retrieved 8 August 2016 from http://www.channel4.com/news/somali-pirates-journalists-jamal-osman-time-magazine-kenya.
4. Potential health harms are mainly relatively minor, such as insomnia and dental health problems, but excessive use is linked to a condition known as 'khat psychosis', and the risk of heart problems (see ACMD 2013 for an overview).
5. See file in the Kenya National Archives: KNA – VQ/11/4.
6. See file KNA – VQ/11/4.
7. See article 'Increase in Drug Taking Alleged' in *East African Standard*, 19 September 1955.
8. See Jubat, A. (2013). 'How Illicit Trade in Guns, Sugar Thrives Along Porous Border', *The Standard*, 1 December 2013. Retrieved 8 August 2016 from http://www.standardmedia.co.ke/m/?articleID=2000099083&story_title=How-illicit-trade-in-guns-sugar-thrives-along-porous-border.
9. Given that not all groups in Somalia are pastoralists, or indeed camel pastoralists, the common assertion that 'we Somalis drink camel milk' serves to reify a particular Somaliness, screening out other identities, such as those of cattle pastoralists, agriculturalists or fishing people.
10. There are other Islamic commodities sold in the estate, including religious books, alcohol-free perfume, prayer mats and so forth.
11. Shoes tend to come through different circuits, many pairs being brought from Ethiopia by Garre and others who live or have contacts in Moyale.
12. Gikomba has not escaped the insecurity that has affected Eastleigh, as witness a bombing in May 2014.
13. Mitumba clothes also often originate in Asian factories, but their circuits take them first to the West. Further demonstrating the intricacy of such networks, the raw materials such as cotton used to make these clothes are often grown in the USA.
14. Marks and Spencer suits are especially popular, which seems odd to the authors, being from the UK and knowing that brand as fairly middle of the road. There is a branch of Marks and Spencer in Hong Kong, which may explain why Chinese factories so often copy it.
15. Electronic items are of course key commodities in Eastleigh, and such hubs of trade as Eastleigh supply many of Africa's mobile phones and other items of electronic necessity and aspiration.
16. Or 'sweep-up' as the July 2012 government-instigated 'Operesheni Fagia Wageni' ('operation sweep up foreigners) exercise attests.

References

Advisory Council on the Misuse of Drugs (ACMD). 2013. *Khat: A Review of Its Potential Harms to the Individual and Communities in the UK*. London: ACMD. Retrieved 16 November 2017 from https://www.gov.uk/government/uploads/system/uploads/attachment_data/file/144120/report-2013.pdf.

Akou, H.M. 2011. *The Politics of Dress in Somali Culture*. Bloomington, IN: Indiana University Press.

Anderson, D.M., and N.C.M. Carrier. 2011. *Khat: Social Harms and Legislation: A Literature Review*. London: Home Office Occasional Paper 95.

Anderson, D.M., et al. 2012. 'Camel Herders, Middlewomen, and Urban Milk Bars: The Commodification of Camel Milk in Kenya', *Journal of Eastern African Studies* 6(3): 383–404.

Appadurai, A. (ed.). 1986. *The Social Life of Things: Commodities in Cultural Perspective*. Cambridge: Cambridge University Press.

Campbell, E.H. 2006. 'Urban Refugees in Nairobi: Problems of Protection, Mechanisms of Survival, and Possibilities for Integration', *Journal of Refugee Studies* 19(3): 396–413.

Candea, M. 2007. 'Arbitrary Locations: In Defence of the Bounded Field-Site', *Journal of the Royal Anthropological Institute* 31(7): 167–84.

Caplan, P. (ed.). 1997. *Food, Health and Identity: Approaches from the Social Sciences*. London: Routledge.

Carrier, N.C.M. 2005. 'The Need for Speed: Contrasting Timeframes in the Social Life of Kenyan Miraa', *Africa* 75(4): 539–58.

———. 2007. *Kenyan Khat: The Social Life of a Stimulant*. Leiden: Brill.

———. 2014. 'A Respectable Chew? Highs and Lows in the History of Kenyan Khat', in G. Klantschnig, N.C.M. Carrier and C. Ambler (eds), *Drugs in Africa: Histories and Ethnographies of Use, Trade and Control*. Basingstoke: Palgrave Macmillan, pp. 105–23.

———. 2017. *Little Mogadishu: Eastleigh, Nairobi's Global Somali Hub*. London, New York: Hurst, Oxford University Press.

Carrier, N.C.M., and E. Lochery. 2013. 'Missing States? Somali Trade Networks and the Eastleigh Transformation', *Journal of Eastern African Studies* 7(2): 334–52.

Cassanelli, L.V. 2010. 'The Opportunistic Economies of the Kenya–Somali Borderland in Historical Perspective', in D. Feyissa and M.V. Hoehne (eds), *Borders and Borderlands as Resources in the Horn of Africa*. Woodbridge: James Currey, pp. 133–50.

Elliott, H. 2014. 'Somali Displacements and Shifting Markets: Camel Milk in Nairobi's Eastleigh Estate', in A. Hammar (ed.), *Displacement Economies: Paradoxes of Crisis and Creativity*. London: Zed Books, pp. 127–44.

Gregory, C. 2014. 'On Religiosity and Commercial Life: Toward a Critique of Cultural Economy and Posthumanist Value Theory', *HAU: Journal of Ethnographic Theory* 4(3). Retrieved 5 June 2016 from http://www.haujournal.org/index.php/hau/article/view/hau4.3.005.

Hammar, A. (ed.) 2014. *Displacement Economies: Paradoxes of Crisis and Creativity*. London: Zed Books.

Hansen, K.T. 2000. *Salaula: The World of Secondhand Clothing and Zambia*. Chicago: University of Chicago Press.

Hecht, E.D. 1987. 'Harar and Lamu: A Comparison of Two East African Muslim Societies', *Transafrican Journal of History* 16: 1–23.

Kopytoff, I. 1986. 'The Cultural Biography of Things: Commoditization as Process', in A. Appadurai (ed.), *The Social Life of Things: Commodities in Cultural Perspective*. Cambridge: Cambridge University Press, pp. 64–91.

Lin, Y.-C. 2011. *Fake Stuff: China and the Rise of Counterfeit Goods*. London: Routledge.

Little, P. 2003. *Somalia: Economy without State*. Oxford: James Currey.

———. 2014. *Economic and Political Reform in Africa: Anthropological Perspectives*. Bloomington, IN: Indiana University Press.

Marcus, G. 1995. 'Ethnography in/of the World System: The Emergence of Multi-Sited Ethnography', *Annual Review of Anthropology* 24: 95–117.

Mathews, G. 2011a. *Ghetto at the Centre of the World: Chungking Mansions, Hong Kong*. Chicago: University of Chicago Press.

———. 2011b. 'Review of "Fake Stuff: China and the Rise of Counterfeit Goods"', *Asian Anthropology* 10: 164–6.

Mintz, S.W. 1986. *Sweetness and Power: The Place of Sugar in Modern History*. London: Penguin.

Rasmussen, J. 2017 'Sweet Secrets: Sugar Smuggling and State Formation in the Somali Borderlands', *DIIS Working Paper* 2017: 11.

Rasmussen, J., and A. Wafer (forthcoming). 'Documentary Evidence: Proving Identity and Credibility in Africa's Urban Estuaries', *African Studies*.

Taussig, M.T. 2010. *The Devil and Commodity Fetishism in South America*. Chapel Hill: University of North Carolina Press.

Whittaker, H. 2015. 'A New Model Village? Nairobi Development and the Somali Question in Kenya, c. 1915–1917', *Northeast African Studies* 15(2): 117–40.

Chapter 5

Capital Mobilization among the Somali Refugee Business Community in Eastleigh, Nairobi

John Mwangi Githigaro and Kenneth Omeje

Introduction

The present volume focuses on the 'mobile urbanity' of Somalis in East Africa. One critical component of this mobile urbanity is the capital that flows through Somali networks within the region and beyond, capital that is itself highly mobile and capable of bringing great urban transformation as seen in places like Eastleigh. This chapter is centrally concerned with an analysis of the local and international capital mobilization strategies adopted by the Somali refugee business community in Nairobi, Kenya. It explores the various sources of business capital they access both locally and transnationally. The research was conducted in an environment shaped by persisting and often negative discourses about Somali refugees, who constitute a large proportion of the Eastleigh business community. There is a general tendency to depict refugees as 'freeloaders' and unwanted elements in the host nation (Loescher and Milner 2004). They are accused of being dependent on the state and are associated with underground economies such as narcotics trade, small-arms trafficking and so forth (ibid.). Somali refugees residing in urban areas and designated refugee camps such as Dadaab in Northern Kenya have been particularly securitized[1] by both media and government officials in the past as constituting a security risk or a terror threat (see Lindley 2011; Omeje and Mwangi 2014). Furthermore, that a place associated with refugees can become a place of wealth has puzzled many, leading to sensationalized explanations of the Eastleigh phenomenon, such as linking it in its entirety to tax fraud or Indian Ocean piracy.

This chapter counters these arguments, showing relevant and more innocent sources of capital that refugees in Eastleigh have been able to tap into, and observes that contrary to the negative perceptions held about refugees in general and Somalis in particular, their mobile capital and urbanity in Eastleigh has brought much opportunity and revenue to Kenya. The chapter reinforces the view that the Somalian urban refugees are not necessarily an economic burden to the state but are considerably relevant to the economy for their contribution to and influence on retail growth and large infrastructural developments (Campbell 2006). Of course, Eastleigh is not just a 'refugee economy' and links strongly to the wider Kenyan and Kenyan-Somali economy, but its refugee population has proved extremely influential, justifying the focus on them.

The chapter is structured as follows. The first part is concerned with the conceptual foundations of the paper focusing on the 'social capital' exploited by Somalian refugees in Eastleigh, the second part examines the various sources of capital mobilization, before ending with a short discussion.

This chapter is based on fieldwork carried out between April 2011 and April 2012 as part of a larger study examining forms of capital mobilization among the Somali refugee community in Eastleigh, Nairobi. During this time 60 Somalian refugees (both male and female), who run small and medium scales enterprises such as barbing salons, small eating joints, clothes stalls, cyber cafes and road vending, were interviewed. The study furthermore included a sample of 31 Kenyan businesspeople (again both men and women), of whom 12 belong to the Asian minority.[2]

Social Capital and Business Support

Understanding the Eastleigh transformation and its sources of capital requires an understanding of the aspects of Somali society that have emerged in the wake of the state's collapse in the early 1990s. It also requires an understanding of how particular Somali forms of 'social capital' have been transplanted to Eastleigh in this time period. The Somali state collapse in 1991 led to the formation of mini-states within its territory and to a rejuvenation of clan based support systems for political power but also for business investment (Hoehne 2016). Indeed, the clan/lineage lines both locally and in the diaspora have continued to be useful in business support and capitalization exploiting as it does the sense of moral and social obligation that individual members attach to their clan (Lindley 2009), although there is a concurrent push against 'clannism' by many Somalis who see it as divisive and emphasize instead shared Somaliness and Islam in their business dealings (Carrier 2017). The Somali refugee business community has tapped into lineage-based social capital, which helps this community in their entrepreneurial activities in Kenya and globally (see Omeje and Mwangi 2014; Grant and Thompson 2015). There exist multiple nodes of connections and various transnational ties in the sense of 'multiple ties and interactions linking people or institutions across the borders of nation states' (Vertovec 1999: 447), and Somali cultural values and structures play a part in all this, easing the mobility of capital through these networks. This study demonstrates these nodes and links of various diasporic connections that Somali refugees and wider Somali society has leveraged to build a vast trade network across the globe.

Social capital in the context of this study refers to the contacts people have to those who supply them with information, labour, capital and skills, often people with whom they share ethnicity, that is, their fellow 'ethnic entrepreneurs'. The mobilization of social capital has been useful in solidifying the business success of immigrant communities such as the Chinese and the Turkish in Finland, the Somalis and the Tamils in Norway, as well as the Somali refugees operating in Gauteng province South Africa (Katila and Wahlbeck 2011; Grant and Thompson 2015; Schiller, Basch and Blanc 1995: 4). Amisi (2009), drawing on a case study of Congolese refugees in South Africa, argues that as refugees in South Africa have to cope with xenophobia and tightened labour and immigration policies, they tap into social networks not only for their (economic) survival, but to also cope with discrimination.

Membership of such a network can create multi-functional bonds, which can be a source of support (though a source of liabilities too). From a number of empirical studies about Somalian refugees in Eastleigh, Nairobi, (such as Carrier and Lochery 2013; Omeje and Mwangi 2014) it is apparent that material support through kin or clan networks often has multiplier effects leading to further economic activity and investment. Similarly, Somalis doing business in South Africa largely use co-ethnic networks (with members who also have similar class affiliations), in contrast to other immigrant groups, which rather try to blend with the South African urban population (see Grant and Thompson 2015). These resources provided by co-ethnic business networks include, among others, start-up capital, tips on business opportunities, access to markets, and a disciplined labour force (Portes 1998: 13).

One of the most important elements running through these transnational co-ethnic networks is money in the form of remittances. Lindley (2009) offers an extensive analysis of the motivating factors that encourage the Somali diaspora to send remittances to their relatives in Somalia and elsewhere. Key among the motivating factors behind sending remittances, the author argues, are ideas of reciprocity and social pressure. The Somali diaspora feels obligated to 'reciprocate' various forms of assistance accorded in the past, ranging from being brought up, to enabling school attendance or to migrate overseas. This social assistance can be considered as a generalized reciprocity typical among their kin but one without obligation to repay in the near future (Lindley 2009). Furthermore, Somalis in the diaspora can feel 'shamed' when unable to support their relatives back home, be they blood relatives or clan members (following a patrilineal descent). Remitting is thus a social practice that is not based on an individual's choice (Page and Mercer 2012).

An empirical study of remittances sent by Somalis in Norway by Tharmalingam (2011) showed that this moral obligation to remit can also take a religious angle, when this particular act differentiates a 'good' Muslim from a 'bad' one. Remitting thus becomes part of fulfilling a religious commitment to fellow Muslim Somali refugees. This strong sense of social obligation translates into a form of 'forced transnationalism', a transnationalism not brought about merely by the will to maintain social networks across national boundaries but enforced by those living in other regions by social pressures. This sense of forced or obliged transnationalism arises out of the moral and religious obligations to assist their kin wherever they maybe. This practice, implying a lack of choice on the remitter, can also include those not part of the same clan or ethnic group, drawing on cross-cutting ties. Cross-cutting ties, as elucidated by Hoehne (2016: 1379), transcend ethnicity and clans to include connections that may for instance arise out of marriage, friendship or residence. Implicitly this analysis also shows the importance of socio-economic status. Those with access to more economic capital or opportunities have a higher sense of obligation and derive symbolic capital from these interventions, gaining honour, prestige and recognition in the eyes of the community (Tharmalingam 2011). The notion of 'Somaliness' in terms of identity and connections is thus reinforced by multiple ties of attachments and belonging that cut across national borders but also ethnic or clan boundaries.

In Eastleigh, our research showed the dominance of clan ties, for diasporic remittances flowing along clan lines, but also locally for providing support to new entrants to the Eastleigh trading space. For contextual clarity, those interviewed as part of this study run small scale and micro enterprises. The following field excerpt of a 25-year-old single Somali business woman is illustrative of this local support:

> I have been running a small-scale tea-vending business for the past two years. I ran away from the Somali conflict in 2013. When I came to Eastleigh, I met a Somali lady from my clan who loaned me three thousand Kenya Shillings (roughly USD 38 as at December 2013 exchange rates). I was able to start this business and I returned the loan 3 months later without interest ... Going to the bank for business support was not an option given my 'refugee status'.[3]

The above excerpt points to how clan connections can support new entrants into the Eastleigh business space with becoming self-sufficient, especially if they do not have the support of immediate relatives when they arrive. In addition to the direct support of acquaintances, specific funds are set up within clans to avail business capital to needy members and also to help them meet other social needs, especially paying for their children's education. This is a form of social capital in practice, fulfilling parts of the obligation of being a clan member. This observation is also consistent with findings from a similar study in South Africa. Drawing on fieldwork with Somali refugees in Mayfair in Johannesburg, South Africa, Sadouni (2009) posits that clan affiliations are a pivotal consideration in providing business support for the Somali.

A significant majority of the fieldwork respondents mentioned that they are part of, or have access to some community contingency funds (such as *ayuuto*) within their Nairobi-based clans and beyond (those funds are discussed in detail later in the chapter).[4] In addition, some wealthy Somalis proudly mentioned their support for Somali businesspeople not belonging to their own clan. In connection to that it has to be underlined that the importance of clan connections in the pursuit of social, economic and political goals has increased since the breakdown of the Somali state (see Hoehne 2016: 1406).

Somali utilization of social capital to leverage business capital and other entrepreneurial opportunities is comparable to the practices of the Indian business community in Nairobi. The Indian community, often described as the main business competitor for Somalis, also runs its businesses along kinship networks. These typically involve uncles, fathers, sons and in some cases daughters running joint or large family business enterprises. This structure has been tenaciously cultivated and perpetuated since the early twentieth century, when they first settled in Nairobi and other urban areas in significant numbers. Based on the 2009 national population census, the roughly 100,000 Indians in Kenya (a rather small number compared to the 40 million inhabitants of Kenya and the 2.4 million Kenyan Somalis officially acknowledged [Kenya National Bureau of Statistics, KNBS, 2010]), mainly live in urban areas such as Nairobi, Mombasa and Kisumu. The major types of support among the Indian business community include business start-up capital, credit referencing and the sharing of information, especially with regard to the nature of the business environment, potential opportunities within and outside the country, trade regulations and relevant government policies.

Clan support is also critical in providing new entrants to Nairobi a foothold in business. This typically happens through the provision of apprenticeship opportunities as well as the facilitation of seed capital to start new enterprises, similar to the support structures of Somalis in South Africa (Sadouni 2009). The economic support being relied upon here depends on two strands of relationships. One is drawing on family ties, which could range from siblings to cousins, often from the patrilineal side. The other draws on support linked to clan affiliations on various levels, or in certain instances the region of origin in Somalia.

Local and International Sources of Capital Mobilization

Thus, Somali society has a strong social infrastructure of support that gives Somalian refugees access to local, as well as transnational social and economic capital. This section now looks at the varied forms of financial resources available to the Somali refugee business community in Nairobi which partly runs through this infrastructure – transnational remittances, rotating savings and credit associations (Roscas), community contingency funds, personal savings through apprenticeships, business partnerships, bank loans, previous business capital from Somalia and last but not least loans and cash grants from non-governmental organizations.

Remittances

Diasporic remittances received by respondents from their kin abroad were a key source of transnational capital mobilization for a significant proportion of Somali refugees (both female and male). These remittances, mostly sent through the informal and highly efficient *hawala* (an Islamic money transfer system), are used for new business start-ups, injecting capital into existing business or meeting a multiplicity of various social needs (see Carrier 2017; Lindley 2009). They are sourced from siblings, relatives (relatedness in this context usually means ties of 'blood' that traditionally draw from patrilineal ties) and spouses spread out transnationally, and could be periodic (monthly, bi-annually) or one-off payments to meet a particular need such as setting up a business. Remittances, as Lindley (2009) has elucidated, are deeply woven into social textures. Through sending money cultural and familial ties are reaffirmed. The following narrative of a 28-year-old Somali refugee, running a spare parts shop in Eastleigh, is illustrative of the transnational reach of their businesses and the mutuality and trust shared amongst their kin.

> I fled Mogadishu six years ago for Nairobi in the thick of the Somali civil war. I then stayed in Nairobi for three years and shortly thereafter left for Canada where I was until recently. It has been four months since I came back to Nairobi from Canada. While in Canada I worked in a petrol station where I managed to save some money and sent it to my brother in Nairobi to start a motor spare parts business that is now up and running … This spare part business is a partnership with my brother. I trust him to run the business in my absence, as I will be relocating back to Canada soon.[5]

The above excerpt also indicates that remittances are not only considered as a form of business capital for those who stay in the region, but also as an investment in countries of the Global South such as Kenya for those who remain settled in the

Global North. The day-to-day running of the business is left to a blood relative, invoking a sense of community trust which is discussed among Somalis as a key asset of their business practice (see Carrier 2017). The above excerpt also points to the reliance on social capital in setting up a business enterprise.

Rotating Savings and Credit Associations' (Roscas)

Somali businesspeople in Eastleigh also make use of rotating savings and credit associations, or ROSCAs, though they term this form of communal saving *ayuuto*, *hagbad* or *shalongo*. Roscas have been studied in great detail in other parts of Africa. For instance, among the Yoruba of southwestern Nigeria, *esusu* (meaning savings) operates as mutual self-help organizations that assist scheme members in meeting a number of obligations such as funerals, weddings, religious ceremonies, businesses and so forth. *Esusu* has historically permeated all sectors of the Yoruba social life and the credit scheme does not stratify between the rich or the poor in its membership (Adebayo 1994).

Also in East Africa Roscas are utilized for a variety of social and business-oriented needs, such as for conducting marriage ceremonies, settling hospital bills, paying tuition fees for pupils in school and so forth, or for investment capital (see Benda 2013: 233). Roscas are typically informal financial institutions found mainly in economies of the Global South where access to the formal credit markets are slim or non-existent, filling existing gaps and contributing to financial inclusion (Gugerty 2007: 251). They have become particularly popular because, in contrast to bank loans, no assets as collateral security are needed, a stipulation which tends to disadvantage the majority of the population from accessing the formal credit market.

While their modes of operation differ, most Roscas are organized as a system whereby members contribute a fixed sum to a kitty for a certain period. Members then take part in a simple random draw to determine the sequence of the rotational disbursement. Another system used by some Roscas is a bidding procedure whereby a member of the group can pay more than the set amount to the kitty to ensure his or her priority in the payment scheme. Roscas members are usually closely-knit associates or members of a face-to-face community who have reasonable knowledge of one another, an essential factor for saving systems based on mutual trust and integrity in order to minimize their rates of default, especially by those who have already benefitted from the rotational pay out (see Besley, Coate and Loury 1993: 794; James 2015).

Our research shows that Somali businesspeople in Nairobi, and among them especially women, use *ayuuto* for business start-ups and expansion. These female entrepreneurs' ran diverse businesses ranging from clothing, ornaments, to small and medium scale food restaurants. This study did not come across a case of male entrepreneurs engaged in *ayuuto*, even though men have been known to join such groups as well. Usually *ayuuto* members make regular contributions (ranging from daily to monthly payments), with the raised amount benefitting group members on a periodic rotation basis. When members receive their share of the disbursement (normally the full or a substantial percentage of the total contributions over the set period), they often use the proceeds to expand their business. To this end, a female respondent with a seven-year experience in the clothes trade noted as follows:

> I belong to an *ayuuto* with some of my friends. Every month, each member contributes USD 200. We are ten of us. In a month two *ayuuto* members are each given USD 1,000. This assists us in boosting our businesses. When one is in an *ayuuto*, you are not charged any interest on the money paid out, unlike a bank that would have to charge one an interest or commission for this kind of support.[6]

The contribution of a monthly amount of USD 200 is an interesting pointer to the large volume of trade turnover of some of the Somali-owned businesses in Nairobi, including small and medium scale enterprises operated by women.

Ayuuto groups are usually set-up by women who know each other and work in the same line of business, such as those in the clothing trade. They can be interpreted as a form of self-help development. In forming *ayuuto*, they are in part navigating the challenges of unfavourable bank rates by seeking an interest-free mode of capital mobilization. *Ayuuto* is not limited to clan affiliations but also cuts across clans. The members of an *ayuuto* usually agree on a simple 'constitution' that sets out the terms and conditions of benefitting from the kitty, including the regularities of contributions, and elect office bearers of this savings group (chairperson, secretary and treasurer). It is instructive to note that the *ayuuto* cater to varying levels of business. The following excerpt of a 35-year-old businesswoman in the tea vending business is illustrative in the small scale of the contributions compared to the clothes trader mentioned above:

> I am member of a Rosca where we contribute 50 Kenyan Shillings daily (equivalent to USD 0.5). I am in a group of ten women. The contribution may be small, but when it is your turn to receive, it can boost your business ... we believe in starting small.[7]

The above interviewed woman had dreams of setting up a permanent food restaurant as she grew her business with the support that her *ayuuto* offered.

Respondents' accounts indicate that *ayuuto* among female Somali entrepreneurs hardly records any defaults, ostensibly because the schemes are deeply embedded in social structures of the closely-knit business community. Defaulting would have undesirable consequences for one's reputation and credit history, especially should the person require any form of financial support for purposes of business expansion in the future.

Drawing from fieldwork data, it is notable that *ayuuto* membership among the Somali refugee business community is much more prevalent among women than men. This could be the result of the large proportion of single women in small and medium scale enterprises, who often lack access to other means of financial capital. Especially women without kin either in Nairobi or in the diaspora find it more difficult than men to access remittance networks or community constituency funds, they are also unable to approach formal banking institutions for loan facilitation as they lack the collateral security. Fieldwork data from the local Kenyan business operators (mostly ethnic Kikuyu) indicate that they practice Roscas more or less like the Somali refugee community, except that membership bridges the gender divide. The Kenyan Indian business community (both male and female), in contrast, does not have a Rosca tradition.

Community Contingency Funds

Members of the Somali refugee business community in Eastleigh reported the setting up of community funds (known as *qaran*) to meet various obligations, especially for business support (see chapter by Ritchie, this volume). These community based self-help schemes are mobilized along clan or lineage lines and work within the Eastleigh context – they are only open to the clan/sub-clan individuals that subscribe to it. The contingency funds operate by way of members contributing a flexible amount of cash monthly to a kitty dependent on the liquidity and generosity of the member.

There are a number of differences between *ayuuto* and contingency funds. While *ayuuto* groups are mostly composed of a few women who know each other well, often independently of clan lines (therefore building financial capital through social capital), contingency funds assemble a bigger group of mostly men along clan lines. Financial support in the *ayuuto* resembles a saving scheme and is highly egalitarian, everybody spends the same amount of money and receives the same amount of money. In case of the contingency fund the actual amount contributed depends on a member's financial means. The amount of money given correlates with gaining status, prestige and honour – financial capital is therefore used to create further social capital, maintaining or establishing hierarchies. Beneficiaries of the funds are not necessarily those who contributed most, but money is distributed according to needs (and to a certain extent the social networks of the beneficiary) and resembles a loan.

The funds obtained from these community kitties are generally interest-free. The funds are managed and disbursed by a committee consisting of respected community leaders drawn from the sub-clan or clan. They determine how much a beneficiary should receive. Fieldwork narratives pointed to a range of financial support between 5,000 KSh and 40,000 KSh (around USD 55–440). When respondents were asked about defaulting experiences, they mentioned that the fund hardly received any defaults from borrowers, as defaulting would bring shame to them and also dent their reputation in the community and related business circles. The respondents also value the funds' continuity and as such regularly contributed to the fund they belonged to. According to an Isaaq respondent:

> Our clan pools resources on a monthly basis for the community contingency fund. We have created this fund to assist newcomers or clan members that might require assistance in any way, e.g. medical bills, wedding expenses, travelling abroad, business needs, etc. Each member of the fund contributes a certain amount voluntarily. In my own case, I contribute ten thousand Kenyan Shillings monthly (about USD 110) to the fund.[8]

In addition to providing business support, one male refugee businessman mentioned that the fund could also be utilized to pay 'bribes' to extract fellow clan members from detainment in light of frequent police raids in the neighbourhood.

Apprenticeships

Personal savings originate either from formal employment or from stipends earned during apprenticeship opportunities provided by kinsmen. The Somali refugee community in Nairobi, as elsewhere, offers business apprenticeships to new entrants in their small and medium size enterprises. The first priority is given to relatives of patrilineal descent followed by clan or sub-clan affiliation, though also other forms of relatedness might link a shopkeeper with their apprentices. Besides facilitating practical business skills, the apprenticeship also allows new entrants in the field of trade to progressively save their stipends and allowances paid by the shopkeeper to set up their own businesses. Over time they might also get more formally employed.

These savings can be matched with remittances from their kin in the diaspora (siblings, first cousins, or spouses). The following excerpt on the role of savings in starting a business narrated by a 28-year-old Somali woman who is a proud owner of a cosmetic shop in Eastleigh is illustrative:

> I have been running this cosmetic shop since 2008. Before then, for three years I used to sell clothes for my aunt who came to Kenya much earlier. I raised a significant sum of my business capital by saving commissions from that trade. It was relatively easy for me to save because I stayed with my aunt and therefore never incurred daily living expenses such as rent, bus fare or food. In starting my own business, I took a small loan from my aunt to top up my savings. I repaid the loan in instalments without interest.[9]

Similarly, a 36-year-old Somalian man running a textile shop in an up-market mall in Eastleigh further adds credence to the role that apprenticeships can play in not only building up business capital but also the required entrepreneurial acumen:

> I joined a business through an apprenticeship opportunity at my uncle's (from my father's side) shop in 2007. In addition to learning some tips of the trade, I saved one year's worth of allowances and set up a small hawking business. Over time, my business expanded and I was able to rent my own stall where I operate from...[10]

The above excerpts on the contribution of savings illustrate instances of community-based support for new entrants. This itself demonstrates the application of social capital in supporting new entrants to gain a foothold in business through on-job training.

Business Partnerships

In the Somali refugee community business partnerships also play an important role in capital mobilization. The partnerships or joint ventures are set up by businessmen both locally and by those living in the diaspora. The amount contributed is then used to determine each individual's stake in the business venture. These business partnerships allow for a wider pool of resources, which are helpful for risk-taking, and large margins of discounts. Given their vast diaspora connections and therefore wider access to business capital, Somali entrepreneurs tend to have significant advantages over their local Kenyan counter-parts. 'I have family members in the US who are partners in my business ... and they send remittances regularly whenever there is a good business opportunity to invest in' asserts a refugee businessman.

The following narrative of a Somalian refugee mobile phone dealer in his early 30s, shows how important partnerships can be for setting up a business:

> This shop is a partnership between me and my distant cousin from my father's side in Dadaab (northeastern Kenya). I sincerely cannot tell how we are related, but back in Somalia we lived in the same extended family homestead... I approached members of my clan [Darood] here in Nairobi and was able to raise 30 per cent of the capital and my cousin raised 70 per cent ...; we then got my cousin's friend to partition a small space for us at the front of his shop where we sell phones. At the end of the month, we pay a little fee to the shop owner.[11]

Another respondent who identified himself as a Hawiye noted that 'in the raising of capital clan considerations come into play ... In my own case, I am in partnership with a fellow Hawiye. This has to do with trust in one's clan.'[12] The three examples show the critical roles that trust, clan and friendship play in business networks among the Somalian refugee community – social capital is activated through clan networks and then translated into financial capital. Tapping into diasporic networks affords the entrepreneurs much-needed capital and also helps in market intelligence of products and ventures, again demonstrating the importance of such social capital.

Bank Loans

Eastleigh has seen a proliferation of banks in its geographical space, all offering Islamic banking products. The latter have been on the rise since their introduction in Kenya in 2005 within the existing formal banking institutions as a fully-fledged autonomous banking arrangement (Ngugi 2011). Islamic banking products are preferred by the majority of Somalis, who consider these facilities to align to the Islamic faith that prohibits interest (*riba*) in credit disbursements. Notable banks in Eastleigh offering Islamic banking to the business community include Chase Bank, Barclays Bank and Gulf-African Bank. All of them also reach out to the non-Islamic community. These banks operate in several towns and have a wide clientele base offering conventional banking products.

Fieldwork in Eastleigh pointed to a sizable percentage of the refugee community using some of the banks for saving accounts or for loans, especially when setting up or expanding businesses. To qualify for bank loans, they usually call on their wealthier kinsmen to act as their guarantors at the bank. The following excerpt of a 31-year-old Somalian documented refugee is illustrative: 'I went to a recently established Islamic bank and applied for a loan of 30,000 Kenya Shillings [USD 330] to expand my clothing business. I got a guarantor to support this application who hails from my clan ... I shall need to repay the loan in a year's time.'[13] Only documented refugees can access the loans due to stringent bank regulations that require valid identification documents. Some of the refugees are undocumented but nevertheless are in business to make a living, and therefore cannot seek bank loans. The following excerpt of a 35-year-old man who operates a barber's shop in Eastleigh exemplifies this: 'I can't get a loan from a bank given that I have no identification documents with me. I don't even possess a refugee status ... coupled with this, I am not even familiar with the procedures.'[14] However, in the wider Eastleigh economy, bank loans are becoming more common, and some large-scale ventures including malls and hotels – principally those owned by Kenyan Somalis – involve bank financing (Carrier 2017: 92–94).

Previous Business Capital from Somalia

Some Somalian businesspeople interviewed for this study indicated that they acquired capital by selling their enterprises and property they owned in Somalia.

Respondents narrated that they used the proceeds to start an entirely new life in a similar or different line of business. One businessman recounted how he sold his thriving business enterprise in Somalia shortly before the collapse of the Somali state in 1991 and used the proceeds to establish a new business in Nairobi. He had to rely on his relatives' networks and guidance to gain business foothold on his arrival in Nairobi:

> I used to be an entrepreneur in Mogadishu where I had a clothes shop and a wholesale business. I left Somalia before the civil war broke out on a full scale. I had a bad feeling that my business would not survive if I stayed longer. I immediately sold my business and crossed into Kenya and in particular to Eastleigh where I had my patrilineal cousins that operated businesses at the famous Garissa Lodge. I lodged in a hotel with my family before my new business venture could take off. I presently own three mini-marts and a textile shop.[15]

A section of Somali refugees thus bring prior business experience to Nairobi and only need support from their resident kinsmen to build up new social networks to establish their business. The above quote highlights a salient point; that refugee entrepreneurs are not necessary in business for their survival but are businesspeople by long-term vocation, bringing the considerable asset of prior business experience (see Ram, Theodorakopoulos and Jones 2008). Carrier (2017: 61) writes too of some of the earliest traders at Garissa Lodge who were from an ethnic group called the Reer Hamar ('the people of Mogadishu'), a group much involved in commerce in pre-war Mogadishu. They thus came to Eastleigh with much in the way of business acumen and trade networks that they could transplant to Eastleigh, as well as capital from selling their original businesses.

Non-Governmental Loans/Cash Grants Facilitation

There are also several non-governmental organizations operating in Nairobi that provide urban refugees with livelihood options through business training and financial capital support. This business support also targets Nairobi-based Congolese and Oromo refugees. One of these NGOs is Refuge Point, headquartered in Cambridge, Massachusetts, which aims to support vulnerable urban refugees in Nairobi on their path towards self-reliance. They claimed to have provided at least 1,500 refugees with available resources to establish micro-enterprises ranging from textile trade, to tailoring, amongst other interventions. There are two ways for refugees to receive loans for starting a small scale venture or to nurture an existing enterprise: there is a cash grant option ranging from 20,000–30,000 KSh (equivalent to USD 200 to USD 300 as at December 2015 exchange rates) provided, and there is the Kiva model based on online crowdsourcing ideas.

The following narrative describes the process of acquiring the Refuge Point grant and the typical support it offers to refugee entrepreneurs in Nairobi:

> Beneficiaries for this program are identified through our outreach urban refugee program. We provide business training covering modules such as record keeping, cash flow management before the grant is disbursed. The requirements include a feasible business plan with prior business experience being put into consideration. I have to point out that a major barrier for self-sufficiency among vulnerable urban refugees remains the lack of business capital and this is where our model fits in.[16]

The second strand that Refugee Point applied was the Kiva Zip model based on the non-profit online crowd funding platform Kiva, where trustees present entrepreneurs profiles and lenders can commit to funding a business without taking interest.[17] Refuge Point acted as trustee until the program had to be stopped in mid-2015 due to feasibility challenges, such as delays in loan disbursement to beneficiaries and repayment challenges. Nonetheless the program facilitated the uptake of fifty-two loans within the three years of existence to various refugee enterprises in Nairobi. These enterprises have ranged from food kiosks, clothing and textile business, to small retail shops. Most refugee entrepreneurs received a maximum of 10,000 KSh (about USD 100) through the Kiva Zip program, the highest amount possible for a first loan. The recipients were required to reimburse the money within 12 weeks to qualify for another loan. It is pertinent to note that the Kiva Zip model has nevertheless been of considerable benefit to a number of Somali refugees interviewed in October and November 2015.

Conclusion

This chapter argues that solid kinship ties, working mainly within clans, are the main social connections along which financial capital is mobilized by the Somali refugee business community in Nairobi. All these sources of capital have combined with other sources in the Eastleigh economy (especially from Kenyan Somali businesses) to fund much of the urban transformation witnessed in the estate.

This research shows that diasporic remittances remain significant as important sources of business capital. This support mainly originates from North America and Europe. Multiple transnational ties have proved useful in mobilizing not only business capital but also information that is useful for their entrepreneurial success. The diaspora also engages in business partnerships. Other localized forms of support include the utilization of clan and kinship ties as well as ties of friendship, and work to initiate and grow businesses through models such as *ayuuto* and community contingency funds. Formal sector credits are also sought from banks, preferably Islamic banks, because of the diverse advantages they hold for this predominantly Muslim community. It is remarkable that members of the community are reported to rarely default in their repayment of loans or in the reciprocation of any transactional obligations amongst themselves, even when there is no written or binding agreement as is often the case. Increasingly non-governmental organizations have also joined in the support of this refugee community by facilitating small interest-free loans and cash grants to improve the livelihood options for vulnerable groups.

This chapter remains consistent with global literature on the role of transnationalism in supporting immigrant entrepreneurs to start-up and grow their business enterprises. The support offered across the Somali business landscape drawing on clan ties in facilitating remittances and business partnerships is not a unique phenomenon. It has been documented across various immigrant communities that support their kin in new lands, such as Chinese Immigrants in the US, Turkish immigrants in Finland, or Congolese immigrants in South Africa. These aspects of social membership are useful globally in providing economic, social and human capital to immigrant entrepreneurs and hence are critical ingredients to their business success. In the case of Somali refugees in Eastleigh, the transnational network of support formed through the spread of lineages across the globe means that many can access the mobile capital so important for the story of urban transformation witnessed in Eastleigh.

John Mwangi Githigaro is Lecturer in Peace and Conflict Studies at St. Paul's University, Limuru (Kenya). He holds a PhD in International Relations from the United States International University Africa (USIU-A) Nairobi, Kenya. His research interests revolve around peace and security studies, refugee studies and media portrayals of terrorism with a specific focus on the Horn of Africa. He is a Nextgen Social Science Research Council New York (SSRC) fellow (2016–2019).

Kenneth Omeje is Research Fellow at the Centre for African and Gender Studies, University of the Free State, South Africa; Visiting Professor at the Institute for Peace and Security Studies in Addis Ababa University, Ethiopia; Visiting Professor at the University for Peace Africa Programme in Addis Ababa and Visiting Professorial Fellow at the Nigerian Defence Academy, Kaduna, Nigeria. He has previously held the positions of Professor of International Relations at the United States International University in Nairobi, Kenya and Senior Research Fellow at the John and Elnora Ferguson Centre for African Studies (JEFCAS), University of Bradford, UK.

Notes

1. This chapter is based on material, which has partly been used in Omeje and Mwangi (2018). Securitization is defined as a process whereby those in authority frame certain social issues as existential threats to the state and thus justify extraordinary responses (see Buzan and Wæver 2009 and the chapter by Wandera and Wario in this volume).
2. The study benefitted from additional fieldwork and literature review in August and September 2014, and in September and October 2015. The research was funded by a research grant from the Institute for Money, Technology and Financial Inclusion (IMTFI) at the University of California Irvine. The researcher also gratefully acknowledges the staff of Refuge Point Nairobi office for support with fieldwork facilitation in 2014 and 2015.
3. Interview with a female Somali refugee trader on 28 October 2015 in Nairobi.
4. *Ayuuto* is a Somalized Italian word (*aiuto*) that simply means 'help'. In Eastleigh, *ayuuto* refers to a form of revolving saving fund, which distributes fixed interest-free rates of money among members.
5. Interview with Somali refugee businessman on 19 July 2011 in Nairobi.
6. Interview with female Somalian trader on 14 July 2011 in Nairobi.
7. Interview with a female Somalian trader on 16 November 2015 in Nairobi.
8. Interview with a male Somali refugee trader on 12 July 2011 in Nairobi.
9. Interview with a female Somali refugee trader on 11 July 2011 in Nairobi.
10. Interview with Somali refugee businessman on 17 November 2015 in Nairobi.
11. Interview with a male Somali refugee trader on 19 July 2011 in Nairobi.
12. Interview with Somali refugee businessman on 19 July 2011 in Nairobi.
13. Interview with a 31-year old male refugee trader in Nairobi, conducted on 31 October 2015.
14. Interview with a 35-year old male barber in Eastleigh, conducted on 16 November 2015.
15. Interview with Somali male refugee trader on 22 July 2011 in Nairobi.
16. Interview with a senior officer of Refuge Point on 25 September 2014 in Nairobi.
17. See www.kiva.org for the history and working of the Kiva Zip model.

References

Adebayo, G.A. 1994. 'Money, Credit and Banking in Pre-colonial Africa. The Yoruba Experience', *Anthropos* 89: 379–400.

Amisi, B.B. 2009. 'Between Home's Rock and South Africa's Hard Place: Non-Nationals Experiences, Livelihood Strategies and Choice to Remain in Post-2008 South Africa', *Policy Studies Bulletin* 10(3): 15–21.

Benda, C. 2013. 'Community Rotating Savings and Credit Association as an Agent of Well-Being: A Case Study from Northern Rwanda', *Community Development Journal* 48(2): 232–47.

Besley, T., S. Coate and G. Loury. 1993. 'The Economics of Rotating Savings and Credit Associations', *The American Economic Review* 83(4): 792–810.

Buzan, B., and O. Wæver 2009. 'Macrosecuritisation and Security Constellations: Reconsidering Scale in Securitisation Theory', *Review of International Studies* 35: 253–76.

Campbell, E.H. 2006. 'Urban Refugees in Nairobi: Problems of Protection, Mechanisms of Survival and Possibilities of Integration', *Journal of Refugee Studies* 19(3): 397–413.

Carrier, N. 2017. *Little Mogadishu: Eastleigh, Nairobi's Global Somali Hub*. New York: Oxford University Press.
Carrier, N., and E. Lochery. 2013. 'Missing States? Somali Trade Networks and the Eastleigh Transformation', *Journal of Eastern African Studies* 7(2): 334–52.
Grant, R., and D. Thompson. 2015. 'City on Edge: Immigrant Businesses and the Right to Urban Space in Inner-City Johannesburg', *Urban Geography* 36(2): 181–200.
Gugerty, K.M. 2007. 'You Can't Save Alone: Commitment in Rotating Savings and Credit Associations in Kenya', *Economic Development and Cultural Change* 55(2): 251–82.
Hoehne, M. 2016. 'The Rupture of Territoriality and the Diminishing Relevance of Cross-Cutting Ties in Somalia after 1990', *Development and Change* 47(6): 1379–1411. DOI: 10.1111/dech.12277.
James, D. 2015. '"Women Use their Strength in the House": Savings Clubs in an Mpumalanga Village', *Journal of Southern African Studies* 41(5): 1035–52.
Katila, S., and O. Wahlbeck. 2011. 'The Role of (Transnational) Social Capital in the Start-up Processes of Immigrant Businesses: The Case of Chinese and Turkish Restaurant Businesses in Finland', *International Small Business Journal* 30(3): 294–309.
Kenya National Bureau of Statistics (KNBS). 2010. *Kenya Population and Housing Census*. Nairobi: KNBS.
Lindley, A. 2009. 'Between "Dirty Money" and "Development Capital": Somali Money Transfer Infrastructure under Global Scrutiny', *African Affairs* 108(433): 519–39.
———. 2011. 'Between a Protracted Refugee and a Crisis Situation: Policy Responses to Somali Refugees in Kenya', *Refugee Survey Quarterly* 30(4): 14–48.
Loescher, G., and J. Milner. 2004. 'Protracted Refugee Situations and State and Regional Insecurity', *Conflict, Security & Development* 4(1): 3–20.
Ngugi, W.R. 2011. 'Kenya', in Sanket Mohapat and Dilip Ratha (eds), *Remittance Markets in Africa*. Washington, DC: The World Bank, pp. 155–83.
Omeje, K., and J. Mwangi. 2014. 'Business Travails in the Diaspora: The Challenges and Resilience of Somali Refugee Business Community in Nairobi, Kenya', *Journal of Third World Studies* 31(1): 185–217.
Omeje, K., and J.G. Mwangi. 2018. 'Capital Mobilization among the Somali Refugee Business Community in Nairobi, Kenya', in B. Maurer, Smoki Musaraj and I. Small (eds), *Money at the Margins: Global Perspectives on Technology, Financial Inclusion, and Design*. Oxford, New York: Berghahn, pp. 44–65.
Page, B., and C. Mercer. 2012. 'Why Do People Do Stuff? Reconceptualising Remittance Behaviour in Diaspora Development Research and Policy', *Progress in Development Studies* 12(1): 1–18.
Portes, A. 1998. 'Social Capital: Its Origins and Applications in Modern Sociology', *Annual Review of Sociology* 24: 1–24.
Ram, M., N. Theodorakopoulos and T. Jones. 2008. 'Forms of Capital, Mixed Embeddedness and Somali Enterprise', *Work Employment and Society* 22(3): 427–46.
Sadouni, S. 2009. 'God Is Not "Unemployed": Journeys of Somali Refugees in Johannesburg', *African Studies* 68(2): 235–39.
Schiller, N.G., L. Basch and C.S. Blanc. 1995. 'From Immigrant to Transmigrant: Theorizing Transnational Migration', *Anthropological Quarterly* 68(1): 48–63.
Tharmalingam, S. 2011. 'A Long Distance Navigator? Remittance as a Transnational Practice among Tamils and Somalis in Norway', *Forum for Development Studies* 38(2): 177–96.
Vertovec, S. 1999. 'Conceiving and Researching Transnationalism', *Ethnic and Racial Studies* 22(2): 447–62.

Chapter 6

Challenging the Status Quo from the Bottom Up?

Gender and Enterprise in Somali Migrant Communities in Nairobi, Kenya

Holly A. Ritchie

Somali influence on urban Kenya is nowhere more visible than in Eastleigh, the estate that features much in this present volume. The estate is famous for its entrepreneurship and its commercial growth, and for the link of this growth to its refugee population – indeed, Eastleigh in some ways is an example of a 'refugee economy'. In such refugee settings, the development of economic activities is viewed as crucial for fostering 'social and economic interdependence' in local communities, and rebuilding social networks (Jacobsen 2002), boosting both refugees and their host environments. In camp situations, refugees have been further described as 'untapped' resources that can be potential 'entrepreneurs' and 'innovators', particularly if linked to commercial partnerships (Betts 2013; Betts et al. 2014). Meanwhile, transnational migrants have been celebrated as entrepreneurs that can be 'agents of social change' (DeHart 2010). To this end, 'entrepreneurship' is often perceived as the best means for promoting refugee livelihoods, self-reliance and local integration towards improved 'human security'.[1]

Yet, the literature on entrepreneurship also suggests a need for caution in promoting such initiatives for poverty reduction or social change. Poor entrepreneurs may be either 'survival-oriented' or 'growth-oriented' (Berner, Gomez and Knorringa 2009), influencing the scope of enterprise developments and potential economic outcomes. Naude (2007) cautions particular attention to fragile environments with few formal institutions.[2] Economic development can also result in the perpetuation of economic forms and institutions that may be negative, fostering unproductive and destructive enterprise. In a context of precarity, as

Eastleigh is for refugee groups, such caution is especially necessary. Indeed, while many sought peace and safety on Kenyan soil, and a steady platform for continued business (including the relocation of major businesses from Mogadishu), Somali refugee lives have remained turbulent and uncertain. Evolving Kenyan policies and attitudes have made it difficult for most Somalis to lead a stable 'productive life in exile' and fulfil their entrepreneurial aspirations, as there 'the right to life has been bought at the cost of almost every other right' (Crisp 2002: 9). In particular, in cities such as Nairobi, despite their 'long-term presence' and 'active contribution', Somali refugees often feel like outsiders, living their lives on the periphery of the greater Kenyan reality (Pavanello, Elhawary and Pantuliano 2010: 8).

Building on earlier doctoral research in conflict-ridden Afghanistan (Ritchie 2016a, 2016b), this chapter focuses on female Somali entrepreneurs, looking at gender through the lens of social change in Somali migrant communities in Eastleigh. Gender relations and roots of inclusion and exclusion are embedded in evolving patterns of institutions (The World Bank 2013). In less structured developing contexts, with few formal institutions, informal institutions such as habits, customs and norms tend to guide economic behaviour (Harriss-White 2010; Steer and Sen 2010). In refugee settings, new economic needs (or demands) can precipitate social change for migrant women and this can arguably be challenging for family men, as they strive to adjust to women's changing gender roles and negotiate 'respectable masculinity' (Kleist 2010).

This chapter builds not only on desk research, but also on six weeks of qualitative field research in Eastleigh, Nairobi, from January to March 2014. Techniques included observation, semi-structured interviews and focus group discussions, with a total of over eighty respondents.[3] Research drew on the critical realist's approach (Lawson, 1997)[4] to explore Somali refugee women's economic engagement in Eastleigh and related socio-cultural dynamics. The investigation aimed to add further insights into gender and institutional change in less certain environments. The discussion highlights the precarious nature of refugee women's evolving economic practices under strained displacement conditions, with little community negotiation and acceptance. Yet the paper draws attention to the development of social structures in Eastleigh that may reinforce the stability of these 'new' institutions. Thus, this chapter shows the ambiguities that the enterprise opportunities in Eastleigh offer from the perspective of some of the estate's most vulnerable refugee residents: it emphasizes the economic contribution of refugee women working at the lower end of the Eastleigh economy, while also highlighting the social challenges they face, especially in a context where conservative gender norms and values persist amongst refugee groups (with the 'mobility' of Somali urban culture), and where more rigid forms of Islam are taking greater hold. Before looking in more detail at the economic lives of refugee women, the chapter begins with a look at changing gender relations among Somalians in the context of exile and diaspora.

Somali Gender Roles in the Kenyan Migrant Communities

Conflict and displacement has shaken up the social, economic and political fabric of Somali society, particularly in terms of gender roles, as Somalians redefine themselves at home and abroad (Bryden and Steiner 1998). In Kenya, Somali cultural identity appears strong amongst Somalians, with a firm sense of belonging (Lambo 2012: 16), demonstrating the non-dependence of cultural identification on geography (Brun 2001; Griffiths 2002).

Somali society can be described as patriarchal, socially-conservative and restrictive for women (Bryden and Steiner 1998), with women's social, economic and political rights, and societal roles limited. Upon marriage, women are expected to adopt their husband's clan. This contributes to a political marginalization, fostering perceptions (amongst men) of 'women's divided loyalty'.[5] Nonetheless, women play a significant role as the 'bearer of loyalties between lineage, clan, or kin' (Bryden and Steiner 1998). Somali women – as nomadic pastoralists – for a long time did not pursue practices of seclusion and veiling common in many Muslim countries, apart from a small urban elite (Kapteijns 1995). There was, however, a 'high level of de facto segregation by sex' (An-Na'im 2002: 68). Yet since the civil war in the 1990s, and the establishment of Islamic Courts in the subsequent security void, conservative Islam has taken root in Somalia, and has accordingly been politicized (Marchal 2007). With this, more austere obligations around gender norms have slowly crept into mainstream urban Somali society (and law), creating stricter boundaries and behavioural rules for women. This has been predominantly influenced by Muslim trends in Arab countries (Murray 2000 in An-Na'im 2002), and driven by (Saudi) 'Wahhabist' elements within Somalia itself ('Salafism'), particularly returning to 'Awan Muslimi'[6] as part of an 'internationalization of more conservative interpretations of Islam' (Abdi 2007).

It is argued that the relative position of Muslim women and their 'Islamic norms' is embedded in 'post-independence trajectories of modern states' and variations in Islam linked to 'different nationalisms, state ideologies and oppositional social movements' (Kandiyoti 1991). In Somalia, new Islamic norms that emerged in the late 1990s clashed with parallel contradictory trends in women's roles in society that had begun during the civil war when women 'acquired new importance as merchants, providers, and heads of families' as a result of the absence of men (Bryden and Steiner 1998: 4). Somali women perceived this new order as both a threat to these advances, and a challenge to their greater 'freedom of movement, association and dress' and their 'autonomy' enshrined in Somali culture (Abdi 2007). This included for instance their 'right to be consulted' if their husband was considering a new wife. Despite Somalis distancing themselves from Middle Eastern Muslims with their (typically) superior attitudes,[7] Somalis now look towards the Arab world for security, religious guidance and economic support. Yet the evolving dynamics of Islamic conservatism in Somalia remain

Figure 6.1 Three Somali refugee women taking part in an NGO training course on business development skills (BDS) in Eastleigh, January 2014 (photo: H. Ritchie).

contradictory, with the dual discourse of extremist religious groups, such as Al-Shabaab, often appearing to both venerate female submissiveness, as well as to encourage female economic activity and political presence outside of the home, if women simply ensure that they wear the '*hijab*' (Islamic head covering).[8]

Outside of Somalia, in regional diaspora communities[9] – as is often the case within immigrant groups – the threatening, and/or unfamiliar foreign setting has tended to generate a desire for Somalis to re-assert their evolving cultural identity and norms. For Somalis, religion is a dominant force in this regard, with greater Islamic activism observed in the Somali diaspora in Kenya and Ethiopia than in Somalia itself (Menkhaus 2002: 111).[10] Religiosity has also been encouraged through trading and links to the Gulf, and evolving business practices. Indeed, religious and political Islam is considered to represent 'one of the few universal points of reference for Somali society' in a greater context of uncertainty (Bryden and Steiner 1998). In some Somali diaspora communities in the US, this has led to women and girls being encouraged to veil by their families and communities, and to adopt conservative behaviour (De Voe 2002). This increasing religiosity has even been argued to strengthen their position in such settings (Berns McGown 1999), possibly in the face of perceived 'loose' western morals and behaviour (and community concerns over women's potential dating and sexual conduct). Yet simultaneously in US communities, there have also been more open attitudes related to female genital mutilation (FGM)[11] (ibid.), and women's economic practices (e.g. in the workplace). It has therefore been contended that religiosity (including an outward increase in veiling) and the participation of women in Islamic movements does not necessarily preclude women's agency to challenge and resist social norms (even if, and as they inhabit them) (Mahmood 2004). The emergence of new Islamic norms (such as female participation in Islamic preaching through technologies such as the radio) may further permit both female religious mediation and authority, although the sociocultural context warrants appreciation (Schulz 2012). For women, a closer association with Islam can also create a stronger platform for combining a Muslim identity with economic career aspirations (Schulz 2013). Beyond religion, and creating an opposing dynamic, the increased trading of the plant stimulant 'khat' has also notably influenced gender patterns at home and in Somali diaspora communities (Anderson et al. 2007), with the increasing role and participation of women.

In the context of Nairobi, and particularly Eastleigh, conservative versions of Islam are perceived to carry both influence and security (Abdi 2007). The increasing 'Wahhabist' influence has even led Kenyan Somalis to cover: 'our dress used to be open and free but now we must cover or be stoned'.[12] This creates new tensions with the Kenyan public, as they are perceived as conservative, different, or labelled as the fundamentalist Islamic terrorists Al-Shabaab. With little media and public support, Somalis have typically retreated and their reaction to persistent public hostility is 'to keep their heads down'.[13] Non-Somali Kenyans even blame Somalis themselves for the current situation by not speaking up enough, apart from the vocal efforts of the popular Kenyan Somali, Yusuf Hassan (Eastleigh MP).[14]

Somali Refugee Livelihoods: Fragile yet Strong (Clan-Based) Support Mechanisms

Whilst there may be a degree of integration (and self-sufficiency) in Eastleigh with significant business engagement of Somali refugees, these groups still often remain 'temporary citizens' in Kenya, with elusive rights and entitlements. According to an NGO livelihood survey (DRC and UNHCR 2012), up to two thirds of Somali refugee households (45–65 per cent) were categorized as low income. This includes 'very poor' households, constituting 10–20 per cent of the community (earning approximately USD 100 per month); and 'poor' households, comprising between 35–45 per cent (earning approximately USD 200 per month). Very poor households are described to meet only 70 per cent of the 'survival threshold' (food/non-food), thus relying on local handouts and remittances (in some cases, these can be considerable). In the survey, approximately 50 per cent of Eastleigh households were reported to be women-headed, indicating a further degree of vulnerability, particularly in terms of access to markets, services and resources. Yet Somali clan and family networks 'remain strong' and have enabled Somalis – men and women – to survive and cooperate, and even prosper (ibid.). Poverty may thus be high, but social support mechanisms can be significant, including from Somali family/clan diaspora in other countries (in the form of remittances), and from within the community itself (local contributions or support from the mosque) (Pavanello, Elhaway and Pantuliano 2010: 21). And with a strong Somali cultural identity (and the observance of rituals and festivals) even in exile, there is high degree of solidarity 'families look out for one another'.[15] Yet there appears to be a simultaneous lack of trust, particularly outside of clans/immediate networks.

Eastleigh's Poor Backbone: Somali Women 'Entrepreneurs'

Somali women are in fact extremely 'visible entrepreneurs' in Eastleigh, and have been described as the 'backbone of Somali [Eastleigh] society' (Jacobsen 2011: 37). Women are not only the 'head[s] of the household', but also the 'primary breadwinner[s]' and responsible for the 'allocation of resources' (ibid.).[16] Many of the refugee women fled without husbands or male family men (divorce is common amongst the Somalis). Yet the research indicates that some women do in fact arrive in Kenya accompanied by men (brothers, paternal uncles, or husbands), but that these male companions then promptly leave to work as migrants, either within Kenya or in regional locations such as South Sudan (due to the scarcity of decent work beyond road-side trading). The women's extended family or clan may often, initially, offer them shelter. However, there were also (less common) reports of non-Somali and Somali Kenyan businesswomen in Eastleigh giving Somali women board and lodging, in exchange for domestic work support.

On first glance in Eastleigh, Somali women appear to be 'successful' entrepreneurs, particularly in terms of their prevalence in the marketplace (Bille 2013). Participating in Eastleigh's commercial rise in the 1990s, a few exceptional women are even now present in the more elite aspects of the Eastleigh economy, as shopping mall owners (Carrier and Lochery 2013). However, the majority of Somali refugee women in Eastleigh's economy struggle with a rather different reality. These poorer women tend to work as petty traders, domestic labourers and tea and coffee sellers (Pavanello, Elhawary and Pantuliano 2010: 21). There is a notable absence of men in such work (Somali or otherwise) in contrast to other commercial areas of Nairobi. Basic livelihood surveys indicate that the Somali women entrepreneurs face various challenges in this work. This includes an absence of proper documentation (with various 'fines' imposed by local authorities if caught); a lack of access to credit (including to buy a business licence and formalize their business); illiteracy and poor capacity (limited marketing, management and organizational skills); and limited relevant language skills (Refugee Consortium Kenya 2008; Bille 2013). More entrenched social barriers that have been highlighted included the pressures of household obligations, 'cultural' factors (related to gender norms), poor access to social networks, and local insecurity (Bille 2013). Raddatz (2013) expands on Somali women's insecurities, as both related to 'daily worries', such as harassment on the street, in addition to a larger 'fear of repatriation to camps', where women are reported to suffer from sexual violence, exploitation, a lack of work/financial autonomy and a loss of networks.

'In Somalia, We Used To Be Housewives…'

By examining this phenomenon closer, this research can shed further light on the precarious lives of poor Somali women entrepreneurs in Eastleigh. Initially, it is important to elaborate on the general characteristics of poor Somali women 'entrepreneurs', and the nature of their evolving work in Eastleigh. Correlating with Jacobsen (2011), the research indicated that approximately eighty per cent of local Somali women engage in some form of work in Eastleigh. The 'entrepreneurs' met were based around the central market Garissa Lodge area, and were largely involved with informal trading/petty trading activities such as operating market stalls (often in clusters of women stalls) or door-to-door trading (in residential areas).[17] Typical items sold included textiles (scarves/clothes), cosmetics, fruit and vegetables, honey and snacks.

Profile of a typical Somali refugee woman goods trader in Eastleigh:

> I am 30 years old and am divorced with no children. I live with my mother, brother and other relatives. I arrived in Kenya 5 years ago. I have a basic market stall in Eastleigh and sell women's headscarves.

> On a good day, I can make between 400–600 Kenyan Shillings (USD 4–6) per day with the sale of two to three scarves. I buy these from a wholesale agent in Eastleigh, and sell these to local residents. I work alone with little protection from local intimidation and harassment, and terrorization by local gangs such as Superpower. I also face constant problems from both the police and City Council, and must pay a daily bribe to avoid being arrested.[18] I am keen to formalize my business and open a shop one day …[19]

Others worked as 'tea ladies', although this was considered to be the lowest and least respectable type of work with pressure to only serve female clients ('If I sell to men, they will abuse me and people will gossip …').[20] Inevitably the tea ladies do have male customers and have to contend with persistent 'hassle' from the sheikhs (holy men). This might include verbal abuse and intimidation. A Kenyan Somali elaborated on the business of tea ladies further:

> The tea ladies tend to congregate around the mosque and Garissa lodge area (main Eastleigh shopping street), and work both day and night, although nighttime work has been curtailed with the recent curfew. To sell their tea, they must almost act like geisha [in being charming and equally in having great tasting tea] to attract the men, as they are in competition with other tea ladies. Hence society looks down on these girls that are seen as prostituting themselves, even when they are not.[21]

With frequent local abuse and harassment, Eastleigh Somali women described entrepreneurs trying to avoid working in areas in which they lived, particularly the 'controversial' tea ladies. Turnover from market stalls and trading was reported to be low, on average 200–400 Kenyan Shillings per day (less than USD 5). Less commonly, Somali women may work in the kitchens of restaurants. To boost their meagre incomes, some enterprising women reported combining different types of work, for example, working as a tea lady in the morning, and as a door-to-door tradeswoman in the afternoon. Women described certain jobs/trades however being simply 'off limits' for Somali women due to either their heavy work, or their being too 'public' (and thus 'against Islam'). This included large factory work, transport and labour-related jobs.

A Somali refugee woman 'multiple entrepreneur' expanded on her background and work life in Eastleigh:

> I am a 34-year-old and a widow with three children, and arrived in Kenya seven to eight years ago. I work as a tea lady in addition to door-to-door clothes trading in Eastleigh. I wake up at 5 a.m. every day and start to make camel-milk tea at home. I make approximately 12 flasks and my

nephew[22] (16 years old) – who is like my adopted son – supports me in taking them to the Garissa Lodge area. We work together and sell the tea to shopkeepers, both men and women. My nephew helps with new customers and they respect me. He also stops any potential harassment including intimidation by my late husband's family. At twelve-noon, I return home with my nephew. I make more tea if needed, and my nephew takes the extra flasks to the market and continues selling these independently over the rest of the day. In the afternoon, I then sell clothes door-to-door and sometimes cosmetics. I buy these in the local markets in Eastleigh. My customers are local residents. If I am lucky with these different businesses, I can make between 500–1000 Kenyan Shillings (USD 6–12) per day. I face problems in my work every day from the police and City Council ... My nephew broke his arm fleeing from the City Council last week ...[23]

From the research, the refugee entrepreneurs tended to be largely uneducated and illiterate (more than 80 per cent), non-English or Kiswahili speaking and most lacked any previous experience in 'business' and living 'like Arabs' in Somalia (practicing gender segregation), particularly after the wave of conservatism in the mid-nineties. Yet in a few cases, women simultaneously reported working with their mothers in Mogadishu during the nineties war, forced into economic activities by circumstances.[24] Over three quarters of the women interviewed were single mothers (divorced or widowed), aged between 25 to 45 years, and had mostly fled Somalia in the past 3 to 10 years. They reported having few local social networks and notably lacked any male authority or support in Eastleigh. Typically, the women worked alone – except for those organized into enterprise-oriented 'Self Help Groups' (rotating savings and credit associations)[25] by the International Rescue Committee (IRC) – and thus they described strong competition between themselves as they endeavoured to market their products and services.

Unravelling Women's Enterprise Challenges

In correspondence with the literature, the major reported challenge in the women's businesses included foremost a lack of legal documents, leading to daily harassment from Nairobi City Council and the police. This has notably increased since 2012, particularly as legal documentation has been more difficult to come by. The City Council charges market stalls approximately 30 Kenyan Shillings per day (if they have basic UNHCR documentation), or imposes a larger 'fine' of up to 3,000 Kenyan Shillings (for those without documentation): 'as soon as they come, everyone packs up'.[26] More sporadically, police are described to impose random fines for a lack of documents or as a means of intimidation.

Due to this, many established shopkeepers try to keep these informal women traders 'off their patch' to avoid potential trouble by the police. This daily harassment and uncertainty not only constrains the women's business activities, but also affects their potential mobility beyond Eastleigh to pursue enterprise development in other less clustered city locations (for fear of both higher visibility, as well as local xenophobia). Women also described being intimidated by local gangs ('superpower'),[27] and occasionally by conservative people. The latter are normally married Somali women, who are mostly 'homebound'. This behaviour appears to be motivated by the desire to uphold 'Islamic standards' of women's acceptability, threatened by the entrepreneur's work without a male authority. Women also spoke of intimidation from their ex-husbands in their course of their work, and particularly suffered from their ex-husband's family's attempts to take back/kidnap the children.[28] Many women in the focus groups elaborated on this, with female relatives (of the husband) often involved in the intimidation of the women, and abduction of the children to 'return them to Somalia'. One Somali tea lady was beaten up, and harassed several times over the research period by her ex-husbands' female relatives in an attempt to pressurize her to give up her two young children.[29] According to An-Na'im, (2002: 74), Islamic family law in Somalia considers the husband to 'hold all rights over children born within marriage' and it is thus 'his decision' with whom they will live. This has the effect of divorced women living in constant 'fear and anxiety' for both herself and her children, further adding to a sense of instability ('When you lose [mental] peace, you lose everything…').[30]

In delving deeper into the refugee women's lives and work, it is clear that the various women 'entrepreneurs' have set forth precarious new work norms, although myriad social and economic issues influence the nature and scope of their work. In the starting phases, the women described much courage in initially 'setting up their businesses', with little advice and guidance on how to operate. Engaging in market activities took them beyond the 'safe' realm of the home, and pushed social boundaries, yet without traditional (male) authorization. Women thus not only face business-related constraints such as a lack of relevant skills (marketing, language and literacy), access to micro finance and legal permits, but also 'very serious' cultural issues including the pressures of domestic obligations, and gaining social acceptance and respect from the community.[31] Notably, whilst most NGOs channel support to existing petty traders, some agencies have pursued enterprise development projects with married homebound women (with husbands present in Eastleigh), and stumbled more directly on these underlying social issues ('most married women [that want to work] face the problem of "culture"').[32] On a personal level, refugee women also stated facing extensive and persisting physical and psychological health issues related to war trauma, sexual violence and female circumcision, inhibiting their work. The displacement context has in fact generated new perspectives on circumcision amongst the refugees and even a rejection of the practice (or its more severe forms) for their daughters (Jinnah and Lowe 2015).

Evolving Motivations yet Impeded Development?

In Somali communities in Eastleigh, single women and their families can in fact draw on community charity and remittances for basic survival, although there still remains a high degree of uncertainty in this strategy:

> Somali women can survive on literally nothing as families and clans look out for each other ... They can live alone but eat breakfast in one apartment, lunch in another and dinner in a third ... and someone will also pay the rent of the room.[33]

Endeavouring to go beyond this, female 'entrepreneurs' described their determination to 'start a business' as inherently economically driven to 'support their households', with some emphasizing that single poor women were now generally 'expected' to work to provide for the families.[34] And with men absent, they also felt ultimately compelled to 'take up men's duties' to look after their families. Women further describe 'a sense of wanting to be independent, to do something "for themselves"'.[35] This economic imperative, coupled with a sense of both obligation and the desire for independence, spurs enterprise initiatives, but these usually remain 'survivalist' ventures (Berner, Gomez and Knorringa 2009) amongst the refugees (meeting basic needs), with activities constrained due to local harassment and intimidation. However, those female entrepreneurs that are motivated and able to foster more growth-oriented enterprises face further constraints to formalize/scale-up their business (lack of access to business licence, credit). Interestingly, enterprise in such hostile conditions may also be driven by social motivations in vein with Ritchie (2016a). In Eastleigh, there were a few exceptional growth-oriented entrepreneurs that indeed leant towards social activism, particularly those that led groups, influencing women's business development as well as community processes (see below).

Women Helping Women through New Networks

Aid agencies have emphasized the strength of Somali culture, customs and networks as unique among the various refugee groups in Kenya (this includes the Congolese, Sudanese and Ethiopians).[36] Yet, for some Somali women entrepreneurs in Eastleigh, there appear to be additional emerging – and interesting – socio-cultural trends. Traditionally the women would seek protection from their husbands and male relatives, and through them their clans ('your clan are your people ... they are everything, and look out for you').[37] Whilst direct clan support still remains significant in day-to-day survival and resolving conflicts,[38] the women indicated that male relatives (apart from sons and nephews) have not helped in the establishment of their work. And as mentioned above, ex-husbands in particular have created additional stress, through intimidating the women, and trying to kidnap the children from the marriage, particularly through senior female relatives. Whilst local instability in 2012–2014 led to the establishment of further (male-led) associations in Eastleigh (councils of elders, businessmen), the specific situation for refugee women (extreme poverty and the frequent absence of men) has prompted the crucial proliferation of non-clan based women's groups. This appears to grow out of older traditions of *madax shub* whereby Somali women used to maintain women's associations based on solidarity, and beyond family/kin connections (Bryden and Steiner 1998). In some cases, this may take the form of a regular weekly meeting with around 10 or 15 married women that are linked through friendship, typically held in one of the women's homes. In other cases, it may only take place to celebrate special occasions such as marriage.

Whilst some women's enterprise groups have been deliberately formed by NGOs such as the IRC (notably including a mix of Somali and non-Somali women in Self-help groups), women entrepreneurs in the research elaborated on the locally-led initiation of several Somali women's groups in the past two years.[39] These groups gather together existing and interested women petty traders, and essentially act as solidarity groups. They both troubleshoot business issues and provide critical social support. They also facilitate women's collection schemes (*qaran*) for women starting up business. The *qaran* is a pivotal – and now evolving – Somali practice, whereby people cooperate to collect funds from the community to support households in need (as a donation). The establishment of some of the women's groups has been in part motivated by external support mechanisms by NGOs that are offering micro-grants and BDS/vocational training for 'women entrepreneurs' (particularly in groups).[40] Whilst the grants are limited in size,[41] the women are said to be 'happy' to receive these, with Somali men not interested in such 'low money'.[42] This sheds light on the women's background and motivations: the women are often desperate and just trying to make ends meet. Women are reported to also 'jump' at any chance of training,[43] although it is not always clear if they will do much with it. Perhaps they hope for potential handouts, or simply, more social interaction and support?

As an interesting indicator of the emerging strength and potential impact of some of the groups, women described establishing rules/regulations to guide their new collaboration: 'you must be active, on time, well-behaved, be prepared to raise your head, work together to solve problems'.[44] With a predominant focus on business, groups provide strategic guidance for women working: 'be careful with your working hours, and local gangs. Avoid work as tea ladies as this is really dangerous.'[45] Women described actively encouraging other women to pursue new economic norms, and engage in enterprise as both 'their duty' and 'within

Somali culture': 'all women should work and be empowered, open their eyes and get out of the house, you are born with a strength and it is *halal* (permitted in Islam) … Feel the sweetness of work, think about your future and don't wait for things to happen'.[46] Women emphasized the importance of obtaining 'respect' through model and exemplary work. They also encouraged one another with important social and religious messages: 'everything we do, we have a religious quote and Somali proverb to support it!'[47]

For many of the women, joining these groups was described as the 'best day of their lives'.[48] The groups have encouraged new women to start their businesses with the safety of a network around them. Beyond business, the groups provide a much-needed comfort (after individual war-related traumas), and opportunities to share and exchange life challenges and events, boosting individual confidence and morale: 'I now believe I can do anything … Before many of us were desperate and had suicidal thoughts',[49] and have made them more open and mobile. Single entrepreneurs already in business expressed how both participation in enterprise and now these emerging groups had completely changed their 'way of thinking and being'. These groups have provided important solidarity for the women entrepreneurs, particularly as life in Eastleigh has become more difficult in recent times. And notably, for women's problem solving in the community, the enterprise groups have often been used to replace the male *guurti*: 'without men, women have to become like men'.[50] Local Somali men were aware of some of these new groups, and assumed that they were only NGO-support motivated, and thus did not appreciate their evolving impact. They further bemoaned the fact that NGOs only appeared to support women.

> Before the war, men would solve the problems … now women have to become strong and solve their own problems.[51]

As shown in the research, the women's groups have essentially led to new cooperation between Somali women entrepreneurs, and encouraged the pushing of social boundaries. Many of the groups emphasized how engagement in such groups was now 'vital', and how 'all women entrepreneurs' should participate in these groups to support each other, but also to participate/access potential NGO courses. Yet, beyond the group, some of the stronger groups now also engage in broader community conflict resolution and peace-making, indicating a wider impact on social cohesion and stability. Such emerging women's forums were cited as powerful vehicles for unleashing women's agency in other Somali contexts (such as Puntland and Somaliland) towards greater community strength and harmony, particularly with women's roles as community peacemakers (Dini 2009). Several aid agencies in Nairobi discussed the 'power' of such women's groups to transform the fragile refugee society in Eastleigh, after years of war and trauma, enabling Somali female refugees to collaborate and navigate extreme poverty and local xenophobia. Participation and cooperation in women's groups has also exceptionally galvanized lead entrepreneurs and group heads to campaign for their broader human rights (related to social respect, FGM, political rights) in the local media (e.g. Star FM). These 'social' entrepreneurs, or 'Trailblazers' (Ritchie 2016a) have influenced women's participation in business in their own groups, access to services (courses, bank accounts)[52] and increased women's voice and power. In a context of instability and uncertainty, it is also worth noting that some of the heads of groups were less socially-inclined, particularly beyond the realms of their group, and sought instead to focus on competing with the other groups (particularly around NGO funds) and maximizing their own personal power.

Reflecting on Social Change and Gender in Eastleigh

Economic pressures in the Somali migrant setting of Eastleigh have induced changes in Somali refugee women's social and economic norms, as women engage in new business activities, fostering an alternative, Somali micro-culture. Yet this 'empowerment' remains deliberately linked to a strong abidance of Islam and Islamic practices (Mahmood 2004), and a Muslim identity (Schulz 2013). Despite this religious framing by the women, social acceptance of these new norms remains limited, with little support in the local Somali community for women's new mobility and work. This is arguably due to the absence of any sort of community renegotiation of these new practices (Horne 2001), critical in such (physically) unstable, and (socially) conservative environments (Ritchie 2016a). Nonetheless, with encouragement to form business groups and associations by local NGOs and civil society, Somali women petty traders are setting forth further cultural trends within the resident Somali community through new forms of social cooperation and decision-making, often led by more dominant women micro-entrepreneurs, linked to the ritual of the *guurti*. Resistance and change may be further galvanized through traditions such as poetry, central in Somali culture,[53] in vein with the use of music by women in Swahili coastal communities (Askew 1999). In addition, Somali micro-entrepreneur activists are creating demands for social justice that go beyond their cultural subgroup, with broader impacts on the wider immigrant and Kenyan community (for example, through FGM campaigning on the local radio).

The high degree of female-headed households – alongside the absence of men (who are often working as migrants), and the high numbers of single women (widowed or divorced) – has been a major factor prompting women to seek work. Poor Somali women described the remaining men in the area as often high on 'khat',[54] and becoming 'useless',[55] with now less reliance on male support (and decision-making through the traditional *guurti*). Arguably, women's work engagement in Eastleigh has ultimately led to a distinct 'sub-culture' (or even 'counter-culture'),[56] notably different to mainstream Somalia, the refugee camps and other more Kenyan Somali areas in Nairobi. From the perspective of the broader Somali community, Somali households in Eastleigh are now considered 'non-traditional', with women both as household heads and working. Somalians in Nairobi often differentiate between Somalian women: those that reside in the 'desperate' and insecure situation of Eastleigh, versus those that live in other Somali districts such as South C that are safe and better off. In Eastleigh, women are considered to be poor, mostly divorced and working.[57] Meanwhile, in the more middle class South C, Somali women tend to be wealthier, comfortable and married ('enough wealth for women to be housewives and to focus on having babies...').[58] Yet with wealth, there is more opportunity for family conservativism. This mirrors similar observations in fragile contexts such as Afghanistan (Ritchie 2016a), where middle class urban families tend to impose stricter gender norms on (younger) women and girls, particularly related to work and public life. Adolescent girls in South C are encouraged to attend an Islamic finishing school (sponsored by Arabs), and are not permitted to work on the streets, but may work within formal offices. As a further contrast to Eastleigh and South C, in the refugee camps, Somalis are described as maintaining a particularly conservative and controlling subculture, where the 'men rule' through customary *guurti*-s, and where the women (still) have little power and voice (they may have their own committees but these fall under the men's councils). It is in fact very hard for women to survive in the camps without a 'male protector'.

Further reflecting on social change, this subculture of work in Eastleigh remains tentative, although it has recently gained further strength and momentum through the development of the women's groups, boosting confidence and individual and collective agency, and fostering new forms of cooperation. Whilst most Somalis believe that women can work, this is traditionally only carried out with the authorization of men. Women are expected to seek cooperation with a male figure (husband, brother or father) to gain societal acceptance in all (public) activities to ensure their 'virtue' (although even if gained, a husband may never fully recognize what she does).[59] For the single women entrepreneurs without such authorization, the groups have endeavoured to guide evolving work norms themselves to support 'how they may go about their business' with implicit rules: fulfilling their domestic duties, abiding by Islamic norms, ensuring conservative dress and careful interaction with men, and keeping to work in daylight hours. Amongst the entrepreneurs in Eastleigh, there are observed variations in gender segregation and veiling reflected in dress, mobility and attitude with younger women remaining highly veiled, and the most vulnerable without any form of male protection.

Thus, whilst Somali women refugees often remain proud of their evolving societal roles, and give a positive spin to the desperate situation that has led them to now engage in work (and in some cases, cooperate in groups), 'entrepreneur' women that are divorced or single still face significant social challenges in pursuing new economic norms, as they are viewed negatively and suspiciously by the community (compared to married women).[60] With evolving religious dynamics (particularly Salafism), fundamentalist sheiks in Eastleigh are also preaching that education and empowerment is unnecessary for women,[61] and look on with disapproval at (refugee) women working. Focus groups elaborated further on new religious trends, in the recent proliferation of *madrasas* (Islamic instruction schools) in Eastleigh led by 'closed-minded clerics', where children are segregated and dressed conservatively: 'no-one knows what they are teaching ... ?[62] There seems to be a concern that this might nurture religious radicalization amongst the youth, as well as fundamentalist values. Meanwhile, despite a general lack of male support for (refugee) women's work, some men were equally described to be even jealous of their endeavours (if successful).

Concluding Remarks

Towards a nuanced understanding of Somalian livelihoods in the East African diaspora, and refugee enterprise (Betts et al. 2014), this chapter has examined Somali refugee women's evolving economic lives in Eastleigh, Kenya, and drawn attention to both formal institutional constraints and more complex social trends. Whilst living under strained conditions, Somali refugee women's emerging work practices in petty trading have led to women's economic empowerment, with social ripple effects into the broader Kenyan community. Yet these new practices remain vulnerable, with such women living on the 'fringes' of a dynamic but fragile society,[63] where both Kenyan law and order, and local Somali cultural acceptance remain uncertain. The latter may be particularly linked to changing religious beliefs, with women forced to negotiate the 'imported fundamentalist Islamic doctrine' of Salafism (Bryden and Steiner 1998) that continues to challenge Somali culture at home and abroad (Abdi 2007, 2015). Salafist ideas tend to promote gender segregation; and despite the claim that there is space for politically and economically active women (Mahmood 2004), this is arguably within rigid Islamic framed constraints. This often more austere, aggressive brand of Islam competes with the traditional, moderate and (mostly) peaceful Sufi Islam (Jansen, Wandera and Peter 2013).[64] And while 'Sufi' Islam may still be conservative, and reinforce gender hierarchies, its ideals remain more fluid and less radical.

The present dominance of Salafist Islamic beliefs – with a less flexible societal narrative, and stricter norms and values – in a volatile environment threatens the sustainability of Somali refugee women's work as petty traders. This jeopardizes the women's evolving economic practices and gains as 'entrepreneurs', as well as their future more inclusive economic engagement (e.g. access to services such as training courses and banking). However, refugee women's emerging social structures in the form of enterprise groups may strengthen support for evolving norms, in addition to charismatic women leaders' socio-political initiatives, as broader community peacemakers (Dini 2009) and activists.

It is useful to reflect on the research findings and refugee women's empowerment in fragile and uncertain social settings, particularly with broader gender dynamics, and pressures on refugee men (Ritchie 2018). Indicators of expanding women's agency may relate to 'women's sense of self-worth and social identity; their willingness and ability to question their subordinate status and identity; [and] their capacity to exercise strategic control over their own lives' (Kabeer 2008: 27). In addition to women's recognition of their own individual power, traditional feminists and recent empowerment researchers have highlighted the importance of women's active collaboration in promoting pathways of empowerment (Cornwall 2016) at both a local level and through their influence on laws and policies that can promote gender equality. In hostile displacement contexts, such cooperation between women can enable critical solidarity and bolster support for refugee women's new socio-economic practices, as well as provide a platform for women's individual and collective action.

As Somalis continue to 'redefine' themselves (Bryden and Steiner 1998), and garner collective strength from their local and global networks (Carrier and Lochery 2013), Eastleigh may begin to gradually stabilize, creating a new trust within and beyond the community, as well as a support for evolving gender roles and relations. To this end, Somali refugee women entrepreneurs and leaders may present both instrumental allies for local integration, and a broader force for social change (DeHart 2010).

Holly A. Ritchie's research focuses on institutional change in enterprise and value chain development, gender and links to human security in fragile environments. Her PhD from the Erasmus University, Rotterdam (The Netherlands), examined institutional transformation and construction in women's enterprise development in Afghanistan, and its implications for broader economic development.

Notes

An earlier version of this chapter first appeared as a research paper (Ritchie 2014).

1. Human security may be understood in terms of 'creating structures and enabling environments that provide building blocks for survival, dignity and resilient livelihoods' (Christoplos and Hilhorst 2009).
2. This includes areas where the state is weak, unwilling or absent, influencing local security and the provision of basic services (Rijper 2013).
3. Respondents included refugee enterprise women, their friends and neighbours, key community and business representatives, researchers and representatives of NGOs and the UNHCR.

4. An exploratory approach that takes a special focus on examining social phenomena, with 'reality' assessed through a broad range of methods and sources.
5. Informal written comments from a researcher on Somalia, Peter Chonka, Nairobi 2014.
6. This is the name given to Somalis that have spent time in Arab countries and return mirroring Arabian styles and religious conservatism.
7. In the research, Somalis described Saudis treating them 'like animals' (Interview with Somali resident, South C Nairobi, February 2014).
8. Informal written comments from a researcher on Somalia, Peter Chonka, Nairobi 2014.
9. It is worth noting that there are ethnic Somalis in both Kenya (Northern Kenya) and Ethiopia (Eastern and Southern Ethiopia) that tend to have mixed identities and potential loyalties.
10. Menkaus (2002) draws particular attention to the Islamic militarism of the Ogaden clan that reside on the borderlands in northern Kenya and eastern Ethiopia.
11. This relates to 'all procedures that involve partial or total removal of the external female genitalia, or other injury to the female genital organs for non-medical reasons' (WHO online, retrieved 19 May 2014 from http://www.who.int/mediacentre/factsheets/fs241/en/).
12. 'My sisters were born free [in Kenya], but have lost their rights and freedom, particularly when they married Somali[born] men', Interview with Kenyan Somali, 28 January.
13. Interview with Kenyan Somali, 28 January.
14. The Kenyan Somali MP Yusuf Hassan has been an active campaigner for Somali causes in recent years (including Somali refugees), but was then injured in the Eastleigh mosque bombing in mid-2013, reducing his public work.
15. This was reiterated several times by different respondents during the course of the research.
16. In some cases Somali women work, and even support men elsewhere, and are described locally as 'sugar mums' (Interview with Somali housewife in Eastleigh, 5 February 2014).
17. Interview with Somali housewife, Eastleigh.
18. This relates to the city council 'charge' for a market stall (with UNCHR documents).
19. Interview with female entrepreneur (case study 1), February 2014.
20. Female tea lady, Garissa Lodge, February 2014.
21. Interview with Kenyan Somali woman, 28 January 2014.
22. This usually pertains to a young male relative from the entrepreneur's paternal family.
23. Interview with female entrepreneur (case study 2), February 2014.
24. Women entrepreneurs' Focus Group 2, 11 February 2014.
25. A highly successful concept developed in rural India, Self Help Groups (SHGs) are a model employed by NGOs to organize people with similar wealth backgrounds into groups (approximately 15–20 members per group) to engage in saving and lending activities, and then to initiate/expand economic activities and enterprise. This concept is closely associated to revolving savings and credit groups in Kenya, common in urban areas in recent years.
26. Group interview with selected case-study entrepreneurs, Eastleigh, 13 February 2014.
27. 'Eastleigh's Youth Gangs – Super Power Gang', *Radio Africa*, 29 July 2013. Retrieved 26 April 2016 from https://www.youtube.com/watch?v=Hm1LvSt6jVA.
28. Interview with female entrepreneur, Garissa Lodge, February 2014.
29. Interview with female entrepreneur (case study 3), February 2014.
30. Ibid.
31. Interview with Eastleigh women's business consultant (for NGOs)/University lecturer, 7 February 2014.

32. Women entrepreneurs Focus Group 1, 11 February 2014.
33. Refugee Consortium Kenya (RCK) interview January 2016.
34. Women entrepreneurs Focus Group 2, 11 February 2014.
35. RCK interview, 7 February 2014.
36. RCK interview, 7 February 2014.
37. Interview with entrepreneur case study 3, January 2014. For married women, the clan tends to relate to their husband's clan. For single and divorced women, the clan is usually their birth clan, with support given by their brothers and direct relatives.
38. Particularly if women belong to the dominant Somali tribes such as the Darood, Isaaq or Hawiye.
39. There were at least 4–5 women's groups identified in the research, with 20–30 members each.
40. This includes organizations such as JRS, Heshima Kenya, RCK, and IRC.
41. Such grants were usually less than USD 500.
42. Interview with UNHCR officer, 28 January 2014.
43. In the research, women seemed to attend several different types of available business training.
44. Interview with female entrepreneur (case study 1). She was the head of the Women's Association 'Single Mother Group', Eastleigh.
45. Women's Association *Kolmere*, Eastleigh.
46. Women entrepreneurs Focus Group, 30 January 2014.
47. Group interview with selected entrepreneur (case studies), 13 February 2014. Proverbs included: 'Before a flood reaches you, create a barrier' (i.e. protect yourself before it is too late), and 'a camel follows a camel' (i.e. you should ensure model behaviour for all).
48. Women entrepreneurs, Focus Group, 30 January 2014.
49. Entrepreneur from Focus Group 2, 11 February 2014.
50. Interview with Somali housewife, Eastleigh, 7 February 2014. It is now not uncommon to find groups of (family) women living together, with men absent as migrant workers.
51. Women entrepreneurs, Focus Group, 30 January 2014.
52. Yet whilst many of the women have now become interested in opening bank accounts, this has been constrained by their lack of legal documentation.
53. *Somali Heritage Week Kicks off in Nairobi Daily Nation*, 18 November 2015. Retrieved February 2016 from https://www.youtube.com/watch?v=1tVatk_9BFg.
54. Narcotic stimulant leaf.
55. Interview with Kenyan Somali, 28 January 2014.
56. UNHCR interview, 28 January 2014.
57. Interview with Kenyan Somali, 28 January 2014.
58. Interview with Kenyan Somali, 28 January 2014.
59. Interview with Somali media specialist, Nairobi, January 2014.
60. Women entrepreneurs Focus Group 2, 11 February 2014.
61. Interview with female community activist in Eastleigh, February 2014.
62. Men's Focus Group, Eastleigh, February 2014.
63. Interview with local researcher, Rosalind Raddatz, 11 February 2014.
64. The revolt of Mohammed Abdullah Hassan, known as the 'Mad Mullah', demonstrated the capacity for conflict within Sufi ideology.

References

Abdi, C. 2007. 'Convergence of Civil War and the Religious Right: Re-Imagining Somali Women', *Signs: Journal of Women in Culture and Society* 33(1): 183–207.

———. 2015. *Elusive Jannah: The Somali Diaspora and a Borderless Muslim Identity*. Minneapolis: University of Minnesota Press.

Anderson, D.M., et al. 2007. *The Khat Controversy: Stimulating the Debate on Drugs*. Oxford: Berg.

An-Na'im, A. 2002. *Islamic Family Law in a Changing World: A Global Resource Book*. London: Zed Books.

Askew, K.M. 1999. 'Female Circles and Male Lines: Gender Dynamics along the Swahili Coast', *Africa Coast* 46(3–4): 67–102.

Berner, E., G. Gomez and P. Knorringa. 2009. *Helping a Large Number of People Become a Little Less Poor*. The Hague: ISS.

Berns McGown, R. 1999. *Muslims in the Diaspora: The Somali Communities of London and Toronto*. Toronto: University of Toronto.

Betts, A. 2013. 'Put Innovation at the Heart of Refugee Protection Work', Global Development Professional Network. *The Guardian*. Retrieved 1 May 2016 from http://www.theguardian.com/global-development-professionals-network/2013/jan/04/refugees-camp-innovation-creativity.

Betts, A., L. Bloom, J. Kaplan, J. and N. Omata. 2014. *Refugee Economies: Rethinking Popular Assumptions*. Oxford: University of Oxford: Refugee Studies Centre, Oxford Department of International Development.

Bille, A. 2013. 'Doing Business Amidst Constraints: A Case Study of Somali Refugee Women Entrepreneurs in Eastleigh Area', MA thesis. Nairobi: University of Nairobi.

Bryden, M., and M. Steiner. 1998. *Somalia Between Peace and War: Somali Women on the Eve of the 21st Century*. Nairobi: United Nations Development Fund for Women (UNIFEM).

Brun, C. 2001. 'Territorializing the Relationship between People and Place in Refugee Studies', *Geografiska Annaler Series B, Human Geography* 83(1): 15–25.

Carrier, N., and E. Lochery. 2013. 'Missing States? Somali Trade Networks and the Eastleigh Transformation', *Journal of Eastern African Studies* 7(2): 334–52. http://dx.doi.org/10.1080/17531055.2013.776275.

Christoplos, I., and D. Hilhorst. 2009. *Human Security and Capacity in Fragile States*. Netherlands: Wageningen University.

Cornwall, A. 2016. 'Women's Empowerment: What Works?', *Journal of International Development* 28(3): 342–59.

Crisp, J. 2002. 'No Solutions in Sight: The Problem of Protracted Refugee Situations in Africa', The Center for Comparative Immigration Studies University of California, San Diego, *Working Paper 68*. San Diego: University of California.

DeHart, M. 2010. *Ethnic Entrepreneurs: Identity and Development Politics in Latin America*. Stanford: Stanford University Press.

De Voe, P.A. 2002. 'Symbolic Action: Religion's Role in the Changing Environment of Young Somali Women', *Journal of Refugee Studies* 15: 234–46.

Dini, S. 2009. 'Women Building Peace: Somali Women in Puntland and Somaliland', *ACCORD Conflict Trends* 2: 31–37.

DRC and UNHCR 2012. *Promoting Livelihoods to Build the Self-Reliance of Urban Refugees in Nairobi*. Nairobi: United Nations High Commissioner for Refugees and the Danish Refugee Council.

Griffiths, D. 2002. *Somali and Kurdish Refugees in London: New Identities in the Diaspora*. Burlington, VT: Ashgate.

Harriss-White, B. 2010. 'Work and Well-Being in Informal Economies: The Regulative Roles of Institutions of Identity and the State', *World Development* 38(2): 170–83.

Horne, C. 2001. 'Sociological Perspectives on the Emergence of Norms' in M. Hechter and K. Opp (eds), *Social Norms*. New York: Russell Sage Foundation, pp. 3–34.

Jacobsen, A. 2011. 'Making Moral Worlds: Individual and Social Processes of Meaning-Making in a Somali Diaspora', Ph.D. dissertation. Washington, DC: Washington University.

Jacobsen, K. 2002. 'Livelihoods in Conflict: The Pursuit of Livelihoods by Refugees and the Impact on the Human Security of Host Communities', *International Migration* 40(2): 95–123.

Jansen, W., J. Wandera and C. Peter (eds). 2013. *Mapping Eastleigh for Christian-Muslim Relations*. Limuru, Kenya: Zapf Chancery Publishers Africa Ltd.

Jinnah, Z., and L. Lowe. 2015. 'Circumcising Circumcision: Renegotiating Beliefs and Practices among Somali Women in Johannesburg and Nairobi', *Medical Anthropology* 34(4): 371–88. http://dx.doi.org/10.1080/01459740.2015.1045140.

Kabeer, N. 2008. 'Paid Work, Women's Empowerment and Gender Justice: Critical Pathways of Social Change', *Pathways Working Paper* 3. Brighton: IDS.

Kandiyoti, D. 1991. *Women, Islam and the State*. Philadelphia: Temple University Press.

Kapteijns, L. 1995. 'Gender Relations and Transformation of the Northern Somali Pastoral Tradition', *International Journal of African Historical Studies* 28(2): 241–59.

Kleist, N. 2010. 'Negotiating Respectable Masculinity: Gender and Recognition in the Somali Diaspora', *African Diaspora* 3: 185–206.

Lambo, I. 2012. 'In the Shelter of Each Other: Notions of Home and Belonging amongst Somali Refugees in Nairobi', *New Issues in Refugee Research, Research Paper* No. 233. Geneva: UNHCR.

Lawson, T. 1997. 'Realism, Explanation and Science', in T. Lawson (ed.), *Economics and Reality*. London: Routledge, pp. 15–26.

Marchal, R. 2007. 'Warlordism and Terrorism: How to Obscure an Already Confusing Crisis? The Case of Somalia', *International Affairs* 83(6): 1091–1106.

Mahmood, S. 2004. *Politics of Piety*. Princeton: Princeton University Press.

Menkhaus, K. 2002. 'Political Islam in Somalia', *Middle East Policy* 9(1): 109–23.

Murray, K. 2000. 'Shar'ia Is the Only Rule of Law in Somalia', *Reuters News Service*. 13 October.

Naude, W. 2007. 'Peace, Prosperity and Pro-Growth Entrepreneurship', *UNU WIDER Discussion Paper* No. 02. Helsinki: UNU-WIDER.

Pavanello, S., S. Elhawary and S. Pantuliano. 2010. 'Hidden and Exposed: Urban Refugees in Nairobi, Kenya', HPG Working Paper.

Raddatz, R. 2013. *The Moved and the Shaken: How Forced Relocation Affects the Lives of Urban Refugee Women and Girls*. Nairobi: Heshima Kenya.

Refugee Consortium Kenya (RCK). 2008. *Self-Settled Refugees in Nairobi: A Close Look at Their Coping Strategies*. Nairobi: RCK.

Rijper, A. 2013. *Fragile States or Hybrid Societies: Engaging in Fragile Settings*. NL: The Broker, retrieved on 1 April 2014 from http://www.thebrokeronline.eu/Articles/Fragile-states-or-hybrid-societies.

Ritchie, H.A. 2018. 'Gender and Enterprise in Fragile Refugee Settings: Female Empowerment amidst Male Emasculation – a Challenge to Local Integration?', *Disasters*, 42(S1): S40-S60.

———. 2016a. *Institutional Innovation and Change in Value Chain Development: Negotiating Tradition, Power and Fragility in Afghanistan*. London: Routledge.

———. 2016b. 'Unwrapping Institutional Change in Fragile Settings: Women Entrepreneurs Driving Institutional Pathways in Afghanistan', *World Development* 83: 39–53.

———. 2014. 'Rethinking "Entrepreneurship" in Fragile Environments: Lessons Learnt in Somali Women's Enterprise, Human Security and Inclusion', *Occasional Paper* 9. Wageningen University, IS Academy.

Schulz, D. 2012. 'Dis/Embodying Authority: Female Radio 'Preachers' and the Ambivalences of Mass-Mediated Speech in Mali', *International Journal of Middle East Studies* 44: 23–43.

———. 2013. '(En)Gendering Muslim Self-Assertiveness: Muslim Schooling and Female Elite Formation in Uganda', *Journal of Religion in Africa* 43: 396–425.

Steer, L., and K. Sen. 2010. 'Formal and Informal Institutions in a Transition Economy: The Case of Vietnam', *World Development* 38(11): 1603–15.

The World Bank. 2013. *Inclusion Matters, New Frontiers of Social Policy*. Washington, DC: The International Bank for Reconstruction and Development.

Chapter 7
Reinventing Retail
'Somali' Shopping Centres in Kenya
Tabea Scharrer

Introduction

When I was in Kenya for the first time in 2004 I followed a Kikuyu friend to her mother's 'shop' – a table in a big room on the ground floor that had been the original store, sharing the space with at least eight other tables. All of the 'shop owners' sold more or less the same goods, clothes coming from Dubai. These shops inside a shop seemed to be something in-between an open-air market or street trading and a European style shop. While trying to trace the beginnings, the driving forces, the actors, the models, the different steps and the diffusion of these spatial innovations I encountered oblivion. Nurrudin Farah wrote something similar about the history of the Tamarind market in Mogadishu: 'try as you might to trace things to their origins, you will find that nobody has the slightest idea … in a city with … a memory far more complex than the lives of the peoples currently residing in it' (Farah 2010: 10).

What seems to be clear is that these spatial transformations were not only a development following a vision but also a necessity. Three parallel processes led to this change: the liberalization of the business sector, urbanization processes and the migration of business people from Somalia to Kenyan cities as refugees. Coming mainly from Mogadishu with hardly more than their knowledge on how to do business, they constituted an important element for the transformation of the trading sector by a reconfiguration of the way space is used for business. Hotel rooms became shops during daytime, bigger shops were subdivided into smaller stalls and later on shopping centres were built, where every inch is made useful. The best example of this reconfiguration of space is the now famous 'Somali' neighbourhood Eastleigh (Nairobi). It was taken up as a model quickly and similar developments took place in other urban centres in Kenya. The change of usage of business space by the subdivision or compartmentalization of shops also contributed to a change in the rules of how trade is done. Locally it is even argued that it allowed more people to participate in the economy by 'democratizing' trade.

The economic activities linked to the 'Somali' shopping centres are set within the structures of what can be described as urban informal economies. Even though the term 'informal' has been criticized frequently, it is nonetheless used here to designate economic activities taking place to a large extent invisible to and unregulated by the state bureaucracy and which are characterized by a high degree of uncertainty and unpredictability (see Hart 2010). Somali traders have established themselves in what is now Kenya from pre-colonial times onwards (see the chapter by Whittaker in this volume, but also Kitching 1980). They were mostly active in smaller scale trading activities, such as shopkeeping (including butcheries) and the livestock trade. Also in Somalia, trading networks linking the urban centres, the Indian Ocean and the hinterland have long operated (Reese 1996). Like many other African countries, Kenya and Somalia experienced an informalization of their business sectors in the 1980s and 1990s, driven by economic decline and liberalization policies (for Africa in general see Meagher and Lindell 2013, for Kenya Foeken and Owuor 2001 and for Somalia Mubarak 1997). In the case of Somalia this development was reinforced by the breakdown of the central state in 1991 (see for instance Little 2005).

This chapter will first summarize the developments in Eastleigh that were the starting point for the transformation of the retail sector, and which serve as a distinctive prototype (or model) for the changes taking place in other Kenyan cities. In the second part of the chapter I will present the example of 'Somali' shopping centres in Nakuru,[1] a city about two hours from Nairobi. Even though it is the fourth biggest city in Kenya, it is one of the largely understudied second-tier urban areas. How these shopping centres were set up and how the traders working in them operate will be shown. The following section will focus on the reconfiguration of space and how this affects the way business is done. It will compare the shopping centres with (often informal) open-air markets and European or North American style shopping malls, showing that they share some features with each of these two retail structures. Finally, two questions will be discussed. Firstly, it will be argued that while these developments are mainly attributed to the presence of Somali refugees in the country since the beginning of the 1990s, this conception does not comprehend the complexities of reality. However, in a changing economic structure they played a pivotal role in establishing a new model for retail trade. Secondly it will be asked if the new way of using retail space is really part of a process that leads to a 'democratization' or 'demystification' of business, a term coined by a Kenyan colleague. The material used is based on standardized interviews in Somali shopping centres in Nakuru, as well as lengthy anthropological fieldwork in Nakuru and Eastleigh from 2010 onwards.

Eastleigh – A Distinctive Prototype for the Reconfiguration of Space

Beside other factors, including the opening up of the Kenyan economy, the rise of Dubai and China as new centres of trade, and the increased elevation of Kikuyu and Kalenjin to Kenya's business elite, the activities of successful Somali businessmen, be they from Somalia or from Kenya, changed the economic landscape of Kenya tremendously. Centre stage in this change was Eastleigh. This quarter of Nairobi had some very distinctive characteristics that made it fertile ground for Somali business. On the one hand its infrastructure was comparably well developed in contrast to other areas in the city. Even though it had deteriorated over time, its colonial spatial outline was rather generous, making it easier to modify and develop the existing building structure, adjusting it to the needs of the growing business community. And even though its transport infrastructure had been dilapidated, Eastleigh was still well connected to important trading routes. On the other hand it was a cosmopolitan area, with a high number of Somali inhabitants, which provided the base for its becoming a refuge for Somalian forced migrants from the beginning of the 1990s onwards. Often without having the right papers, they could hide among all the other migrants that came to this part of the town, providing safety in numbers.

At this time Eastleigh became a 'city in a city' in several aspects. First of all as a refuge, Eastleigh soon became a crowded place, where rents were rising, as so many people looked for a place to stay. Space became a valuable good. In this context low storey buildings were demolished and multi-storey houses built. Eastleigh is of course only one example of the global phenomenon of urbanization and the developments observed here resemble those underway in other places where density changed the pattern of the usage of space, like Hong Kong, Japan or newly-built Chinese cities.

Economically Eastleigh developed into a kind of unofficial 'special economic area', where more and more goods and money were turned over. Already in the late 1970s Eastleigh was known as a place where you could get anything.[2] Since the early 1990s, Eastleigh had become crowded not only with migrants, but also with mushrooming businesses. With the economic success that was achieved 'casually in the absence of any formal security arrangements', insecurity heightened (ibid.). When the infrastructural situation became worse due to the rise in the population, Eastleigh even became a kind of semi-autonomous space in matters of urban administration, run in part by its well-organized Eastleigh Business District Association. In 2010 the High Court ruled that Kenya's

160 *Tabea Scharrer*

Figure 7.1 Construction work does not prevent trade (Eastleigh, Second Avenue) (photo: T. Scharrer).

Nairobi City Council should not collect council permits from the more than 3,000 traders in Eastleigh for failing to offer requisite services (Abdikarim 2010). Only a year later the City Council promised to invest heavily in Eastleigh's infrastructure, resulting for instance in repair works on the 'Eastleigh Second Avenue' beginning in 2011.

Garissa Lodge and the Founding Myth of Eastleigh

How much the economic changes taking place in Eastleigh were linked to spatial reconfigurations becomes clear when looking at the founding myth of Eastleigh – the rise of the Garissa Lodge shopping centre. During its earlier days in the 1980s Garissa Lodge was a small hotel. At the end of the 1980s/beginning of the 1990s the hotel was used by Somali traders, among them Benadiris from long established trading families from Mogadishu. They made popular an already existing, but at that time rather clandestinely used, business model by turning the hotel rooms during daytime to shops, while still sleeping in them at night (Carrier and Lochery 2013: 336–7). Most of the merchants had neither the requisite papers nor other facilities to set up businesses. But they brought with them the knowledge of how to run a successful trade, the money to invest in goods and the networks to acquire commodities to sell. In 1992 a Kenyan Somali businesswoman bought the building, kept the old name but turned over the rooms into business stalls, 92 inside and 92 surrounding the outside of the mall (ibid.: 337). That is how the first shopping centre in Eastleigh was born. The second one was opened already in 1993 and in 2012 there were about forty shopping centres in Eastleigh, very fancy new ones as well as some already looking run-down. In addition there are uncountable street side stalls, giving the centre of Eastleigh, between the First and the Second Avenue, the feel of a huge open-air market. Adding to the modification in the trading sector there are numerous banks that now have a branch in the neighbourhood, as well as shining hotels like the Grand Royal that came up in the last decade. There is also an expansion of residential apartments, contributing to the tremendous change of the urban landscape in Eastleigh.

Soon it became both a prototype for doing business and for the reconfiguration of urban space. On the one hand, a similar destruction of old buildings and the creation of new residential buildings (often for Somali refugees) took place in other cities, for instance in Mombasa's old town. The new houses use every inch of space, often obstructing old passageways, which leads some people of Mombasa to moan about the loss of 'their' town (Karama and Kitito 2011). On the other hand, all over Kenya 'Somali' shopping centres were built similar to the ones in Eastleigh, for instance in Nakuru, which will be discussed in detail in the next section. The same spatial logic also featured in non-Somali exhibition centres, such as Freemark limited (registered in Nairobi in 1994),[3] which started by subdividing the plenary hall at the Kenyatta International Conference Centre (KICC) 'into open-plan stalls of as little as a table of four feet by two feet'.[4]

Somali Shopping Centres in Nakuru

Nakuru, the fourth biggest city in Kenya, was coined the 'fastest growing town in Africa' some years ago, its number of inhabitants rising from less than 200,000 in 1995 to over 300,000 in 2010. As a regional centre positioned along the main Kenyan trading route it is economically vibrant and has a well-developed infrastructure. These features make the town attractive for many different groups of migrants. Quite a lot of them have no chance to work in the public sector or the bigger companies in Nakuru and therefore try to set up their own businesses.

The Shopping Centres

Before talking more about the traders, I would like to take the reader on a small tour through the different 'Somali' shopping centres in Nakuru, all of them located in the middle of town, in very close vicinity to the Jamia mosque. The Al-Mujtahid Shopping Centre,[5] which was opened in 1995, is the oldest one in Nakuru. It is situated in a run-down two-storey building from the 1970s, which belongs to an Arab family. This family has lived in the town for more than 50 years. After seeing what happened in Eastleigh and through the initiative of a Kenyan Somali who had lived in Nakuru for a couple of years they leased the building, which served before as a lodge, to a Garre man from Nairobi,[6] who gave it the name 'Al Mujtahid'. This man himself owns a big electronics shop on the ground floor. This shop is the only sign for what is happening in the building. To reach the other shops one has to enter the building through a small open entrance and go up a narrow, uninviting staircase. In the two upper floors there are 42 shops. The owner is leasing the building for 5 years and pays about USD 1,400 a month.[7] The shops cost on average about USD 75 each in rent in the same period, adding to USD 1,750 after the deduction of costs. That means that both men earn a substantial amount of money just by leasing the shopping space.[8] In the upper floor of Al-Mujtahid, where the rents are a bit cheaper, all the traders are women who sell clothes, shoes and handbags. Only two of the women are Somali, one from northeastern Kenya and one from Somalia. The latter already came in the 1970s to Kenya, because she married a Kenyan Somali in Nairobi. Most of the other women are Kikuyu traders. The shops on this floor are quite dark and crammed.

In the middle floor most of the traders are Garre men from Kenya (a few of them are from Somalia), many of them belong to the extended family of the owner. While most of them also trade in clothes (mainly suits and other clothes for men), there are also a few electronics shops on this level (on the goods sold by Somali businesspeople see the chapter by Carrier and Elliot, this volume). The shops here are bigger and lighter and the products are displayed in a very neat and ordered way.

In the next couple of years more Somali shopping centres were opened including the Mandera Shopping Centre (1997) just around the corner of the

Figure 7.2 Upper floor in Al-Mujtahid Shopping Centre, Nakuru (photo: T. Scharrer).

'Al-Mujtahid', the Old Garissa Shopping Centre (1998) on the same road and the old Dubai Shopping Centre (2000). All three are operated by Kenyan Somalis. The buildings are single-storey and consist of long corridors from which the shops can be entered. In the first stalls after entering the building, which are rather big, mainly textiles are sold. These shops are followed by others where clothing and bags can be bought. Men run most of the shops, but there are also a few female traders in the building. In the back of the building there are non-Somali tailors who produce clothes from the material that can be bought closer to the entrance. One branch of the *hawala* company Dahabshiil also operates from one of these buildings.⁹ The stalls are bigger than in the Al-Mujtahid Shopping Centre and also more expensive. For instance, in the Old Garissa Shopping Centre stalls cost between USD 90 and USD 115 in 2012. Two years later the rents had already risen to USD 100 to USD 130. In two cases the physical structure belongs to an Arab family, and the buildings are leased by the founders of the shopping centres. The connection between the Arab owners of the structure and the Somali leasers are purely business – beyond these concrete business partnerships they are rather competitors. In 2000 the owner of the Mandera Shopping Centre opened another one in the same area. The small shops are arranged in a way which gives the building a maze-like feel. Contrary to the other shopping centres most of the traders in this building are not Somali.

The Dubai Shopping Centre, which was opened in 2010, is the first one in Nakuru that was actually built as a shopping centre, following a basic version of a European or North American style mall. The building itself belongs to a Kikuyu who leased the structure to a Garre family for thirty years. This family of five brothers, one of whom was the mayor of Nakuru between 2011 and 2013, transferred the lease to the same Arab family who owns the al-Fatah building (reportedly for 90 million KSh/ around USD 1 million)¹⁰ in 2013. Most of the traders working in this building are again Garre but there are other shop owners as well, many Somali but also a number of non-Somali traders. The main items sold are again shoes, clothes and handbags, as well as perfumes and other commodities. This three-storey building accommodates not only shops, but also a few NGOs, for instance the Nakuru Islamic Propagation centre. In the first year the Dubai shopping centre resembled a basic, yet compared to the surrounding buildings conspicuous, version of a North American mall. The shops were spacious and the building had a touch of luxury, even though already at this time only local traders were running the shops inside and there were no branches of large chain stores in this building. But already by the second year the shops were cut into several smaller shops and outside shops came into existence, at the ground level surrounding the building and also inside using the aisles. While the rents for the normal shops were a bit higher than in the other shopping centres, an aisle shop only cost about USD 30. The revenue reported was however considerably smaller than for a normal shop.

And the Traders

The case study of Nakuru shows that in some of the 'Somali' shopping centres the majority of traders fall under the category of Somali, but that this is not always the case. Altogether around forty traders were interviewed in 2012, thirty of them having their shops inside one of three different Somali shopping centres. There were also some interviews done with traders who have small stalls not

Figure 7.3 The Dubai Shopping Centre in Nakuru (photo: T. Scharrer).

within one of these facilities, but outside the mosque area, to have a comparative view on different modes of (small) retail businesses. However, as my research focused on Somali migrants,[11] I interviewed only a small number of non-Somali traders. The results of the research can therefore not be transferred to other groups of traders without further investigation.

Among the Somali traders in Nakuru, most came from the northeastern part of Kenya, which corresponds to the composition of the Somali community in

Nakuru. While among the Garre traders the overwhelming majority were men, in the group of the other Somali traders women and men were equally represented. Most of the traders, Somali and non-Somali alike, were between the ages of 25–45. The majority of the traders work on their own, only a few employing one other person. The employed person was either a member of the family, or in two cases a person from the same religious community. Likewise most traders operate only one shop, although a few have a second shop either in Nakuru or elsewhere in Kenya.

The majority of the traders I talked to indicated a monthly revenue or turnover fluctuating between about USD 175 and about USD 375,[12] a few earning much more and a few much less. The revenue seems to be almost the same, no matter if the trader rents a big or small shop. Although the shops do not cost that much, there are a number of other expenses. The license for a small shop, for instance, costs about USD 50 a month. Additionally, of course, the traders have to buy their stock. To buy a complete set of shoes with all sizes and designs will cost more than USD 3,000. That means that the actual income of the trader, taking the numbers given above, is only between USD 30 and USD 230 a month. To provide for a whole family with this income is difficult. It does work when the business season is good, but it becomes problematic in times of uncertainty, whether these be times with less customers or when the trader is not able to attend to their shop (for instance due to illness).

Comparison to Nakuru Street Traders

Even though there is now a large number of traders operating in one of the newly founded shopping centres, there are still many traders having a small stall outside on the street. In a report published by 'Women in Informal Employment: Globalizing and Organizing (WIEGO)' (Lubaale and Nyangoro 2013), the number of informal street traders in the Nakuru municipality in 2012 was estimated to be more than 10,000. Eighty per cent of them were located in the Central Business District, where the Somali shopping centres are also situated.[13] There the largest population of potential buyers is to be found, people who pass through the town as well as people who come directly for shopping from the outskirts of the city or the surrounding regions. For the street vendors the main business site is the bus stage, followed by the main streets of Nakuru (Lubaale and Nyangoro 2013: 6). For over ninety per cent of men and almost seventy-four per cent of women interviewed for the report, their business was the main source of household income.

The traders reported a monthly turnover (total value of sales, without taking into account the total costs of running the business) comparable to those in the Somali shopping centres: between 20,000 KSh. and 30,000 KSh. inside the stage and 40,000 KSh. to 50,000 KSh. outside the stage (Lubaale and Nyangoro 2013: 34). This finding corresponds to statements by traders in the Somali shopping centres, when they were asked about the different income opportunities of their businesses compared with those of the street traders.[14] That means that street traders might have even better chances of profit compared to people working in the Somali shopping centres, as they have a comparable turnover, but fewer overhead costs (shops inside the shopping centres cost about 15 to 20 times more). Yet one woman selling perfume from a street stall in the middle of the city told me that her main aim is to get enough money to build up her business inside one of the shopping centres. The question of why people opt to work in the Somali shopping centres despite the at times lower chances for profit will be discussed at the end of the chapter.

Links to Eastleigh
Eastleigh is central for almost all of the traders in Nakuru, as most of them go there to buy their goods. Only one of the interviewed traders reported going to Dubai directly and selling in bulk himself. Eastleigh therefore functions as a huge outdoor and indoor distribution centre. The goods imported into Kenya are sold from here to traders hailing from all over Kenya, most of them non-Somali.[15] The main goods resold to traders outside of Eastleigh are clothing, shoes, textiles, perfumes, watches, spices, electronics, carpets, foodstuffs, cellphones, *abaya* veils and other religious articles. As mentioned earlier, the products are not only imported from Dubai, China or Indonesia, but also Turkey, whose higher quality goods hold much appeal for those who can afford them. Not all products only transit through Eastleigh; some of them are also produced there. Like the tailors in the back of the Garissa shopping centre in Nakuru, the artisans working in Eastleigh are in most cases non-Somali. While for a long time it was possible to get almost all goods in each of the shopping centres, now they are more specialized. The traders from Nakuru often have one or two permanent middlemen in Eastleigh, where they always buy their goods. Some of them go to Eastleigh every week; others wait until their seller calls them and tells them that new goods have arrived. Others travel there once a month to buy the goods they expect to sell during that time.

Spatiality and Business

Lacking the glamour of 'Western' shopping malls the 'Somali' shopping centres have one or more floors with traders either renting a shop, a table in a shop, or a place outside a shop. While open-air markets are open, public places these 'new' kinds of shops are privately owned, often with a rather long chain of brokers, owners, leasers and subleasers. In these new 'exhibitions' or 'shopping centres' mainly cheap textiles, leather and electronics, imported from Dubai, Turkey, Thailand, Indonesia and China, are sold.

The spatial innovations under consideration here concern three new ways of utilizing pre-existing structures. In the shopping centres all three different modes of building up shops can be found:

1) Firstly there are shops inside a shop. As in the example given at the beginning of this chapter, a shop of a 'normal' size is sublet to several traders; each of whom has a table which functions as their own shop. Often all the merchants sell the same kind of goods. Sometimes a shop is subdivided by building up very thin walls, retaining the idea of a 'real' shop – this was done in the Dubai Shopping Centre. Kinyanjui describes a similar development of subdividing shops in the Taveta Road in Nairobi that started in the late 1990s. (Kinyanjui 2014: 89–90)
2) Secondly there are shops outside of shops. Street vendors build up their business directly in front of another shop, often dealing in similar goods but at cheaper prices. These outside shops can also be found inside Somali shopping centres, either on the ground floor outside the building or inside the building on the aisles.
3) And thirdly there is the shopping centre itself. One- or multi-storey buildings are used to build up a kind of privately owned indoor market. As the example of the Al-Mujtahid shows, the buildings used as shopping centres were at the beginning not necessarily erected as such. In the last couple of years there was a trend towards building more fancy looking shopping centres that look more like malls. However, these buildings are often used in a similar way to that described in the first two modes as the example of the Dubai Shopping Centre in Nakuru has shown.

Concerning the logic of buying and selling, the shopping malls more closely resemble open-air markets than European or North American style shopping malls. The shops are run by small-scale traders (often working alone or having only one employee), not by multinational corporations. The goods sold are rather cheap, you can buy a pair of shoes for approximately USD 10–15 or a piece of clothing for something like USD 6–10. These goods are also part of global consumption, but are not brands produced for and bought by the rich (see also chapter by Carrier and Elliot this volume). The products in the shopping centres do not feature much variety; often the traders in one area sell the same items, very much like at bigger markets. In some shopping centres only one kind of product is sold, clothes, for example. On the one hand this means that comparison between the different offers is easier and therefore prices can be negotiated (which is normally not the case in shopping malls). On the other, buyers and traders often have longstanding relationships and the building up of trust plays a big role in such business.

The access to the shopping centres is normally not restricted, which means that not only people belonging to the local middle class or elite can enter the shops, as in the case of North American style shopping malls. Also 'undesirables', such as the urban poor, homeless, street children and informal traders can enter the building, in contrast to other examples of rather state-driven urban reconfigurations that try to create 'civilized', modern cities by promoting the building of glamorous malls (one example of the demolition of a market and its resurrection as an up-scale shopping mall in Vietnam is given by Endres 2014). However, the poor seldom can afford the products even though they are rather cheap, and therefore they have no reason to go into the shopping centres. That also means that contrary to the big malls, which can be seen as symbols of increasing inequality and injustice, the Somali shopping centres are locally often discussed as a symbol of the economic dynamism of Kenyan society.

Mathews calls places like that '[m]arts of low-end globalization' (2011: 20). With the mall as the 'epitome of the American Dream' they share private ownership. Often the owner of the building is somebody else than the owner of the shopping centre. The newer shopping centres are established in buildings directly designed for this purpose (see also Carrier 2017). In the latter cases the name and the architectural appearance often resemble the European or North American style shopping mall, projecting the urban traders' dreams of wealth and progress.

What distinguishes the shopping centres from both the market as well as the mall is their functional focus on processes of selling and buying. Markets are often open places where people meet, exchange news and discuss politics. They can even be used as a stage for political or religious rallies and are therefore public arenas. In the case of shopping malls they are not designed as public places, but as they are also places for recreation, urban dwellers appropriate the malls for uses other than consumption in processes of publicization, a re-making of private spaces into public ones. The shopping centres on the other hand are highly specialized places where the pragmatism of trade dominates. In the case of the Nakuru shopping centres there are no 'slow spaces' (Le Roux 2009: 1), areas where you can eat or drink something, where people can sit down and chat. There is no space for gatherings as the shops and hallways are small and crammed. This might be partly due to the location of the shopping centres in Nakuru, as they are all built in an area that already has a number of those 'slow spaces', but it is also a result of the very economic usage of space.

The Role of the State in These Privately Driven Developments

Trying to trace the origins of this space-saving way of doing retail trade, I encountered two different stories of its origins – both of them following a similar logic. One of the explanations sees the genesis in Somalia. Some claim that Siad Barre openly supported Somali hawkers against the felt superiority of 'Asian' (Indian) traders.[16] Together with the economic breakdown in Somalia in the 1980s and the already established links to the new global trading centres on the Arabian Peninsula rising in the 1990s, this policy led to the rise of a new

Somali trading spirit. Trading activities were carried out to a large extent in the growing parallel market, aided by the *franco valuta* system through which migrant workers were able to remit parts of their income as goods to Somalia (see Mubarak 1997). The second explanation places the origin even earlier in Uganda, where the subletting of shops was said to have started in the1970s when Idi Amin expelled the majority of the Asian community. Both explanations therefore trace this reconfiguration of business space to an afro-centrist policy, directed against long-established Asian traders.

Interestingly there have been very similar developments in South Africa. The shopping centres described by Le Roux (2009) follow a comparable spatial and organizational logic. She traces their origin back to Ethiopia (and therefore also to the wider region of Eastern Africa) as it was traders from the Ethiopian diaspora who created the first shops in the modernist buildings in the inner city of Johannesburg at the end of the 1990s, possibly after having stayed in Eastleigh for some time (see Carrier and Kochore, this volume).

An interesting aspect of these two explanations is the role the state plays in this reconfiguration of space. Contrary to other areas of the world (like for instance the building of malls described by Endres 2014), the Somali shopping centres are not the result of direct state interventions in form of planning or building activities. They are likewise not the outcome of processes in the framework of state-directed privatization. Having said this, they are also not spontaneously developing out of nowhere, but are created in a climate of far-reaching economic liberalization on the one hand and under the influence of state actors on the other.

Already the colonial state used the policy to license hawkers as a way to control them, largely with the aim of keeping Africans out of the city (Robertson 2007; Kinyanjui 2014). During and after World War II there was a short period of a tremendous growth of the hawking sector in Nairobi, with many hawkers working illegally and not in the 'few African markets allowed' (Robertson 2007: 28). During the Mau Mau era in the 1950s, licenses were heavily reduced and hundreds were arrested for hawking without a license or for hawking outside the permitted areas. At the end of the 1950s there were almost no licensed traders left in Nairobi (ibid.: 33–34). This changed during the early 1960s, when, after lifting the emergency restrictions on population movement, thousands of traders went to Nairobi. As there was not enough market space, many formed illegal markets, called '*uhuru* [freedom] markets' (ibid.: 35–36). In 1973 there were 2,252 licensed hawkers in Nairobi (266 of them sold clothing), but also some 10,000 unlicensed hawkers, many of them also offering services (Kinyanjui 2014: 24–25). Kinyanjui explains this tremendous growth of the hawking sector not only through economic factors, but also through post-colonial thinking: 'individuals ... had strong desires to negotiate their own livelihoods rather than work for someone else: working for someone else was associated with slavery, drudgery and oppression and therefore freedom from working for someone else was one of the ideals of the liberation struggle' (ibid.: 32). However, the state soon started to see street vending again as a problem, it was obstructing pathways, posing health risks and an aesthetic nuisance to the modern city. Markets were developed as a way to keep street vendors out of the city centre. The open-air markets, however, were not supposed to have permanent structures, resulting in hawkers building them on their own, and soon facing conflict with the municipality. As a concession the state started to build permanent structures (for example the Wakulima market in Nairobi, completed 1966). The enclosed markets not only proved too costly, but many street vendors also did not want to move in, because they did not want to lose their places in the central business district (ibid.: 28–29).

This meant that with the onset of neoliberal political thinking, the informal sector was very much established in Kenya, as was its demonization as a menace for society. Two things changed in the 1980s and 1990s: on the one hand there was an influx of many people into economic informality, due not only to the worsened economic conditions, partly arising from the structural adjustment programs, but also a result of rapid urbanization, not least triggered by the decline of agricultural commodity prices which hit rural economies (Kinyanjui 2014: 37); on the other hand a stronger interlinkage between the informal and formal economies could also be observed. Kinyanjui (2014: 9) gives the examples of Coca-Cola adopting kiosks as part of their distribution network, as well as Safaricom's reliance on kiosks and hawkers, further blurring the boundaries between these two modes of business. Even though the increase in the number of small traders is often seen as a sign of poverty, Pedersen argues for Kenya that this assumption is problematic, because it can also mean that there is a growing market for the products they offer (Pedersen 2005: 13). There are further aspects that militate against the assumption that economic informality is the last resort for the urban poor. Studies for Nairobi and Nakuru observed that the educational level of the street traders was not as low as expected – 73 per cent (Kinyanjui 2014: 79)[17] and 40 per cent (Lubaale and Nyangoro 2013: 9)[18] respectively had a secondary school or higher certificate.[19] Furthermore, 24 per cent of the female hawkers in Nairobi owned their own houses of residence (Kinyanjui 2014: 89), about the same number as other Kenyan town dwellers (Kenya National Bureau of Statistics 2015: 16).

In addition to the changing economic structures, the arbitrariness of policies concerning street traders also increased in the 1980s. The era after the foiled coup against Moi in 1982 was a time of political tension and competition, as well as of heightened violence and insecurity. While until the mid-1980s the erratic course of government comprised of arrests and demolitions, but also of efforts to help some traders, the political competition now led to a strict anti-hawker policy. This went so far that all Nairobi 'central city illegal markets were bulldozed'

(Robertson 2007: 40) in 1990. This move was linked to protests against the massive slum demolition in the 1980s and 1990s, especially of residential areas thought to be involved in the multiparty movement (ibid.: 40–41). Especially in the 1990s, but also still in the 2000s, there was surging criminality and gang activity, some of it sponsored by businesspeople for protection or to harm rivals (Kinyanjui 2014: 54).

The first Somali shopping centres emerged in the early 1990s. As it has just been shown, the economic competition and the political insecurity made business difficult for street vendors at this time. The Somali shopping centres offered a new way of trading, new commercial networks as well as a secured space for doing business. They can therefore be described as an indirect outcome of neoliberal policy.

Neoliberal urban spatial reconfigurations are often discussed in terms of 'gentrification', '… a form of class-based socio-spatial segregation' (Fernandes 2004: 2421) that excludes the urban poor from public visibility (existence) in certain areas and replaces them with middle-class and high-end consumers. This is to a certain degree also true in the case of the Somali shopping centres, especially in the area of Eastleigh. But, following the historical development in Kenya, it can also be argued that this is far from a new phenomenon.

Even though the Kenyan state itself questions the notion of differentiating between a formal and an informal economy, the Somali shopping centres are in most cases described as part of an informal economy.[20] As most of the traders are working on their own they are subsumed under the category of Micro and Small Enterprises (MSE) which again in Kenya is often used interchangeably with the term 'informal sector' or *jua kali* (Swahili: working under the hot sun) (e.g. Mitullah 2003: 3). Kinyanjui (2014) as well as Lubaale and Nyangoro (2013) discuss the entanglement of the informal and formal, for instance its combined allocation and distribution networks. Some traders manage to move from the informal to the formal sector, this nuance providing them with more security and in most cases higher earnings. Some women entrepreneurs who started at Freemark, for instance, later owned sizeable upmarket shops in Nairobi's malls.[21]

When looking closer at the setup of the Somali shopping centres, it also becomes obvious that the formal–informal divide is often not very clear-cut (see Potts 2008). Firstly, the traders are registered with the state and have to pay licenses, the amount being determined according to shop size – and this is also true for many of the street vendors. According to one definition of informal businesses, which includes only unregistered enterprises (Meagher 2013), paying licenses would place them in the formal sector. At the same time, most of the shop owners in the Somali shopping centres are exempted from paying value added tax (VAT), and therefore from disclosing accounting, in contrast to bigger traders. Currently the Kenyan Revenue Authority (KRA) aims to include more traders into the latter group.

Secondly the (local) state is deeply involved in the sphere of the Somali-run trade, even though often not directly. As the economic, the political, as well as the religious realm often seem to be part of the very same sphere of business, some actors appear in all three domains. In Nakuru the most visible example were the owners of the Dubai Shopping Centre – one of whom served as a mayor at the same time and a second of whom was tightly linked to the Muslim community of the city.

The Somaliness of 'Somali' Shopping Centres

The success story of Eastleigh is often ascribed to Somalian refugees, meaning to Somali nationals, a term often equated with ethnic Somaliness. However, as can be seen in the case of the Benadiri traders from Mogadishu, they can be 'Somalians', but in the strict sense not ethnic Somalis.[22] Among the inhabitants and the successful businesspeople in Eastleigh are likewise many Kenyan Somalis from the northeastern part of the country, and members from other minority groups from the northern part of Kenya and its bordering neighbours, like Garre and to a lesser extent Oromo (many of them also coming from Kenyan families) as well as Ethiopians.

Another myth surrounding the success of Eastleigh is its attribution to piracy money on the one hand and tax evasion on the other hand. Without excluding the possibility that cases like this might exist,[23] the example of Garissa lodge shows that many traders of the 'founding period' were already successful traders in Somalia, coming from relatively rich families, either with a long-established trading background or having been involved in other economic activities. But it was not just money such families had acquired before the fall of Somalia that served as a source for investment, but also funds that were gained during the beginning of the 1990s when there was a wave of humanitarian aid and military assistance coming to Somalia. Most international and humanitarian organizations relied on local counterparts to deliver goods. In this period of gold-rush mood, which is still talked about among businesspeople, many Somalis made a lot of money. Another important source of money is the diaspora, specifically the *hawala* system which allows money to be more mobile than other forms of ethnic capital (see chapter by Githigaro this volume). Here again especially people from former elite families or people who managed to gain from the war are able to source money for use in places like Eastleigh and Nakuru. Lastly, the very art of making business, sharing spaces and acquiring goods in bulk, gave Somali traders an advantage over other businesses in the beginning. Because they were so successful with their model, it was taken up quickly not only in other places but also by many non-Somali business people as the example at the very beginning of this chapter showed.

When talking about Eastleigh and the Somali-run trade in Kenya, the crowding out of Asians by Somalis is another topic often alluded to. However, as mentioned above, Eastleigh was since early on not only an Asian living quarter, but also a Somali one. Some Asians already moved out of Kenya in the 1980s, some of them because of anti-Asian riots after the foiled coup in 1982 and others from 1987 onwards to regions that were economically more promising (see Herzig 2006: 26). While many Asians who stayed in Nairobi moved upwards in their socio-economic position and therefore relocated to wealthier parts of Nairobi, the inhabitants of the quarter that were really affected by the rising prices were Kenyan Somali families living in Eastleigh. While many Asians owned property and therefore gained from the developments, not all of the Somali families were as well off. Some moved to other, poorer parts of Nairobi, others moved to Europe as 'refugees'. Another group that gained from the developments in Eastleigh were other Kenyans, mainly Kikuyu, business people who had bought property in Eastleigh.

What seems to be true, however, is that the logic of retail followed by Asian traders is a different one than the logic the Somali traders applied so successfully. The South Asians had dominated the retail sector through a low volume, high mark-up model, which is closer to the way business is done in European or North American style shopping malls. This went hand-in-hand with their usage of space – their retail takes place mainly in spacious front shops along the streets. With market deregulation and liberalization other groups of traders entered the arena of low and medium quality product retail and occupied these segments of the market (see Kantai 2012).

Conclusion – 'Demystification of Business'?

I heard the term 'demystification of business' the first time from a Kenyan colleague.[24] He compared it with the 'demystification of religion' by reformist groups (Salafi or Wahhabi groups as well as the Tablighi Jama'at). People no longer had the feeling they needed an intermediary, a holy man, to communicate with God. Something similar, he said, had happened due to the Somali traders – they had shown that it is possible to start a business with few resources. Not only Asians (and influential Kikuyu) were able to be economically successful, but everybody had the possibility to become a successful businessperson. He linked this change to a transformation in the usage of space. As has been shown in this chapter this narrative is too simple, but a change in the composition of the retail sector took place for sure in the 1990s, and with it a concomitant change in the rules governing how this business works.

With the space-saving arrangements described above, rents are much lower than in a room-size shop or a European or North American style mall respectively, and even with a small investment it is now possible to build up a permanent and respectable business in one of the shopping centres. An opening up of the options for doing business for a broader range of people can be observed.

This change is not the direct result of governmental interventions or public planning, but of private investments by businesspeople, who in many cases live in precarious situations, either as Somalian refugees without the permission to stay in the urban areas or as Kenyan Somalis often politically marginalized. What they created for themselves as well as for the traders doing business in the Somali shopping centres is a realm of security, a closed yet open, secluded yet visible space. This might also be the reason why traders opt for doing business in the Somali shopping centres instead of trading in the streets, even though the chances for profit might be lower in the former. What they gain from the Somali shopping centres is security, a storage space and shelter. The diffusion of the Eastleigh model might therefore not be so much a 'democratization' of trade, as the provision of a space more suited to the informal sector upon which so many in Kenya are reliant.

Tabea Scharrer is a postdoctoral researcher at the Max Planck Institute for Social Anthropology, Halle (Germany). She has conducted research in Tanzania and Kenya on Islamic missionary movements as well as on migration-related issues in refugee camps as well as in urban areas. Her publications include the monograph *Narrative islamischer Konversion: Biographische Erzählungen konvertierter Muslime in Ostafrika* (transcript, 2013) and a co-edited volume on *Middle Classes in Africa* (Palgrave, 2018).

Notes

1. The term 'Somali' is written in quotation marks to highlight the complexities linked to it.
2. Goldsmith, P. (2008), 'Kenya: Eastleigh Goes Global', *The East African*, 17 August. http://allafrica.com/stories/printable/200808190301.html; retrieved 26 January 2010.
3. *Kenya Gazette* 97(15): 524, 24 March 1995.
4. 'Founder of City's Stalls Business Was Left Crying', Roy Gachuhi, 29 December 2013. Retrieved 18 February 2016 from nairobinews.nation.co.ke/news/nelson-kajuma-founded-citys-stalls-business-but-left-crying/.
5. A *mujtahid* is a person qualified to exercise *ijtihad*, which is translated as independent reasoning (important especially in the reformist Islamic discourse) and constitutes one of the key concepts in Islamic jurisprudence. As a fire in mid-2014 destroyed the upper floor of the building (which has not been repaired since), the arrangements in the building are now different from what is described in this chapter.
6. If Garre are categorized as Somali or not, depends on the situation, the person you are talking to and the time in which the discussion takes place (see also Schlee 2009). By most Kenyans (and many researchers) they are seen as Somalis, even though in Nakuru they live apart from the other 'Somalis' in different areas.
7. Most prices given in this chapter date back to 2012 when the most comprehensive gathering of data was done. In some cases, when indicated, the numbers relate to prices in other years. The prices were always given in Kenyan Shilling and were converted to its current value in USD by the author of the chapter.

8. In some of the new shopping centres, the traders have to pay goodwill in addition to rent (in one example in Nakuru this amounted to USD 3,300 for a small shop). This money is mostly used for building or leasing the trading centre.
9. *Hawala* (*xawaala* in Somali spelling) is an informal money transfer system, which has existed for a long time in Islamic trade networks. In the Somali context it became an important tool in the 1980s when many Somalians worked in Arab countries and transferred parts of their income back to Somalia. Some of the big *hawala* companies, such as Dahabshiil, cannot be considered informal anymore but rather resemble other banks.
10. E-mail communication with a Kenyan Somali resident of Nakuru, 1 April 2015.
11. I use the term 'migrant' in a broad sense – my research encompassed families who came with the British colonial power from Somaliland at the beginning of the twentieth century, people who came as refugees from Somalia since the beginning of the 1990s, ethnic Somalis from the northeastern part of Kenya who came at about the same time as part of an urbanization process as well as Somali returnees from Western and Arab countries. Many of the latter are in the possession of foreign passports and want to combine the closeness to Somalia with the security and convenience of Kenya. Most of this migration took place in the last twenty years. Before 1995 only about 500 Somalis lived in Nakuru. Many of them were from Isaaq families living in Kambi ya Somali, a quarter founded by the British administration for its Somali employees in the 1920s. As of 2012 there were about 10,000 Somalis living in the town, 2,000–3,000 of them having come from Somalia.
12. As the numbers the traders indicated were very similar, the answers seem to be reliable. Furthermore, the mother of my research assistant is a trader herself, which helped to contextualize the interview results.
13. The following numbers are based on the research cited. The results of that research derive from interviews with about 140 street traders in Nakuru.
14. Interestingly the report also showed that men worked almost twice as many hours as women (more than 50 hours compared to slightly more than 30 hours a week) (ibid.).
15. Goods are also sold to Somali shop owners outside of Kenya, for example in Europe, as I witnessed in a Somali shop in Salzburg (Austria).
16. Interview with high-ranking Somalian politician and businessman in Mombasa, July 2011.
17. She argues that this is a development of the 2000s, as in older studies conducted in the 1990s the educational level of the street traders seems to have been considerably lower (ibid.). A certain bias can of course also occur during research, depending on the traders and trading sites covered by a survey.
18. The Kenyan census of 2009 recorded an educational level of secondary school attainment for 50 per cent of the Nairobi population and 45.5 per cent for Nakuru (Kenya National Bureau of Statistics 2010).
19. These numbers can also be interpreted in a more pessimistic way, using them to show how difficult it is even with a secondary school education to find employment.
20. The newer malls in Eastleigh certainly fall somewhat out of this assessment, however Eastleigh as a quarter is nonetheless discussed in these terms.
21. 'We Were Not Always Businessmen, But We Have Learnt Fast', Joyce Nyairo, *Daily Nation* Online, 21 November 2015.
22. The Benadiri are a group somewhat similar to the Swahili that developed from African as well as Arab roots. They are not part of the Somali clan system, even though they can get incorporated as quasi-clans.

23. A World Bank report from 2013 argues against this myth by stating that the entire money generated from piracy activities is dwarfed by bank credits and remittances flowing to the real estate sector (p. 73–5).
24. Thanks a lot again to Kadara Swaleh for showing me around in Eastleigh and for the inspiring discussions we had that in the end resulted in a workshop on Eastleigh in Nairobi in 2014.

References

Abdikarim, A.M. 2010. *City Council of Nairobi Stopped from Collecting Rates from Eastleigh Traders*. 18 June 2010. Retrieved 12 June 2013 from http://english.alshahid.net/archives/7950.

Carrier, N. 2017. *Little Mogadishu. Eastleigh, Nairobi's Global Somali Hub*. New York: Oxford University Press.

Carrier, N., and E. Lochery. 2013. 'Missing States? Somali Trade Networks and the Eastleigh Transformation', *Journal of Eastern African Studies* 7(2): 334–52.

Endres, K.W. 2014. 'Downgraded by Upgrading: Small-Scale Traders, Urban Transformation and Spatial Reconfiguration in Post-Reform Vietnam', *Cambridge Anthropology* 32(2): 97–111.

Farah, N. 2010. 'Of Tamarind & Cosmopolitanism', in E. Pieterse and N. Edjabe (eds), *African Cities Reader: Pan-African Practices*. Cape Town: Chimurenga Press and African Centre for Cities, pp. 9–12.

Fernandes, L. 2004. 'Politics of Forgetting: Class Politics, State Power and the Restructuring of Urban Space in India', *Urban Studies* 41(12): 2415–30.

Foeken, D., and S.O. Owuor. 2001. 'Multi-Spatial Livelihoods in Sub-Saharan Africa: Rural Farming by Urban Households. The Case of Nakuru, Town, Kenya', in M. Bruijn, R. Dijk and D. Foeken (eds), *Mobile Africa: Changing Patterns of Movement in Africa and Beyond*. Leiden: Brill, pp. 125–40.

Hart, K. 2010. 'Informal Economy', in K. Hart, J.-L. Laville and A. D. Cattani (eds), *The Human Economy: A Citizen's Guide*. Cambridge, Malden: Polity Press, pp. 142–53.

Herzig, P. 2006. *South Asians in Kenya: Gender, Generation and Changing Identities in Diaspora*. Berlin: LIT Verlag.

Kantai, P. 2012. 'Eastleigh and the Rise of Somali Diaspora Capital'. Retrieved 12 June 2013 from http://pesatalk.com/eastleigh-and-the-rise-of-somali-diaspora-capital/#st-hash.6KNvxc0m.dpuf.

Karama, M., and K.O. Kitito. 2011. 'The Changing Cultural Faces of Mambasa in Relation to the Influx of Somalis Into Mambasa Old Town', *The Development, Geopolitics and Cultural Exchange in the Indian Ocean, Zanzibar, 26–28 May 2011*. Zanzibar Indian Ocean Research Institute (ZIORI) and Research Network on 'The Indian Ocean as a Visionary Area'.

Kenya National Bureau of Statistics (KNBS) 2010. *Population and Housing Census 2009*.
———. 2015. *Kenya Demographic and Health Survey 2014*.

Kinyanjui, M.N. 2014. *Women and the Informal Economy in Urban Africa: From the Margins to the Centre*. London: Zed Books.

Kitching, G. 1980. *Class and Economic Change in Kenya: The Making of an African Petite-Bourgeoisie*. New Haven, London: Yale University Press.

Le Roux, H. 2009. 'Coffeemanifesto: Sampling Instant and Slow Spaces in the African City', *African Perspectives 2009, The African Inner City: [Re]sourced, International Conference, Pretoria 25–28 September 2009.* University of Pretoria. Retrieved 17 October 2018 from https://repository.up.ac.za/handle/2263/59966.

Little, P. 2005. 'Unofficial Trade when States Are Weak: The Case of Cross-Border Commerce in the Horn of Africa', *Research Paper*, UNU-WIDER, United Nations University (UNU), 2005/13. Helsinki: UNU-WIDER.

Lubaale, G.N., and O. Nyangoro. 2013. *Street Vendors in Nakuru, Kenya.* Cambridge, MA: WIEGO.

Mathews, G. 2011. *Ghetto at the Center of the World: Chungking Mansions, Hong Kong.* Chicago, London: University of Chicago Press.

Meagher, K., and I. Lindell. 2013. 'ASR Forum: Engaging with African Informal Economies: Social Inclusion or Adverse Incorporation?', *African Studies Review*, 56(3): 57–76.

Meagher, K. 2013. 'Unlocking the Informal Economy: A Literature Review on Linkages between Formal and Informal Economies in Developing Countries', *WIEGO Working Paper* 27. Cambridge: WIEGO.

Mitullah, W. 2003. 'Street Trade in Kenya: The Contribution of Research in Policy Dialogue and Response', *Urban Research Symposium on Urban Development for Economic Growth and Poverty Reduction, Washington, 15–17 December 2003.* Washington, DC: The World Bank.

Mubarak, J.A. 1997. 'The "Hidden Hand" behind the Resilience of the Stateless Economy of Somalia', *World Development* 25(12): 2027–41.

Pedersen, P.O. 2005. *Trade in the Small- and Micro-Enterprise Sector in Kenya and Other Countries in Eastern and Southern Africa.* Copenhagen: Danish Institute for International Studies (DIIS).

Potts, D. 2008. 'The Urban Informal Sector in Sub-Saharan Africa: From Bad to Good (and Back again?)', *Development Southern Africa* 25(2): 151–67.

Reese, S.S. 1996. *Patricians of the Benaadir. Islamic Learning, Commerce and Somali Urban Identity in the Nineteenth Century.* Philadelphia: University of Pennsylvania.

Robertson, C.C. 2007. 'Whose Crime? Arson, Class Warfare and Traders in Nairobi, 1940–2000', *Crime, Histoire & Sociétés* 11(2): 25–47.

Schlee, G. 2009. 'Changing Alliances among the Boran, Garre and Gabra in Northern Kenya and Southern Ethiopia', in G. Schlee and E.E. Watson (eds), *Changing Identifications and Alliances in North-East Africa: Ethiopia and Kenya.* New York, Oxford: Berghahn, pp. 203–23.

World Bank. 2013. *Pirate Trails: Tracking the Illicit Financial Flows from Pirate Activities off the Horn of Africa.* A World Bank Study. Washington, DC: World Bank.

Part IV
The Politics of Somali Mobility

Chapter 8

Perpetually in Transit

Somalian Refugees in a Context of Increasing Hostility

Lucy Lowe and Mark Yarnell

> What rights do you have? [pause] Come on, as refugees here in Kenya, what rights do you know about that you can claim to have? Can you give me any examples? [pause] Do you have any rights as refugees?
>
> —Arthur, a Kenyan legal advisor

In a small windowless office in Eastleigh, Arthur, the Kenyan legal advisor who had been invited to give a presentation on refugee rights, was met with nervous stares and reluctant answers from the assembled group of refugees from Somalia, Ethiopia, Democratic Republic of Congo, Rwanda and what is now South Sudan. The participants, individuals selected to be community representatives who could disseminate information from NGOs, were rather shy and reluctant to speak up, but some offered suggestions of the right to free speech, access to healthcare, to vote and to live. The legal advisor hummed awkwardly around some of the responses before providing his own answer:

> There are some important rights that you do have, such as the right to protection, the right to a fair trial, the right to seek asylum, the right to be considered innocent until proven guilty. Then there are some rights that are human rights in the UN Declaration, that you don't have in this country, like the right to vote or the right to free movement, and there are some rights even we [Kenyans] do not have as rights in this country. Sexual orientation, things like that.

This statement, and particularly the forthright acknowledgement that refugees and asylum seekers are subject to substantially different laws, policies and treatment by the state than both citizens and other migrant groups is illustrative of how refugees are considered to exist completely separately from everyone else in Kenya. While all migrants face certain restrictions as non-citizens, such as the right to vote, refugees and asylum seekers are subject to an encampment policy that restricts and monitors their movement within the country. They lack access to basic human rights, are subject to different laws and regulations, and are governed by separate and hybrid sources of power from the often uncomfortable alliance of Kenya's now disbanded Department of Refugee Affairs and the UNHCR, thereby constructing a theoretically enclosed and isolated existence. With this in mind, refugees in Kenya can be and have been excluded and isolated from other migrants as 'an object of intervention and discursivity by international aid institutions that administer to them as an aggregate with basic human needs. They are simultaneously inside and outside the national' (Peteet 2005: 24). Despite this, many refugees regularly traverse this line, between the legal and the illegal, the encamped and the 'free'. In this chapter we will explore the ways in which this excluded insider is embodied in the often-silenced yet conspicuously visible Somali refugee population that resides in the Eastleigh estate in Nairobi.

Eastleigh has long been home to Somalis,[1] both Somalian nationals and ethnically Somali Kenyans, and has been central to a long historical discourse that has emphasized the foreign, immigrant status of Somalis within Kenya. Increasingly, this often-xenophobic national and international discourse has depicted Eastleigh as a hub of Islamic fundamentalism and terrorism. Indeed, Eastleigh is frequently referred to as a distinctly Somali neighbourhood, with many Kenyans referring to it as an annex of the Somali state, or joking that they needed passports in order to enter. Many others expressed a fear of both Eastleigh and its Somali residents. The wave of terrorist attacks in Kenya, many of which occurred within Eastleigh itself, has sharpened the political and media focus on the presence of foreigners in the capital city. This conflation of the label 'Somali' with both 'refugee' and 'terrorist' has blurred the lines between objects of humanitarian concern and national security threat. Demands for the deportation, or at least encampment, of refugees in remote camps speaks to the complexities of this relationship. In spite of these constant threats – and Kenyan government policies that seek to restrict freedom of movement and access to livelihoods – many Somali refugees cope and benefit through 'mobile urbanity'. In this chapter, we will focus on the more recent tensions that have shaped experiences of forced migration among Somalis living in Kenya, including Operation Usalama Watch and the recurring threats to close Dadaab refugee camp.

Lucy Lowe conducted ethnographic fieldwork in Eastleigh between November 2009 and June 2011, returning periodically in 2012, 2013 and 2014. Her initial research focused on the interplay between reproductive health decisions, displacement and onward migration. This chapter draws on both interviews and participant observation conducted while living in Eastleigh. Mark Yarnell works for Refugees International, an independent advocacy organization based in Washington, DC. In July 2014, he interviewed Somali refugees in Eastleigh and Dadaab in the wake of Kenyan government orders for all urban refugees to report to refugee camps. Drawing on Yarnell and Lowe's different yet complementary research aims, methods and backgrounds, this chapter seeks to provide an insight into the lived experiences of Somalis in Eastleigh, and examine the strategies for navigating their protracted displacement.

The Refugee Context

Due to its geographical position and relative stability, Kenya has long been a major refugee receiving country, and it currently hosts refugees from Somalia, Ethiopia, South Sudan, DRC, Eritrea and more historically from Uganda, Rwanda and Burundi. Despite a move by the United Nations refugee agency (UNHCR) in 2009 to recognize and support the widespread existence of urban refugees, Kenya has maintained an encampment policy since the early 1990s, which requires all refugees to be registered and living in one of two large refugee camps, Kakuma in the northwest or Dadaab in the east. Both of the camps are in remote, arid and underdeveloped parts of the country, and Dadaab, near the border with Somalia has the unfortunate reputation of being one of the largest, oldest and most over congested refugee camp complexes in the world. The population of the three original camps within the Dadaab complex (Ifo, Hagadera and Dagahaley) peaked in 2011 at almost 500,000, leading to the opening of two further camps in the area (Ifo II and Kambioos). The numbers of officially registered refugees has surged and declined in response to various periods of conflict and natural disasters and relative stability. In 2018, the population of the Dadaab camps was reduced to below 210,000, with returns to Somalia facilitated by UNHCR and promoted by the Kenyan government (Refugees International 2016). Lawful travel by refugees from the camps to other parts of Kenya is restricted by the government, which issues movement passes on a case-by-case basis.

Yet it is important to recognize that camps do not exist in isolation from the countries and communities in which they are situated, despite their often remote locations (Turner 2016b: 141). As is clearly the case in Kenya, both refugees and local Kenyans move in and out of the camps for diverse reasons, including access to trade, education and healthcare (Jansen 2016). Indeed, dispersing families across multiple locations is an essential strategy to cope with displacement (Horst 2006). Even when possibilities are explored in Nairobi or other parts of the country, the camps provide a fallback option they can return to if they are unsuccessful. Bram Jansen also urges caution when perceiving camps solely as zones of isolation or warehousing, and suggests that a refugee camp in a protracted crisis can transform over time into an 'accidental city', where humanitarian spaces, structures and engagements are normalized over time (Jansen 2016: 150). As Marc-Antoine Perouse de Montclos and Peter Mwangi Kagwanja note, 'after a certain period of time, refugees appear to be some sort of "urban dwellers in the making" and camps to be a preliminary step towards urbanization' (2000: 206). Trade networks develop, market systems are established, and population density increases. According to a 2010 study commissioned by the Kenyan, Danish and Norwegian governments, there are around 5,000 camp-based businesses in Dadaab (mostly traders and vendors) with annual sales reaching around USD 25 million annually (Enghoff et al. 2010: 9).

Liisa Malkki (1995) suggests that refugees, as those situated simultaneously inside and outside the national order, are unsettling to the state. Refugee camps therefore represent an attempt to bring normality to chaos, order to disorder. Camps are, however, glaringly absent from the 'durable solutions' that have been identified by UNHCR – repatriations, resettlements and local integration – and their residents are instead left without a solution, in what Simon Turner has termed an 'indeterminate temporariness' (2016b: 142).

In practice, the enforcement of the encampment policy has been extremely haphazard, and this is one of the reasons that thousands of refugees have long been able to live in other parts of the country. In the camps, registered refugees can live legally, with basic housing, rations, education and healthcare provided for free – through the United Nations and its implementing partners.

Despite this, many people leave the refugee camps or circumvent them altogether, and instead choose to live in a legally ambiguous context where the everyday cost of living is extremely high and insecurity and harassment are commonplace. As Simon Turner argues in relation to Burundian refugees, 'Nairobi for them is also a non-place between the past and the future, where they do not want to put down roots but are preparing for a future either in Burundi or in Europe or North America' (2016a: 37). For many Somalis, Nairobi and particularly Eastleigh are not non-places, but have come to be defined as important diasporic hubs. Unlike Burundians, Somalis do not, for the most part, live on the outskirts of the city. In Eastleigh they are highly central to it, in both geographic and economic terms, and Somalis more broadly occupy a particular position in the Kenyan political imagination. Additionally, the presence of Kenyan Somalis, as well as those Somalian nationals who have established businesses and family networks that suggest some degree of permanence in the city, highlight the tensions that many people face when imagining their futures.

Because this legal ambiguity is coupled with the apparent wealth in Eastleigh, which has developed into a booming regional trading and business hub (Carrier and Lochery 2013), Somalis – both Somalian refugees and Kenyan Somalis – have long been a target of corrupt authorities. Encounters, directly or indirectly, with the police are ubiquitous in Eastleigh, and the questioning and detention of Somalis on the street is a common occurrence. Reports of arbitrary detention, extortion and physical assault are widespread. For young people in particular, the anxiety of everyday life coupled with a fervent awareness of life 'outside', in Europe and North America, incited the desperation to leave Kenya and seek security elsewhere.

As Elmi, a Somali man in his mid-twenties stated, 'I can't die here. I can't get old here. I can't have my body put in the cemetery here.' For Elmi the prospect of living out the rest of his days in Nairobi was simply not a possibility he would or even could consider. For this young man, as well as many other Somalis, the difficulties that were an everyday aspect of life in Kenya – the lack of opportunities, the regular police harassment and the general sense of insecurity and uncertainty – were so great that there was no way in which he could think about his current living situation as anything more than temporary.

This absolute belief that he would eventually leave Kenya should be put into context by the fact that he had been in Kenya for seventeen years, having fled Mogadishu as a child with his mother and siblings. During this time, he had lived in the Dadaab and Kakuma refugee camps, as well as having spent nine years in Nairobi. As an adult he had worked informally for his uncle in order to provide financial support for his relatives in Nairobi and Dadaab. He had seen many friends leave Kenya, some had returned through choice for visits or through deportation, others had never returned. Some had gone back to Somalia during periods of relative peace, in many cases so as to reclaim land and property, only to return to Kenya once more due to renewed conflict or drought. Others had died, in Kenya, Somalia, further afield, or – as many feared – en route, trying to get out. The fact that so many friends and a number of close relatives now lived 'outside', in countries in Europe and North America that were generally considered to have more opportunities and were therefore generally 'better', further fuelled his desire to move abroad.

For many people like Elmi, living in Eastleigh presented an alternative to the refugee camps. If life in the camps was defined by dependence and enclosure, Eastleigh could be seen as a way out: a transit point on the journey of forced migration. Anxiety surrounding life within Kenya and the desperation to move 'outside' was pervasive in Eastleigh. It came up in conversations every day, often framing how people understood their lives, as migrants, as refugees and as Somalis. It was central to how people spoke about their relatives, and often, their sources of financial support.

During the time of this research Elmi was detained by the police on several occasions, and either paid a bribe to be released or managed to talk his way out of it by pretending to be Kenyan. On one occasion, when a friend of his was detained, Elmi attempted to intervene on his behalf, but was beaten by the policemen, using the butts of their guns. Nothing was particularly unusual about these experiences, and many young men living in Eastleigh echoed them. Another young man stated,

> When they catch you, they begin by talking to you in Kiswahili to try to immediately catch you out. If you don't understand then they know they've got you. But if you can answer then you have to try to talk to them nicely. I speak good Kiswahili so I act like I'm *siju*.[2] There was one time, we were all sitting chewing [khat] and the police came in and I tried to act like I'm helping them, I told other people to bring their IDs. Kenyans are somehow slow, so you can distract them. But otherwise, if they just catch you, they pick you up by this [belt loop] in the back of your trousers. They pull so hard, as though they're lifting you by your ass. It's so embarrassing. They want everyone to look, so everyone knows what's happening. Or if there are more of you together, they handcuff you all together, like animals. Then they tell you, 'phone someone.' That's when you have to start making calls to collect money.

Numerous people complained that Somalis were treated like 'slaves' or 'animals' who could be captured, bought and sold; as one man phrased it, 'they catch us just so they can sell us like goats to our own people.' Locally-made Somali–Kiswahili phrasebooks were a sad reminder of the ubiquity of police persecution. Rather than beginning with basic forms of greetings, introductions and asking where the bus station is, the books readily available from small kiosks begin with more locally pertinent phrases such as 'police', 'show your ID', you are under arrest', and the ever useful *kitu kidogo* ('something small' – a bribe). Presence in Eastleigh, coupled with stereotypical Somali features, including lighter skin and 'softer' hair, make many Somalis easy to pick out in public spaces. For some, the ability to speak fluent Kiswahili and Sheng (Swahili-based slang) enabled them to 'pass' as ethnically Somali Kenyans, thereby avoiding or minimizing police harassment. Many young men told me that they avoided wearing clothes that marked them as 'new arrivals', including the *macawis* (male sarong, looped around the waist) or particular styles of shirts and trousers, preferring the jeans and t-shirts that are more popular among young urban Kenyans. As one man commented 'they see you dressed like that [identifiably Somali], they immediately know they will eat well today!' Women, who almost universally wore the Islamic *jilbaab* and *hijab*, also used language in an attempt to pass as Somali Kenyan, and many reported casually flirting with policemen in an attempt to escape persecution. One woman in her early twenties who had lived in Eastleigh since she was a child explained,

> You have to smile nicely for them, be like '*Sasa, niaje...* [Sheng greetings]'. If you run they will chase you and then they know that they can ask for big money, because if they arrest a woman the family will pay

quickly. So you have to be so nice and talk sweetly, but not too much or they will start to like you and think that they can take advantage [sexually].

These fears of persecution and the gendered strategies people adopted to mitigate them were embodied in everyday life in Eastleigh. Continual police harassment, a widespread mistrust of and hostility towards Somalis unsurprisingly reinforced the sense of temporariness and transience of life in Eastleigh for many Somalis.

In practice, urban refugees in Kenya often fall between the gaps of protection by UNHCR, which is internationally mandated to provide protection for refugees and asylum seekers. As discussed above, Kenya maintained an official policy of encampment for years, yet tacitly accepted the presence of refugees in cities. To be clear, government agencies seized with national security issues promoted the enforcement of encampment, but other government entities, particularly the former Department of Refugee Affairs (DRA), perceived the presence of refugees in Nairobi as 'both legitimate and inevitable' (Campbell, Crisp and Kiragu 2011). In fact, the government did not even formally gazette and designate Dadaab and Kakuma as refugee camps until 2014.

When the UNHCR launched a global urban refugee policy in 2009, the agency worked with the DRA to expand the rights of refugees living in cities. At the heart of the policy was the notion 'that cities are recognized as legitimate places for refugees to reside and exercise the rights to which they are entitled'. By 2012 over 55,000 refugees were officially registered in Kenya's cities, the vast majority in Nairobi, and aid organizations established programmes to help improve access to local services like health care and education. Further, UNHCR partnered with Kenyan legal aid organizations to bolster legal representation for urban refugees and expanded its direct outreach and engagement with refugee populations. Despite this institutional move towards support for urban refugees, the vast majority failed to register at all. During interviews in Eastleigh, some Somalis who were present during this period explained that they had attempted to register but had never received their documents, while others received ID cards with the photographic image blanked out, and others that had already expired. Far more suggested that the process was futile, given that they were already living and in many cases working in Eastleigh quite successfully without registration. As one woman who had lived unregistered in Nairobi for fourteen years explained, 'the Kenyan government will only bring problems. Better to stay away from them.' The gains that were made during this period have since been dramatically reversed.

Citing national security concerns, the Kenyan government has transitioned from tacit acceptance of refugees in cities to overt antagonism, periodically announcing directives that order all urban refugees to report to camps. Such directives have become more commonplace and aggressive since 2011. Far from achieving the implementation of its encampment policy, however, urban refugees have become exposed to heightened levels of abuse and extortion at the hands of Kenyan security services. Refugee informants told us that the security services regularly disregarded official refugee documentation papers (including UNHCR mandates and Department of Refugee Affairs refugee certificates), sometimes confiscating the documents or even ripping them up on the spot. Numerous refugees said that they felt abandoned by the UNHCR and that it became evident that possessing money to pay bribes was far more essential to ensuring one's protection and freedom than any kind of refugee registration document.

In the face of this perceived abandonment, the UNHCR received scathing criticism from human rights organizations due to its reluctance to publicly condemn the Kenyan security services. For example, following a police crackdown in late 2012/early 2013, Gerry Simpson with Human Rights Watch stated,

> There has been a deafening silence from UNHCR on these abuses, even though they happened within a half-hour drive from their Nairobi offices. For 10 weeks, police were free to rape, assault and steal from over 1,000 refugees and asylum seekers without a single public word from the one international agency legally mandated to protect refugees. (2013)

Though the UNHCR is mandated to protect refugees, it is important to note that the UNHCR itself is not, in practice, an independent organization. Not only is it dependent on voluntary contributions from donor governments for its operating costs (Horst 2006), it also carries out those operations as the guest of a particular host country. To illustrate, when the High Commissioner selects a new UNHCR representative, the host government can decide whether or not to accept the representative – similar to the accreditation of ambassadorships. Similarly, the host government can also decide to expel UNHCR staff already in country, let alone the whole organization, which would certainly compromise ongoing activities. As such, the UNHCR does not exist in a political vacuum and there is a constant evaluation of how the agency's relationship with the host government might impact its ability to operate. For example, would a public condemnation of Kenyan police behaviour in Eastleigh cause the government to restrict the UNHCR's operations in Dadaab – particularly when the UN's staff rely on Kenyan police for security escorts in and out of the camp blocks? This is not to evaluate the UNHCR's response to rights violations against urban refugees, but rather to acknowledge the constraints that exist within the modern international refugee regime.

In Kenya, a rise in terrorism – combined with public rhetoric that conflates the threat of terrorism with the presence of Somali refugees (see Wario and Wandera, this volume) – has given license to security services to intensify harassment and violence against Somalis. For their part, Somalis are forced to find ways to cope and navigate day-to-day life in the context of growing hostility and xenophobia – without being able to rely on the international refugee regime for protection.

On 6 May 2016, the Kenyan government made its most startling refugee announcement to date. Citing national security concerns, the Ministry of Interior Principal Secretary Dr. Eng Karanja Kibicho declared that the 'hosting of refugees has come to an end' and that both the Kakuma and Dadaab would be closed. Toward that end, the government moved immediately to disband the DRA. Shortly thereafter, government officials withdrew the threat to close Kakuma, but Dadaab, which houses mainly Somali refugees, remained slated for closure. In February 2017, Kenya's High Court actually struck down the government's order to close Dadaab. Judge John Mativo found, 'The government decision specifically targeting Somali refugees is an act of group persecution, illegal, discriminatory and therefore unconstitutional' (Mativo 2017). Unfortunately, the Kenyan leadership has shown no intention to abide by the ruling. As of March 2017, Kenyan President, Uhuru Kenyatta, had continued to reiterate publicly that Dadaab would be closed,[3] and new demands into that direction have been made after the 12 Riverside attack in January 2019.[4] The Kenyan government representatives have made such threats in the past only to back down following international pressure.

Beyond violating Kenya's obligations as a signatory to the 1951 Refugee Convention and the 1967 Protocol, as well as the Organisation of African Unity (OAU) convention on refugees, physically shuttering a camp as large and established as Dadaab and forcing refugees to return to Somalia could very well be logistically impossible. Nonetheless, the announced policy is having a real impact. On 13 June 2016, the rights group, Amnesty International noted that it 'continues to receive reports of arrests, detention and harassment of refugees by the police in many parts of Kenya since the government's plan to close the camp was announced in May' (2016). Significantly, the one government department charged with refugee protection, the DRA, no longer exists. Further, the DRA's responsibilities included issuing movement passes for refugees who required short-term departures from Dadaab for particular circumstances, like accessing specialized medical treatment or attending university classes, and the issuance of such passes was abruptly halted when the DRA was eliminated. While other government officials subsequently began carrying out some of the tasks for which the DRA was responsible, under the auspices of a newly established entity known as the Refugees Affairs Secretariat, the disbandment of the agency is significant. No matter what happens in the future, the rights of Somali refugees in Kenya have been significantly eroded.

The uncertainty surrounding the future of the camps illustrates the tension in Simon Turner's argument that refugee camps can be understood 'as exceptional and hence temporary measures to be taken before normality is restored once again in the future' (2016b: 140). As the illusion of temporariness has increasingly faded from the camps in Kenya, the threat of permanence has pressed heavily on Kenyan political discourse.

As that discourse evolves, and as the government's emphasis on refugees as a national security threat ebbs and flows, Somali refugees are caught in a constant state of uncertainty about their place in Kenyan society. Remarkably, only weeks after President Kenyatta's March 2017 statement that Dadaab would be closed through 'our efforts to hasten the repatriation and resettlement of refugees',[5] the government appeared to reverse course – at least on paper. At a summit convened by the Intergovernmental Authority on Development (IGAD), Kenya endorsed a declaration that called for not only upholding the rights of refugees, but also for the integration of refugees into longer-term development efforts. According the declaration, Kenya agreed to 'progressively … facilitate the free movement of refugees and their integration into national development plans and access to services' (IGAD 2017). Since then, the government has refrained from overt calls for the premature return of refugees to Somalia and subsequent drafts of the Garissa County Integrated Development Plan, wherein Dadaab is located, have included refugees. However, as history demonstrates, political and security developments within Kenya and the region may render these positive developments moot.

Sanitizing Eastleigh

As Jeff Crisp describes, 'Security has been a central concern of Kenyan refugee policy since the colonial period. But that concern derived from a preoccupation with the security of the state, and the perception that state security is jeopardized by the presence of refugees' (Crisp 1999: 17). Kenya's historically tense relationship with Somali populations in the border regions exacerbates the perceived threat of Somali refugees in particular (Horst 2006). However, the Kenyan government's promotion of the refugee/terrorist narrative has reached a new level of intensity and impact in recent years.

In October 2011, Kenyan troops entered Somalia, apparently in response to a growing sense of insecurity in the region that was blamed on the Somali-based terrorist organization Al-Shabaab. On 24 October 2011, a week after Kenya sent their troops, two explosions occurred in the centre of Nairobi. With apparently little evidence at the time, these explosions were immediately attributed to Al-Shabaab, and to Somalis more generally.

Telephone conversations, texts and emails with interlocutors in Eastleigh confirmed that the residents of Eastleigh were feeling the ramifications of what was happening in Somalia and Nairobi. As predicted by many people, there was an increase in the police raids that were already a familiar aspect of everyday life in Eastleigh, and each night certain streets were blocked off and anyone unlucky enough to be outside was arrested or extorted. As one informant said,

The streets are dead. By 7 o'clock you can see everyone is rushing home, no one wants to be caught after dark. So we're staying at home and waiting. For now it's just the streets, but soon they'll be going house-to-house.[6]

A few weeks later, with little notice, the government began demolishing homes in Eastleigh. They claimed that they were too close to the military airbase that borders the length of Eastleigh, despite many of them having been built entirely legally and with permission over a decade earlier. Although these demolitions affected low-income Kenyans, Somalis and other non-Somalis alike, this was yet another reminder of the power of the Kenyan government and the continuation of their displacement. As one friend stated matter-of-factly over the phone as he frantically searched for somewhere for his family to move to, 'no one cares about what happens to us, no one cares about Somalis'. The Kenyan media reported that the demolitions were halted by a court ruling in which the judge described the government as 'a monster'. Rumours, however, abounded that it was when officials realized that following through with their plan would involve demolishing both a church and a mosque that they reconsidered the matter.

In December 2012, the Kenyan government ordered that all refugees must reside within Dadaab or Kakuma, on the grounds that they posed a terror risk. Further, all urban registration centres were closed, and aid agencies were instructed to cease programming for refugees in cities. This directive was eventually overruled by the High Court in July 2013, stating that it violated the Kenyan Constitution, which enshrines the country's obligations to ratified conventions, such as under the 1951 Refugee Convention. In particular, the Court concluded, the directive violated refugees' rights to dignity and freedom of movement.

Despite this ruling, Somalis in Kenya continued to endure harassment. These tensions were renewed in September 2013 when Westgate, a Nairobi shopping mall popular with expatriates and wealthy Kenyans, was attacked by gunmen, killing sixty-seven people. The four-day attack rapidly gained international media attention as footage of the burning mall foreshadowed the catastrophic damage to the building and its contents. Al-Shabaab quickly claimed responsibility via social media, while conflicting statements were made from various individuals and offices in the Kenyan government, including accusations that British, Norwegian, Sudanese and Somali nationals were amongst the attackers. It is widely believed that there were four attackers, all of whom were killed during the standoff, but only one has been officially identified as Hassan Abdi Dhuhulow, a Somali refugee who had grown up in Norway. Much of the damage to the building and the protraction of the siege, days after the attackers are believed to have been killed, was a result of looting by Kenyan soldiers. Despite the enduring confusion around the events, the Kenyan government have persistently blamed the attacks on Somalis and specifically those living in the Dadaab refugee camps.

A number of other security incidents in and around Eastleigh finally led to a reissuing of the order for all refugees to return to the camps in March 2014, this time bolstered by a popular imaginary of refugees and terrorists as synonymous. Simultaneously, the government launched a security operation called 'Operation Usalama Watch' (Operation Peace Watch) – or as it was referred to within the government, 'Operation Sanitization of Eastleigh' (Refugees International 2014) and within Eastleigh, 'Osama Watch' – which ostensibly aimed at ridding Nairobi of Al-Shabaab supporters (for more on Operation Usalama Watch see Wario and Wandera, this volume).

What ensued was two months of daily harassment, abuse, extortion and even deportations. Thousands of Somalis – Somalians and Kenyan Somalis – as well as other regional immigrants were rounded up and held in makeshift detention centres. Several thousand were forcibly sent to the refugee camps, while at least 259 were sent by plane to Mogadishu (Refugees International 2014). Stories were rife throughout Eastleigh of the brutality that ensued. Children abandoned at home after their parents were detained, including the separation of breast-feeding women and young babies, a pregnant woman forced to jump out of a third floor window, another woman in hospital having been thrown down the stairs after failing to produce a bribe, because she had given everything she had on the two previous nights. Unlike the street harassment that was an everyday aspect of life in Eastleigh, the ferocity of Usalama Watch reached into people's homes. Consecutive nights were spent hiding in silence and profound fear, with the sound of heavy metal doors being kicked in and windows shattering in the background. During a visit in April 2014, well-prepared building managers explained to Lowe how they collected money from each apartment, so it could easily be passed on to the police upon arrival, thereby preventing the door-to-door banging that often resulted in costly property damage.

This brutal ethnic profiling was not limited to the police and military forces. On the streets of Nairobi, Somalis were refused entry to *matatus* (public transport) and service in cafes, and in Eastleigh roadblocks were set up to ensure that anyone attempting to enter or exit was subject to searches. During this period the cost of freedom rocketed from a couple of hundred shillings, to around 50,000. During this period, a Somali acquaintance was arrested in front of Lowe, much to the delight of the policeman who turned to her and said 'if you want your friend back, bring some of your British pounds'.

By July of 2014, when Yarnell conducted interviews with Somalis in Eastleigh and Dadaab, the security operations had abated somewhat but tensions remained high. Though several thousand refugees had indeed been rounded up and forcibly relocated from cities to the refugee camps in the north, the majority of those refugees had in fact returned to Eastleigh and other urban centres in Kenya – many by paying bribes to bus drivers and police along the route.

One informant interviewed in Nairobi explained that she had been detained and sent to Dadaab but managed to return to Nairobi after only several days. She said that despite the risk of severe police abuse and daily harassment, she had no intention of staying in the camp because life in the city offered greater opportunities for her and her family. She could earn money selling tea in Eastleigh and she believed that her children had access to better education in the city. In the immediate term, however, she and her children did not plan to leave their house. She was too scared to return to work, and without income, she could not afford the fees to send her children to school. She said she was hopeful that the situation in Eastleigh would soon return to 'normal', but intended to avoid all potential interactions with the police until then.

Other refugees said they planned to return to their daily lives – such as attending classes at a local college – but that they would take carefully chosen *matatu* routes around Nairobi that were least likely to encounter police roadblocks. One Somali refugee woman who, after the height of the crackdown, returned to selling fruit at an outdoor kiosk in Eastleigh said that she would run inside a nearby shop whenever she saw police patrolling the street.

Even as the intensity of Operation Usalama Watch waned, however, and the hum of commerce and activity in Eastleigh resumed, a concern among many interviewees was not *if* there would be another major police crackdown against Somalis, but *when*.

Reasons to Stay, Reasons to Go

The anxiety of everyday life in Eastleigh, and the ferocity of violence during peaks of political panic in Kenya, as exemplified by Usalama Watch, beg the question – why does anyone stay in Eastleigh? As this chapter has highlighted, an escalation of insecurity is often coupled with a sudden exodus, as many people face the risks of re-encampment, onward migration, or even return to Somalia as a preferable option to remaining in Nairobi. Yet, as this chapter has also emphasized, many people also often choose to return to Eastleigh when the disquiet has subsided. In the final part of this chapter, we would like to further explore the crucial reasons why people chose to remain.

As noted above, the camps represented a singularly dependent relationship for many people. A life of rations, immobility and essentially – waiting. In a stark description of the restrictions imposed on refugees whom he interviewed in Dadaab, Ben Rawlence notes, 'They were forbidden from leaving and not allowed to work … confined to camps for generations, their children and then grandchildren born in the open prison in the desert' (2016: 3).

This is not to downplay the complex nature of life in the Dadaab camp. There, residents are constantly seeking to adapt to the externally imposed restrictions by, for example, participating in the camps informal market system (Montclos and

Kagwanja 2000), by seeking one of the few minimally paid 'incentive worker' jobs with aid organizations, and by engaging in income generating trainings and schemes. Ultimately, however, as Cindy Horst describes, 'Due to the scarce economic opportunities in the region, combined with policies of care and maintenance rather than self-sufficiency, the refugees in Dadaab have, from 1991 until now, largely been dependent on rations provided by the international community' (2006: 81).

Further, even though food rations are indeed delivered at no cost to the recipients, the quantity provided to each household is regularly reduced (sometimes cut in half!) due to World Food Programme funding constraints. Additionally, while education for the Dadaab camp residents is technically free, the demand far outstrips the availability with around 25 per cent of school aged children and youth enrolled in school, according to a 2013 study by the Danish Refugee Council, with minimal opportunities for secondary education (Kamau and Fox 2013: 17). These challenges are exacerbated by widespread insecurity and crime, including sexual and gender based violence, which are commonplace in displacement settings. As Horst continues, 'if the camp environment is unfavourable, the goal of self-sufficiency can remain remote and unattainable, no matter how committed the refugees might be to the principles of independence and self-sufficiency' (2006: 106). While life in Eastleigh clearly presents significant barriers as well, there exists the perception for (if not the real attainment of) greater life opportunities, both in Kenya and beyond.

Somalis in Eastleigh are enmeshed in large diaspora networks of family and friends; and through their computers and mobile phones, their use of Facebook, Instagram and WhatsApp, they are acutely aware of the possibilities and luxuries that might await them if they were able to leave Kenya. Although refugees in camps similarly engage with such networks, the sense of spatial freedom and independence marked a different relationship with the rest of the world and, crucially, with the humanitarian regime. Jansen suggests that, in refugee camps, 'people strategize and/or find themselves, as individuals or as part of social networks, in different proximities to humanitarian action' (2016: 151). With the same logic, refugees in Nairobi are situated in varying degrees of proximity to many options and strategies – camps, Eastleigh, diasporic networks and possibilities for onward migration. Opportunities to leave are far less prevalent than the desire to do so. Official resettlement by UNHCR and their implementing partners is the dream of many, yet achieved by only a tiny fraction. (In fact, globally, only about one per cent of registered refugees are ever resettled.) Others must rely on their own transnational kinship networks to achieve onward migration, through the facilitation of visas or family reunification, or through more illicit modes of border crossing, again, often dependent on their relatives for the financial means to do so.

If camps represent containment, and the apparent luxuries of the affluent West represent an imagined freedom, security and potential for opportunities, then Eastleigh could be situated somewhere in between – a stepping stone to a more desirable future. To live in Eastleigh might expose people to particular forms of state violence, yet it freed them from the structural and physical violence of refugee encampment. In the camps they were refugees, but in Eastleigh they were Somalis.

The majority of interlocutors had lived in cities in Somalia before leaving, and many associated this with a desire to not live in the arid areas of Northern and Eastern Kenya where the camps were located. Living in Eastleigh allowed people to distance themselves from this negative category of refugees, and to live within a largely self-sufficient Somali community. During interviews people would often explicitly state that they were not refugees, and frequently referred to their experiences of living within Dadaab or Kakuma as 'when I was a refugee…' On multiple occasions, Lowe was emphatically told by young women and men not to label them as 'refugees' when using their image or quotes in publications or presentations. Their perception of a refugee was of a victim, dependent on aid, echoing popular stereotypes in media and political discourse.

People often expressed to both authors that they did not want to be dependent on aid agencies for their livelihoods. Furthermore, they felt trapped within the camps, and expressed feeling like prisoners or caged animals. This speaks to the critique of refugee camps in protracted emergencies such as this one, which essentially constitutes the warehousing of people. As Yarnell encountered, in an effort to maintain the notion that the Dadaab camp is 'temporary', the Kenyan government has prevented the establishment of infrastructure such as plumbing, an electric grid, or even permanent roads (see also Rawlence 2016). Therefore, the perennial 'care and maintenance' approach to the camp further entrenches the dependency of camp residents on humanitarian service delivery.

Significantly, in Nairobi people were still dependent in one way or another. At the time of this research Kenya did not provide work permits for refugees, and although many people were able to access employment illegally, often relying on Somali Kenyan business owners or illegal documents, many others were reliant on remittances sent through transnational kinship networks. This form of familial dependence was seen as completely different from dependence on refugee agencies.

It should be noted that the kinship networks that were often essential for life in Eastleigh were not available for all, and frequently reflected broader social and ethnic inequalities within Somali communities. Abduwahab, a young man in his late teens, expressed enormous frustration and dejection at the obstacles of life in both Nairobi and Dadaab. He had grown up and completed his education in the camp, then found himself unable to find any work that could help support his family. He travelled to Nairobi in search of work, and was sleeping in a *madrasa*. He explained that he was from a small clan and had no contacts in Nairobi who might help him find work. He had sought help at a number of mosques, but had been told that as a man he must find a way to support himself, and not look to the community for help. Without an income he had little choice but to return to Dadaab, where he would still be unable to work, but would be able to rely on the organizations for basic support. For Abduwahab, neither option seemed viable in the long-term. For most people, Nairobi represented opportunities that were lacking in the camps, thereby providing some sense of hope and possibility for the future. It was evident in this case, however, that to live in Eastleigh required access to a certain level of support or access to livelihoods that most often materialized through clan networks. Anna Lindley suggests that, 'for many, Eastleigh is a staging post to an uncertain future' (2010: 111). For Abduwahab, the weakness of his kinship networks meant that attempts to secure his future in Eastleigh had been unsuccessful. Others spent years, even decades, trying to find ways in which to move forward from this point of uncertainty. Strong networks were a means through which people sought to navigate and cope with the uncertainty that was inherent in displacement. At the same time, the effectiveness of such networks destabilize understandings of communities as spatially bounded (Lindley 2010; Basch, Schiller and Blanc 1994), as families, as sources of emotional, physical and economic support were often dispersed across multiple countries and continents.

For people like Abduwahab, with limited access to resources and networks, hope was a distant and intangible concept to hold on to. For many others, however, Eastleigh, with its large and dense Somali population, its thriving business community and its many mosques, represented a space of hope where they could live as Somalis, connected physically, economically and virtually to a much larger network of diaspora communities. In reference to young Palestinian students, Hage suggests that 'nothing symbolizes social death like this inability to dream a meaningful life' (2003: 79). This was echoed among many informants who dreamed of a future in a 'better' place, but had only the vaguest sense of what that life would entail. When asked, the most common responses were 'I will study' or 'I will get a job', but when pushed for details the overwhelming response was 'I can't know until I get there'. As one young woman stated 'I am desperate to go. I want to go to America and leave Kenya forever, but until that happens I can't think of anything else but getting there.' The descriptions of Dadaab and Kakuma by people in Eastleigh resonated with Hage's depiction of social death. Living in Eastleigh presented a means to escape that death, and the ability to dream of a meaningful life somewhere better.

Conclusion

The intensification of violence towards Somalis and other refugees in Kenya, such as that encountered during Operation Usalama Watch should not be understood as a series of singular events. Rather, it can be situated on a continual spectrum of harassment, exploitation and containment that are everyday realities for the residents of Eastleigh, including many of those Somalis who are legal Kenyan citizens. Despite this, Nairobi, and more specifically Eastleigh, presents displaced Somalis with an alternative to refugee camps, where life is often perceived as static and limited. As Simon Turner suggests 'Nairobi may not be a pleasant place to live, but it opened up opportunities – or at least promised the dream of opportunities – to do better in the future' (2016a: 45). Living in Nairobi, and specifically within a predominantly Somali neighbourhood has allowed many people to purchase their existence as non-refugees. While rejecting the insufficient 'humanitarian' services provided in camps, many people choose to live in Eastleigh where, through private businesses and corruption, they are able to purchase goods, healthcare, education and even a particular sense of freedom – they choose 'mobile urbanity'. It is in this sense that they identified themselves as independent and therefore not refugees. The appropriated space of 'Little Mogadishu', and the perception by Kenyans and non-Kenyans that the estate – the landscape itself – is ethnically Somali, has established an environment in which people can be Somalis, rather than refugees. The temporariness of this space, which could be understood as rented rather than owned, the ambiguous legality of residency and the ubiquitous insecurity meant that the boundaries and definitions of who is or is not Somali have to be continually reinforced.

This commodification of freedom is, however, only available at a cost, and while many people are willing to pay this – through expensive rents, healthcare, education and through the not uncommon cost of paying bribes – this particular form of freedom in displacement relies on access to both financial resources and kinship networks that can be relied upon for both physical and financial security.

Lucy Lowe is a social anthropologist working at the University of Edinburgh (UK). She received her PhD from the same university for her research about the relationship between forced migration and reproductive health decisions among Somalis living in Eastleigh.

Mark Yarnell works at Refugees International. For this organization he has led field assessments to Somalia, Kenya, Ethiopia, South Sudan, the Central African Republic, Nigeria and Greece, as well as conducting research in Burkina Faso, Niger, Burundi and the Democratic Republic of the Congo. Prior to joining Refugees International, Mark was a Stimson Center Congressional Fellow, based in the office of US Senator Richard Lugar.

Notes

1. The distinction between Somalian nationals and ethnically Somali Kenyans is often problematic and there is some degree of fluidity between the two. In this chapter we refer to 'Somalis' and specify when we are explicitly discussing 'Kenyan Somalis'. It should be

noted that the term 'Somalis' is also to reflect the fact that, despite differences in citizenship, they frequently receive the same treatment in terms of profiling and harassment.
2. A term used by Somalians for Kenyan Somalis, from the Swahili word *sijui*, 'I don't know'.
3. *Capital News*, 'President Kenyatta Tells UN Chief Dadaab Must Close', 8 March 2017; retrieved 3 October 2018 from https://www.capitalfm.co.ke/news/2017/03/president-kenyatta-tells-un-chief-dadaab-must-close/.
4. E.g. *The Standard Digital*, 'For the Sake of Security, Dadaab Refugee Camp Should Be Dismantled', 11 February 2019; retrieved 7 March 2019 from https://www.standardmedia.co.ke/article/2001312660/for-the-sake-of-security-dadaab-refugee-camp-should-be-dismantled.
5. E.g. *Capital FM*, 'Rights Groups Urge Reopening of Kenya's Borders to Somali Refugees', 24 March 2017; retrieved 3 October 2018 from https://www.capitalfm.co.ke/news/2017/03/rights-groups-urge-reopening-kenyas-borders-somali-refugees/.
6. Interview with 29-year-old male Somali refugee, Nairobi, 2012.

References

Amnesty International UK. 2016. *Kenya: Talks about Closure of Dadaab Must Result in Concrete Action to Protect Refugees*. Retrieved 26 September 2016 from https://www.amnesty.org.uk/press-releases/kenya-talks-about-closure-dadaab-must-result-concrete-action-protect-refugees.
Basch, L., N.G. Schiller and C.S. Blanc. 1994. *Nations Unbound: Transnational Projects, Postcolonial Predicaments, and Deterritorialized Nation-States*. London: Routledge.
Campbell, E., J. Crisp and E. Kiragu. 2011. *Navigating Nairobi: A Review of the Implementation of UNHCR's Urban Refugee Policy in Kenya*. Geneva: UNHCR Policy Development and Evaluation Service.
Carrier, N., and E. Lochery. 2013. 'Missing States? Somali Trade Networks and the Eastleigh Transformation', *Journal of East African Studies* 7(2): 334–52.
Crisp, J. 1999. *A State of Insecurity: The Political Economy of Violence in Refugee-Populated Areas of Kenya*. Geneva: UNHCR.
Enghoff, M., et al. 2010. *In Search of Protection and Livelihoods: Socio-Economic and Environmental Impacts of Dadaab Refugee Camps on Host Communities*. Royal Danish Embassy, Norwegian Embassy.
Hage, G. 2003. '"Comes a Time We Are All Enthusiasm": Understanding Palestinian Suicide Bombers in Times of Exighophobia', *Public Culture* 15(1): 65–89.
Horst, C. 2006. *Transnational Nomads: How Somalis Cope with Refugee Life in the Dadaab Camps of Kenya*. New York and Oxford: Berghahn.
Human Rights Watch (HRW). 2013. *Kenya: Police Abuse Nairobi's Refugees*. Retrieved 26 September 2016 from https://www.hrw.org/news/2013/05/29/kenya-police-abuse-nairobis-refugees.
Inter-Governmental Authority on Development (IGAD). 2017. *Nairobi Declaration on Durable Solutions for Somali Refugees and Reintegration and of Returnees in Somalia*. Retrieved 3 October 2018 from https://igad.int/communique/1519-communique-special-summit-of-the-igad-assembly-of-heads-of-state-and-government-on-durable-solutions-for-somali-refugees.
Jansen, B.J. 2016. '"Digging Aid": The Camp as an Option in East and the Horn of Africa', *Journal of Refugee Studies* 29(2): 149–65.

Kamau, C., and J. Fox. 2013. *The Dadaab Dilemma: A Study on Livelihood Activities and Opportunities for Dadaab Refugees*. Danish Refugee Council.

Lindley, A. 2010. *The Early Morning Phone Call: Somali Refugees' Remittances*. New York and Oxford: Berghahn.

Malkki, L. 1995. 'Refugees and Exile: From "Refugee Studies" to the National Order of Things', *Annual Review of Anthropology* 24: 495–523.

Mativo, Judge J. M. 2017. *Kenya National Commission on Human Rights v The Hon. Attorney General of Kenya, Constitutional Petition No. 227 of 2016*. Nairobi: Republic of Kenya in the High Court of Kenya in Nairobi.

Montclos, (Perouse de) M.-A., and P.M. Kagwanja. 2000. 'Refugees Camps or Cities? The Socio-Economic Dynamics of the Dadaab and Kakuma Camps in Northern Kenya', *Journal of Refugee Studies* 13(2): 205–22.

Peteet, J. 2005. *Landscape of Hope and Despair: Palestinian Refugee Camps*. Philadelphia: University of Pennsylvania Press.

Rawlence, B. 2016. *City of Thorns: Nine Lives in the World's Largest Refugee Camp*. New York: Picador.

Refugees International. 2014. *Between a Rock and a Hard Place: Somali Refugees in Kenya*. Washington, DC: Refugees International.

Refugees International. 2016. *Refugee Returns from Kenya to Somalia: 'This Is about Fear... Not about Choice'*. Washington, DC: Refugees International.

Turner, Simon. 2016a. 'Staying out of Place: The Being and Becoming of Burundians Refugees in the Camp and the City', *Conflict and Society* 2(1): 37–51. DOI: 10.3167/arcs.2016.020106.

———. 2016b. 'What Is a Refugee Camp? Explorations of the Limits and Effects of the Camp', *Journal of Refugee Studies* 29(2): 139–48.

Chapter 9

Framing the Swoop

A Comparative Analysis of Operation Usalama Watch in Muslim and Secular Print Media in Kenya

Joseph Wandera and Halkano Abdi Wario

Introduction

Eastleigh stands alongside other volatile urban spaces in Kenya that have featured prominently in recent travel advisories issued by Western countries. Foreigners in Kenya have been warned to avoid unnecessary visits to an area seen as a hotbed of radical Somalia-based militant groups. These advisories, facilitated by secular and religious media, have immensely impacted the business community of Kenya and Somalis within Kenya. The making and remaking of Eastleigh as a 'no go-zone' has developed gradually over the past decade. Following terror-related violence, including the Westgate siege which took place on 21 September 2013, intermittent grenade attacks in Nairobi and Mombasa and in parts of northeastern Kenya, the security forces of the Kenyan Government embarked on a large crackdown on the Eastleigh estate in 2014 – Operation Usalama Watch (see chapter by Lowe and Yarnell in this volume).

There was unprecedented media coverage of the operation, with the government and political opposition assuming positions at variance with each other. Within the government itself, as well as within the opposition, there were heated debates regarding claims of ethnic marginalization, collective criminalization and profiling of ethnic Somalis in Eastleigh. Secular and faith-based media channels covered the government's action in diverse ways. This chapter's main argument is that how the news is reported and framed depends not only on the target audiences and the print media's editorial policy, but also on unfolding consequences of media events over a period of time and on prior circumstances related to these media events.

Incidents of terror-related violence escalated following the rise of the Al-Qaeda-linked Al-Shabaab group in Somalia in 2006 after the ousting of the Islamic Courts Union, which had attempted to create a semblance of order in a country stateless since the collapse of the Siad Barre government in 1991. In October 2011, following kidnappings and cross-border attacks attributed to Al-Shabaab, the Kenya Defence Forces pursued the militant group into Somalia, displacing them from key towns and ports in southern Somalia. The entry of Kenya's Defence Forces as part of the African Union-backed African Mission in Somalia (including armed units from Uganda, Burundi, Djibouti and Sierra Leone) elicited threats of violence, several grenade attacks, including at a University in Garissa (Kenya) in April 2015.

The growth in terror-related attacks in Nairobi and Somalia as well as the alleged radicalization and recruitment of youth in urban Kenya to join militant groups fighting the internationally-supported Somalia government has led to massive security operations in Muslim majority areas, including closure or close supervision of worship places and educational institutions. Police surveillance and subsequent arrests of some Muslims at the Riyadh Majengo and Masjid Musa Mosques in Nairobi and Mombasa among others are reported in both secular and Muslim media outlets, categorized by the latter as continued infringement by the state of the rights and freedoms of Muslim communities.

Kenya has a vibrant media landscape with numerous television and FM radio stations, secular and faith-based newspapers owned by people of various religious backgrounds, and a large user base of social media (Odhiambo 2002; Goldberg et al. 2014; Mbeke 2010; Gathara and Wanjau 2009). While some have argued that the Kenyan media is among the most vibrant in the region (see Maina 2006), others see it as deeply co-opted by successive governments in terms of editorial policy (Nyamnjoh 2005; Mbeke et al. 2010) leading to partial coverage. In 2016 the *Daily Nation* dismissed Editor Denis Galava allegedly for writing a highly critical editorial about Uhuru Kenyatta's performance as President (*Daily Nation*, 1 January 2016).

Applying the Copenhagen School's securitization theory, we shall attempt an analysis of the conceptual framing of the 'swoop' in Eastleigh and the ensuing discussion in the *Daily Nation*, a leading secular newspaper as well as in the *Friday Bulletin*, a weekly mosque newsletter.[1] This chapter seeks to demonstrate both the possibilities and the limitations of media engagement in the public sphere and thus contribute to a growing literature on the public role of the media and interdisciplinary studies of religion and media.

The methodological basis of the chapter is a textual analysis of articles, government statements, opinions and editorial columns, readers' commentaries and news items in the months preceding the April 2014 swoop, during it and a few months following in the *Daily Nation* and the *Friday Bulletin*. We employ the term 'swoop' in this chapter to indicate a sudden and quick move by security forces to conduct operations that include large-scale arrest and incarceration and controlled mobility in and out of a locale resulting in closure of business and restrictions of other mundane social interactions. The period chosen clearly demonstrates shifts in framing strategies by the two media houses before, during and after the swoop. As a case study on the ongoing global attention given to coverage of news and articles on the 'War on Terror', the African media in general and the Kenyan media scene in particular is a fascinating phenomenon, being in a state of constant fluidity and flux, subject to governmental or advocacy persuasions. Media reporting on terrorism varies between critical reviews of ongoing events, to support for government counter-terrorism strategies, to provision of critical information to the growing literate audiences across the country.

Securitization Theory (ST) has been employed in the analysis of terrorism and related security issues (Coşkun 2012). The theory defines securitization as a successful speech act 'through which an intersubjective understanding is constructed within a political community to treat something as an existential threat to a valued referent object, and to enable a call for urgent and exceptional measures to deal with the threat' (Buzan and Wæver 2003: 491; Stritzel 2007: 358). The theory is influenced by J.L. Austin's theory of speech acts as utterances (Austin 1962), hence grounded in the concept of performativity (or 'textuality'). As Ole Wæver puts it, 'by uttering "security" a state-representative moves a particular development into a specific area, and thereby claims a special right to use whatever means are necessary to block it' (Wæver 1995: 55; Stritzel 2007; Buzan et al. 1998). Three different elements play a crucial role in the process of securitization; the speech acts itself, the securitizing actor(s) and the audience. The actor performs a securitizing move by uttering a security speech act and the audience may accept or refuse the move through 'negotiation'. Buzan and Wæver (2003) added the notion of 'facilitating conditions' that point to the legitimacy and authority of the securitizing actor(s) in declaring an issue as deserving extraordinary measures to convince the audience using power politics (Stritzel 2007; Roe 2012; Floyd 2011; Buzan 2006). It should be noted that 'the complexity of determining the assent of the audience is further compounded by the fact that, in many instances, there is not one single audience but rather several possible audiences' (Balzacq, Leonard and Ruzicka 2015: 8–10).

In the case under discussion, the Kenyan State and its security forces have been engaged in an ongoing struggle against what it defines as foreign (Somalia-based) and local variants of terror groups. The threat posed by the militants is seen as existential to the referent object (the state), as previous acts of violence attributed to such groups have led to loss of lives and damage to property, challenged the state's monopoly of violence, sovereignty and control of its borders, and negatively affected its economy (Buzan 2006). The Kenya Defence Forces are a part of African Union's 22,000 security personnel in the reconstruction of post-war Somalia; hence the state does not foresee an imminent end to the threat that it faces from the terrorist groups. There has been a growing concern that certain urban suburbs are becoming the hub for recruitment and radicalization of youth as well as the source of financial funds for terror groups. These include Majengo and Eastleigh in Nairobi and Majengo and Old Town in Mombasa, places predominantly inhabited by the Somali and Swahili. The discussion that follows examines selected scholarly works on the question of Somalis in Kenya. It demonstrates the contested nature of the issue in order to show that the security operation in Eastleigh and the media coverage of it are part of a longer historical process that predates independent Kenya.

Locating the Swoop

There have been significant scholarly works on the question of Somalis in Kenya. Emma Lochery (2012) has examined the history of Somalis in Kenya through the lens of a screening exercise organized by the Kenyan government in 1989 to distinguish citizens from non-citizens. Lochery demonstrates the delicate nature of Somali citizenship status in Kenya and how this is located in the 'institutionalization of state power in Kenya and the way social relations have mediated power' (Lochery 2012: 615). Godwin Murunga (2012) has documented the colonial context of the place of Somalis in urban Nairobi showing how Somalis negotiated their habitation of Nairobi. Murunga argues that Somalis had been reluctant to occupy Pangani or the Bazaar, urban districts within Nairobi, in big numbers because of their desire to 'carve out an identity separate from the larger group of "natives"' (Murunga 2012: 473). Indeed, Murunga continues '… they [Somalis] fought to be defined as "non–native" rather than "native"' (Murunga 2012: 473; see also the chapter by Whittaker in this volume). Such quests for non-native definitional status, according to Murunga, were based on the preferential treatment some local groups such as the Arab–Swahili received. Indeed, the colonial state allowed Somalis to occupy sites other than the 'native' locations (Murunga 2012: 473). The theme of the occupation of Somalis within Nairobi is also discussed by Hannah Whittaker (2015). She analyses the contestation between Somalis in Nairobi and the colonial state regarding attempts to resettle them from the 'villages' to M'bagathi eight miles from the city centre. Arguing that Somalis are fully native to Kenya, Whittaker suggests that the manner in which Somalis related with authorities in that period finds some parallels in present day Kenya (Whittaker 2015).

The Shifta War in Kenya (1963–1967) during which hundreds of Kenyan Somalis were killed and their livestock decimated has remained central to Somali contestation with the state (see Whittaker 2014). This has been further worsened by the collapse of the Somalian state and the resultant influx of Somalian refugees across the vast porous borders. At the centre of the Somali question have been the issues of citizenship and belonging, fluid identities and loyalties, resource allocation and development and representation in national political and social matters. In this frame, Lochery argues that 'Kenyan Somalis have long experienced precarious access to citizenship' (Lochery 2012: 1). Lochery further argues that '…dynamics of inter-ethnic and intra-ethnic competition shape the production of citizenship in Kenya' (ibid.: 3), which in turn influences the 'distribution of rights and resources amongst different groups of citizens' (ibid.). The development of insecurity in Kenya and the surrounding regions has exacerbated the general animosity of the state towards Somalis.

Issues of insecurity categorized as terror have a long history in Kenya. In February 1975, two explosions occurred in Nairobi at Starlight club and travel bureau near Hilton, during the same year a blast occurred at OTC bus terminus killing thirty – all three bombings seem to have been linked to the assassination of J.M. Kariuki. In February 1980, a blast took place at the Jewish-owned Norfolk Hotel killing twenty people, with the Palestinian Liberation Organization (PLO) claiming responsibility for an act believed to be a revenge for Kenya's supporting role in Israel's Operation Entebbe. In August 1998, Al Qaeda attacked the US Embassy in Nairobi killing 222 people while injuring thousands. On 14 November 2002, terrorists attacked an Israeli-owned hotel in Kikambala, Mombasa killing 15 people including three Israelis.

A new wave of attacks occurred after the beginning of Operation Linda Nchi (Protect the country) in October 2011, following kidnappings and cross-border attacks attributed to Al-Shabaab. The entry of the Kenya Defence Forces into Somalia was followed by a large number of attacks on Kenyan soil. It started with small attacks in 2011 that became more frequent in 2012. These attacks targeted mainly churches, bars and public transport facilities in Nairobi and Mombasa, but also the North Eastern Province inhabited mainly by Kenyan Somalis, the refugee camp Dadaab situated there, as well as Eastleigh.

Operation Usalama Watch (also known as 'Operation Sanitize Eastleigh') started on 2 April 2014, at first in Eastleigh but later extended to other areas in Nairobi where many Somalis live, such as South C, Langata, Kawangware and Kasarani. The operation also took place in other Kenyan towns. In the weeks that followed, more than 4,000 people, mainly 'ethnic' Somalis and Somalians had their citizenship status reportedly checked by the Police. The *Daily Nation* of 17 April 2014 indicated that 1,136 suspected illegal immigrants, most of them Somalians (782) and Kenyans (242), were screened at the Safaricom Stadium in Kasarani in April. Following outcries from human rights organizations and other Kenyans over the legality of using a stadium as a 'detention' space, two weeks after the 'screening' started the stadium was gazetted as a police station.[2] At one point, over six thousand security personnel, more than those deployed in Somalia, including administration police (a paramilitary security unit), General

Service Unit (a paramilitary wing of the Kenyan police) and blue grey berets (Kenya Air Force, from Moi Airbase) were active in carrying out the swoop in Eastleigh (Bruzzone 2014).

Operation Usalama Watch corresponds to the securitizing move through 'performative utterance' by the main securitizing actor – the Kenyan state. This utterance entailed the popularization of convincing narratives by the said actor to the larger public audience and other organs of the society through elaborate use of media and concurrent performance of swoops on suburbs of Nairobi seen as posing an existential threat to law and order and the sovereignty of the state. Its pronouncement was accompanied by actions in the forms of swoops, arrests, detentions and deportations, all extraordinary measures said to contain lawlessness and to restore peace and stability.

As demonstrated, purported security measures such as forceful evictions and later movement of hundreds of persons to a national stadium were used. An important question concerns the reactions of the audience or audiences to the securitizing move. Were those who accepted the securitizing move convinced through coercion and persuasion? How about those who were opposed to the securitizing move from the very beginning as a result of strained relations with the securitizing actor due to past similar moves? The arena through which these discourses were deliberated was the media, both private and public and this is therefore the focus of the remaining part of this chapter.

This swoop bore certain similarities to previous swoops in Kenya's history, such as 'Operation Anvil' launched by the British colonial government in central Kenya around sixty years ago. It mainly targeted members of the Kikuyu community thought to be involved in the Mau Mau movement and aimed at taming the bigger Kikuyu community. The Kenyan state had used this approach of 'rounding up and screening' as well after independence – very similar military mobilizations were used to suppress and eliminate insurgencies during the Shifta wars (Whittaker 2014) or later in the Mount Elgon region (Simiyu 2008). These examples are evidence of a historical pattern of securitizing moves by the state that led to extraordinary measures of all-out military operations within the national borders.

The Swoop in the Eyes of the Media

The media coverage of Operation Usalama Watch was unprecedented, with newspapers, television stations, online sites and social media all reporting on the operation. There were dozens of commentaries, blogs, and Facebook-based pictures and commentaries on the operation. Although Operation *Linda Nchi* by the Kenyan Defence Forces in Somalia already had strong military performative components evident in the broadcasting of its operations on Kenya's main television stations, the publications in various newspapers, as well as the adorning of military fatigues by President Kenyatta on key military occasions, the attention to Eastleigh was even more intensive. Its proximity to many Kenyans generated considerable interest.

The role of the media in this process was 'reminiscent of Kenya's state-controlled media in the 1970s and 1980s prior to the winds of change in the 1990s' (Bruzzone 2014: 1) when media houses reported events using a similar script and exercising utmost care not to cause offense to the state. In that period, some media houses were highly controlled by the state, with some including the *Kenya Times* being mouthpieces of the then Kenya African National Union (KANU) led government (see Bruzzone 2014).[3] During the initial phase of the operation, leading media houses characterized it in a positive light, arguing that it would rid Eastleigh of terrorists. In this regard, a Somali novelist, Abdi Latif Ega, wrote '…[t]he current Kenyan imagery, hard driven by the media, is that Eastleigh is just another country at our doorstep, the barbarian at the gate' (Warah 2014: 1).[4]

The National Police Service produced a 'documentary on terrorism' for the purposes of mobilizing Kenyans to support the operation. It was aired on April 15 and 16 at prime time on all major TV stations: KBC, KTN, Citizen TV, K24 and NTV. This documentary *On the Heels of Terror: A Documentary on Terrorism* framed Operation Usalama Watch in a positive light as the 'rapid and effective' response of security forces about six months after the Westgate attack. Additionally, the documentary framed and portrayed the terror attacks as a clash of religions. Missing from the documentary was a critical assessment of the operation in terms of the gross human rights abuses that the security forces committed in Eastleigh.[5] The timing of the documentary, coming two weeks after the operation began, was as a result of protests from human rights organizations such as the Kenya National Commission on Human Rights (KNCHR), Muslim Human Rights (MUHURI), and Human Rights Watch (HRW), over alleged gross violations meted out against Somalis in the conduct of the operation. The documentary was part of the state's and its agents' (securitizing actors) measures to strengthen public support and undo the damages done to the operations by vocal human rights lobbies and Muslim media.

It will be analysed below, how voices of different media, in this case, the *Daily Nation* and *Friday Bulletin*, approved or refused to buy into the securitizing move by the state.

The *Daily Nation* and Its Coverage of the Operation

The *Daily Nation* is arguably Kenya's (and the wider east African region's) most influential newspaper with a daily circulation of about 180,000 copies. Its readership is most likely even higher because more than one person reads each copy. The Englishman, Charles Hayes, launched it in 1958 as a Swahili weekly called *Taifa*. In the following year Prince Karim Aga Khan IV, the spiritual leader of the global Ismaili Community, acquired *Taifa*. This newspaper has remained secular in its coverage and reporting. In January 1960 it became a daily newspaper called *Taifa Leo* (Swahili for 'nation today'). The first English language edition was published on 3 October 1960, thanks to the efforts of a former editor of the British News Chronicle, Michael Curtis (Loughran 2010).

In terms of relations with the government, the newspaper has continually shifted its positions. During the pre-independence days in the early 1960s the *Nation* was the voice of the Independence movement supporting African efforts to fight for emancipation from colonial rule. Following Kenya's independence in 1963, the newspaper argued for the consolidation of the gains of *uhuru* (independence). Later in the aftermath of the murder of politician J.M. Kariuki, the newspaper's stature as a voice for the voiceless took a beating for what many perceived to be a lie to the country that J.M. Kariuki was in Zambia. In the 1980s the *Nation* began to recover its voice as a beacon of hope and a voice for the second liberation of Kenya. However, compared to other publications such as *The Weekly Review* and *Society*, the newspaper remained more cautious in its criticism of government. During the fight for multi-party politics in the 1990s, the *Nation* took an active role in the struggle. With the demise of single party rule and the ascendancy of Mwai Kibaki to power, the newspaper adopted an establishment orientation, which continues to date.

We shall focus on articles that were published in the *Daily Nation* between March and May 2014 in order to demonstrate how the paper framed the situation before the swoop and the operation in Eastleigh itself. We begin with articles that helped to frame the swoop in a positive light, written mainly in the early phases of the operation, and move then to articles that were critical of the human rights abuses in the course of the swoop.

Following the numerous terror attacks in and beyond Eastleigh, media reporting of the situation depicted the attacks as acts of terror that needed a decisive response. In an article published on 3 March 2014 after bombs were found in a Mosque in Mombasa, its title was 'Mosques Turned to Avenues for Recruiting Youth into Terrorism'. The headline of another article published on 20 March 2014, read 'Are We Just Going to Sit Around and Wait to be Blown to Bits by Terrorists?' The author's remark that '…no one seems to share these fears' might point to the fact that he feels rather alone with this thinking in terms of the state's lack of a decisive response to the attacks. The titles of these articles captured the general public's feelings regarding the terror activities taking place in the country at the time, appearing to offer justification for the activities of the police. However, the writer depicted his feelings as isolated in order to convey the image of a helpless *mwananchi* (Swahili: citizen) facing imminent danger in the face of an inept and indecisive government. Thus, the writer, Mutuma Mathiu, Managing Editor at the Nation Media Group, wrote: 'It would appear that every little, two-bit Somali has a big dream – to blow us up, knock down our buildings and slaughter our children'. The article argued that terrorists intended to blow up the lives of Kenyans. The editor concluded his article, '[w]e are at war. Let's start shooting'.[6] The article depicted terrorism as an existential threat to Kenyans that needed a swift armed response. In another article published on 22 March 2014, the title was 'Alarm as Radical Youth Take Over Key Mosques'. The article argued that this development could result in more terror attacks and cited an investigative broadcast by Nation Television that attributed the expulsion of certain Muslim clerics to the radicalized youth.

Following the mass arrests of Somalians as well as Kenyan Somalis in Eastleigh, the *Daily Nation* of 7 April 2014 carried a report, 'Police Hold Hundreds in Kasarani Stadium'. The story explained that 'those without identity documentation were among those rounded up and detained at the Safaricom Stadium, Kasarani'. The question of the abuses that reportedly took place in the conduct of the arrests did not feature in the newspaper's reports. Similar portrayals of the swoop in a generally positive light followed: 'Police Alert on Fleeing Suspects' on 9 April 2014 and '82 Somalis Deported in Security Operation' on 10 April 2014. The latter article reported about the deportation of Somalians back to Somalia following the security swoop. The newspaper reported that the operation was due to 'continuous attacks' and that 'most suspects arrested did not have appropriate documents and were detained in several police stations'.[7]

A columnist for the *Daily Nation*, Kwamchetsi Makokha writes a satirical column in which he comments mainly on political issues. Thus, in an article the opening line stated, 'Arresting 657 Somalis in Eastleigh, holding them in cages at Kasarani Stadium and taxing them for illegal presence in Kenya should teach terrorists a lesson'.[8] The writer also argued, '… the government has allowed these relatives of Al-Shabaab to invest in the country, constructing tall buildings, trading and practicing their religion, oblivious of the poor pay the police receive'. While the satirical nature of the article was not in doubt, the literary gap between the writer and ordinary *mwananchi* could lead to divergent interpretations of the text. Further, the general mood of the country could have helped the writer understand the possibility of the article generating xenophobic acts in the country, such as non-Somalis attacking Somalis.

The general framing of the swoop in Eastleigh could also be noticed in the way the various stories were physically laid out on the pages of the *Daily Nation*. For example in April 2014, the main story featured a report about a speech the National Assembly Majority Leader Aden Duale had given in Eastleigh, in which he had apparently talked in a questionable way about terrorism.[9] On the far right of the same page there were shorter articles entitled: 'Westgate Witnesses Testify in Camera', '12 Found Without IDs Deny Being Somalis' and 'Man Facing Explosive Charges Granted Bail'. Therefore, it was not only the headings of the article and the content that was framed in a particular way, but also the layout of the respective stories that spoke to the prevailing biases. The location of the various articles, all focusing on the operation in Eastleigh and appearing to present Somalis as guilty by association or actually engaged in terror played a role in influencing public perceptions.

The raid on Eastleigh elicited heated condemnation from national and international human rights organizations as well as from Muslim organizations and activist groups, which influenced significantly the *Daily Nation*'s shift in its coverage of the security operation. Organizations that condemned the human rights abuses meted out on the Somalis during the raid included the Kenya National Commission on Human Rights, Amnesty International, the Council of Imams and Preachers of Kenya, Muslim Human Rights and various churches in Kenya, among others.[10] Thus one could sense a change in the way the *Daily Nation* now reported the swoop. The narrative shifted from that of labelling terror suspects to that of citing human rights violation. The Somali community and other Kenyans were recognizing Somalis as 'victims' of the operation. Thus, on 22 May 2014, Mutuma Mathiu wrote in the *Daily Nation*:

> Chances are that the next Somali you meet has absolutely nothing to do with Al-Shabaab and is as much in danger of being blown up in a grenade attack as you are. Therefore, if you have profiled him or her, then he or she is a victim twice over. This is not only unfair and unjust, it is also an unhelpful reaction based on blind fear. We must also make an effort to understand the circumstances of Somali émigrés in our midst. The bulk of them are running away from a violent and dangerous place.[11]

Interestingly the above article still framed Somalians as outsiders, with little consideration in the media for the rights of Kenyan Somalis.

Following different publications focusing on the human rights abuses, Kenya's Independent Policing Authority (IPOA) initiated investigations into allegations of human rights abuses in the conduct of the operation Usalama Watch. On 4 July 2014, *Daily Nation* reported that Kenya's Independent Policing Authority had identified 29 police officers accused of taking bribes and harassing civilians during Operation Usalama Watch. The economic aftermath of the security swoop was also noted. On Saturday 14 June 2014 in an article by Justus Wanga entitled, 'Eastleigh Traders Relocate with Billions in Crackdown' the writer reported that 'investors in Nairobi's Eastleigh area are moving billions of shillings into neighbouring countries in the aftermath of a security swoop …' In the same newspaper a story was published entitled, 'Landlords Stare at Empty Houses as Tenants Leave'. Clearly the *Daily Nation* was now focused more on the negative effects of the swoop.

The *Friday Bulletin* and Its Coverage of the Operation

In the last decade no publication has covered issues concerning the Muslim communities in Kenya as thoroughly as the *Friday Bulletin* (Mwakimako 2007). The Bulletin is produced by an editorial board comprised of three to four individuals selected by the Nairobi Jamia Mosque Committee, a body mandated to administer this very important Kenyan mosque. It labels itself as 'the weekly Muslim news update' and ranges from eight to twelve pages. Apart from news and analysis of weekly events, the Bulletin also carries regular columns of *da'wa* (Arabic: invitation, proselytism), religious teachings for special constituencies such as women, youth and children, announcements about mosque lectures and talks as well as an assortment of advertisements from Muslim commercial enterprises. It is funded by the Jamia Mosque itself, which runs a number of rented business premises that generate income near the operation. The editorial team has been mandated to prioritize issues affecting the faith community and appropriate religious knowledge content.

The *Bulletin*, though it purports to represent a wide-range of Muslims notwithstanding diverse ideological affiliations, holds rigid Salafist positions on matters of religious beliefs. This is evident in its stance on the place of religion and politics and the nature of selected religious knowledge, themes appropriated from online articles and blogposts by leading global voices of Salafist/and Islamist ideologies.[12]

It reaches dozens of mosques in the country by means of elaborate distribution networks, is available for download on the main website of Jamia Mosque and is sent to dozens of individuals and institutions in digital format through email subscriptions.[13] The *Bulletin* is accessed and distributed free of charge in contrast to mainstream newspapers which charge between 50 and 60 Kenyan Shillings (equivalent of USD 0.5) per copy. The *Friday Bulletin* is an English language publication, a choice that is informed by the prominent use of the language in Kenya's print media scene (Mazrui 2009) and targets urban Muslims who have proficiency in the language.

The *Bulletin* sees its role as defending the right and freedom to speak to the state and its agencies by publishing their pertinent issues on a weekly basis. This aim also becomes apparent in its self-description as playing an active role in revitalizing the Muslim media and countering 'negative media propaganda'.[14] This role is one reason behind the publication's attraction for readers.

Prior to the rise of the *Friday Bulletin* as a regular publication, there had been only a few Muslim print media in Kenya. These included *al-Islah* (1930s), *Sauti ya Haki* (1970s) and *Nuru* (1980/90s), and among others. These precursors were characterized by intermittent production and their lack of consistent content and form. In recent years *Friday Bulletin* competes with publications such as *The New*

Dawn, produced by the Kenya Muslim Youth Alliance (KMYA), an organization close to the Supreme Council of Kenya Muslims (SUPKEM).[15]

Since the 8 August 1998 simultaneous bombing of the United States embassies in Nairobi and Dar es Salaam and subsequent terrorism-related attacks, there has been a growing perception among Muslim communities that the state unfairly targets its members under the pretext of fighting terror. Special legislations such as the Prevention of Terrorism Act of 2012 and the establishment and operations of an Anti-Terrorism Police Unit (ATPU) have elicited opposition from human rights organizations, sections of the Muslim community and the *Bulletin* (Kenya National Commission on Human Rights 2008).

The period preceding the swoop shows the continued engagements by the *Friday Bulletin* regarding the legality and abuse of the counter-terrorism strategies by the state and other challenging issues. Even though the *Bulletin* also condemns acts of terror and advises its readership to avoid militant groups, it often chooses to focus on the consequences of the state's counter-terrorism actions. The swoop coverage was important as it was conducted in Kenya's capital city and was also in the focus of national and international media outlets.

From April to August 2014, the *Friday Bulletin* published varied news items relating to Operation Usalama Watch. All weekly issues during the months of April and May were dominated by the analysis of the swoop as main news headlines, while editorial expositions and letters from readers condemned the security operation and appealed for an end to the suffering of the residents in Muslim majority estates in Nairobi.

To emphasize the gravity of the swoop and the broader concerns from sources beyond the Kenyan Muslim community, the editors consistently included varied opinions, press statements, reports and international coverage from very different organizations, such as the UNHCR, Amnesty International, the Kenya Human Rights Commission, the International Federation of Human Rights or the Kenya's security watchdog Independent Police Oversight Authority (IPOA)[16] as well as an assortment of local secular NGOs engaged in human rights advocacy, but also appeals from select individual members of the US Congress and Senate, diplomats and the government of Somalia. For instance, the UNHCR is reported to have raised the illegality of arbitrary arrests, detention and the resultant deportations to an unstable country of origin contrary to international laws that protects refugees whether or not they are legal.[17]

The *Bulletin* was also among the first to highlight extortion by the security agents of the Somali residents of Eastleigh and South C estates.[18] It concluded that those incarcerated at the Kasarani Stadium comprised Kenyan Somalis, genuine legal immigrants, undocumented refugees as well as those unable or unwilling to pay bribes.[19] The editors described the conditions – complete with photos – as akin to a 'concentration camp'. The phrase Kasarani Concentration Camp gained currency among users of social media.[20] In subsequent issues of the

Bulletin the editorial team also argued that such swoops were excessive as they had the effect of heightening distrust between Muslims and the state, thus hindering opportunities for collaboration on security matters and only stimulating further radicalization.[21]

The Bulletin observed that the flow of millions of shillings through the once vibrant Eastleigh came to a standstill due to fear of raids and extortion and loss of rental income due to movement of tenants to other estates. It also hinted that the swoop was used, as a side-effect, for economic sabotage by rival non-Muslim/Somali groups aiming at dislodging the Somali business empire. The *Bulletin* also reported capital flight and mass emigration of Somali entrepreneurs to Kampala, Uganda (see Iazzolino, this volume) where there was a better investment environment. Similar reports on the economic impact of the swoop were also featured in the *Daily Nation* during the month of May 2014. An unfavourable effect noted by the *Bulletin* included ethnic profiling of Somalis and discrimination against Muslims by non-state actors and an emerging Islamophobia within the larger non-Muslim populace during the swoop.[22] The headline of a commentary in the *Friday Bulletin* on 23 May 2014 (Issue No. 577) was titled 'Religious and Ethnic Intolerance – A Time Bomb'. Citing reports, the *Bulletin* detailed strained relationships and threats against the Somali community from neighbours of Muslim religious and education institutions, ejection of Somalis or Muslims from public means of transport and cases of hate speeches by some politicians[23] against Somalis and Muslims as sympathizers of terror groups.[24] The *Friday Bulletin* included the opinions of its readers on the swoop, including appeals from local and diasporic Muslim readers to the head of state to end the ongoing security operations.

The period of the swoop coincided with the first annual 'Journey of Faith – Africa. International Islamic Conference' which is an extension of Journey of Faith (JoF) conferences founded by Sheikh Said Rageah and held annually in Toronto, Canada.[25] Most speakers, both Kenyan Muslim leaders and prominent scholars from outside the country, called for moderation in faith, and the embodiment of peace, good character and morality as a way of calling others to the faith during the event held at Kenyatta International Conference Centre.[26]

Contrasts and Convergence in Coverage of the Operation

The introduction of political pluralism in the early 1990s was accompanied by the opening of media spaces in Kenya, which played a constructive role in the development of a broad movement for democratic change that challenged the Moi autocracy (Middleton 2009; Mbeke 2010; Ogola 2011). Nevertheless, effective and impartial media operations in Kenya are still hampered. A report about 'Kenya media vulnerabilities' points out that '… corruption is endemic in all media and cuts across all levels of staff. Journalists, editors and owners are politically co-opted and openly show editorial bias' (Mbeke et al. 2010: 7).

Operation Usalama Watch in Eastleigh and its coverage by secular and religious media in Kenya raise important questions about the changing relationship between the government and the media. Although Kenya's secular media is reputed to be the most sophisticated in the region and over the past decade has enjoyed massive expansion in terms of ownership diversity and coverage, its reporting on Operation Usalama Watch was dictated by a variety of factors. These included the government position regarding the swoop and later reflected human rights and civil society sentiments. The operation provided a context in which one could identify the limits and potential of the media to engage in the public sphere. It demonstrated how media houses could easily slip into a negative mode of engagement despite their rich tradition of critiquing human rights abuses. In addition, increasing securitization as part of counter-terrorism strategies by the state is slowly impacting on how media outlets approach incidents like the swoop. The relations between the media and the state risk being further strained by clauses that may inhibit investigative reportage of issues deemed state security priorities.

There are multiple audiences to the government-initiated securitizing move through the swoop and the subsequent incarcerations at a national stadium. The state as the securitizing actor had a relatively easy time in reaching some levels of intersubjective understanding of the threat that the allegedly illegal residents of Eastleigh and South C estates pose to the stability and security of Nairobi in particular and Kenya in general. Due to mass media framing, during terrorist attacks and subsequent crackdowns the image of Eastleigh conjured among ordinary Kenyans has been that of a den of terrorists. This, however, subsides as the commercial district picks up its business momentum afterwards. Operation Usalama Watch was launched right after a series of terrorist attacks in various parts of the country and no tangible measures were taken by the state to avert further attacks. Hence it easily garnered public support and allowed the state to use the measures it deemed best to address run-away crimes of terror. The *Daily Nation* tapped into an existing narrative targeted at the public in the initial phases of the swoop and, going by the analysis, [27] some of the writers appeared to drum up support for the state and commend the operations as long overdue. Being a prominent publication with nationwide coverage, its narratives played a crucial role in marshalling large sections of the audience. The *Friday Bulletin* in contrast has been relentless in condemning the actions of the state particularly in regards to the 'War on Terror' and the relations between the state and Muslim communities in general. From the very start of the swoop to the end, it maintained a critical stance against the state agencies involved. The *Friday Bulletin* and its readers fall under groups that are unconvinced and oppositional to the performative speech act and subsequent actions of the state, the principal securitizing actor.

Therefore, as a result of the current power structures in the field of security it is likely that some voices will be excluded from the speech act process, thus limiting the opportunity for dissent from those who may be most affected by the security policy. This exclusionary aspect becomes particularly evident if we accept that, as it currently stands, once 'security' is uttered it limits the space for democratic contestation (Balzacq, Leonard and Ruzicka 2015). It is only much later that *Daily Nation* also shifted to the oppositional side of the securitizing move. This was based on numerous narratives and pictures from the swoop that depicted those arrested as subject to discrimination, harassment, extortion, deportation and assault. The paradigmatic shift in the framing of the swoop in the *Daily Nation* was also influenced by similar critical reviews of the swoop by leading human rights organizations, independent state-related police supervisory committees and its own first-hand accounts from field assignments. Was the securitizing move successful? Did the state succeed in establishing intersubjective assent among multiple audiences to an existential threat to itself that allowed extraordinary measures? The answer is elusive. However, as long as the swoop exists in the memory of some its most ardent oppositional audiences as a series of repressive actions against its constituents, and as long as it is documented and critiqued by non-sectarian lobby groups and organizations, the media will continue to play a crucial role in shaping public responses to similar future operations.

Conclusion

In this chapter, we have discussed the framing of the swoop in Eastleigh by the *Friday Bulletin* of the Jamia Mosque Nairobi and the *Daily Nation*, a leading secular newspaper. Based on the Copenhagen School's securitization theory, we have attempted a conceptual framing and analysis of the swoop in Eastleigh and the ensuing discussion by the *Daily Nation* and the *Friday Bulletin*. In the wake of the government's 'securitization' of the swoop in Eastleigh by framing terror attacks as a threat to state security, an inter-subjective understanding was successfully constructed within Kenya's political community to treat the attacks as an existential threat calling for urgent and exceptional measures. In this context, the *Daily Nation*, in the initial phase of its reporting bought into the government's narrative and generally framed the swoop in a positive light, adopting an uncritical 'nationalistic stance'. One could argue that during the first phase of its coverage of the swoop, the *Daily Nation* had been co-opted by the state, reporting the effort by government as a security measure. Although the actor performs a securitizing move by uttering a security speech, the audience may accept or refuse this move through 'negotiation'. In this frame, the Muslim *Friday Bulletin* saw itself as standing up against state authoritarianism and defending Muslim rights while drawing on a variety of sources both local and international to depict the swoop's indiscriminate nature. Unlike the *Daily*

Nation, in its initial coverage of the swoop, *Friday Bulletin* offered alternative narratives highlighting three areas. Firstly, it framed the process as one in which the government was using the ongoing anti-terrorism operation to collectively target and marginalize the Somali community, and deduced from this a targeting of the Muslim community in general (see Kresse 2009). Secondly, it consistently provided an economic frame of analysis pointing out the negative effects that the operation was having on the Eastleigh economy. This angle, missing from the first phase of the *Daily Nation*'s coverage, was to later emerge clearly during the second phase in the latter newspaper as well. Finally, the *Bulletin* invoked human rights in regard to the operation, noting the numerous reports by local and international agencies regarding gross violations of such rights.

This chapter demonstrates the fluid nature of the media coverage of the swoop. While the two media houses differed in their coverage of the operation, they also converged later on. In response to the protest against the violation of human rights, the *Daily Nation* in its second phase of reporting appeared to acknowledge the principles of public interest and impartiality, balancing the competing interests, sympathies and susceptibilities of different audiences in Kenya. Like the *Friday Bulletin*, violation of human rights became a major concern for the *Daily Nation* in the later phase of its coverage.

Joseph Wandera is a Bishop at the Mumias Diocese of the Anglican Church of Kenya. Until 2017 he worked as a senior lecturer at the Department of Religious Studies, St Paul's University (Kenya). His PhD is from the University of Cape Town, South Africa. His publications include *Mapping Eastleigh for Christian–Muslim Relations* (Zapf Chancery Publishers Africa, 2013) and *Public Preaching and Interface Relations: The Influence of Muslim and Pentecostal Leaders in Western Kenya* (Borderless Press, 2018).

Halkano Abdi Wario is a lecturer in the Department of Philosophy, History and Religion at Egerton University (Kenya). He holds a PhD from the University of Bayreuth, Germany, for research focusing on the transnational Islamic movement Tablīghī Jamāʿat in Kenya. His research interests include religious knowledge, religious transnationalism, Islamic reformism in Eastern Africa and emerging trends in Islamic law in Africa and dynamics of countering violent extremism in the Horn of Africa.

Notes

1. *Friday Bulletin* is a weekly publication from the Nairobi Jamia Mosque and one of the leading Muslim print media in Kenya in the last decade. *Daily Nation* and *Sunday Nation* are owned by the Nation Media Group that also manages a number of other broadcast television and radio stations.

2. Gazette notice 2719, *Kenyan Gazette* Vol. CXVI No. 50, p. 1039, 17 April 2014, retrieved 7 March 2019 from http://kenyalaw.org/kenya_gazette/gazette/notice/143379.
3. For the history of media in Kenya, see also Ogola (2011).
4. Cited by Rasna Warah (2014).
5. *Daily Nation* of 17 April 2014 commented on a recent film entitled 'Terror at the Mall' produced by British filmmaker Dan Reed on the eve of the first anniversary of the Westgate attack, and especially the role of Kenya's security forces: 'Kenya's Security agencies appear to score poorly in this film … The commentator describes Kenya's soldiers and police officers as confused and lacking a comprehensive plan.'
6. *Daily Nation*, 'Are We Just Going to Sit Around and Wait to be Blown to Bits by Terrorists?', by M. Mathiu, 20 March 2014.
7. *Saturday Nation*, 5 April 2014.
8. *Daily Nation*, 'Turning Screw on Somalis will Force Them to Reveal Attacks', by K. Makokha, 11 April 2014.
9. *Daily Nation*, 'Eastleigh Rally Clip Puts Duale in a Tight Spot', by R. Abdi, 10 April 2014.
10. See for example, *Daily Nation*, 14 April 2014, 'Muslim Leaders Rally against Clampdown' and *Daily Nation*, Tuesday 15 April 2014, 'Clergy Call for Humane Police Operation'.
11. *Daily Nation*, 'When You Meet the Next Somali or Muslim, Hug Him; He's also a Victim', by M. Mathiu, 22 May 2014.
12. The *Friday Bulletin* reveals a strong inclination toward works and treatises of prominent conservative religious scholars with a bias towards Salafist and Islamist ideologies; they include among many others Muhammad Saalih Al-Munajjid, a prominent Saudi Islamic scholar, and Yusuf al-Qaradawi, a famous Egyptian theologian and media personality.
13. The *Bulletin* was for a long time available to download from the former website of the Nairobi Jamia Mosque.
14. *Friday Bulletin*, 09 May 2008 (No. 262): 2.
15. The Supreme Council of Kenya Muslims was founded in 1973, and officially recognized by the Kenyan government as representative of Kenyan Muslims in 1979 (Oded 2000).
16. *Friday Bulletin*, 18 July 2014 (No. 585), carries a headline 'Police on the Spot Over Flawed Eastleigh Operation' reporting about the IPOA investigation of 29 police officers for harassment, extortion and assaults.
17. *Friday Bulletin*, 11 April 2014 (Issue No. 571).
18. In *Friday Bulletin*, 18 April 2014 (Issue No. 572), in a news item entitled 'Security Operation Moves to South C'.
19. *Friday Bulletin*, 17 January 2014 (Issue 559) quotes an official of SUPKEM saying 'Eastleigh has been turned into an ATM (Automated Teller Machine) by officers whose main work is to harass innocent residents and force them to pay bribes to secure their freedom'.
20. In Issue No. 584, 11 July 2014, the *Bulletin* reports an online campaign dubbed '*#Kasaraniiftar*' to feed Muslim inmates at the Stadium and various Police cells. Kasarani remained a spatial enclave for unlawful incarceration for an extended period of a few months after the swoop.
21. The Wajir women's representative lamented that the operation only targeted the Somali community remarking 'Is this how the government wants to win the fight against terrorism? Actually they are creating more terrorists and radicals' (*Friday Bulletin*, 18 April 2014 (Issue 572)).
22. *Friday Bulletin*, 09 May 2014 (Issue No. 575).

23. *Friday Bulletin*, 23 May 2014 (Issue No. 577), quotes Moses Kuria from the ruling *The National Alliance* coalition 'I think it is just a matter of time before Kenyans start violence against *perceived* terrorists, their sympathizers, their financiers and those issuing travel advisories (Western countries) without sharing intelligence. Choices have consequences.' (author's emphasis) on the front page and analyses the growing threat of what it considers as Islamophobia in the country.
24. On a positive note, the *Bulletin* demonstrated the agency of the Kenyan Somalis to counter rising incidences of stereotyping by an initiate, dubbed 'Kenya, I Am Not a Terrorist', *Friday Bulletin*, 02 May 2014 (Issue No. 574).
25. Sheikh Said Rageah was born in Somalia. After his family lived in Saudi Arabia for a while, they moved to North America in the late 1980s.
26. *Friday Bulletin*, 02 May 2014 (Issue No. 574), 'Be Ambassadors of Peace'.
27. The work of a securitizing actor to give an 'issue sufficient saliency to win the assent of the audience' (Balzacq, Leonard and Ruzicka 2015: 3) is what ultimately empowers the appropriate authority to act.

References

Austin, J.L. 1962. *How to do Things with Words*. Cambridge: Harvard University Press.
Balzacq, T., S. Leonard and J. Ruzicka. 2015. '"Securitization" Revisited: Theory and Cases', *International Relations*: 1–38. DOI: 10.1177/0047117815596590.
Bruzzone, A. 2014. 'Kenya's Security Crackdown and the Politics of Fear'. Retrieved 11 November 2014 from http://focusonthehorn.wordpress.com/2014/04/23/kenyas-security-crackdown-and-the-politics-of-fear/.
Buzan, B. 2006. 'The "War on Terrorism" as the New "Macro-Securitization"', Oslo Workshop, Oslo, 2006.
Buzan, B., and O. Wæver. 2003. 'Regions and Powers: Summing Up and Looking Ahead', in B. Buzan and O. Wæver, *Regions and Powers: The Structure of International Security*. Cambridge: Cambridge University Press, pp. 445–60.
Buzan, B., O. Waever, F. Hampson and J. Wilde. 1998. 'Security: A New Framework for Analysis', *International Journal*: 798–98.
Coşkun, B. 2012. 'Words, Images, Enemies: Macro-Securitization of the Islamic Terror, Popular TV Drama and the War on Terror', *Turkish Journal of Politics* 3(1): 36–51.
Floyd, R. 2011. 'Can Securitization Theory Be Used in Normative Analysis? Towards a Just Securitization Theory', *Security Dialogue*: 427–39.
Gathara, P., and M. Wanjau. 2009. 'Bringing Change through Laughter: Cartooning in Kenya', *Media and Identity in Africa*: 275–86.
Goldberg, A., T. Simon, L. Aharonson-Daniel, D. Leykin and B. Adini. 2014. 'Twitter in the Cross Fire – The Use of Social Media in the Westgate Mall Terror Attack in Kenya', *PLoS ONE* 9(8): e104136. doi:10.1371/journal.pone.0104136.
Kenya National Commission on Human Rights. 2008. 'On the Brink of the Precipice. A Human Rights Account of Kenya's Post-2007 Election Violence. Final Report'. Nairobi.
Kresse, K. 2009. 'Muslim Politics in Postcolonial Kenya: Negotiating Knowledge on the Double-Periphery', *Journal of the Royal Anthropological Institute* 15: S76–S94.
Lochery, E. 2012. 'Rendering Difference Visible: The Kenyan State and It's Somali Citizens', *African Affairs* 111(445): 615–39. DOI: 10.1093/afraf/ads059.
Loughran, G. 2010. *Birth of a Nation: The Story of a Newspaper in Kenya*. London: I.B. Tauris.

Maina, L. 2006. *African Media Development Initiative, Kenya: Research Findings and Conclusions*. London: BBC World Service Trust.
Mazrui, A. 2009. 'Language and the Media in Africa: Between the Old Empire and the New', in N. Kimani and J. Middleton (eds), *Media and Identity in Africa*. Edinburgh University Press, pp. 36–48.
Mbeke, P.O. 2010. *Mass Media in Kenya: Systems and Practice*. Nairobi: Jomo Kenyatta Foundation.
Mbeke, P.O., et al. 2010. *The Media We Want: The Kenya Media Vulnerabilities Study*. Nairobi, Kenya: Friedrich Ebert Stiftung. Retrieved 7 July 2017 from http://library.fes.de/pdf-files/bueros/kenia/07887.pdf.
Middleton, J. 2009. *Media and Identity in Africa*. Edinburgh: Edinburgh University Press.
Murunga, G. 2012. 'The Cosmopolitan Tradition and Fissures in Segregationist Town Planning in Nairobi, 1915–23', *Journal of Eastern African Studies* 6(3): 463–86.
Mwakimako, H. 2007. *Mosques in Kenya: Muslim Opinions on Religion, Politics and Development*. Berlin: Klaus Schwarz Verlag.
Nyamnjoh, F. 2005. *Africa's Media Democracy and the Politics of Belonging*. London: Zed Books.
Oded, O. 2000. *Islam and Politics in Kenya*. London: Lynne Rienner Publishers.
Odhiambo, L. 2002. 'The Media Environment in Kenya Since 1990', *African Studies* 61(2): 295–318.
Ogola, G. 2011. 'The Political Economy of the Media in Kenya: From Kenyatta's Nation-Building Press to Kibaki's Local Language FM Radio', *Africa Today* 57(3): 77–95.
Roe, P. 2012. 'Is Securitization a "Negative" Concept? Revisiting the Normative Debate over Normal versus Extraordinary Politics', *Security Dialogue* 43(3): 249–66.
Simiyu, R. 2008. 'Militarization of Resource Conflicts: The Case of Land-Based Conflict in the Mount Elgon Region of Western Kenya', *ISS Monograph* No. 152. Pretoria: Institute for Security Studies.
Stritzel, H. 2007. 'Towards a Theory of Securitization: Copenhagen and Beyond', *European Journal of International Relations* 13(3): 357–83. doi: 10.1177/1354066107080128.
Warah, R. 2014. 'Eastleigh Crackdown Offers Major Opportunity for Bribe-Taking and Harassment by Police', *Sahan Journal*. Retrieved 11 November 2015 from http://sahanjournal.com/eastleigh-crackdown-offers-major-opportunity-bribe-taking-harassment-police/#.VGJXOVYRbwI.
Wæver, O. 1995. 'Securitization and Desecuritization', in R.D. Lipschutz (ed.) *On Security*. New York: Columbia University Press, pp. 46–86.
Whittaker, H. 2015. 'A New Model Village? Nairobi Development and the Somali Question in Kenya, c. 1915–17', *Northeast African Studies* 15(2): 117–40.
———. 2014. 'The Shifta Conflict, 1963–68', in H. Whittaker, *Insurgency and Counterinsurgency in Kenya*. Leiden: Brill, pp. 69–88.

Chapter 10

Beyond Eastleigh
A New Little Mogadishu in Uganda?

Gianluca Iazzolino

Introduction

Research on Eastleigh has mostly highlighted the significance of the neighbourhood for Somalian refugees and Kenyan Somalis in Kenya and its central position within transnational migrant and commercial networks. As argued previously in this volume, this literature has examined the economic and spatial practices that make the neighbourhood, simultaneously, a commercial hub and an urban space in which refugees (not only from Somalia) pursue livelihood strategies and wait for resettlement to third countries (see chapter by Ripero-Muñiz in this volume). However, in doing so, these studies have mostly focused on the links with Somalia or with other centres of low-end globalization, particularly outside of Africa. Less discussed is the role of Eastleigh as a regional stepping stone, particularly to neighbouring countries which not only offer refugees a safe haven during troubled times in Kenya, but also provide both Kenyan Somalis and Somalians with opportunities to pursue education or branch out into new businesses. The purpose of this chapter is to contribute to filling the gap of knowledge on regional connections spanning from Eastleigh to the rest of Africa, examining in particular an increasingly important link between the Somali areas of Nairobi and of Kampala, Uganda (on Uganda see also Iazzolino and Hersi 2019). Indeed, according to Uganda's Office of the Prime Minister (OPM), the main administrative body which deals with refugee affairs, between 2008 and 2017 the number of registered Somali refugees in the country soared from 8,239 to 41,234, with 43 per cent of the total registered in Kampala and the rest in the Nakivale refugee settlement.[1] The overwhelming majority of them were previously refugees in neighbouring Kenya, but once they reached the border, they re-applied for refugee status in Uganda. Others have applied as refugees in Uganda for the first time after illegally venturing through Kenya from Somalia. Moreover, this number does not account for unregistered Somalians, for Somalis with foreign passports and Somalians regularly travelling between Somalia and Uganda.

This chapter thus examines why, and how, in the past years Uganda has become at the same time a safe haven in troubled times and a place where many Somalian refugees wait for resettlement to a third country, advance their education, manage their business in the region and closely follow Somalia's winding path to recovery.

The argument of this chapter is that, despite the recent spike, the Somali route to Uganda and its significance should be looked at within the long history of Somali mobility across East Africa. While regional Somali migrations are not a new phenomenon (Kleist 2004; Hammond 2014; Bakewell and Binaisa 2016), the novelty of this steady influx to Uganda lies in its specific push and pull factors acting as key mobility drivers at a regional level:[2] the growing pressure on Somali refugees in Kenya, where state security concerns have increasingly permeated public discourses on refugee issues (as described in the chapters by Lowe and Yarnell and by Wario and Wandera, this volume); the implementation of Uganda's 2006 refugee law; and ease of access to neighbouring areas, particularly the Uganda–DRC borderland, Rwanda and, until recent upheavals, South Sudan, where fresh business opportunities had drawn the interest of resourceful refugee entrepreneurs – but also to Somalia, thanks to direct flights connecting Entebbe airport to Mogadishu, and to a visa policy which allows Somali passport-holders to re-enter Uganda. These drivers define the socio-political landscape through which Somali refugees navigate, according to individual skills and aspirations, but also to pre-existing configurations of power, mostly depending on clan affiliations.

Some caveats are in order: a main purpose of this chapter is to tease out the complexity of Somali mobility patterns, which challenge clear-cut separations between categories such as forced and voluntary migration and survival and business networks. This is why the empirical focus of this chapter is on both migrants and refugees and on the way practices on the ground challenge policy and scholarly frameworks.

Also, as this research is based on fieldwork conducted over a timeframe spanning from January 2013 to May 2014, it grapples with a specific moment shaped by the interplay of factors that exacerbated a volatile situation. Since then, the tensions have partially abated and many of those who had made their way to Uganda during my research have returned to Eastleigh. However, Kampala's Kisenyi area, dubbed by Ugandan media 'Kampala's Little Mogadishu', has since become a major Somali commercial hub in the region, with stronger links to Eastleigh in terms of flows of Somali businesspeople and students, goods and capital. This chapter thus highlights the interplay of individual aspirations, social networks and institutional settings in shaping complex transnational and translocal strategies. The dynamics at play which are here described are therefore far-reaching and provide insights not only for the understanding of Somali mobility patterns in East Africa, but also for the scholarly debates on migration in Africa and migrant agency. Indeed, although smaller by size when compared to the Somalian refugee population still in Kenya, Ethiopia and Yemen (to mention only countries close to Somalia), the study of the Somali diaspora in Uganda fits a stream of research, stemming from a recent surge in interest in African migrations (primarily motivated by European policy concerns), which have challenged many assumptions about trajectories and drivers of human flows originating in the continent (Flahaux and De Haas 2014). Particularly significant are the empirical studies tackling intra-African migratory flows (Sander and Maimbo 2003; Bakewell and Bonfiglio 2013; Bakewell and De Haas 2007) and shedding light, on the one hand, on the variety of forms of mobility in Africa; on the other, on the complex interweaving of factors shaping mobility patterns. The case here discussed thus challenges the rigid boundaries between the categories of forced and voluntary migrations (Bakewell 2010), not denying their policy relevance, but emphasizing the strategic role of migrant networks to garner the resources through which they move between these two categories. Furthermore, examining the emergence and the transformation of the Somali community in Uganda brings to the fore the significance of desires and aspirations, generally overshadowed in the analysis of migratory phenomena by the prominence attached to the dimension of coping, ascribed to conditions of displacement.

This chapter opens with an overview of the debates to which this chapter aims to contribute by describing the background against which this Somali route to Uganda has emerged, briefly describing the factors which have precipitated the deterioration of Somali refugees' living conditions in Kenya. Subsequently, it retraces the historical origins of the Somali presence in Uganda and the emergence of a Somali community in Kampala's Kisenyi area. Then, it narrows the focus on the current situation, analysed in the light of the legal framework which regulates the rights of refugees in Uganda, and on the heterogeneous population, which constitutes the Somali diaspora in urban Uganda, particularly students and businesspeople. Finally, it discusses the implications for Somalia, looking at its relations with Uganda, and its wider migratory flows.

A Time of Uncertainty

On 12 December 2012, all urban refugee operations in Kenya were stopped following a directive of the Kenyan Department of Refugee Affairs (DRA) stemming from the decision of the Government of Kenya (GoK) to enforce its fitfully applied encampment policy. Although the directive addressed refugees from all nationalities residing in Kenyan urban areas, the move was largely perceived as particularly targeting Somalian refugees, who made up the largest refugee population in the country. The directive raised the alarm for Somalian urban refugee communities across Kenya, although it did not come completely as a surprise. Since Kenya launched *Operation Linda Nchi* (Protect the Country) against Al-Shabaab strongholds in Southern Somalia in 2011, terror attacks on the Kenya–Somalia borderland and in Nairobi had escalated. As a result, fears of terrorist infiltrations added to the deep-seated suspicion against the large Kenyan Somali minority that has accompanied Kenyan post-colonial history. Security concerns seeped into refugee policies, to the point where public discourses in Kenya conflated the two issues, and Somalian refugees were increasingly portrayed by Kenyan politicians and media as a potential 'fifth column' of Al-Shabaab (Okungu 2011; see also Wandera and Wario, this volume). Besides, and related to this heightened anti-Somali rhetoric, the anxiety of the Somali population was exacerbated by a spate of bombings that hit Eastleigh between August and December 2012, killing 18 people and injuring at least 41. On at least one occasion, the attack had triggered an anti-Somali riot and, in the ensuing battle between Kenyan and Somali residents of Eastleigh, local Kenyan Somali-owned shops were looted (Gogineni 2012). The attacks were attributed to Al-Shabaab and added to a broader situation of uncertainty. Indeed, at the beginning of 2013, Nairobi's main roads were punctuated by large political billboards, exalting Kenyan diversity and trumpeting the word '*Amani*', 'Peace' in Swahili. However, ahead of the political elections, scheduled on 13 March 2013, there were fears across Kenya that this could remain just a word on billboards. The shadow of the violence that had marred the previous elections, between December 2007 and February 2008, in which 1,500 were killed and over 600,000 were displaced, loomed large. Despite the approval of a new constitution in 2010, many issues remained unresolved. The risk that political violence would flare up again was felt particularly in some areas of Nairobi. Eastleigh was among these. Unlike during the 2007 post-electoral violence, when the Somali community was left unscathed by the riots, this time there were fears that, in case of fresh turmoil, the neighbourhood's shopping facilities could be targeted by looters.

From the Tripartite Agreement to Operation Usalama Watch

Although the DRA directive was put on hold by Kenya Supreme Court in July 2013, the position of Somali refugees in Kenya remained precarious as the security situation continued to deteriorate because of an escalation in terrorist tactics. On September 2013, Al-Shabaab gunmen raided an upscale shopping mall in Nairobi's Westlands, an area mostly frequented by upper-class Kenyans and expatriates, and in the ensuing three days siege more than 60 people lost their lives. Faced with controversies over the handling of the crisis, the government of Uhuru Kenyatta pandered to widespread anti-Somali feelings among the general public, and, on 10 November 2013, signed a tripartite agreement with its Somali counterpart and the United Nations High Commissioner for Refugees (UNHCR). The document established the legal framework for the repatriation of more than 500,000 Somalian refugees currently living in the country, to be carried out according to an unspecified timeframe and, to formally abide by the principle of 'non-refoulement', in a 'voluntary' way (UNHCR 2013). However, the most immediate effect of the provision was to further exacerbate the Somalian refugees' vulnerability by propelling the ethnic profiling of the Somali population in Kenya and implicitly giving the police free rein to harass and extort money (Human Rights Watch 2014). Stoking pre-existing communal tensions, particularly in the coastal region,[3] and fuelled by belligerent op-eds[4] and diplomatic rows between the Kenyan and the Somali government,[5] the security crackdown escalated between March and April 2014 when the government launched Operation Usalama Watch. In the course of a massive security swoop across Kenya, the police arrested over 4,000 people, restricted the movement of refugees to camps and began the repatriation of dozens to Somalia.[6] The operation not only was punctuated by gross violations of human rights, but also proved ineffective at curbing the violence: large scale attacks were staged, allegedly by Al-Shabaab, in the region of the former North Eastern Province (NEP) again in June and then in November and December 2014.

Should I Stay or Should I Go?

Against this background, many Somalis were pondering whether to leave Eastleigh, or even Kenya, for the time being. Some Kenyan Somalis as well as Somalian refugees were planning to move to Garissa, or to other locations in the NEP, a Kenyan region mostly inhabited by ethnic Somalis, where relatives could temporarily host them. Others were heading to the Kenyan coast, hoping to find protection among Muslim fellows. A few wealthy Kenyan Somalis were about to leave for the United Arabs Emirates (UAE). Finally, a significant number turned their attention westwards, across the border with Uganda. Kampala was on many people's lips, suggesting an established pattern, which, however, had gone largely unnoticed in the academic literature. Apart from a few media articles in the Ugandan press, this route seemed to not have been yet properly examined.

While for many the decision to move to Uganda had been triggered by the recent events, and they were thus seeking a shelter for the time being, others were considering a long-term plan. A young refugee businesswoman named Ferdowsa running a small textile business from the small flat she shared with her mother and four siblings in Eastleigh, for instance, claimed: 'what happened here [in

Eastleigh] a few years ago, it is happening there right now', meaning that the same economic dynamism that drove the rise of Eastleigh as a major trade hub in East Africa was currently perceivable across the border with Uganda. She acted as intermediary between wholesalers in Mombasa, where fabric rolls from Dubai were shipped, and retailers in Kampala.

When, a month later, I followed the trail of her fabric rolls 650 kilometres west to a street linking Old Kampala to the Owino market, in the Kisenyi-Mengo area of the Ugandan capital, I found a Somali community still at a fledgling stage. There were only a few clearly recognizable Somali shops and restaurants clustered around a mosque. At the time, Ferdowsa's words sounded an overstatement. However, when I returned to the same area in May 2014, her prediction seemed closer to reality: many new Somali shops were evident, and the Somali presence in the neighbourhood had become more conspicuous. Cars packed with Somalis were arriving from the Kenyan border every morning before dawn. Some Somalian refugees settled in Kampala, while others continued their journey to the Nakivale refugee camp, in the south of the country. Ferdowsa was not among the newcomers. Still a single woman, she found it easier to keep a low profile in Eastleigh, particularly since the growing Somali presence in Kampala guaranteed a steady income from her transnational fabric trade. Although, at the time of the interview in early 2013, the combined effect of terror attacks and the increasingly repressive response of the Kenyan security forces against the Somali population in Kenya had caused a drop in the number of customers visiting the area, the number of orders from Kampala had increased.

The Route to Kampala

To understand the significance of Uganda within Somali regional trajectories, it is useful to adopt a historical perspective in order to identify continuities and changes in the dynamics shaping this increasingly busy route. Indeed, the first Somali community in Uganda traces back to the early twentieth century and consisted of Somali soldiers from British Somaliland embedded in the British army, and mostly hailing from Isaaq and Darood Harti (Dhulbahante, Warsangeli and Marehan),[7] and their families. However, it was only in the late 1970s that the community eventually found its heart in Kisenyi, a shabby and ill-famed area of Kampala's Mengo Municipality, mostly inhabited by menial workers at the nearby Owino market. There, a Darood Dhulbahante Imam from Northern Somalia, Sheik Abduhani, who was well connected to local authorities, was granted a concession to build a mosque. Sheik Abduhani was a reference point for other Somalis – mainly from Darood Harti clans – interested in setting up entrepreneurial activities in Uganda, or using the country as a gateway, mainly to Zaire.

During this period, local Somali entrepreneurs linked to the Gulf through Northern Somalia, began amassing their fortunes, consolidating their control over strategic business sectors such as transport. Among them, there was Ahmed Omar Mandela, owner of the Mandela Group – a cars and trucks spare parts company established in the 1980s – and later of the fuel supply company City Oil and the Java Café chain. In 2004, Ahmed Omar Mandela was appointed Minister of State for Management and Development of the Royal Treasury of the Buganda Kingdom, an achievement that still today young Somalis, hailing particularly from Harti clans in Northern Somalia, regard with pride in Uganda. Another notable Ugandan Somali was Hussein Shire, born in the 1930s in Tororo, where he started building up his transport company by ferrying passengers on a blue Peugeot 504 between Tororo and Malaba, on the border with Kenya. In the 1980s, the transport business expanded into a 100-vehicle buscompany, Gateway, and an oil company, Shire petroleum, a store chain, Hussein stores, real estate development and agribusinesses (Odeke 2014).

Somali business networks across Africa thus began taking shape prior to the collapse of the Somali state. They relied on a physical infrastructure for long-haul transport, punctuated by oil stations and along which money and goods circulated. Moreover, transport tycoons and truck drivers of Somali origin developed ties which also proved helpful during volatile times, such as in 1989, when a screening to determine citizenship status in Kenya prompted the flight of almost 15,000 Somalis to Uganda, who obtained temporary political asylum from the Ugandan government. After 1991, most of these Kenyan Somali returned to Kenya, as the incipient refugee flow from Somalia heralded future business opportunities.

The Beginning of the Refugee Phenomenon

Between 1991 and 1994, over 400,000 people crossed the border from Somalia into Kenya (Milner 2009) prompting Kenyan president Daniel Arap Moi to request the intervention of international donors and lift the state of emergency imposed on the North Eastern Province in 1964 (ibid.). The UNHCR became responsible for determining and granting the newcomers a status, and recognized hundreds of thousands of Somalians as 'prima facie' refugees on a group basis and offered temporary protection in camps.[8] This approach overturned the pre-1991 refugee policy, according to which freedom of movement was granted to refugees to facilitate their integration in the national economy. Although relinquishing responsibilities to UNHCR for the management of humanitarian affairs, the GoK officially adopted a policy of 'abdication and containment', obliging refugees to reside in a camp while awaiting a more durable solution (Milner 2009: 88). Refugee camps were located in the borderland regions. The main shelter was established on the outskirts of Dadaab village, in the Garissa district and at around 100 kilometres from the Somali border. It soon expanded into three UNHCR facilities, Ifo, Dagahaley and Hagadera, turning Dadaab into one of the largest refugee complexes in the world and an icon of the protracted Somali refugee situation (Horst 2006; Agier 2011). Other camps were established across Kenya, including on the coast, but were subsequently closed. Although the UNHCR declared that the emergency was over (Lindley 2011), repatriation from Kenya to Southern Somalia was hindered by security concerns. Many of those Somalians who were repatriated ended up in IDP camps in the surrounding of the urban centres (Hammond 2014: 6).

Settling in Uganda

In 1994, the Ugandan government allowed the UNHCR to settle recently arrived Somali refugees in Nakivale refugee camp, but not in urban centres (Bagenda, Naggaga and Smith 2003), although refugees from Darood Harti and Isaaq clans with connections and resources settled in Kampala and Jinja. However, many among those who moved to town registered in Nakivale because of the widespread, yet according to UNHCR officers unfounded, belief that being registered in a refugee camp would speed up the resettlement process.

Although Kampala already featured a big mosque funded by the Libyan leader Muammar Gaddafi on the top of the Old Kampala hill, in 1994 a larger mosque with an annexed '*madrasa*' (college for Islamic learning), named Al-Tawheed, was inaugurated by Sheik Abduhani, who had been raising funds among the local business community, keen to leave a testament to the growing economic success of Somalis in Uganda. Around the new Kisenyi mosque the first Somali hotels and restaurants opened. On top of that, the neighbourhood offered the most affordable accommodations close to the Central Business District, despite poor infrastructure and widespread petty crime, and allowed easy access to bus and truck terminals. Here, young refugees arrived looking for employment in the transport sector. In the 1990s, the Ugandan government started implementing privatization policies, which further boosted Somali businesses in capital-intensive activities such as fuel supply. Somali remittance companies grew central within the local economy and, at the end of the 1990s, a branch of Amal, a money transfer operator from Puntland, opened in Kisenyi. Interestingly, Sheik Abduhani was appointed local manager – a key factor for the success of the company in Uganda. The easier access to transnational financial networks enabled Somali businessmen to raise capital for large-scale investments and seize control of strategic businesses, such as the petroleum trade. The oil was usually purchased by clusters of entrepreneurs, who arranged its shipping from the Gulf to Mombasa. From there, it was funnelled to Eldoret through a pipeline and transported by truck to Uganda and further on, to the DRC, Rwanda and Burundi. Fuel companies and ancillary services providers gradually became major employers of Somalis in Uganda.[9] On top of that, the introduction of the East African passport in 1999 eased border crossing for East African citizens, thus facilitating the transit of 'suitcase traders' (informal traders characterized by transporting small quantities of goods, often in suitcases), notably from Eastleigh. Throughout the 2000s, Uganda continued to attract mostly refugees, but also Kenyan Somalis and Somalians with pre-existing connections there. The country was indeed considered a profitable market especially for big businesses, while lower salaries than in Kenya discouraged many refugees. However, this disadvantage was gradually offset by the increasing cost of living in Nairobi and by a changing regional configuration.

A New Little Mogadishu Takes Shape

As mentioned above, 2006 marked a watershed for both the refugee policy in Uganda and the conflict in Somalia, and the resulting outbound human flows. On 24 May, the Ugandan parliament passed a new Refugees Act, tabled in 1998, which repealed the previous Control of Alien Refugees Act (CARA), in place since 1964 and an object of criticism for the UNHCR and other advocacy organizations. Hailed as 'progressive [and] human rights and protection oriented' by advocacy organizations (Refugee Law Project, n.d.), the new law embraced refugee rights in conformity with the 1951 Refugee Convention, of which Uganda, like Kenya, is a signatory country. The 2006 Refugee Act therefore allowed refugees the right 'to an identity card or travel document, to remain, to non-discrimination, to administrative assistance, to freedom of religion, to freedom of association, to access the courts, and to freedom of movement' (Refugee Law Project, n.d.). On top of that, it recognized, among other rights, the rights to movable and immovable property, transfer assets, education, the right to set up a commercial enterprise, have their professional qualifications recognized and practice their religion.[10] As for the right of association, the Refugee Act states clearly that refugees 'have a right of association as regards non-political and non-profit making associations and trade unions' (Refugee Law Project, n.d.) – a provision that would pave the way, as discussed later, to the vibrant Somali student activism. The act was set to enter into force in 2008. However, its approval contributed to building trust between the Ugandan state and the refugee population, particularly as it stood in sharp contrast with the more restrictive refugee act passed the same year by the Kenyan parliament. Approved in December 2006, this act shifted the responsibility for the management of refugee matters to the Government of Kenya through the creation of a Department of Refugee Affairs (DRA), in charge of the administrative processes of refugee status determination. The law draws a distinction between statutory (those who have gone through the status determination process), and 'prima facie' refugees and states the right to seek protection within 30 days from the entry, whether by legal or illegal means, into Kenya. It also upholds the principle of 'non-refoulement', the prohibition against forcibly repatriating those fleeing countries in which their lives or freedom may be threatened because of race, religion, nationality, political opinion or membership in a particular social group. An important provision of the Kenyan Refugee Act concerns the residence requirement within camps, although this encampment policy is at times rather loosely implemented (Grant, Kimotho and Gerstner 2012).

The Beginning of the AMISOM Phase

Also in 2006, Somalia experienced a renewed outburst of violence following the Ethiopian invasion, with a resulting fresh wave of displaced people – both within Somalia and outside. A large number of refugees poured into the Dadaab refugee complex and Eastleigh. New peaks in the refugee flow were reached in 2007 and 2008, when 80,000 displaced people poured into UNHCR refugee camps (Simpson 2009). Ugandan media increasingly began turning their attention to the local urban Somali community,[11] as the Ugandan government of Yoweri Museveni was discussing the deployment of the Ugandan People's Defence Force (UPDF) to Somalia – a discussion in which the same Somali community in Kisenyi participated (Musamali 2007). In March 2007, the first Ugandan troops were deployed to Somalia under the command of AMISOM – a move to which Al-Shabaab threatened to retaliate against targets in Uganda (Jaramogi 2008). In response, the Ugandan army publicly called on the Somali population to cooperate with security agencies (ibid.), but, on 7 November 2008 a bomb detonated in Kisenyi, killing two (Jaramogi and Wagawulo 2008). The Ugandan government – particularly the OPM and the Ministry of Internal Affairs – intensified the collaboration with local Somali organizations, particularly the Somali Community Association in Uganda (SCAU).

Established by a group of refugees from Southern Somalia in 2006, SCAU became a key partner of the government, in charge of monitoring the burgeoning Somalian refugee population and collecting intelligence on militants' activities in Somalia to be used by the UPDF troops in the field. It should be noticed, though, that the authority of the SCAU was not acknowledged by all Somali refugees in the country. Indeed, the association was dominated by Somalis from South-Central Somalia. Northerners were active in large businesses and were mostly connected to Ugandan Somali families who had arrived in the early 1900s, principally Darood Harti from the Puntland region.

Following the implementation of the Refugee Act in 2008, a growing number of Somalian refugees crossed the border from Kenya into Busia and Malaba. There, they were required to declare their status to the border authorities. They would be then given 30 days to register either at Old Kampala police station or at the Office of the Prime Minister's Department of Refugee Affairs.

If they declared that they had a sponsor in an urban area, they were allowed to reside in a city. Otherwise, they would have been resettled in Nakivale refugee camp. However, upon arrival in Kisenyi, where Somali guesthouses were located, they would have had to register at the SCAU in order to be pre-screened by the security officer of the association.

The cooperation between the Somali community – often outspoken in supporting the Ugandan mission in Somalia (Kajoba 2009) – and the Ugandan government was tested again in the aftermath of the 11 July 2010 terror attacks, when 74 people were killed by three bombings in Kampala – one in Kabalagala's Ethiopian Village, a venue packed with football fans watching the World Cup Finals, and twin blasts in Nakawa's Kyadongo Rugby Club.[12] The attacks were claimed by Al-Shabaab and, although stirring fears of ethnic profiling among the Somali population (Wesonga 2011), the impact was limited to stricter vetting procedures for new arrivals from Somalia, requiring applicants for refugee status intending to live in an urban site to be accompanied by a guarantor at the Old Kampala police station for further verification.[13] This cooperation yielded a number of arrests on suspicion of terrorist activities but the positive response of the Ugandan authorities strengthened the perception that Uganda was a friendly place for Somalis.

A Student Destination

Among the new arrivals in Kampala there were many youths, attracted by the greater freedom of movement, the lower cost of living compared to Nairobi and the possibility of pursuing higher education in Ugandan institutions. Refugees were entitled to the same fees as Ugandan citizens in both public and private universities, whose number had skyrocketed since late 1990s to tap into the booming demand for enrolment. Moreover, student cards had the same legal value as state or UNHCR issued IDs, thus providing an additional document, which many young refugees were particularly eager to produce as an alternative to the refugee card. In terms of self-perception, many students felt that through university enrolment, they were distancing themselves from the limitations inscribed in the condition of refugees. The fact that the most popular degrees were in business, development studies and public policy reflected the likeliest career trajectories for Somalis in Somalia and East Africa. It is worth pointing out, though, that most refugee students came from better off families, able to support them through remittances.

Also, young Somalis with Kenyan passports found student life in Kampala easier than in Nairobi. For instance, Abdi, a 20-year-old born in Kismayo, but today a Kenyan citizen, decided to move from Eastleigh and enrol at Kampala International University at the suggestion of his father, who had already lived in Kisenyi in the 1980s, when he was engaged in the sugar trade from Brazil to Somalia and then across East Africa. Abdi had attended primary school in Kampala and then had moved with his entire family to Kenya. Later on, his father had set up a construction company in Thika, a town 40 kilometres northeast of Nairobi, but had stayed in touch with Sheik Abduhani. In the last few years, Abdi had studied and worked in an uncle's shop in Eastleigh, but, following the latest developments in Kenya, his father sent him to Uganda. The initial plan was to wait for the situation in Kenya to settle down, but in Kampala new opportunities arose. Although his goal remains to move to China to study medicine, he began trading watches from Eastleigh to Somali and Ugandan customers.

Student associations proved critical loci for expanding social networks. Student associations have animated Somali political life since colonial times, particularly in Northern Somalia. Indeed the first unions in Uganda were initially established at the end of the 2000s, by Darood Harti students aiming to help prospective and current students from the same clans with information and contacts. Technological innovations had a crucial role in facilitating networking and relocation of students. For instance, the mobile money service Safaricom M-Pesa, launched in Kenya in 2009, was widely used by students to receive money in Kampala. Even though Safaricom and MTN's tie-up network agreement excluded mobile money services, M-Pesa transactions occurred 'under the counter': users did not send money from their mobile wallets but instead paid the agents, who had Kenyan Shillings in their M-Pesa accounts, to perform the payment in roaming on their behalf. Some Somali students became informal money transfer agents by simply 'renting out' their M-Pesa mobile wallets to colleagues who needed to receive money but wanted to bypass official money transfer agencies, tariff-wise or, in the case of *hawala*, for avoiding undue attention. Moreover, since 2011–2012 Facebook became very popular among Somali students, and Somali student associations' pages proliferated on the social network. In these online communities, prospective students could get in touch with friends and relatives and obtain useful information before moving to Uganda. Although clan names were not made explicit, social relations were mostly along clan lines, intersected with more mundane memberships, revolving around the attended universities or even football clubs.

These associations fulfil two main functions: 1) giving support to prospective and current students, especially in providing information on relocation in Uganda and university enrolment and coursework; 2) establishing connections with the Somali business community. This latter aspect was particularly relevant: Somali businessmen financially helped student associations or offered scholarships to students from their own clan, mainly to find trustworthy individuals to employ, but also to create loyalty bonds and groom future political leaders. The funds were deposited in the student associations' accounts in *hawala* branches (which guaranteed greater accountability) and were used to pay for the associations' offices and catering at student conventions. Student associations' elections held in Kampala's various universities were thus major political events in which young and ambitious refugees would run for office and display their oratory skills and political adroitness.

Regional Connections

The Somali presence increased around Kampala International University, Cavendish and St. Lawrence, in areas such as Kabalagala, Kasanga and Mengo Rubego. However, Kisenyi remained the centre of the Somali community in Kampala, which became more conspicuous with the opening of shops and eateries with a clear Somali identity. At the same time, daily bus connections between Eastleigh, Nairobi's 'Little Mogadishu', and Kampala's counterpart, and the possibility of using M-Pesa in roaming, sustained a growing community of Somalian refugee entrepreneurs relocating from Nairobi to the Ugandan capital and living on the small trade of a wide range of goods, from camel milk to clothes. Yet, the high fees of commercial licenses hindered the proliferation of business activities. The cost of a business license for a medium size shop was about USD 2,000 and only those able to raise the necessary capital could rent a shop. Thus, although Kisenyi was now commonly dubbed 'Little Mogadishu' by the Ugandan press, it was hardly comparable to Eastleigh in terms of scale, particularly for the lack of its iconic large shopping malls (similar to those described in the chapter by Scharrer, this volume), and consequently, trade volume. Instead, rising business opportunities in neighbouring countries turned Kisenyi into a regional hub that allowed Somalis to operate across borders.

A main destination was South Sudan, which, since its independence in 2011, had seen a large availability of hard currency brought in by international organizations, NGOs and foreign companies.[14] Somali businessmen started investing heavily in construction and trade, particularly in the capital Juba and in Bor, Jonglei State. Kisenyi became a transit point for the trucks coming from Mombasa through Nairobi and travelling to South Sudan. However, in June 2013, following the decision of the South Sudanese Central Bank to limit the provision of hard currency to commercial banks, many Somalis reduced their investments in the country lest they would get stuck with South Sudanese Pounds (SSP). The decision was subsequently reversed in November but after violence broke out in South Sudan in December 2013, the flight of Somali businessmen accelerated. Around 500 Somali citizens were flown to Mogadishu by the Somali government,[15] but the majority moved to Kampala from where they continued to run their businesses.

Rwanda and the DRC also increasingly became areas of interest for Somali businessmen, despite the local linguistic barriers (in both case the dominant language is French) and – particularly in the case of the latter – their insecurity. Yet, in the case of Rwanda, Paul Kagame's government adoption of English as another official language of the country facilitated the access for Somali entrepreneurs. In general, Kampala provided a central location in the region from which Somalis could manage an extensive network of business services, mainly long-haul transport and fuel supply. This network straddled as far as Kisangani, in the DRC – where some were engaged in timber extraction and trade – and Zambia.

Furthermore, after the election of Hassan Sheikh Mohamud as president of Somalia on 10 September 2012, Uganda started accepting the Somali blue passport at its borders, becoming the first country since 1991 to do so.[16] The document was issued either in the Somali capital or at the Embassy of the Republic of Somalia in Kampala. On 8 July 2013, Air Uganda began operating between Entebbe and Mogadishu, the second national air company, after Turkish Airlines, to re-establish the connection with the Somali capital. This helped many in the Somali diaspora – with either Somali or foreign passports – to travel from Entebbe to Mogadishu and back for the first time in many years, often on reconnaissance trip to meet relatives, check up on family's properties and pursue business opportunities.

Improved security and growing economic expectations had started fuelling a building spree across Mogadishu (Hammond 2013) and boosted land acquisition in fertile areas of the country, particularly along the rivers Shabelle and Juba. Yet, the situation on the ground remained volatile, and Somali entrepreneurs were reluctant to move back to Somalia with their families. Instead, even refugees based in Kenya benefitted from the greater ease of travelling back and forth between Entebbe and Mogadishu, travelling to Uganda as refugees and then to Somalia as Somali citizens. When going back to Nairobi as refugees became more difficult, some decided to resettle in Kampala. The Somali population therefore became more heterogeneous, encompassing not only students but also families. As Kenya intensified the deportations to Somalia, many flew back from Mogadishu to Entebbe, this time not as refugees but as Somali citizens.

Diaspora and Geopolitics

The Ugandan government has found in the local Somali associations a crucial ally not only in managing internal security, but also in advancing a geopolitical agenda at a regional level. It is worth remembering that, at the time of writing, Uganda is the top troop contributor to AMISOM, with approximately 6,200 soldiers of the UPDF deployed in some of the flashpoints, such as Banadir, Lower and Middle Shebelle, Bay and Bakool.[17] At the onset of the mission in 2007, Uganda was viewed by Somali warring parties as unbiased, not having a large Somali minority, nor direct stakes in Somali politics (Hansen 2013). According to some analysts, the reasons for Ugandan participation in the AMISOM mission are multifaceted and include concerns of a 'domino effect' of instability in East Africa, and a desire to appease the army, whose officers and privates would benefit from higher pay than at home – therefore lowering the pressure of the armed forces on the regime; and the will to strengthen the relations with the US and in general to bolster its international prestige (ibid.).

Following the 2010 Kampala bombings, Uganda's commitment against Al-Shabaab on Somali soil became a matter of national security, but in pursuing this strategy the Ugandan authorities have been unwavering in their support for both legitimate institutions in Somalia and Somali grassroots organizations in Uganda. The Somali diaspora in Uganda has been providing intelligence both in Uganda and in Somalia on potential threats to Ugandan civilian and military targets and have been regularly employed as consultants for 'cultural awareness' trainings, funded by the US Embassy and aimed at UPDF troops being deployed in Somalia. Additionally, Uganda has been able to leverage its leading role in the mission at an international level. For instance, in November 2012, Uganda threatened to pull its troops out of Somalia in response to a UN report, which claimed that its government was supporting the M23 rebel group in the DRC.[18] In the following days, the Ugandan media dedicated coverage to the Somali diaspora – particularly to those affiliated to the SCAU – who voiced their concerns over this possibility. As the diplomatic outcry over the report abated, Uganda continued to project its influence over the international mission in Somalia. On 15 May 2014, a United Nations Guard Unit (UNGU), formed by 410 UPDF soldiers, was deployed for the first time to protect UN personnel and installations in Mogadishu.[19] At the same time, the edgy relation between Kenya and Somalia increasingly made Uganda a privileged regional partner of Hassan Sheikh Mohamud's government, as became clear on 12 May when a large Somali delegation, including the President, the Minister of Defence and other top generals, travelled to Entebbe upon invitation of Ugandan President Yoweri Museveni.

Conclusions

This chapter has traced the transformations of the Somali presence in Uganda in the light of recent developments at the regional level. It has described the regional context against which recent Somali mobility patterns have emerged, emphasizing that mobility is not just a reaction to the Kenyan government's securitization of Somali refugees and, in general, to crises, as is often suggested by studies on displacement, but it is also a strategy to pursue opportunities in settings shaped by the interaction of pre-existing linkages and institutional frameworks. It would thus be useful to conclude the discussion by briefly outlining future scenarios for the Somali population in Uganda and suggesting possible lines of inquiry for further research.

A preliminary consideration is that the local Somali population is largely perceived – by Ugandans and Somalis alike – as being under the personal protection of President Museveni and therefore its security is seen as inextricably bound to the President's or to his son – often tipped as a likely successor to his father – Muhoozi Kaneirugaba's political future. This belief is a source of anxiety for many long-term members of the Somali diaspora, who admit to having feared the end of the Museveni era during the 2011 elections. This is also a reminder that the current Ugandan refuge could come to an abrupt end. Aware of this possibility, the SCAU has been lobbying since 2007 to have Somalis recognized in the Constitution as a Ugandan tribe, supporting this claim through the argument that Somalis have been living in the Ugandan territory for a century.[20] On top of that, a growing number of refugees, backed by the legal advocacy organization Refugee Law Project, are seeking to become Ugandan citizens by challenging the Department of Immigration in court. They demand the implementation of a provision in the 2006 Refugee Act that grants Ugandan citizenship to those who fulfil a specific set of requirements (Walker 2008).[21] Whatever will be the outcome of this claim, it will be useful to examine how Somali migratory flows will adapt to shifting regional scenarios and what will be, in the long run, the impact on the academic and policy conversation of forced and voluntary migrations, in Africa and elsewhere. It also remains to be seen how, and to what extent, different Somali groups will be able to cope with volatility or reap the benefits from the opportunities arising out of growing regional integration, thanks to the diffusion of mobile phones to communicate and transfer money, and means of transport that enable faster and more efficient communications. Further research may eventually seek to highlight the implications for Somalia, where the on-going state-building process is still poised between encouraging signs of reconstruction and disheartening acts of terrorism.

Gianluca Iazzolino is a research fellow in the International Development Department and the Firoz Lalji Centre for Africa at the London School of Economics. He has a PhD from the Centre of African Studies (CAS), University of Edinburgh, where he wrote a thesis on Somali transnational networks based on fieldwork conducted in Kenya, Uganda and Somaliland. Furthermore he has consulted on mobile money and digital financial inclusion for, among others, UNCDF, FSD Kenya, FAO Somalia and the Rift Valley Institute. Prior to his PhD, he worked as a freelance journalist in the Middle East, India, Latin America, Russia and East Africa.

Notes

1. Source: Uganda's Department of Refugees – Office of the Prime Minister. UNHCR/OPM. Profile of Somali refugees in Uganda, 28 February 2017. Retrieved 1 September 2018 from https://igad.int/attachments/article/1513/FactSheet_Uganda.pdf.

2. Van Hear, Bakewell and Long (2012: 7) define drivers as 'the factors which get migration going and keep it going once begun' and suggest a classification of drivers based on the functions they fulfil in migration processes.
3. *BBC* (2014), 'Kenya Terror Charges After Mombasa Police Raid Mosque', 03 February. Retrieved 25 August 2016 from http://www.bbc.com/news/world-africa-26013964.
4. *Daily Nation* (2014), 'Are We Just Going to Sit Around and Wait to be Blown to Bits by Terrorists?', 20 March. Retrieved 25 August 2016 from http://www.nation.co.ke/oped/Opinion/Are-we-just-going-to-sit-around-and-wait-to-be-blown-to-bits/440808-2252048-7t44r5z/index.html.
5. *BBC* (2014), 'Somali PM Angry Over Diplomat's Arrest in Kenya', 28 April. Retrieved 26 August 2016 from http://www.bbc.com/news/world-africa-27190887.
6. *BBC* (2014), 'Kenya Sends Back "Illegal" Somalis After Nairobi Raids', 9 April. Retrieved 26 August 2016 from http://www.bbc.com/news/world-africa-26955803.
7. Clans and subclans' names are spelled differently according to the source.
8. The *prima facie* refugee status applies to applicants for asylum coming from regions affected by generalized conflict, such as Somalia (though Kenya stopped recognizing Somalis as *prima facie* refugees in 2016).
9. Still in present times, petrol stations of companies such as CityOil, Delta and Hass in Ugandan major cities are the gathering points of the Somali community.
10. Refugee Act, 4 August 2006.
11. *New Vision* (2009), 'Uganda: Kisenyi – a Haven for Somali Tranquility or Scams?', 27 September. Retrieved 30 August 2016 from http://www.newvision.co.ug/new_vision/news/1218656/kisenyi-haven-somali-tranquility-scams.
12. *BBC* (2010), '"Somali Link" as 74 World Cup Fans Die in Uganda Blasts',12 July. Retrieved 2 September 2016 from http://www.bbc.com/news/10593771.
13. This provision was eventually dropped in 2013.
14. The pursuit of hard currency is a common mobility driver of the Somali business diaspora, as explained to the author of this chapter by many Somali entrepreneurs in Eastleigh, Kisenyi and Hargeisa. Accruing hard currency enables traders to retain values not only across time, but also across space, since it facilitates cross-border trades.
15. *Dalsan Radio* (2014), 'Third Flight Carrying 200 Somali Citizens Arrive Mogadishu [sic] From South Sudan', 15 January. Retrieved 2 September 2016 from http://allafrica.com/stories/201401151195.html.
16. A passport with a blue cover had been issued by the Transitional Federal Government since September 2011, to replace the previous green passport, in use during Siad Barre regime, therefore declared obsolete.
17. AMISOM (n.d.). 'Uganda – UPDF. http://amisom-au.org/uganda-updf/, retrieved 11 November 2015.
18. *Al Jazeera* (2012), 'Uganda Threatens Somalia Troop Withdrawal', 2 November. Retrieved 5 September 2016 from http://www.aljazeera.com/news/africa/2012/11/2012112165833950535.html.
19. UN News Centre (2014), 'Somalia: UN Deploys New Special Force to Protect Staff in Mogadishu', 18 May. Retrieved 21 November 2015 from http://www.un.org/apps/news/story.asp?NewsID=47820#.U3seAfmSySo.
20. The *New Vision*. 28 October 2007. 'Uganda: Somalis Demand Recognition'. Retrieved 28 September 2016 from http://www.newvision.co.ug/new_vision/news/1216592/somalis-demand-recognition.

21. According to the *Uganda Citizenship and Immigration Control Act* (UCICA), the following criteria must be met under art. 16(5): 'The qualifications for naturalisation are that he or she (a) has resided in Uganda for an aggregate period of twenty years; (b) has resided in Uganda throughout the period of twenty-four months immediately preceding the date of application; (c) has adequate knowledge of a prescribed vernacular language or of the English language; (d) is of a good character; and (e) intends, if naturalized, to continue to reside permanently in Uganda' (Uganda Citizenship and Immigration Control Act cited in Walker 2008: 4).

References

Agier, M. 2011. *Managing the Undesirables: Refugee Camps and Humanitarian Government*. Cambridge: Polity Press.
Bagenda, E., A. Naggaga and E. Smith. 2003. 'Land Problems in Nakivale Settlement and the Implications for Refugee Protection in Uganda', *Working Paper* 8. Kampala, Uganda: Refugee Law Project.
Bakewell, O. 2010. 'Some Reflections on Structure and Agency in Migration Theory', *Journal of Ethnic and Migration Studies* 36(10): 1689–1708.
Bakewell, O., and H. de Haas. 2007. 'African Migrations: Continuities, Discontinuities and Recent Transformations', in L. de Haan, U. Engel and P. Chabal (eds), *African Alternatives*. Leiden: Brill, pp. 95–118.
Bakewell, O., and A. Bonfiglio. 2013. 'Moving Beyond Conflict: Re-framing Mobility in the African Great Lakes Region', *Working Paper for the African Great Lakes Mobility Project, IMI Working Paper* 71. Oxford: International Migration Institutes, University of Oxford.
Bakewell, O., and N. Binaisa. 2016. 'Tracing Diasporic Identifications in Africa's Urban Landscapes: Evidence from Lusaka and Kampala', *Ethnic and Racial Studies* 39(2): 280–300.
Flahaux, M.-L., and H. De Haas. 2014. 'African Migration: Exploring the Role of Development and States', *IMI Working Papers Series* 105. Oxford: International Migration Institutes, University of Oxford.
Gogineni, R. 2012. 'Police Raids Alienate Kenya's Largest Ethnic Minority', *Voice of America*, 23 November. Retrieved 12 April 2015 from http://www.voanews.com/content/violent-eastleigh-police-raids-alienating-kenyas-ethnic-somali-minority/1551714.html.
Grant, K., R. Wangui Kimotho and E. Gerstner. 2012. *Asylum under Threat: Assessing the Protection of Somali Refugees in Dadaab*. Refugee Consortium of Kenya.
Hammond, L. 2013 'Somalia Rising: Things are Starting to Change for the World's Longest Failed State', *Journal of Eastern African Studies* 7(1): 183–93.
———. 2014. 'History, Overview, Trends and Issues in Major Somali Refugee Displacements in the Near Region', *New Issues in Refugee Research, Research Paper* No. 268. UNHCR.
Hansen, S.H. 2013. 'Opposing Interests? The Geopolitics of the Horn of Africa', in E. Leonard and G. Ramsay (eds), *Globalizing Somalia: Multilateral, International, and Transnational Repercussions of Conflict*. New York: Bloomsbury Academic.
Horst, C. 2006. *Transnational Nomads. How Somalis Cope with Life in the Refugee Camps of Dadaab, Kenya*. Oxford and New York: Berghahn.
Human Rights Watch. 2014. 'Kenya: End Abusive Round-Ups'. Retrieved 13 May 2015 from http://www.hrw.org/news/2014/05/12/kenya-end-abusive-round-ups.

Iazzolino, G., and M. Hersi. 2019. 'Shelter from the Storm: Somali Migrant Networks in Uganda between International Business and Regional Geopolitics', *Journal of Eastern African Studies*, DOI: 10.1080/17531055.2019.1575513.
Jaramogi, P. 2008. 'Uganda: Army Warns Somali on Terror', *The New Vision*, 12 October.
Jaramogi, P., and C. Wagawulo. 2008. 'Uganda: City Explosion Kills Two in Kisenyi', *The New Vision*, 7 November.
Kajoba, N. 2009. 'Uganda: Somalis Commend Peacekeepers', *The New Vision*, 29 July.
Kleist, N. 2004. 'Nomads, Sailors and Refugees: A Brief History of Somali Migration', *Sussex Migration Working Papers* 23: 1–14.
Lindley, A. 2011. 'Between a Protracted and a Crisis Situation: Policy Responses to Somali Refugees in Kenya', *Refugee Survey Quarterly* 30(4): 14–49.
Milner, J. 2009. *Refugees, the State and the Politics of Asylum in Africa*. Basingstoke: Palgrave Macmillan.
Musamali, G. 2007. 'Uganda: Somalis Want UPDF Deployment', *The New Vision*, 12 January.
Odeke, F. 2014. 'Gateway Bus Founder Dies in South Africa', *The New Vision*, 30 June.
Okungu, J. 2011. 'Is Al Shabaab Head in Somalia or Nairobi?', *The Star*, 28 October. Retrieved 22 May 2015 from http://www.the-star.co.ke/opinions/jerry-okungu/46694-is-al-shabaab-head-in-somalia-or-nairobi.
Refugee Law Project. n.d. 'Critique of the Refugees Act 2006'. Kampala.
Sander, C., and S.M. Maimbo. 2003. 'Migrant Labor Remittances in Africa: Reducing Obstacles to Developmental Contributions', *Africa Region Working Paper Series*. Washington DC: World Bank.
Simpson, G. 2009. 'From Horror to Hopelessness. Kenya's Forgotten Somali Refugee Crisis'. New York: Human Rights Watch.
UN High Commissioner for Refugees (UNHCR), *Tripartite Agreement Between the Government of the Republic of Kenya, the Government of the Federal Republic of Somalia and the United Nations High Commissioner for Refugees Governing the Voluntary Repatriation of Somali Refugees Living in Kenya, 2013*, 10 November 2013. Retrieved 1 March 2019 from https://www.refworld.org/docid/5285e0294.html.
van Hear, N., O. Bakewell and K. Long. 2012. 'Drivers of Migration. Migrating out of Poverty', *RPC Working Paper* 1. Migrating out of Poverty Consortium, University of Sussex, Brighton.
Walker, S. 2008. 'From Refugee to Citizen? Obstacles to the Naturalisation of Refugees in Uganda', *Briefing Paper*. Kampala, Uganda: Refugee Law Project.
Wesonga, N. 2011. 'Uganda: Somalis Still Feel Safe in Country Even After Attacks', *The Monitor*, 11 July.

Afterword

Günther Schlee

While this book is ostensibly about East Africa, it is global in scope. The Somali movements on which it focuses form part of wider global patterns of migration, while links between Somalis in different countries and on different continents and their relationships to other migrants and population groups form a very global picture.

One may therefore speak of a global Somali community or of a global Somali diaspora. Both terms are problematic. How much community or commonality is there in this 'community'? A diaspora is normally defined through reference to a lost homeland. However, Somalis have more than one homeland, and these homelands are not lost in a sense of definite deprival. Unlike in the paradigmatic case of a diaspora, the Jewish Diaspora, there have never been wholesale expulsions of Somalis from any of the Somali states or territories and much of 'diaspora' life is characterized by coming and going, by exchange of people and information between northeast Africa, including the predominantly Somali-inhabited areas, and other parts of the world. Somalis have also long lived in territories, which later became part of different nation states in the Horn of Africa (Ethiopia, Kenya, Djibouti etc.). Today they have more than one territorial unit (be it a regional state, a province, or an independent state) to their name. The largest among these, Somalia, comprising or not comprising Somaliland (an issue I am not going to address here), is far from being politically united. It underwent a process of political fragmentation in the 1980s and 1990s and since has never been under the control of a single government or any finite number of well-defined powers. This situation has led to libertarian phantasies of authors who have never been exposed to life without a government, but it is clear that most Somalis would prefer to live in a normal state and to have a regular passport (Schlee 2015). To different degrees, these territories and the subregions composing them are claimed by different clans, not for exclusive use, but as entities with which they are closely associated historically and politically. Outside these territories, clanship plays a role, which is not less important. In the 'diaspora' we find elements of identification shared by many Somalis (language and ethnicity as expressed in the global Somali language entertainment media) as well as Islam (primarily to mark the difference from 'Westerners'), but we also find globalized clans: people aggregating in clan-specific neighbourhoods and maintaining important links with members of the same clans elsewhere. And race is important; a point to which we will return.

In the present collection the historical contribution by Hannah Whittaker makes use of clan names. Clanship also plays a role in the other contributions, but the closer one gets to the present in Somali studies, the more reluctant authors tend to be when it comes to using clan names. They would speak of 'the same clan', 'another clan', or 'rival clans' without naming them, applying the same practice of anonymizing to them as to individual research participants. Why? Under Siad Barre, the president who fled Somalia in 1991, clanship had been officially abolished and the use of clan names was forbidden. By this he might have tried to make it difficult to criticize his own politics, which heavily relied on clan alliances and in the end on just his own clan. So is the taboo around using clan names due to the posthumous influence of Siad Barre? Other factors are also at work. Some Somalis do not want to promote clanship or are afraid of being accused of doing so if they use clan names. 'Whites' are accused of projecting primitivism or tribalism onto the Somalis or, worse, of falling back into colonial patterns. Unintentionally, those who follow this taboo send the strongest possible signal of the importance of clanship, as unimportant things are not surrounded by taboos.

Some authors point to the changing functions of clanship in order to differentiate themselves from the classical or 'traditional' views of the Somalis, with I. M. Lewis being the most prominent father figure subjected to attempted parricide (metaphorically speaking; he died peacefully in 2014). They are right insofar as pasture and water are no longer the only contested resources. Somalis in Somalia fight about strategic resources like airstrips, ports and mineral resources (Hoehne 2014; Schlee 2014). Outside Somalia clan-based networks might compete for resettlement,[1] travel documents, recognized status as refugees or citizens. Clanship has found its way into the contestation of modern resources. But the changes in clanship generally do not comprise its weakening. On the contrary, in situations of escalating violence and precarious survival, patrilineal clanship tends to gain importance at the expense of uterine links, friendship and other binding forces (Hoehne 2016: 1388–89).

In the present volume help from and dependence upon relatives figures prominently in many contributions, and it is a laudable feature of this book that paternal uncles are distinguished from maternal ones or from affinal 'uncles', and different kinds of 'cousins' are distinguished, instead of lumping them together as the English language suggests. Patrilineal links and clanship play a special role in Somali society. In this volume, Githigaro makes clear the extent to which members of the same clan, even on other continents, are preferred over nearby other Somalis or non-Somalis as business partners. He cites one of his interlocutors as explaining that his business partner is a distant cousin from his father's side and that he does not know the precise genealogical link. This strongly suggests that it is actually a shared clan or subclan membership, not a specific dyadic relationship, which is the basis of trust at least in this relationship. That patrilineal support networks can also fail and are not all-encompassing is illustrated by Ritchie (this volume) who describes women who organize themselves on non-clan lines.

Generally, the relative peace in which Somalis (and people who look like Somalis) live in Eastleigh (at least as far as their internal relations are concerned; we shall come back to the relationship with the Kenyan state shortly) seems to favour inter-clan and inter-ethnic cooperation. This seems to confirm Hoehne (2016) *ex negativo*: uterine links, friendship and other binding forces than patrilineal clanship have a chance to gain importance in the absence of escalating violence and threats to survival.

To drop the apparent taboo in Somali studies surrounding clans would help explain settlement patterns in the 'diaspora'. There is anecdotal evidence, to which I have alluded above, that Somalis tend to aggregate and locally cluster according to clanship, but a proper global geography of Somali clans is made difficult by the reluctance to name them. Taboos are neither good for empirical description nor for the analysis of social facts.

There are other levels of identification between 'global Somalis' and shared membership in a clan or subclan. The focus of much of this book is on Eastleigh, a neighbourhood in Nairobi. Kochore and Carrier (this volume) point to the presence of Oromo there, comprising Muslim Oromo who speak some Arabic or even Somali and tend to work for Somali businessmen,[2] but also others who stem from areas of Ethiopia where different branches of Christianity or 'traditional religion' predominate. However, other Ethiopians also live in that area, especially Amhara, who are mostly Christian. What is the common denominator of all these people? Their languages belong to clearly distinct branches of the Afroasiatic family, Semitic and Cushitic, so there is no reason to attribute a strong force to a feeling of linguistic relatedness. How about religion? Christianity and Islam are very similar, but that does not save them from being used as excuses for mortal clashes elsewhere. In my understanding this pattern of local aggregation is best explained by the fact that people feel safer in places where they do not stand out, where there are many others who look more or less like themselves. Apart from tight government control of 'illegal migrants' and suspected terrorists (Wandera and Wario, this volume), ethnic riots and mob justice are not unknown phenomena in Kenya. The anxiety Lowe and Yarnell (this volume) speak of is justified. 'Race', because of the history of the term and the practices linked to it, is, of course, even more difficult to talk about than 'clan', but similar physical appearance seems to be a feature relevant to a very central concern: safety. One feels safer among people who look alike.

The present volume analyses many comparative aspects of Somali studies in a well-chosen, new framework of 'mobile urbanity', given that Somalis have been described in another framework, pastoralism, for quite some time. In anthropology, the Somalis have made quite a career as prime examples of mobile pastoralists who are capable of defending their interests along the principles of a segmentary lineage system and its potential for mobilization. In fact they seem to outdo the paradigmatic case for a 'segmentary lineage system', the Nuer of South Sudan, in all this. They have later turned into the extreme case of 'failed statehood' (a concept which is problematic as long as we do not identify the aims of statehood and its advocates), and they have been found to be unusual refugees who often somehow do not fit the expectation of being destitute and docile. Somalis are often seen as extreme in more than one way. How much in terms of general skills and attitudes is 'Somali' and can be found in Somalis in all these different settings, will remain a topic for a long time.

The continental focus on urban Somalis in Eastern and Southern Africa, important and so far under-researched as it is, highlights only a part of a global picture. One of the many ways in which Somalis appear extreme to observers is the scattered nature of their 'diaspora' which goes far beyond any regional borders or former colonial ties. The times when Britain and Italy were privileged sites for finding Somalis abroad are long gone. Today there are studies about Somalis in Finland and Germany and numerous other countries. Urban Somality or Somali urbanity has become a global lifestyle of Somalis. And there is no evidence for these global urban Somalis ceasing to be Somali and being assimilated into the respective local environments or some globalized Anglosphere marked by consumerism and liberalism. In this, there are, of course, generational differences. I recall a Somali from Finland who attended the 14th Somalia Peace Process in Eldoret, Kenya, and who lamented that his children had become Finns (Schlee 2008: 126). He was probably exaggerating and the ways in which and the degrees to which these children were Finnish or Somali would be an interesting topic of research (like the studies by the late Petri Hautaniemi (e.g. Hautaniemi 2011)).

City size and city scale, that is their degree of regional or global connectedness (Glick Schiller and Çağlar 2011) seems to play a role in the choice of cities. Sure, there are rural Somalis, especially from what was then British Somaliland, in many villages of Kenya and beyond, as livestock and retail traders, with large families whose younger members are often more proficient in the local language than in Somali. Apart from the local language and Somali they would also speak Swahili and are mocked by 'proper' Somalis as people who respond to the question 'Yaa tahay?' (Who are you? Meaning of which clan) with the Swahili phrase 'sijui' - 'I don't know', making them 'Reer Sijui', the 'People of I-don't-know'. They are a common socio-type in rural Kenya, and there are also Somalis in medium-sized towns, as Scharrer's study about Nakuru (this volume) testifies. However, the more recent trend seems to favour large cities, further up in terms of both size and scale. And the Somali communities in these are interconnected and exchange goods, services, knowledge and members. For this reason, the title 'Mobile Urbanity' is well chosen.

The rich descriptions found in this volume offer food for thought about all this, also beyond the topics explicitly addressed. I feel honoured to have been given the opportunity to publish it in my series 'Integration and Conflict Studies' and to add my reflections on the matter at the end.

Günther Schlee is Director at the Max Planck Institute for Social Anthropology, Halle (Germany), where he leads the department 'Integration and Conflict'. He is the author and editor of several books, among them *How Enemies Are Made: Towards a Theory of Ethnic and Religious Conflicts* (Berghahn, 2008) and *Difference and Sameness as Modes of Integration* (Berghahn, 2018). He is widely known for his research on northern Kenya, Ethiopia and Sudan.

Notes

1. Oral information from Sophia Nakueira who currently works on a postdoctoral project on Somali refugee camps in Uganda at the Max Planck Institute for Social Anthropology.
2. Why Somalis often end up as businessmen and Oromo as their employees is a question to which neither Kochore and Carrier nor I have a definite answer. I have tended, following Portes (1994) to privilege 'migrant culture' (or whatever shapes the present situation of people) over 'culture of origin' in explaining what people do. But the pastoralist logic is not so different from the capitalist logic, as the etymology of the language of capitalism implies, which is all about livestock (e.g. capital, stock exchange, or pecuniary from Latin *pecus* 'cattle'). There may be something in their pastoralist past, which pre-disposes Somalis to become good at business. But then – both (parts of) the Oromo and (most of) the Somalis share both a pastoralist past and – in Eastleigh – the same experience of recent migration, so what makes them occupy different economic niches? Carrier (personal communication) relates this question to the observation that Oromo see Eastleigh as a place to pass through, not as a place to settle more permanently, and so not as somewhere in which to invest too much time or money into business. Alternatively, one may look for an explanation in the more pronounced business-mindedness of Somalis, evidenced both in Somali pastoralism (heavily commercialized for long) and in a longer rural and later urban history as traders of parts of the community.

References

Glick Schiller, N. and A. Çağlar (eds). 2011. *Locating Migration. Rescaling Cities and Migrants*. Ithaca, London: Cornell University Press

Hautaniemi, P. 2011. 'Transnational Life Course, Human Development and Diverse Landscapes of Opportunities among Young Somali Men', *Nordic Journal of African Studies* 20(1): 11–27

Hoehne, M.V. 2014. 'Resource Conflict and Militant Islam in the Golis Mountains in Northern Somalia (2006 – 2013)', *Review of African Political Economy* 41(141): 358–73.

———. 2016. 'The Rupture of Territoriality and the Diminishing Relevance of Cross-Cutting Ties in Somalia after 1990', *Development and Change* 47(6): 1379–1411. DOI: 10.1111/dech.12277.

Portes, A. 1994. 'The Informal Economy and Its Paradoxes', in N. Smelser and R. Swedberg (eds), *The Handbook of Economic Sociology*. Princeton, NJ: Princeton University Press, pp. 426–49.

Schlee, G. 2008. *How Enemies are Made: Towards a Theory of Ethnic and Religious Conflict*. Oxford, New York: Berghahn.

———. 2014. 'How Terrorists Are Made', *Annual Report Max Planck Society 2014*: 23–26. Retrieved 5 March 2019 from http://www.eth.mpg.de/4231303/MPGreport2014_schlee.pdf.

———. 2015. 'Customary Law and the Joys of Statelessness: Somali Realities beyond Libertarian Fantasies', in B. Turner and G. Schlee (eds), *On Retaliation: Toward an Interdisciplinary Understanding of a Basic Human Condition*. Oxford, New York: Berghahn, pp. 319–60.

Glossary

Al-Shabaab — Somali: *Xarakada Mujaahidiinta Alshabaab*, lit. 'Mujahideen Youth Movement' is a militant Islamic group based in Somalia, fighting against the Federal Government of Somalia and the African Union Mission to Somalia (AMISOM)

ayuuto — Somali version of a rotating savings and credit association (ROSCA), a form of combined peer-to-peer banking and peer-to-peer lending; from Italian *'aiuto'* (help)

buibui — Swahili for *abaya*, a full-length outer garment worn by some Muslim women

buufis — Somali word indicating a desire to migrate to Europe and North America which can lead to mental instability if unfulfilled

Dahabshiil — *hawala* company (see below entry for *xawaala*) based in Dubai, with strong links to Somaliland

Darood — a Somali clan family spread over southern Somalia, Puntland, the Ogaden in Ethiopia and the northeastern areas of Kenya

Galabbiya — northeast African ankle-length outer garment, usually with long sleeves, similar to a robe

Garre — multilingual Somali clan which some consider related to the non-Somali Oromo; they are often fluent in Oromo, Somali and their own language, Af-Garre; Garre live mainly in southern Somalia, northeastern Kenya and southern Ethiopia

guurti — Somali for wise men, council of elders

Glossary

hagbad	(also *xagbaad* in Somali spelling) another Somali term for *ayuuto*
Hawiye	Somali clan family, living mainly in central and southern Somalia, the Ethiopian Ogaden region and the northeastern part of Kenya
Herti	subclan of the Darood clan family
injera	Amharic term for Ethiopian flatbread made from *teff* flour
Isaaq	Somali clan family mainly to be found in Somaliland, the Ogaden in Ethiopia and Djibouti, as well as in Kenyan urban areas, where they are also known as Isahakia or Ishakia
jua kali	a Swahili term relating to working under the hot sun, denoting informal economic enterprises
khat	more usually known as *miraa* in Kenya, the green leaves of a shrub cultivated mainly in Ethiopia, Kenya and Yemen, which are chewed as a stimulant
kipande	Swahili term for an identity card introduced in colonial Kenya that restricted African mobility
macawis	Somali term for man's skirt of coloured material
madax shub	Somali: anointing of the head, ritual held for expectant mothers
mafrish	(also *merfish*) Somali: place established for the consumption of khat
matatu	Swahili term for privately-owned public service vehicle
mehar	(also *meher*) Somali for marriage contract, bride wealth (paid by the groom)
mirqaan	Somali term for the euphoric effect of khat, also known as *handas* in Kenya
mitumba	Swahili term for second-hand clothes
mukhalas	Arabic term for broker, smuggler
qaran	Somali term for community contingency funds
Reer Hamar	Benadiri, 'people of Mogadishu'
riba	Arabic term for exploitative gains made in trade or business under Islamic law (often equated with interests)
shalongo	another Somali name for *ayuuto*, the Somali version of a rotating savings and credit association (ROSCA)
spaza **shop**	informal convenience store in South Africa, sometimes run from home
xamar	also Hamar; Somali word for Mogadishu
xawaala	Somali for *hawala*, an old system of transferring money used in Arab countries and South Asia

Index

A
African Union Mission in Somalia (AMISOM), 4, 228–29, 232
Al-Shabaab, 4, 6, 29, 41, 49, 53, 58, 105, 138, 139, 190–92, 201, 204, 208–209, 222–23, 228–29, 233
ayuuto, 18, 122, 124–26, 131–32, 133n4

B
Barre, Siad, 4, 169, 201, 239
Brazil, 32, 67, 105, 229
Bulla Karatasi massacre, 29
Burundi, 183–84, 201, 226
buufis, 64, 66, 73n4, 87

C
camel milk, 98, 100, 105, 106–107, 110, 115n9, 231
capital (financial, social), 1, 8–9, 18, 20, 30, 32, 43, 85–87, 97, 100–101, 107, 118–32, 212, 221, 226, 231
China, 10, 32, 105, 110, 112–14, 159, 167, 230
citizenship, 6, 42, 43, 53, 61, 89, 197n1, 203, 204, 225, 234, 236n21
clans, 121–22, 125, 131, 140, 145, 176n22, 224–25, 226, 230, 239–40
class, 6, 11–12, 32, 48, 70–72, 89, 90, 120, 149, 168, 172, 222–23
clothes, 18, 27, 46, 59, 86, 87, 97, 98, 101–102, 110–13, 115n13, 125, 127, 141, 142–43, 157, 162, 164, 168, 186, 231
colonial period, 4, 9, 11–12, 14–15, 27–30, 42–53, 100, 104, 159, 170, 203, 205, 230, 241
commodities, 18, 82, 85, 98–100, 105, 109–11, 114, 115nn10,15, 161, 164
conflict goods, 8
contraband goods, 30
corruption, 20, 88, 197, 212–13
cosmopolitanism, 41, 59–61, 69, 73, 77
counterfeit trade, 113
credit, 87, 90, 109, 122–25, 129, 131, 141, 143, 145, 177
criminal gangs, 19, 142, 144, 146, 172

D
Dadaab, 4, 9, 10, 77, 105, 111, 118, 128, 182–84, 185, 187, 188, 189–90, 191, 192–96, 204, 225–26, 228
Daily Nation, 20, 201–202, 204, 206–209, 212–15, 215n1, 216n5
Darood, 43, 44, 128, 153n38, 224, 226, 228, 230

demographic change, 15, 31, 76, 77
Department of Refugee Affairs (DRA), 182, 187, 188, 189, 221–22, 227, 228–29
deportation, 182, 185, 192, 205, 208, 211, 214, 232
Derg (Ethiopia), 79
detention, 28, 79–81, 84, 185, 189, 192, 204, 205, 211
development, 8, 10, 49, 53, 111, 125, 145, 190, 204, 229
  urban development, 12, 15, 45, 101, 102, 119, 135, 157–59, 225
diaspora, 4, 8, 9–10, 20–21, 21n4, 26, 32, 59, 60, 63, 64, 72–73, 73n4, 76, 83, 84, 88–89, 98, 103, 105, 106, 108, 111, 119, 120, 126, 127, 128, 131, 136, 138–40, 150, 170, 173, 194, 196, 221, 232–34, 235n14, 238–39, 240, 241
discrimination, 41, 120, 212, 214
displacement, 9–10, 12–13, 28, 43, 91n3, 107, 136, 137, 144–45, 151, 183, 191, 194, 196, 197, 221, 233
Djibouti, 22n4, 201, 238, 245
DRC (Democratic Republic of Congo), 20, 27, 44, 78, 120, 130, 145, 181, 183, 220, 226, 231–33
drought, 4, 9, 15, 28, 30, 44, 61, 185
Dubai, 10, 32, 97, 105, 107–108, 110–11, 112, 157, 159, 167, 224
dugsi, 26. *See also* madrassa

E
East Africa Protectorate (EAP), 42, 44, 48
Eastleigh, 6, 14, 15–20, 22n9, 26, 30–33, 41–42, 47, 50–51, 58–59, 62–64, 66, 69, 71–72, 76–90, 97–114, 118–32, 135–51, 158–62, 167, 170, 172, 173–75, 182–88, 190–97, 200–15, 219–24, 227–31, 240, 242n2
Eastleigh Business District Association (EBDA), 32, 159
education, 20, 26, 32, 34, 51, 70, 71, 80, 83, 109, 122, 150, 171, 176nn17–19, 183, 184, 187, 193, 104, 195, 197, 201, 212, 219, 220, 227, 229
electronic equipment, 18, 97, 110, 112–13, 162, 167

entrepreneurship, 18, 31, 35, 43, 58, 119–20, 122, 124–25, 128–32, 135–36, 140–51, 172, 212, 220, 224–26, 232
Eritrea, 80, 82, 183
Ethiopia, 4, 10, 17, 21n4, 28, 30, 31, 41, 44, 45, 52, 61, 65, 68, 79–84, 86, 88, 89, 91n3, 115n11, 139, 152nn9–10, 170, 181, 183, 221, 238, 240
Ethiopian People's Revolutionary Democratic Front (EPRDF), 79
exclusion, 27, 42, 48, 66, 136
exile, 31, 60, 70, 73, 77, 82, 90, 136, 140

F
Female Genital Mutilation (FGM), 139, 148
Friday Bulletin, 20, 201–202, 206, 210–15, 215n1, 216n12

G
Garissa, 6, 26, 28, 34, 101, 106, 190, 223, 225–26
Garissa Lodge, 31, 77, 87, 97, 104, 108, 110, 111, 130, 141–43, 161–62, 173
Garre, 86, 106, 115n11, 162, 164, 166, 173, 175n6
gender, 126, 136–37, 139, 141, 143, 148–51, 194
Gikomba market, 112
globalization, 8–9, 20, 32, 59, 113–140
  low-end globalization, 9, 20, 98, 114, 169, 219
gold, 18, 107–10, 173
governmental organizations, 17, 61–62

H
Hajj, pilgrimage, 4, 104
hawala, 32, 65, 97, 123, 164, 173, 176n9, 230
Hawiye, 43, 44, 54n11, 128–29
Herti, 44–45, 48–52, 54n11
housing, 47, 50–51, 53, 184
human rights, 148, 181, 182, 188, 204, 207, 209, 211, 213, 214, 215, 223, 227
  organizations, 143, 146, 206
humanitarian aid, 13, 20, 173

I
identity, 4, 12, 15, 29, 59–60, 67–72, 76, 82, 98, 106, 121, 137, 139, 140, 148, 151, 203, 208, 231

Index

independence, 9, 12, 14, 15, 34, 42, 44, 52–53, 137, 145, 194, 205, 207, 231
India, 4, 9, 32, 110, 152n25
informality, economic, 20, 30, 43, 85, 90, 107–109, 112, 123–24, 136, 141, 144, 158, 166, 169, 171–72, 175, 193, 227, 230
   informal settlements, 12, 43, 46–47, 73n2
infrastructure, 12, 14, 32, 33, 97, 123, 159, 160, 162, 195, 225, 226
internal migration, 15, 26–28
international organizations, 12, 14, 34, 231
investment, 10, 47, 76, 89, 100, 101, 119, 120, 123–24, 173, 174–75, 212, 226, 231
irredentism, 44, 52
Isaaq, 44–45, 47, 48–52, 54n11, 102, 127, 153n38, 176n11, 224, 226
Isiolo, 30, 44–45, 48, 49, 51, 86, 106
Islam, 26, 33, 78, 86, 90, 104, 109–10, 115n10, 119, 129, 136–39, 144, 148–49, 164, 186, 226, 239
   Salafism, 19, 137, 139, 150, 174, 210
Islamic banking, 33, 129, 132
Islamophobia, 212, 217n23
isolation, 17, 64, 66–67, 183

J
jewellery, 107–109
Johannesburg, 12, 17, 58–60, 62–68, 71–73, 78, 84, 89, 122, 170
jua kali. See informality
Jubaland, 44, 101

K
Kakuma, 4, 9, 77, 111, 183, 185, 187, 189, 191, 195, 196
kambi ya Somali, 29, 176n11
Kampala, 6, 12, 20, 110, 111, 212, 219–21, 223–26, 229–33
Kenya
   census, 21n4, 27, 35n1, 45, 48, 54nn10–11, 122, 176n18
   constitution, 35, 191, 222
   devolution, 34
   Kenya African National Union (KANU), 30, 206
   northeastern Kenya, 10, 15, 77, 128, 162, 200

Kenyan Somalis, 6, 14, 27–29, 41, 43–47, 52, 53, 62, 64, 69, 72, 76, 103, 107, 122, 129, 139, 163, 173, 175, 184, 192, 197nn1–2, 203–204, 208, 209, 211, 217n24, 219, 223, 227
khat, 18, 59, 78, 82, 84, 102–104, 107, 109, 110, 115n4, 139, 148, 186
King's African Rifles (KAR), 44–45
kinship ties, 11, 18, 32, 42, 46, 52, 122, 131, 194–97
kipande, 49
Kisenyi, 20, 220–21, 224, 226, 228–29, 231, 235n14

L
legal status, 17, 18, 43, 48, 52
Libya, 64, 226
Linda Nchi, 190, 201, 204–205, 222
livelihoods, 6, 9, 78–79, 87, 90, 135, 140, 150, 151n1, 170–71, 182, 195, 196
livestock trade, 46, 50, 51, 54n19, 100–101, 102, 158

M
madrassa, 149–50, 195, 226. *See also* dugsi
Malawi, 62, 65
Mandate Refugee Certificate (MRC), 83, 188
Mandera, 6, 28, 34, 81, 105
Mau Mau uprising, 28, 30, 170, 205
Mayfair, 59, 62, 63–68, 71–72, 84, 122
meat (trade of), 30, 33, 100–101, 105–106
media, mass media (stereotyping), 6, 58, 79, 118, 139, 182, 191, 195, 200–203, 205–207, 209, 213–15, 216n3, 222, 228, 233, 239
   Somali voices in the media, 33, 35, 148, 210–12, 216n12, 239
mehar, 108
Meru (people), 78, 102–103
Micro and Small Enterprises (MSE), 119, 121, 124–27, 130, 148, 172
middle class, 6, 32, 149, 168, 172
migration, 3–4, 6, 7–10, 14, 15, 16, 20, 22n6, 41–42, 43, 45, 47, 48–49, 52, 59–61, 62–63, 67, 71, 72, 76, 77, 78, 79, 84, 90, 111, 157, 176n11, 183, 193, 194, 220, 221, 234, 235n2, 238, 242n2
   forced migration, 7–8, 14, 182, 185, 189
   politics of, 3, 10

migration (*cont.*)
    return migration, 8, 26, 48, 89, 183, 185, 193
mitumba, 112–13, 115n13
mobility, 3–4, 6, 7–11, 16, 18, 19, 20, 21n1, 26, 44, 45, 49, 84, 90, 100, 120, 136, 144, 148, 149, 202, 220–21, 233, 235n14
Mogadishu, 9, 19, 62–67, 69, 77, 97, 104, 115n1, 123, 130, 136, 143, 157, 161, 173, 185, 192, 220, 232–33
    'Little Mogadishu', 4, 15, 20, 41, 59, 63, 66, 71, 76–90, 91n4, 98, 197, 220–31
Mombasa, 6, 19, 27, 28, 44, 45, 46, 47, 97, 122, 161, 200, 201, 203, 204, 207, 224, 226, 231
mosque, 31, 82, 86, 140, 142, 162, 165, 191, 195–96, 201, 207–208, 210, 214, 224, 226
Moyale, 79, 81–82, 115n11
Mozambique, 65
muslim organizations, 206, 211

N

Nairobi, 16–20, 26–29, 41–53, 58–65, 68–73, 77–84, 86, 91n3, 97, 101–104, 106–107, 111, 118–20, 122–28, 130–32, 135–36, 139, 141, 143, 147, 149, 159, 162, 161, 168, 176n18, 182–85, 187–88, 192–97, 203–205, 209, 213, 214, 219, 222, 227, 229–32, 240
    Central Business District (CBD), 14, 33, 111, 171
    Kasarani stadium, 204, 211, 216n20
    South C, 33, 63, 149, 204, 211, 213
    terror attacks, 4, 190–91, 200–201, 204, 211
    urban transformation, 6, 10, 12–15, 30–33, 41–53, 100–101, 170–72, 174
Nakivale, 220, 224, 226, 229
Nakuru, 6, 12, 19, 28–30, 45, 51, 97, 158, 159, 161, 162–69, 171, 173, 175n6, 176nn11,13,18, 242
nomadism, 3, 10
non-governmental organizations (NGOs), 8, 70, 123, 130, 132, 138, 140, 144, 146, 147, 148, 152n25, 164, 181, 211, 231. *See also* human rights organizations; muslim organizations

North Eastern Province, 28, 43, 204, 223, 225
Northern Frontier District, 28, 30, 43–45, 48, 51–53
Northern Province Peoples Progressive Party (NPPPP), 53

O

onward migration, 78, 183, 193–94. *See also* migration.
Oromo, 15, 17, 31, 66, 76–91, 91nn3–5,7, 103, 130, 173, 240, 242n2
    Oromo Liberation Front (OLF), 79, 80, 88

P

passport, 20, 29, 68, 70, 98, 176n11, 182, 220, 227, 229, 232, 235n16, 239
pastoralism, 3, 50, 100, 241, 242n2
police, 19, 58, 62, 65, 81–82, 113, 127, 142, 143–44, 185, 188, 190, 192–93, 201, 204–209, 211, 214, 228–29
    harassment, 6, 89, 185–87, 189, 223
poverty, 6, 135, 140, 146, 148, 171
Pumwani, 47, 102–103
Puntland, 64, 68, 147, 226, 228

Q

qaran, 18, 126, 146

R

race, 48, 66, 228, 239, 241
radicalization, 150, 201, 203, 212
Refugee Affairs Secretariat (RAS), 83, 189
refugee camps, 4, 9–10, 14, 19–20, 22nn7,9, 65, 73n4, 83, 111, 118, 149, 182–85, 187, 189, 191, 192, 194–95, 197, 204, 224–26, 228–29
refugee card, 229
refugee status, 83, 91n13, 121, 129, 220, 227, 229, 235n8
religion, 4, 76, 79, 82, 86, 139, 174, 201, 206, 208, 210, 227–28, 240
remittances, 8, 10, 16, 64, 84, 120–21, 123–24, 127, 128, 131–32, 140, 145, 177n23, 195, 229
repatriation, 52, 55n32, 81, 141, 184, 190, 223, 226
resettlement, 16–17, 43, 45, 79, 87–88, 98, 104, 108, 184, 190, 194, 219–20, 226, 239

retail sector, 19, 158, 174
ROSCAs, 123, 124–26
Rwanda, 20, 78, 181, 183, 220, 226, 231

S
Saudi Arabia, 32, 217n25
schools (Somali schools), 51, 53
   integrated schools, 32, 36n9
   school enrolment, 194, 229
secession, 6, 53
second-hand clothes. *See* mitumba
secular, 20, 200–201, 207, 211, 213, 214
securitization, 10, 20, 88, 133n1, 201–202, 213, 214, 233
security, national security, 6, 19, 28–29, 78, 81, 89, 187–90, 200–206, 208–209, 211–14, 216n5, 220, 223, 224, 228–29, 233
   human security, 88, 135, 137, 139, 151n1, 172, 197
sedentarization, 9, 14, 50
segregation, spatial, 47, 172
shifta war, 26, 28, 35, 203, 205
smuggle, 65, 88, 104, 105, 111. *See also* contraband goods
social networks, 14, 59, 67, 101, 109, 120, 121, 126, 130, 135, 141, 143, 194, 221, 230
Somali (language), 4, 26, 73n4, 76, 78, 85–87, 90, 106, 133n4, 239
Somalia, 21n4, 28–32, 45, 52, 61–65, 67, 69–70, 77–78, 81, 86, 98, 115n9, 120, 122, 128, 137–39, 141–44, 149, 162, 169–70, 176nn9,11, 190, 193, 195, 200–201, 203–205, 211, 219–24, 229–30, 232–34, 238–39, 241
   civil war, 4, 9–10, 61, 98, 107, 123, 130, 137, 228
   displacement, 4, 6, 9–10, 15, 28, 31, 41, 61, 114, 183, 185, 189, 225–26, 235n8
   economy, 100–102, 106, 111, 123, 129–30, 157–65, 173, 225
   urbanization, 9–10, 14–15, 195
Somaliland, 21n4, 29, 44–45, 48–49, 52, 81, 91n12, 110, 147, 176n11, 224, 238, 241
Somali National Association, 53
Somaliness, 59, 61–63, 67–68, 70–73, 76, 86, 106, 115n9, 119, 121, 173

Somali separatism, 53
Somali shopping centres, 14, 85, 158–75
South Africa, 10, 12, 14, 59–72, 73n2, 87, 120, 122, 132, 170
South Sudan, 20, 78, 140, 145, 181, 183, 220, 231, 241
space, 3, 15, 19, 20, 27, 34, 35, 59, 63–64, 67, 77, 97, 100, 108, 121, 129, 150, 157–60, 161, 162, 169–70, 172–75, 184, 186, 196, 197, 200, 204, 212, 214, 219, 235n14
stereotyping, 41, 47, 58, 186, 195, 217n24
structural adjustment programs (SAPs), 111–12, 157–58, 170–71, 174, 226
student associations, 230–31
Sudan, 64, 78, 191

T
Tanzania, 4, 6, 26–27, 30, 65, 82, 88
tax, 8–9, 46, 51–52, 118, 172, 173, 208
tea vendors, 121, 125, 141, 142–44, 146, 193
terrorism, terror, 6, 19, 29, 41, 49, 58, 79, 88, 118, 139, 142, 182, 188, 190–92, 200–209, 211–14, 216n21, 217n23, 222, 224, 229, 234, 241
trade, traders, 4, 6, 8–10, 19, 27, 29, 41, 42, 45, 46, 50–51, 52, 77, 82, 90, 97, 98, 100–114, 115nn1,15, 118, 120, 122, 125, 127–28, 130, 141, 148, 150, 158–75, 176nn8–9, 183–84, 224, 226–27, 229–30, 231–32, 235n14, 241–42, 242n2
transit, 13, 64, 72, 103, 167, 181–97, 227, 231
transnationalism, 10, 59, 62, 114, 120, 131, 221
Turkey, 32, 111, 167

U
Uganda, 4, 6, 12, 20, 26, 27, 29, 30, 170, 183, 201, 212, 219–34
   constitution, 234
   Control of Alien Refugees Act (CARA), 227
UNHCR, 61, 68, 82, 83, 84, 88, 143, 182, 183, 184, 187–88, 194, 211, 223, 225–29
United Somali Association (USA), 50–51, 53

urban refugees, 59, 119, 130–31, 183, 187–88
urbanization, 7, 11, 14, 28, 157, 159, 171, 176n11, 184
Usalama Watch, 6–7, 20, 29, 113, 182, 192–93, 196, 200–15, 22–23

V
visa, 20, 194, 220

W
Wagalla massacre, 28, 35n3

Wajir, 28, 34, 45, 216n21
Westgate Shopping Mall, 4, 19, 58, 191, 200, 206

X
xenophobia, 8, 29, 52, 62, 120, 144, 148, 189

Y
Yemen, 31, 102, 221, 245

Z
Zambia, 11, 65, 111, 232

www.ingramcontent.com/pod-product-compliance
Lightning Source LLC
Chambersburg PA
CBHW070916030426
42336CB00014BA/2441